IN PLACE OF SPLENDOR

CONSTANCIA DE LA MORA

In Place of Splendor

THE AUTOBIOGRAPHY
OF A SPANISH WOMAN

HARCOURT, BRACE AND COMPANY   NEW YORK

first edition

Designed by Robert Josephy
PRINTED IN THE UNITED STATES OF AMERICA
BY QUINN & BODEN COMPANY, INC., RAHWAY, N. J.

For Ignacio and Luli

CONTENTS

I. CHILDHOOD IN OLD SPAIN
(1906-1923)

IT WAS cold in Madrid that January day in 1906 when I was born. The beggars squatting on the steps of the Church of Las Salesas in the beautiful Square of the Palace of Justice, just in back of our house, shuddered under the cold wind coming in from the Sierra—the wind that "does not blow out a candle but kills a man."

But my mother's bedroom was close and warm. My father's house was one of the few in Madrid with central heating. Draped curtains of heavy, stiff, blue brocade kept the Sierra winds from my mother as she lay in her great Louis XV bed. The ancient, fat midwife and the family surgeon watched carefully.

In the next room, the young husband paced nervously, brooding over the future of the son he expected momentarily. The child would inherit much. Although my father, Germán de la Mora, was still a very young man, he was already managing director of one of the two most important electric companies in Madrid. He had a good salary beside the small fortune his father had willed him. But more important than these practical considerations—for this was Spain in 1906—the new son would be the first-born of Constancia, one of the daughters of Don Antonio Maura, friend of kings, leader of the Conservative party, many times over Prime Minister of Spain.

My father, thinking of his wife whose faint cries came through the heavy brocades, muffled but poignant, leaned over to inspect her photograph. She sat, in the dark picture, stiffly on a garden bench, a girl of twenty-one in a tight-waisted tailored suit and an enormous hat burdened with violets. The photographer, in spite of himself, had caught something of her charm and beauty. Her black hair and eyes, straight nose, pale skin, and slightly thick lower lip, the proud line of her neck and shoulders, stood out from the graceless background and the hideous hat.

My father had married this gentle girl because—and this was almost a scandal in old Madrid—he loved her. Dutiful, bearing a great name, fortunately she was also everything a Spanish gentleman needed in a wife. She had been strictly brought up by Don Antonio Maura and his exceedingly pious wife. She

3

had gone to the Sacred Heart Convent in Paris to perfect her French—as all fashionable young ladies of her time did. She had, it is true, brought no great dowry, for Don Antonio was one of the few Spanish politicians of the time whom everybody, even his worst enemies, considered an honest man. But in spite of this flaw, my father reflected with satisfaction on his choice of a wife, and on the future of the small son so soon to gasp for his first breath.

The door to the bedroom opened. The family surgeon came in to announce my birth. My father's hopes of a son vanished— he stood stiffly, staring at a wailing infant, raw, red, covered with a dark fuzz. But finally my father smiled. The child, after all, was his own—perhaps it was better to have first a girl, then a boy. For the next several years my parents tried desperately to have a son, but they only succeeded much later. Before that, four girls one after another were brought into the world by my mother, and in that very same room, under the very same blue brocade draperies.

My nurse came down to Madrid from her Galician village in the Northwest of Spain. She left her own newly born baby in the care of her husband to earn, by feeding me at the breast, the food that her husband and child needed during the long winter months when there is no work for a farm hand in Galicia. She arrived just in time to save my life, for my own mother had no milk and Madrid doctors could not make me suck from a bottle.

My mother dressed up my nurse in green velvet and cream-colored lace—she was a strikingly beautiful peasant woman. When she wheeled me out in the pram to the Square of the Palace of Justice, she attracted much attention. People would come up to ask her for a look at the grandchild of Don Antonio Maura. More than once she hid me under the coverlet and pretended that I could not be disturbed because she felt ashamed to show off the ugly baby in the perambulator.

I was only four years old the morning that our mother came into our bedroom to introduce our new Irish nurse, Miss Nora Walsh. The nurse did not understand a single word of Spanish, nor did anyone in the house understand English. Fortunately Miss Nora had no important vices, because during the next three years she had complete control of my little sister's life and my own—for my mother was never able to learn enough English to give Miss Nora orders, nor was Miss Nora ever able to learn enough Spanish to give any reports on her two charges. Doubtless my mother sometimes found this arrangement rather difficult, but English-speaking governesses were the height of fashion in Madrid in those days and my mother was exceedingly fashionable. At least, the language barriers in our household soon forced my sister and me to learn English and in a few weeks we both spoke with a rich Irish brogue, more reminiscent of the Irish peasantry than the London gentry—a fact which fortunately my mother never understood.

Miss Nora was not alone in Madrid. Her sister Maggie was also a nursery governess. Miss Maggie's small charges were of the same age as my sister Marichu and myself and twice a day the two little Valdes-Fauli sisters and Marichu and I trotted up and down the Castellana, the great fine avenue shaded with trees of Spain's capital, in a never-ending series of long walks. The four children marched decorously in front, the two Irish sisters, busily chatting, brought up the rear. Everybody who was anybody at all in Madrid society of those days had an English-speaking governess to look after their children. Walking along the Castellana, you hardly heard another language spoken.

Great rivalry, however, raged among the Irish "Misses," a rivalry which was mimicked by the children. Sometimes the motive for the adult battles was the difference of ages among the nurses, sometimes the social standing of the Spanish families by whom they were employed. I remember a long-standing quarrel with Consuelo and Paquito Andes, or rather with their governess, an elderly lady who for some reason did not approve of the Misses Walsh. For years we sniffed as the baby Andes trotted by us on the avenue—and for years they glared right back as their enemies, the de la Mora infants, approached.

The Andes were quite closely related to us, too—a fact which never healed the feud between our Misses Walsh and the

Andes' English governess. Small Consuelo and Paquito were
our courtesy cousins. My mother's eldest brother, the Count of
Mortera and future Duke of Maura, had married the sister of
the Countess of los Andes—and so rejoiced in half a great Spanish fortune made (but we never talked about that) in a famous
Cuban brewery.

These rolling Latin titles perhaps sound very elegant in
English. At least I think they always impressed the young
women who came from Ireland to bring up the embryo dukes
and countesses and baronesses. Actually, the titles were not as
grand as they sounded or looked in a coat of arms. The Spanish
aristocracy of 1912 and 1913 was in a state of flux. A few ancient titles retained all the glamor of the Renaissance. The
Duke of Alba, for instance, might talk to himself and two dozen
other dukes with perfect comfort—but no one else. These
Grandees owned the estates and olive groves of Spain and lived
in the clubs and casinos of Madrid on the rents their miserable
peasants paid.

After the two dozen Grandees, who were so frozen in family
pride they privately considered the King something of a
nouveau riche, came the rest of Spain's sprawling titled class.
Unlike the British aristocracy with its careful, disciplined
graduations of rank and pride, the Spanish aristocracy had
little form. My grandfather, for instance, was offered a title
over and over again by the Crown—but he disdained a title so
new, preferring to be the most famous statesman of Spain. His
heirs were not so finicky. My uncle was the Duke of Maura
before my grandfather was decently dead.

Our family differed from the rest of the aristocracy of Spain
only in my grandfather's exotic disdain for a "dukedom."
Titles take money to support them, and most of the children
who walked on the Castellana as the sons and daughters of
"counts" and "countesses" came from families who had "re-
claimed," or at least refurbished, their titles within the last two
or three generations. This reclamation process took money and
Spain's aristocracy was the result of the slow industrialization
of a feudal nation. Bankers, owners of coal or iron mines, elec-

tric companies, factories, and shipping combines either married the impoverished daughters of titled families or bought their new title directly from the Crown (this was a great source of revenue to the King), or went back into the past to an ancestor who was born noble but died too poor to pass the title to an heir.

The Grandees were too few to impose their ideas of caste and pride upon the Spanish aristocracy. The richest and grandest and most powerful of the new titles appeared at Court as often and with as much effect as the few genuinely ancient noblemen of old Spain. Among the Spanish titled rich there was much jockeying for position and fame but none of the cold and fierce snobbery that separates an English duke from an English baron, an English baron from an English knight. Within the Spanish aristocracy there was a certain democracy— and beyond it none whatsoever.

For no middle-class child walked on the Castellana. No middle-class mother dared challenge the iron barrier between her small child and a de los Andes or a de la Mora. Spain's comparatively tiny middle class stayed in its set place—and under it, smoldering in starvation and discontent, were the peasants and the workers, the feared, hated poor people.

I do not remember as a small child ever being exactly told that I was a member of Spain's privileged class: the rich. And yet I knew this before I could pronounce the Spanish word for it.

I remember one day walking along the avenue, dressed in a Scotch plaid my mother considered highly fashionable. My sister trotted beside me, well-fed, well-kept, pretty, and clean. Suddenly a little boy appeared from a side street, a child so ragged and dirty and starved that Marichu and I drew back in alarm. Miss Walsh hurried up to us, grabbed our hands. The boy snarled out an epithet, and then jumped in the gutter, snatched a handful of mud, and threw it as he ran. My beautiful Scotch plaid was spattered with the mud, but I cried not for my finery but for the look of hate and contempt in the boy's eyes. He made me afraid.

Every cinema house in Madrid showed a moving picture on the Passion of Christ during Holy Week. When I was six, my grandmother, Doña Regina, bought two boxes at the finest theater and sent part of her household of servants and her three eldest grandchildren to see the film. My two cousins, hardly a year older than myself; the seamstress; Doña Rafela, the elementary school teacher, whose eyes were slightly crossed, a forlorn, homeless and shriveled creature; my grandmother's personal maid; the housekeeper for the big establishment—we all went to the Holy Week movie. The children carried thermos flasks filled with hot milk. The grown-ups took with them a *botijo*—a kind of earthenware jar with twin spouts—filled, I am afraid, with wine instead of the usual water. We all wept buckets at the movie and when I got home I remember having said one of those pretty sentences that "nice" children please their parents with and are repeated for months in the drawing-room.

My mother so decided that the moment had come for me to receive my first communion. So I had to make my first confession. My mother called me into her room and made me kneel down at her prie-dieu. Half frightened, I glanced around at the magnificent blue velvet and mahogany Louis XV furniture. "Look into your soul," she told me. I was a very ordinary child with very little feeling for the supernatural, but all this seemed rather thrilling. Under my mother's prodding, I was able to remember a sin—for in order to make a first confession there must first be a sin to confess. Armed with my sin I trotted off at the heels of Miss Nora to Father Rubio. But, alas, my sin turned out to be hardly worth mentioning. Father Rubio called on my mother to ask her whether she had really properly instructed me—for surely a fib told at the age of six concerning the origin of a certain green lamp in the household was not a very noteworthy business to take to the confessional!

A few months later, however, I had a real sin. Marichu and I had come to know Lulu and Baby, the charges of the other Miss Walsh, very well. After our walks in the Castellana, we often went to their house to play. The Valdes-Fauli family was suddenly, during these months, increased by the advent of twin sisters. We were all four taken to see the new-born babies and the two wet nurses who fed them. For the first time I saw a woman giving her breast to a child. The moment we four children returned to the play-room, we naturally began to imitate as best we could the fascinating process we had just seen. Miss Nora and Miss Maggie, busily chatting in a corner as usual, looked up and to their astonished horror saw what we were doing. Miss Nora, after her first shriek, immediately cried out, "Children, you are committing a mortal sin! You must go to confession!"

I spent the next twenty-four hours quaking in my small boots. None of us children had any idea what a mortal sin was, or why we had offended against God. Marichu felt sure we would all go to hell, although Lulu and Baby, more optimistic, were convinced it would be only prison—"with rats."

The next afternoon we were taken by our pious Irish nurses to the Jesuit Fathers' residence in the Calle de la Flor, and there we asked Father Rubio, who was by now our regular confessor, to listen to our sin. In all fairness, I must say that the Father did not consider our souls in mortal danger. Lulu and I had both to say ten Hail Marys and one Pater Noster—a great relief after the horrid punishments we had both anticipated.

Nobody ever remained in Madrid during the summer—except most of the mere populace. All the rich and fashionable families deserted the capital early in summer.

When we were very young we spent the three summer months in my grandmother's villa at Santander on the seaside. Later on when I was four, my parents took an exciting trip to what was then an almost unknown property in the family, La Mata del Piron.

La Mata was a very large country estate which had belonged to the Crown of Spain. Our family bought it in the nineties. Though the distance from Madrid was little more than seventy miles by road, my grandmother, Doña Regina, had never ventured to visit it. My father as a young man had ridden there on horseback from Segovia, the nearest railway station. My mother liked the place the moment she saw it, and father started building a fine house, stables, and a coach-house the first summer, while his enchanted family took their meals in a big tent and slept in the steward's house.

But even after the La Mata buildings were completed, we always spent the month of August at the seashore—not really because the Castilian sun was too hot, but simply because my mother, after her first week in the country, became terribly bored and longed to go somewhere else.

During many summers, we spent August at the then ultra-fashionable Zarauz, near San Sebastian in the Basque country. We stopped at the one really smart hotel—what summer resort, the world over, has more than one hotel at which a lady of fashion could bear to be seen?—and enjoyed the formidable smiles of Mme. Bringeon, the French proprietress, a woman of ample bosom and dyed black curly hair. Once a simple-minded servant engaged rooms—far superior, cheaper rooms—for my mother at the rival and slightly less haughty hotel across the village square, but we never slept in them. My mother would not hear of such a social breach.

The villagers, the servants, chauffeurs, and valets of the summer guests danced every night in the main square and the night was gay with the Basque music and beautiful with the graceful old *Aurresku* dance. But all this was vulgar and inmates of the Grand Hotel and the villas on the sea would have nothing to do with the fiestas in the square. In fact the only time we put foot on the village streets was when our nurses haughtily paraded us across to the beautiful palace of the Duke of Granada, on the other side of town, where we went to play on rainy days.

In Zarauz I became a rebel against my heritage. Although it took twenty years and more to develop, I remember distinctly that my first feeling of hostility to my surroundings, my people, my life, was born in Zarauz. For this summer resort was almost exclusively peopled by the Spanish aristocracy with a sprinkling of the diplomats accredited to the Court. The deadly boredom of life among the haughty Spanish upper classes settled down over Zarauz like a great damp blanket. And although I played every morning on the beach and every afternoon in the various parks of the Villas with small children bearing the beautiful and sonorous great Spanish names, I always felt, even as a child, something unutterable that kept me from really liking them and being one of them. No Vega, Lécera, Santoña, Catres, or Portago ever came close to my heart. I would probably not remember that uncomfortable feeling of my childhood, except that it followed me all through my girlhood, into mv life as a woman and citizen of Spain.

My father's mother, Doña Regina, died in the summer of 1913. We were at la Mata when a telegram called my parents to Santander. A few days later another telegram told us of her death. I was too young then to remember much about this remarkable grandmother of mine. I only knew she was tall and very dignified, and I had already memorized the most famous of the many stories told about her austere piety.

The story began at the time her second husband, Germán Gamazo, was a Cabinet Minister. My grandmother was bidden to a reception at the Royal Palace, as she had often been bidden before. This time she could find no plausible excuse for not attending, and dressed in her finest black brocades and black satins, she went to the Palace. Her distinguished beauty, and unusual presence attracted a great deal of attention. As she was bowing good night to the Queen Mother Cristina, Regent at the time, she was asked if she had enjoyed herself.

"Very much indeed, Señora; in fact, too much. That is why I shall never come again."

My grandmother considered the austere, stiff Court of the Hapsburg Princess too wicked and gay when everyone else thought it the dullest and most boring in Europe.

On our return to Madrid in the autumn after my grandmother's death, my parents decided to move into a more modern and larger house. With her death we had inherited two properties in the province of Salamanca and by some trick of luck, or of the lawyers, La Mata had also come to my parents in the partition of the inheritance.

The house in Madrid went to my father's eldest brother. But he had also set his heart on La Mata—he liked the house my father had built there—and he resented his bad luck very much indeed. I suppose this was really the major cause for our moving.

Naturally, when we decided to leave the old house where I had been born, we did not dream of renting or buying a new house of our own. Spanish families live with the clan as a matter of course. We left my father's relatives to live with my mother's parents, Don Antonio Maura and Doña Constancia Gamazo. Don Antonio owned a very large house near the Retiro Park, the old gardens that had once encircled the summer residence of the kings. Madrid had grown rapidly, and the graceful Alcalá gates, built by Carlos III and made famous by the Napoleon invasion, no longer marked the limits of the city, but ornamented the residential quarter where my grandfather and his family lived.

The house, near all these parks and gates which became the familiar and beloved landmarks of my childhood, stood on a street then called the Calle de la Lealtad. Later on, it was renamed for my grandfather. Indeed, the portico of the house itself was—when I was still a young girl—to house a marble bust of Don Antonio Maura, a bust which the Primo de Rivera dictatorship decided not to unveil. The unveiling took place without any ceremony one early morning just after dawn when a grandchild of Don Antonio snatched off the cloth covering the bust and then ran for her life. But this was all much later.

When I first saw the house as a little girl of seven, it had been newly partitioned and redecorated to suit Don Antonio's growing family. It was an enormous house, something like a small and smart apartment house in New York. My grandparents lived on the main floor and used half of the ground floor too where my grandfather had his various studies and work rooms and one of the largest private libraries in Madrid. Those rooms are part of a public museum now—then they were the quietest rooms of the whole great house.

The main floor of the house spread around a square open court filled with the usual Spanish palms. During the spring and summer months, the court was covered with a striped awning and everyone used to sit there in the twilight drinking coffee. A wide gallery surrounded this beautiful court and on each of its four angles a door opened into often unused and empty rooms. A hideous gold-and-white drawing room, for instance, opened from the court—a drawing room used once a year—on Don Antonio's feast day. Next to the state drawing room were the suites of my two uncles, Antonio and Honorio, who never used them except when they came from South America with their Argentine wives for brief visits to Madrid.

The large dining room was across the court from the drawing room and in back of that formal and elegant hall was my grandparents' double bedroom, furnished in carved, heavy mahogany. Just off the bedroom was my grandmother's sitting room, and from there you walked straight into her private chapel, the walls of which were decorated with blue and white painted lilies.

We moved into the floor above my grandparents. We had only half the upper part of the house, but even my father's growing family rattled around in the vast rooms. There was a special staircase in our apartment leading to the servants' quarters on the top floors, beside bedrooms, bathrooms, a kitchen, sitting rooms, drawing room, and a huge studio which my father used as a library and office for his two secretaries. Marichu and I each had a lovely bedroom and we shared a large playroom which overlooked the old summer palace, now turned into a museum. We had our meals at a little table and our governess taught us our A B C's in this bright sunny playroom. My smaller sisters had a nursery near by the suite of rooms Marichu and I used, and my father and mother had their bedroom and dressing rooms near the front of the house. My father's family did not exactly "live with" his wife's parents, in the American sense of the word, for our apartment was quite private, we employed our own servants, had our own entrance, and lived our own lives—except that life in the great old house centered directly around Don Antonio, the head of the clan, and his wife.

My grandfather, Don Antonio, who had nearly reached the apex of his career when I first came to know him well, had come from his native island of Mallorca to study law at the university in Madrid. Later on, at the big lawyer's office of Gamazo, he met the young woman who was to become his wife and the mother of his ten children, the sister of his superior in the firm. There was really nothing at all in common between these two human beings—they always appeared to be two polite strangers addressing each other ceremoniously. I never heard them exchange a harsh word, to be sure—but they led completely different lives.

My grandfather was the most beautiful old man I have ever seen. He had pure white hair and a pure white beard. He carried himself with such perfect dignity that he seemed to be surrounded by a halo. Even his grown-up sons addressed him as Don Antonio for they never dared to call him "father." As children we were taught never to interrupt the important flow of his thoughts with our chatter. Most of his life was lived beyond the gates of the house and none of his family, certainly not his wife, ever shared with him the overwhelming burdens of his career. We knew he was Prime Minister of Spain. His wife knew it. Beyond that we knew nothing and even our grandmother did not venture to ask him questions.

My grandmother was totally different. Anything but good looking, her face had a grayish tint and her white hair had been burned into yellow by her faithful hairdresser Julia, who came every morning to do it in a most ungraceful fashion. She sat for hours on end in her sitting room, hunched up in her favorite armchair, knitting, or just staring into space with her hands folded, while her lady companion read aloud the life of some saint. Paralyzed as a result of a dreadful illness, she could hardly move one side of her body and sometimes she lay in bed for months. When she recovered from her worst attacks she would return to her armchair, sometimes walk as far as the dining room for meals, and when she was much better, go out for an hour's drive in the afternoon. She rode in a stately carriage drawn by two horses, because she said she could not stand the motion of an automobile. It was supposed to be an honor for Marichu and me to accompany our grandmother on these afternoon drives. But I think we dreaded the honor—at least I did, because she took this opportunity to pry into our innermost thoughts.

My grandmother's day always began with Mass said in her

private chapel. When she was too ill to kneel in the little church, the doors to her sitting room were doubled back and she could hear and see the chaplain from her bed. At night the whole family—except my grandfather—had to assemble in this same sitting room to say the rosary.

In spite of my grandmother's illness, she took a very lively interest in the varied affairs of her huge family. After the midday meal, her sons and daughters and their wives and husbands assembled in the sitting room and discussed the latest family news. My grandfather, in the meantime, left the table to sit for a while in his great red leather armchair at one end of the huge dining hall. There, every day before we went to school and on Sundays after that, we children were brought to kiss ceremoniously our distinguished grandfather. Then we moved on to our grandmother's room to stand shyly about while the adults gossiped. The signal to stop the afternoon talk was my grandfather's hurried step in his little dressing room just off my grandmother's small parlor. A hush fell over the family as we heard him coming, a second later he marched into his wife's room, his half-extinguished cigar in his hand, ceremoniously kissed first his wife, then his children, finally his grandchildren, and then departed for his Ministry or his study to be engulfed again in his work and his thoughts until the very late dinner hour of Madrid.

I started school in 1915. I was not quite nine. We had lived in the new house for almost two years and I had grown to love the pleasant courtyard, the playroom, and the gardens. My mother might have kept Marichu and me in that great, beautiful house until we were grown up, but in 1915 the last of the English governesses had returned to their war-stricken country. The Spanish upper classes were faced with the problem of educating their daughters, now that the European war had stripped the capital of the anonymous young women from abroad who had for so long tutored the small children of Madrid.

Just at this time, the Hand Maids of the Sacred Heart opened a new convent school for the daughters of the rich and great. The school, patterned after the famous boys' schools run by the

Jesuit order, was supposed to be the most modern and luxurious educational establishment for girls in all Madrid. The building was modern enough, even if tasteless and cold, but the education the children received within its walls was anything but modern.

First of all, we had to wear black woolen uniforms with full pleated skirts, high collars, and silken sashes. It was so hideous that our mother would never allow us to come in and kiss her good evening when we came home from school until we had changed our clothes.

This was only the beginning. Every other morning the school bus would toot five times at our door at seven-fifteen in the morning. We would rush down the stairs, our maid, who had replaced the governess who used to watch over us, carrying some of the clothes and school books we had forgotten in our mad rush. The school bus would be already half full of sleepy-looking little girls and an elderly lady companion who was supposed to keep us in order. She was the only lay person we ever met in our school. Although the rules demanded complete silence, not even good mornings allowed on the bus, the helpless lady companion was always unable to control us. She used to report us only when passersby on the street noticed our wild shrieks and loud talk. Then the whole school would be punished by losing the daily forty-five minutes of recreation after lunch. Most of my entrancing and passionate friendships were developed on those bus rides to school—almost the only bright spots in all my school days.

The early morning rising meant that we were in time for Mass and Holy Communion. The last bit of news had to be imparted before we crossed the threshold of our convent school, for we were not allowed to speak—not even to whisper—during the whole long school day except for our precious forty-five minutes after lunch. As we arrived each morning we went immediately to get our black or white veils hanging outside the chapel. White veils meant that you were ready to receive Holy Communion, a black veil the opposite. And woe to the child who wore a black veil; our teachers demanded a long explanation of such behavior.

After Mass, we had a dreary breakfast of thick chocolate made with water or watery coffee, according to one's choice in the long marble-tabled refectory. We ate breakfast, as we ate all our meals in school, in complete silence.

Lessons started at nine o'clock, and by that time the school buses had made their second round and brought in the rest of the one hundred and forty day pupils. The classrooms in our school were as cold and dreary as the rest of the convent. The little girls sat silently, listening to the monotonous voices of women teaching subjects with which they were not very familiar. After almost six years of convent school life, I found myself with a very slight knowledge of matters like geography, religion, and English literature. History, as taught in our school, both of Spain and of the rest of the world, was more myth than fact, as I learned much later. I was able to subtract and multiply, it is true, and I had followed a two-year course in a subject called "logic," the meaning of which I came to know many years afterwards. Art, my favorite subject, got rather cavalier treatment. I learned about the great painters of Spain, not from the famous museums of Madrid—for we were never taken inside their walls—but from a book in which every plate was carefully altered with a white paint so that we children should not look upon a picture which showed more than head, hands, or feet of a human being. Spanish literature was a subject we never encountered in our Spanish school although I once delivered a long lecture on Cervantes to my fellow pupils and their assembled parents. But the lecture had been written out by one of the nuns and I had been ordered to memorize it.

The largest part of our time in the convent was devoted to hand work. Each child had a covered wicker basket, lined in pink satin, in which she kept her sewing things. To my mother's great distress, I always loathed needlework and embroidery and so when our school settled down to the long silent hours of our never-ending sewing lessons, I always volunteered my services as a reader. I remember these interminable hours of my childhood, the hundred and more little girls, dressed in that stiff and hideous black, bending over the delicate embroidery in their small hands and I standing before a carved lectern reading in the prescribed monotonous voice, the life of some long-dead saint.

We had forty-five minutes of "freedom" every day. During that lovely and beautiful period we could talk out loud, we could play in the school garden. Of course we couldn't shriek or yell or play noisy, unladylike games. And of course we couldn't talk alone to our friends. For the nuns forbade friendships—conversation in those forty-five minutes had to be general.

But no rules, no matter how strict, no matter how strictly enforced, can prevent little girls from making passionate, wild friendships. And indeed, the lonely lives the pupils of this convent led at home as well as at school—for we were all the daughters of the rich—which meant we saw our parents very little—bred rather than discouraged the most fervent attachments between the convent pupils.

I used to write under the lid of my desk, always afraid of interruption, the wildest sort of letters to Maria Vallejo or to Maria Morenes, who were my two dearest friends for years. I named them Florencia and Cornelia and signed myself Patricia in those long passionate letters. Though my two friends were quite fond of me in a way, I always found very little response to my letters. And at last we had to stop our correspondence altogether when Maria Vallejo's mother found a letter signed Patricia addressed to her daughter. The letter expressed pious hopes that Maria Vallejo might drown in order that I could save her and thus demonstrate the depth of my affection for her. Incidentally Maria Vallejo had won the first swimming prize for girls at Portugalete that summer and I could hardly hold myself above water level. Señora Vallejo threatened to take Maria out of the convent school and I had to give up my intoxicating correspondence.

The three of us, the two Marias and I, used to meet every Sunday afternoon, usually at my home, just to talk. We were so accustomed to the rule of silence which we observed for six days of the week that on the seventh we used to chatter almost desperately, trying to get said all the things we might want to say for the entire next week. What malice there could be in schoolgirls' friendship of the most normal kind such as ours was, I could never understand. More than once I sat thinking in school of this matter, and I always wondered what the nuns meant when they said that the devil stood between two people —even two twelve-year-old schoolgirls—when they talked alone.

The world seeped into our convent school, passed the closely guarded walls, circumvented the pious nuns. Even before Marichu and I started going to school, we heard the children chattering about the War—and some of the youngsters who played with us in the sunny garden paths of Retiro Park wore on their smart little coats a button carrying the Spanish slogan then popular: "Don't talk to me about the War!"

My parents went to Bordeaux in 1916 for a vacation. They returned hurriedly, their faces haggard, as if the picture of the War, if only reflected in the nurses' uniforms, the trains full of wounded, and the relatively peaceful towns of Southern France, had been too harrowing for them. The few words they said to my sister and me when they returned, the tight frightened look on their faces, was the first real knowledge I had of the World War. It was a shadow that disappeared and returned again a year later.

The Conservative Government of Spain, headed by Don Eduardo Dato, made a declaration of neutrality soon after the beginning of the hostilities in Europe. The Liberals, the Republicans, and the Socialists set up a great howl of opposition. "Their victory is ours, and their defeat is ours," the pro-Ally people cried. But the rest of Spain, and especially the middle and upper classes, with the army at their head, were opposed to any intervention in the great European War. And while they talked neutrality, they actually favored Germany, for they saw the Central Powers as an even greater stronghold of reaction against the growing freedom of the people.

And the King, new to power, wavered, first apparently pro-Ally, then to the public eye, the Kaiser's friend. The Grandees whispered that his English wife won him over from what should have been his "true" allegiance. The more realistic guessed that the rising Spanish industrial rich put pressure on the wobbling monarch. Alfonso was, indeed, a most unhappy ruler. From the very beginning, he had troubles with the politicians who ruled the reactionary Spanish state. Both the Conservatives and Liberals, who alternated with very slight changes of policy in holding cabinet office, objected to Alfonso's interest in the Army. The Queen Mother had, as Regent, always been able to circumvent the politicians, when she wanted some law passed or some decree put into force which they disapproved, by forming a cabinet headed by a general. This threat had always been enough. The Conservatives, or the Liberals as the case might be, fell into line, passed the law and the Queen dismissed her puppet general.

Alfonso tried to follow his mother's example. But he was constantly warring with the Cortes, and the Cortes in turn were constantly warring with him. Sometimes the various political parties descended to kindergarten level in the free-for-all battle for power and prestige. Once, for instance, an "economy reform" ministry had a solemn announcement made by the speaker of the Spanish Congress.

"In order to economize some thousands of *pesetas* annually . . ." the order began, and it went on to upset the whole system of free candy for deputies to the Cortes. Until this revolutionary bolt, every deputy was entitled to as much free candy as he could eat or carry away from the stately hall of the National Legislature. But, alack, deputies had enormous sweet teeth, and they made such a practice of giving the government candy away to their friends that the reform cabinet complained the cost had become enormous. Under the new rule, there were two types of sweets to be distributed free by the government to its officeholders. Mere deputies got second-grade candy; cabinet ministers got the best, or first grade. I remember that my grandfather, who was very fond of candy, always received sweets of the first category even when he was not in power! And those were the very same sweets he handed out to us children when we came down after lunch to kiss him good day!

But we children heard about the War with a vengeance, one Sunday morning in the early Spring of 1917.

On this particular Sunday, we returned from Mass in the

school bus to find an enormous crowd milling around the door of our home. "Maura Si!" men screamed, "Maura Si! Maura Si!" Marichu and I were badly frightened, but the bus driver grinned and made a path for us through the cheering people.

Once safely inside, the servants told us what was happening. Don Antonio, our grandfather, had made a great speech in the bull ring that morning. He had shouted, in his beautiful Spanish, that "although his country belonged by nature and strategical position to the bloc of western powers, it was and should remain neutral." Nobody had even bothered to tell Marichu and me that our grandfather was making the greatest speech of his career while we dutifully went to Mass.

We stared at the crowd outside our door half the morning, consumed with pride and curiosity, and when we were finally dragged in to lunch, the manservant, Lucrecio, as he put our plates before us, recited whole paragraphs of the speech with enormous enthusiasm. He tried to tell us that our grandfather had placated his right-wing pro-German followers with his firm declaration of neutrality, and at the same time given a sop to the partisans of the Allies.

But alas, Marichu and I understood very little of all this. Our parents did not lunch at home that exciting Sunday. When we came solemnly into the drawing room that night to kiss their hands, and have them make the sign of the cross on our brows, a daily ceremony, they did not speak of Don Antonio's triumph. And our relations with our parents were so formal, even cold, that we felt the silence to be a rebuke to our unasked questions. We never had the courage to ask our mother or father why and how our grandfather had become a hero.

My grandfather had set Spain's foreign policy that Sunday in the bull ring. Shortly afterwards, over the bitter protests of the die-hard Germanophiles, Spain and Great Britain signed a commercial agreement. Spain sent badly needed footstuffs to England and got coal in return and the Allies relaxed, for they could feel sure then that the Pyrenees would not be another frontier to defend.

But the year was 1917—a black and bitter year for Spain. Marichu and I went every day to our silent, cold convent school, dressed in our black uniforms. We lived in a great house surrounded by servants. No one spoke to us of what was happening around the corner in Madrid and yet even foolish, ignorant schoolgirls breathed the uneasy air of Spain in 1917.

For money, great wealth, was pouring into the old, decadent feudal country. Neutral while the rest of Europe died and wasted its fortunes until the third generation on guns and poison gas, Spain was a great coffer for the restless money that needed safety in a world at war. The old landed aristocracy stirred with rage at the sight of the golden stream, for very little of these bags of coins went to the ancient Grandees. Most of the World War profits went to the newly rich industrial aristocracy. Now and then an old aristocrat would be clever enough to leave his uncultivated estate and his illiterate peasants to reach out a hand for some of the stream of new money. But mostly Spain's Grandees sat idle in Madrid, watching disdainfully the nouveaux riches rise to power and prestige.

The first political results of Spain's belated entrance into the industrial and financial world was an Army coup. The reactionary aristocrats controlled the General-ridden Spanish Army from the ground up—and the King with it. Military Juntas, or officers' committees, formed supposedly to defend the interests of the Army soon began to dictate the policies of the Government. The King struggled weakly against this usurpation but in a few weeks he became the captive of his own military force. General Primo de Rivera, the uncle of Miguel who was one day to be the Spanish dictator, was made Minister of War in a new government formed by the Cortes. This didn't please the Military Juntas either. The old general was considered unsatisfactory because he had imbibed some of the "new ideas" of the period. The Army refused to co-operate with the old man.

But now a new—and in our family it was considered dreadful—force came into play. The Military Juntas upset the delicate balance maintained for years between the Liberals, the Socialists, the Republicans, and the Conservatives. The working class of Spain stirred. The Republicans and the Socialists formed a separate and strong block. People muttered in the dark rows of workers' tenements in Madrid and Barcelona.

For times were very hard for the poor about whom we knew so little! The decrepit old aristocrats grumbled at the World War prosperity in Spain but they at least could still dine off their tarnished gold plate, still grind rents out of their tattered peasants. The workers got no share of the new prosperity, either, and they had no coat of arms, no crumbling castle to comfort them. They ate bread and onions and little else, while the war profiteers ate at the luxurious restaurants, a novelty introduced in Spain during that period.

The railway companies set the spark to the tinder. They turned down the claims put forward by the railroad men's unions—claims that only asked a small share of the great war profits the companies were making. They began the strike that in a few weeks was to turn into the largest general strike Spain had known in the twentieth century. The first big popular uprising of the century had taken place in 1909 when my grandfather blackened his record, otherwise perfectly clean as a Spanish patriot and Conservative leader, by signing, together with the King, the death sentence of Francisco Ferrer, an Anarchist idealist. Ferrer was a great and noble personality, but certainly no man of action. He was made a victim by a weak and frightened government for the events of what was known in Spain as the "Tragic Week of Barcelona."

This 1909 uprising was the result of a scandal in the Spanish Army. The Spanish Generals in Morocco lost 1,500 men in a disastrous battle called the "Barranco del Lobo." Immediately, married reservists were called to the colors. The knowledge that only working-class men could not buy themselves free and were to be sacrificed alone in this hazardous venture, fanned the smoldering discontent into a real uprising. Thirty-six churches went up in flames: corpses buried in the convents were paraded in the streets. Children from religious orphanages wandered alone in the city. This ancient tragedy is probably more familiar to Americans than they think. Pictures taken in Barcelona in 1909 were widely used by the Franco Rebel Junta to "illustrate" atrocity stories in 1936 and 1937.

But even the Barcelona riots brought less bloodshed than fear. In that whole week of 1909 only two priests and one nun were killed. The Spanish Civil Guards, in the repression that followed, killed 102 workers and hundreds more went to prison or were legally executed. I mention this only because it is typical.

The 1917 general strike made the Barcelona riots look like child's play. The government shook in its shoes. The King trembled in his palace. For days not a tram moved, not a taxi rolled, not a train pulled out of a station in all of Spain. The aristocrats of Spain had been lulled into a feeling of security, in the years after 1909. Now the working class of Spain rose up again to terrify the old men on their land, the new rich in the cities. I remember the shuddering servants in our house, the worried faces of the nuns.

And then the Civil Guard came, bearing machine guns. Seventy workers died in one day on the streets of Madrid and Barcelona. Two thousand went to jail. Leaders fled abroad. The Army toyed with the noble idea of taking some of the better-known prisoners, like Prieto, Caballero, Besteiro, Marcelino Domingo out of their jail cells to face a firing squad. The hot-headed officers were finally prevented from doing their country this "patriotic service."

My grandfather helped prevent the Army from shooting the Republicans and Socialists the Civil Guard had arrested. But the names of these gentlemen were never mentioned in our family without a surrounding strong smell of sulphur.

In 1918, the next year, the King called upon my grandfather to form a National Government. The Royal ultimatum asked Don Antonio to "save the country" and from that time on our grandfather was always called "the savior."

Marichu and I, indifferent to politics until then, suddenly awakened with a bang. We were celebrities, even in our dank convent school. Everyone, from the chaplain, Don Tomas, to the little sister who opened the locked door that led us to the outside world, treated us with a new deference, for we were the grandchildren of the man the King called "savior."

The National Government was greeted in Spain with great enthusiasm. Our manservant, Lucrecio, one of the dearest friends of my lonely childhood, who played with us more than anyone else in the house, proudly showed us, when he was serving our lunch in the playroom one Sunday, a new shirt he was wearing. The words "Maura Si" were embroidered over his chest. Those two words were the new slogan of Spain.

My grandfather's new success brought him new friends. The Duke of Infantado, one of the haughtiest and proudest of Spaniards, decided to eschew the delights of hunting on his great estates for the even greater delights of helping to "save" Spain. He fell under the spell of my grandfather's remarkable personality and tried to rally the landed aristocrats who were his friends and relatives to Don Antonio's banner. Unfortunately for the enthusiastic Duke, his fellow Grandees were too lazy, too ignorant, and too debauched to take much interest in politics. They were content to pour out their rents on dancers in Madrid or shoot on their ancient estates.

My grandfather appreciated the Duke's efforts, however, and I grew up to know the Duke's family. Two of his daughters went to my convent school, and considering that they had been trained to believe that there were only half a dozen people in all Europe with whom they could speak without condescension, they were quite human.

Marichu and I could not follow the affairs of the government, because our convent school considered such matters carnal and quite beneath the dignity of the teachers, but we spent an intoxicating Winter with our noses in the air and our necks quite out of joint, lording it over the rest of our school friends who were distinctly not the granddaughters of a "savior."

But alas, we learned bitterly that pride goeth before a fall. Suddenly, in the Spring, Marichu and my two younger sisters were withdrawn from school and sent to the country. My parents informed me that I would be a boarder at my convent school for some time. I was twelve then. Nothing could have made me more utterly miserable. I begged to be told why my life was to be changed so suddenly and wept hysterically when my father and mother refused, very sharply, to answer. I thought that some cruel mystery was being hidden from me, I fancied that a terrible disgrace was about to overtake my family, that some fearful tragedy lay in the offing.

At school my friends were shocked by the mysterious change in my fortunes. As a boarder I could not see any of my day school companions. The life I had to lead was totally isolated. The silence that had engulfed my days, for so many years, was now about to overtake me all my waking hours. I had to substitute for the bosom companions of years the unfortunate girls who lived as boarders during the school year in the convent.

They welcomed me, of course, as a diversion in their horribly dull lives. They were mostly girls from provincial towns, daughters of rich families. We were not supposed to talk to each other, silence was the rule in the dormitories of the convent as well as the eating halls and the classes and the corridors. But we managed to whisper a little in spite of the nuns who watched us so closely. The boarders wanted to know why I had been sent away from home and since I couldn't answer because I didn't know, I wept and raged at these sad little girls whom I considered provincial and beneath me.

Then, after two weeks of silence, two weeks of the whispered and agonized attempts to explain why I had been banished from home and my sisters sent away from school, came my first visiting day. My mother appeared in the school parlor. And then the older girls knew instantly why I was a boarder. My mother was pregnant. My parents made my twelve-year-old life a tragedy for nearly two months so that I should not observe the natural growth of life.

The boarders tormented me, after that, with their jokes. They tittered behind their chaste veils and took every opportunity to remind me that I was such a dolt, I had not known that my own mother was going to have a baby. The nuns watched over us with eagle eyes—but they could not prevent the hasty whispers of bored adolescent girls who had nothing on earth to talk about except this rich joke.

When at last my brother was born in June, I was allowed to return home. Seeing my mother in bed with the child in her arms, I did not dare ask her how she felt or what was wrong with her. I was afraid she would lie to me and then I would have to lie to her in return, to go on pretending I did not know the origin of that small wrinkled baby lying on the embroidered silk pillow, when the girls in Madrid's strictest and finest convent school had already told me what my mother might much better have said to her daughter.

Every year during Lent we had a week dedicated to Spiritual Retreat. For seven days we prayed in absolute silence. Four times a day we listened to pious sermons delivered by a Jesuit Father, who followed closely the rule of Saint Ignatius and his four treatises on Spiritual Exercises. The preacher's pet themes were sins committed by young girls, such as dancing, frivolous entertainment, conversations with men, and other such crimes, and the subsequent punishments. We usually had a different preacher every year. Some gloated more over the first part, giving us vivid descriptions of the terrible sins that could be committed when dancing. Others passed lightly over these dangers and excelled in detailing the burning oil and pointed forks that awaited sinners in the Kingdom of Lucifer.

I was a rather nervous child. I had grown too fast for my age, and I could not stand the strain of seven days of continued emotion. My nose bled, I fainted at least once a day, sometimes oftener. Cold perspiration ran down my forehead. The nuns considered my condition a saintly one and I was never excused from any of the long sermons or sessions of prayer in the chapel. The climax came the last day of the Spiritual Retreat when the exercises were over. We were kept for about three hours in the beautifully illuminated chapel, decorated with lilies, listening to the nasal chants of the nuns, the badly played organ, and the last sermon preached by the Jesuit Father. The theme this last day was always of heaven, although the description of Paradise was always less detailed than that of the lower region. A certain feeling of warmth and relief always crept over me and the rest of the children, piously kneeling in the blue-and-golden chapel, and every single one of us, that last day, made a vow of sanctity.

Shortly after our Spiritual Retreat in the Spring of 1919, my mother, who had become the matchmaker in the family, decided that it was time my father's orphaned nieces should be married. My cousins had plenty of money and would have substantial dowries if nothing else that would make them attractive to a husband. My mother had never been to Seville, but she knew it was a great meeting place and fiesta time for the rich and great of Spain, so she took me, a child of thirteen, and my marriageable cousins to be there during Holy Week.

Seville awoke twice a year—as far as the women were concerned. Of course I am not thinking of the women who lived in the miserable huts on the other side of the Guadalquivir—those huts whitewashed again and again to deceive the world—and the women singing or brawling with their neighbors, or screaming at their children, to forget, too, that the belly that carries this year's child has received as nourishment a piece of bread with an onion to make it savory. No, these women lived every day alike.

But the women who lived on the other bank of the river, the rich women: they awoke twice a year for the fair in April and for Holy Week. On these occasions they came out of their old stone houses and lived like human beings. For the rest of the year they dwelt behind bars looking across the narrow streets of their ancient city. The streets of Seville are very narrow because the sun burns in the summer and the Arabs who built them did not have motor cars in mind.

But no one can understand Seville and its women of leisure until he walks through the streets at night—then everything is clear and plain. The same women who walk, in the mornings, with short steps and modestly lowered eyes, dressed in black mantillas, a rosary in their black-gloved fingers, followed by their mothers or old weather beaten companions, to the church around the corner; the same black eyes that looked blankly through the glass window of a carriage driving through the park, forget all their modesty and reticence as soon as night comes over the town.

For every house in Seville has a barred window called a *reja*. The *rejas* are the human safety valves of the inhuman Seville society-code. The mothers in Seville go to bed feeling quite safe about leaving their daughters sitting beside the barred windows on the street level with a piece of embroidery or an innocent novel in their hands. About eleven o'clock, when the big house becomes silent, and all the lights are out, the young girls of the family, whose whole lives are lived in this single hour, listen for a tap on the windowpane. They diffidently open the window. And outside stands their suitor, iron bars between him and his sweetheart—but iron bars that sometimes melt under the soft southern night sky.

The men of Seville find life very different from their sisters or daughters or wives. These men of the South are the perfect type of Spanish *Señorito*. Landowners, sons of rich men, officers in the Army, they are only interested in bull or horse breeding. Perfect wine tasters, they also know how to taste women. In the Calle de la Sierpe, or at the Circulo de Labradores, these men sit in front of the tall, thin wine glasses filled with the golden Manzanilla and thick green olives that come from their own olive groves, discussing the bulls, the horses, and the women. Mostly the women. They talk about the new arrivals at the "houses," about the old ones and the new ones. They talk, too, for this is not outside the code of a Spanish gentleman, about the girls of good family who are waiting for them now at the barred windows.

Then the hour grows later, the wine is finished, the last dishes at the late dinner are taken away. The men of Seville rise, and some of them go to court the girls of good families behind the bars, and some of them go to the famous "houses" where they need not court but only pay. And whether the men visit the virgins in the narrow streets of the rich houses, or whether they go to one of the "houses" they will find women obsessed by piety. For the girls in the brothels are exceedingly religious. In every room of the best institutions there is a reproduction of the famous Virgin de la Macarena, adorned with rich jewelry, dressed in silk and satins, just as she looks when she is brought out for the Holy Week processions. For these poor girls believe that the Virgin helps them to attract and keep their customers. Some of the most expensive jewels the Virgin wears in the procession are gifts from grateful women of Seville's underworld.

This is the world of Seville. I saw it first as a child of thirteen, when I could not even guess what lay under the mysterious surface of the rigid, ancient social life of the beautiful city of Southern Spain. My mother, my cousins, and I arrived at the Hotel Inglaterra on Palm Sunday. We rented the customary landau, drawn by two horses from our hotel, and every morning one of my mother's childhood friends, whom she had known in the convent in Paris and who had since married in Seville, would drive out with us to see the old Andalusian town. My mother's friends always wore beautiful black mantillas perched over high combs, though never as high as in those American pictures supposedly showing Spanish women going to a bull fight. After lunch they would wear hats—for this was one of the two times in the year they had the opportunity. All the rest of the weary months they had to stay like prisoners, within the walls of their houses and gardens.

We saw the city in the daytime—at night we saw Spain under the monarchy, Spain in all its false glamor and corrosive tragedy, Spain set forth explicitly in the Holy Week Processions of Seville. Here in these winding streets marched the Church and the Civil Guards, the rich landowners, and the semi-starved *trianeros*—the men who lived in the huts across the river.

Swaying over their bony shoulders came the scenes of the Passion: beautifully sculptured scenes, some of the eighteenth century; hideously garrulous scenes, very ancient perhaps; the Last Supper with its full-sized figures sitting around the table where real food was laid out; Jesus's last Prayers in the Garden of Gethsemane; the Descent of the Cross; two separate figures of Jesus Christ and his Mother—two pathetic figures bedecked with jewels donated to the images or loaned for the occasion by the rich families of Southern Spain.

The carriers, dressed in sackcloth, were hidden in the shadowy folds of the curtains that hung from the platforms of the Passion Scenes to the ground. The Passion Scenes were heavy; every hundred yards or so the carriers emerged from their black cave of cloth to rest, leaving the Last Supper or the Descent from the Cross parked on its wooden supports while they rushed into a near-by wine shop for liquid refreshment. After a few such rest-stops, the *trianeros* shouldered their eighteenth-century burdens with twentieth-century stimulation under their belts, and the scene began to take on an eerie aspect, the carved figures moving along with remarkable cadence that apparently, seen from the spectator's eye, rose from the very bowels of the earth.

The procession took place at night in the crowded narrow streets of Seville: the only time that the men and women came into close physical contact. Suddenly a piercing cry would ring out, the men and women holding their breaths and in that tense moment very conscious of each other's presence. The *Saeta* is like a dart thrown by a lonely man into the great crowd. It is like a plea from a mother for her child. It is like the shriek of a woman abandoned by her lover. It is a suffering people mingling their sorrow with the tears of the Mater Dolorosa for her son-to-be-crucified. It is agonized man sharing the agony of Christ.

Tourists believe these wailing, piercing songs, seemingly rising from the very hearts of men, to be spontaneous, unrehearsed. Alas, I knew even as a child of thirteen that a twenty-five or fifty *peseta* note, according to the voice of the singer, was all that was needed to make the procession stop opposite the windows of the men's clubs in the Calle de la Sierpe or at the Circulo. My cousins and I watched the procession from this last place. The fair-haired Princess Maximo de Bourbon sat with us. She thought it was all very "pretty," and so did my cousins and I, watching it from the balcony. My mother was bored and sleepy, and after the first night of the processions went to the hotel and left us with a group of friends—and after that I still sat, pleased and charmed, with the enchanting spectacle.

But I learned, later on, that one cannot know the Seville Holy Week from the balcony of a rich man's club. You must stand on the street, fighting for space with the crowd, heated with the rising pulse of excited and feverish humanity, to be able to understand and love or hate these strange, dark, almost horrible ceremonial parades. The crowd was the same that

went to the bull fights—through centuries of black repression
the people had learned to take their pleasure from death. And
in those days they did not know they could hold life in their
hands. That had to be learned much later—and also through
death.

I liked Seville but my cousins did not. For they failed to
encounter the young men who would lead them to the altar,
and so we all returned to Madrid. At school I was able to boast
to my friends about my knowledge of the Murillo paintings
which were what impressed me most in the ancient city of the
South.

Later on in that Spring of 1919, I went to another Spanish
ceremony, this time with my grandfather, then Prime Minister,
and our entire family. King Alfonso was to dedicate a statue of
the Sacred Heart—the occasion was so important that my grandmother appeared in public beside her husband for one of the
few times of her life. We all motored to the Cerro de los An-
geles where stonemasons had erected the statue in the exact
geographical center of Spain near Madrid. My grandfather
made a short speech and then King Alfonso, standing beside
him, stepped forward and in his weak voice offered his country
to the image of the Sacred Heart, with these words:

"Spain, the country of your inheritance and predilection,
prostrates herself reverent before this throne which is raised
for you in the center of the Peninsula. All the races which in-
habit Spain, all the regions which form it, have constituted in
the succession of centuries, through mutual loyalties, this great
nation, strong and constant in love for religion and for the
monarchy."

The grave-faced noblemen, the Grandees, and all the other
titles and their resplendent wives nodded solemnly as they
heard the King of Spain pledge his subjects to the Church and
the monarchy.

The King lifted his hand to pull the veil covering the statue.
The great crowd watching him stirred restlessly. Workmen
bustled forward to assist. The fluttering white cover slipped off
the stone to disclose the graven words, "You will reign in
Spain."

And then the crowd went mad with cheers. And the King and my grandfather and all the noblemen turned pale. For under the huge carved words was another slogan, roughly and hastily scratched on. In Spanish not nearly so elegant as the "You will reign in Spain," were the words, "You may think so, but it will not be true."

The crowd cheered, but the rich and the mighty standing on that bunting-draped platform turned pale and trembled. The day was quite spoiled and we all went home in a somber mood. Next day the story was hushed up, the newspapers attributed the "vandalism" to "street urchins," and everyone I knew pooh-poohed the whole matter.

The World War was over. The Spanish aristocracy swarmed to French seaside resorts for the summer. No fashionable woman could any longer be seen at a Spanish watering place and so naturally we planned to be in the van of the June migration.

At Easter, our whole family went to Biarritz to choose a villa for the summer months. The French coast struck me as very clean and prosperous in comparison to my own country. Everything seemed strange and unfamiliar. We knew nobody. The Carlton Hotel was full of young men who put powder on their cheeks, plucked their eyebrows, and rouged their lips. I sat trembling at a table in the hotel and watched tea dancing for the first time in my life—trembling, for I kept remembering in waves of fear what my teachers had told me (at our last Spiritual Retreat two weeks before) and of the eternal punishment that was awaiting all the young people who were dancing and looking so happy.

I had another shock too. In Biarritz I saw three Protestant Churches, a Russian Church, and a Synagogue. I had been taught that descendants of Adam and Eve were automatically Roman Catholics and although I was thirteen and a half years old, I had never seen a church that was not Roman Catholic and never heard that otherwise decent, respectable folk could be of another religion. It is true that as we walked up the Castellana in our childhood we were told that a funny little building beside the German Embassy was a Lutheran Chapel but I did not understand that people—men and women—actually went to such a place to pray.

I was fearfully shocked by Biarritz and my mother, pious as all Spanish women were, even laughed a little at me. My horror had worn off a little by Summer, however. After our usual month at La Mata we went to the big hotel at Saint Jean-de-Luz. We were practically an army when we traveled in those days. First came my mother and father, then my three sisters and I, then my baby brother, still in arms, and after us the nurses, maids, and menservants.

That summer began as a nightmare for me. I was tall for my age, big and gawky. I disdained playing with the children on the sand, and my mother absolutely forbade me to speak to a boy, so I was cut off from the girls just a little older than myself who played tennis and rode bicycles with the young blades of the resort. Every day I sat brooding in my hotel room reading *David Copperfield* and bemoaning my sad life.

Then suddenly my fortune changed. My mother, who was an incurable matchmaker, even if a totally unsuccessful one, imported her young cousin, Margot, to stay with us at the hotel. Margot was an unusual Spanish beauty. Like my sister, Marichu, she was blonde with blue eyes and dreamed of a prince who would some day come to lead her away from her dull life in Spain—and she was very willing to follow my mother's instructions and meet the young men at the resort.

I was in the way. My sisters were babies, practically, but I was an adolescent. Mother traded me for Margot—I was sent to the villa at Fuenterrabia to stay with Margot's parents and her eight brothers and sisters. Fuenterrabia was no longer fashionable, but since I was not of a marriageable age, my mother decided that I could bear the social disgrace of being seen on the Fuenterrabia beach.

That Summer I spent on the beautiful Spanish seacoast was the one happy and gay vacation of my childhood. The weather was glorious. The great sea beat on the towering rocks, the sun made the wide sand beach golden, the flowers climbed over the little villas. I was thirteen and a half years old, and suddenly I felt happy.

For Francisco Maura and his wife and his huge family, even though they bore our honored name, even though they were proud Spaniards, were really happy. They lived a carefree, jovial life. The children loved their parents and my uncle and aunt petted their youngsters and played with them and talked to them. The older children even ate with the family—and every night I sat down at the dinner table and laughed and joked and had fun. It was the first time in my life I had eaten a meal with adults, and the first time in my life I had had dinner without a governess standing over me to correct my English or French and snarl at my table manners.

The whole big household was filled with warmth and the noise of eight children—nine with me—rough-housing on the staircases and playing in the gardens. Even the servants reflected the informality of the family. The French governess, who chaperoned the older girls, was a pleasant old soul who giggled in her soup and laughed more than she scolded.

Perhaps the Francisco Maura clan was not as remarkable as I thought then—perhaps many people in Spain lived just as they did. But I never had seen such a family before and sometimes I stopped in the middle of my laughter at dinner to wonder if all this was quite proper and decent, was it really permissible for children to ask questions and be answered, to poke gentle fun at their father and get a hilarious answer in return? In my own family, at least, such behavior would have been counted monstrous.

Francisco Maura was a painter, which possibly explained his departure from the strict rules of Spanish upper-class life. I think he was not a very good painter, but he had an important family and was a professor at the Royal Academy of Arts in Madrid. This made him positively exotic in the Maura family —our one Bohemian. He was a handsome Spaniard and looked much like my grandfather, even if he lacked the majesty of that famous man.

After my first shock at being invited to have dinner with my uncle and aunt, I began to listen to the conversation. It was the first real adult conversation I had ever heard and I was quite bowled over at its content. My uncle was a violent anti-monarchist. He hated King Alfonso and to the delight of his huge family used to mimic that weak-brained monarch with the sloping chin. I had been taught by the nuns to revere the monarchy and in all the years of my life I could remember I had never failed to pray every night for the health and safety of the Spanish King. I supposed that every decent person in Spain shared my opinion of his Catholic Majesty—and my teachers in school had told me that my grandfather was the faithful servant of the Spanish dynasty.

So now my eyes nearly popped out when I heard my uncle roar jovially: "Alfonso, that bastard! He'll drive Don Antonio crazy yet. You mark my words, children, that Bourbon half-wit will drive your grandfather to his grave before his time."

My grandfather apparently didn't like the King! Don Antonio, from what I could make out, quarreled constantly with his lord and liege, the King of Spain, and not only quarreled but had his way.

"Don Antonio," my uncle would shout down his long table filled with growing boys and girls, "certainly put a good one over on that dim-wit Alfonso yesterday. Yes, sir, old half-a-chin got a real thumping from your grandfather!"

Of course, my uncle Francisco knew very little about politics and attributed all the ups and downs in my grandfather's career to the stupidity or venality of the King. This was scarcely an accurate picture of Spanish post-War politics but to me it was a great revelation. Fancy an uncle of mine not praying for the King every night! I could hardly wait to get back to school to tell my friends—and I never prayed for King Alfonso again.

My aunt Juana seemed nearly as remarkable to me as her anti-monarchist husband. She must have been beautiful in her youth and even when I saw her she still had golden hair and soft blue eyes. But unlike any Spanish woman I had ever met before, she was filled with energy and an enormous gaiety. She had time to run her household with only four servants—I had never been in a house before that did not at least have seven, besides the governesses and nursemaids. She went often with her husband and children on picnics and walks and parties. I had never seen a Spanish woman of a good family walking out with her children—in Madrid such a thing was unheard of.

To this day I remember with great exactness the morning I arrived at the Maura house when my aunt went into the kitchen and made sandwiches for me and her daughter Susan to take on a bicycle ride. Until then I had thought that cooks, people who could make sandwiches, were a separate race of human beings, absolutely different from my mother and her friends.

Susan was just my own age and my aunt Juana, among the other strange and remarkable ideas she had, believed in some freedom for growing girls. For the first time I put a foot out of a house without the inevitable governess trailing behind me. Susan and I were fiendish bicycle fans that Summer. We went on what we thought were long expeditions, always trailed by half a dozen boys a little older than ourselves. Susan's older sisters scorned us because we were still in pigtails and thick ribbed cotton stockings, but we turned up our noses at the young ladies and their stupid occupations. The squad of fifteen- and sixteen-year-old boys who followed us around with considerable admiration were quite enough for Susan and me. We used to go fishing, always attended by our young men, and take long hikes to an old ruined fort and eat tuna fish and dry bread on the crumbling battlements as we looked out into France across the waters of the Bidasoa.

As the weeks passed, I began to suffer a little for I decided that Susan with her blonde hair and rosy cheeks was pretty, while I with my black hair and olive complexion and soft black eyes was definitely and hopelessly homely. This was very sad for I had made up my mind that I was in love with a handsome man named Pedro, fifteen years of age. Pedro maintained a glum silence on his feeling for me—or lack of it—all Summer and I decided that he was in love with Susan. Alack! I tried to solace my thirteen-year-old heart with a stuttering youth named José. But José was not very satisfactory. He wore short trousers and Eton collars and his old governess popped her head out of the window now and then to order him around as though he were the merest child.

But when I finally returned to La Mata, I recovered my self-esteem. Pedro wrote me a letter! A love letter! And type-written! He assured me that it was his first love letter and also his first effort on the typewriter, a combination of important events that gave his letter a certain historical grandeur. Pedro's letter filled my cup—my Summer had been the most perfect success. And indeed it was hard for me to settle down once more to the stiff, formal life of La Mata and Madrid.

Children are self-centered. While I had been enjoying the first real happiness of my life, my mother had been tasting tragedy. For my father had fallen very ill with ulcers of the stomach and by the end of the Summer my mother faced the fact that she must take him to Germany for a long stay in a hospital.

The Summer had been strange; the Autumn was even more remarkable. My mother and father had gone to Germany. Our section of the house in Madrid was closed and we children stayed on at La Mata with the servants.

One windy Autumn day Marichu and I were running races in a field near the house when our governess hastily called us. Our grandfather had come to see us! This was a most extraordinary event, the first time in my life I had ever really talked to the head of our family. Some of his forbidding coldness slipped away as we all sat around the fireplace talking about the country and I had a glimpse of the man who had made Spain's greatest career in politics.

My grandfather loved the country better than anything else in the world. He was a fine shot. His picture in a shooting jacket and a little felt hat with a feather on the side, sitting on a field chair with the King beside him, was very familiar to all Spanish readers of the illustrated papers. During the closed season he spent his Sundays painting water colors of familiar landscapes he loved. He was not a great painter by any means, but his easel and paint box and brushes took his mind off King Alfonso and the squabbles with the Cortes and his cabinet ministers. Don Antonio's tragedy, which his dignity and hauteur always masked, lay heavy on his heart. He believed that Spain needed a revolution—he said so, daringly, in the Cortes. But he wanted the revolution to come from on top, from the government. And he was the government, but he could not drag his Conservative Party after him.

That Autumn day as he returned to Madrid the gardeners and peasants and stewards, the grooms, the maids, all the servants said, "What a good man he is," and chattered of the moment when he shook hands with all of them. It is true that he was not in the least pompous and perhaps his simplicity and well meaningness, even if he failed to carry through his intentions, made him loved and respected by people who met him. I felt very proud to be his grandchild and in the long evenings of that Autumn at La Mata we used to talk about him with the servants.

For the nights had grown cold and we all, the children and the house servants, sat around the great fireplace in the steward's house. The proper English governess had grown bored and left us. Our Madrid house servants had found excuses to return to the capital. We were left alone with the staff of the estate, the chauffeur and the steward and the housekeeper. We felt free and comfortable and happy. Every night we played cards with the chauffeur who used to beat us with much satisfaction. The steward, Don Antonio Lacalle, told us stories. He had been with our family forty years, had watched the building of La Mata. Now, with all the adults gone, he and his wife somewhat timidly invited us to sit around their fire, much more comfortable than the bleak great hall in the manor house.

Don Antonio Lacalle was a very special person in the life of my sisters and myself. I have always felt sure that he loved us more than our own parents did. He watched over us with fatherly pride and rejoiced in our small triumphs and mourned our tragedies.

He was a good and honest man, fond of telling stories of the days when he fought with the Liberals against the Carlists in Spain's Civil War of the nineteenth century. He had served our family most of his life. Before he came to us he had been steward for my grandmother on another country place of hers. And yet I think that he never really liked his job and stayed all those years because he had to work and it was a job—and he liked the children.

For our steward was the overseer, the rent collector, the landlord's arm among the peasants. He had to grind out the heavy yearly rent payments; he had to prevent the peasants from stealing rabbits when their children were hungry; he had to make sure that not a drop of milk from the cows went anywhere else but to my parents' house where it became whipped cream and butter and thick and rich milk for the children of the landlord.

And these duties were but the beginning. Our steward had to patrol the streams to make sure no one but the de la Moras fished the bright fast-running trout brooks; he had to drive the charcoal workers in the Winter and see that they wasted no time resting; and in the Summer he was forced to be a cruel taskmaster to the peasants in the fields. It was his duty to call the Civil Guards when the need arose. My father had built a barracks for the Civil Guards on his estate—a gesture of generosity to the police force, he said. Actually he built the barracks to have what amounted to a small private army, paid by the government, resident on his country place.

During that Autumn, the tires on one of our old cars were stolen. The Civil Guards were called at once, and they swarmed over the old coach house, converted into a garage, poking their heads, decorated with the two-cornered hats, into every nook and cranny. They couldn't find out who stole the tires. There were no clues. So they picked up a young shepherd boy of about my own age and decided to grind the secret out of him.

I saw them take the boy, half starved, dressed in rags, to our barn. I ran out, in the cold day, but the doors had already been closed. Inside the barn I could hear the loud rough voices of the Civil Guards.

"Who did it?" they growled at the boy. And I heard his shrill voice, trembling with fear, reply that he did not know.

And then suddenly as I listened, my heart beating painfully fast, I heard the boy scream. He screamed horribly and the scream broke into pathetic childish sobs, then flowed fearfully again into another piercing, maddened shriek, followed once more by the breathless, gasping sobs.

"Who stole the tires?" the Civil Guards said and the boy—he was only just thirteen—said through the throaty tears, "I don't know; nobody told me; I never heard."

"You know, you little rat," the Civil Guards said, and then I heard the blow fall and the scream.

I ran to the steward, my old friend, who loved me. I begged him to stop it. "They're killing him," I said, and wept.

He shook his head. "You must learn, little Constancia," he told me, "the authority of the Civil Guard is the authority of your father. One cannot interfere with it."

The screams lasted nearly an hour and they echoed in my heart forever. I tried to cover my ears that terrible afternoon, but I could not shut out the desperate cries of the little peasant boy. I think the steward did not like the Civil Guard, and I think he wanted to save the shepherd boy. But absentee landlords need the Civil Guard to hold their lands for them and peasants must know that the tires of the master cannot be stolen.

Perhaps the shepherd boy did know who stole those miserable tires; if he did, he never told. The Civil Guards could not recover those pieces of rubber from the silent and hostile peasants, but they considered they had fulfilled their duty. A peasant had suffered for the theft; it was enough; they would remember.

I think they did remember. The Civil Guards lived in barracks upon the land, close to the peasants. But no peasant ever spoke to a member of the Civil Guard. No peasant woman ever passed the time of day with the wife of a Civil Guard. The fierce, silent hatred of the peasants frightened the Civil Guards and they never walked out without their guns, and seldom alone.

They always came in pairs to my father's house. The steward gave them wine in his quarters, but the warmth faded away from the room while the men with the gray uniforms, yellow straps, and black patent leather hats sat stiffly talking.

My father wanted Marichu and me with him for Christmas. He was very ill and my mother wanted to follow his wishes. So accompanied by the inevitable governess, French this time, my sister and I started shortly before the holidays for Paris where our mother planned to meet us.

We stopped at the Hotel Edward VII, very smart at that time, all marble and glass. My mother took her two daughters of fourteen and thirteen to dinner that night at the hotel—a recognition that we were growing up. But alas for my mother. The first thing we saw was a wonderful lady, beautiful beyond anything I had ever dreamed of. Even now I remember her costume perfectly. She wore great pearl earrings, a blue feathered hat over her blonde hair, a cloak of blue feathers over her bare shoulders, and under that a shining, glimmering evening dress. I stared, my jaw dropping, but my mother was exceedingly annoyed. She dragged Marichu and me up to our hotel room and when some friends of hers appeared I gathered, from their French, that, alas, I had set eyes upon an actress or—horrors—even worse!

My father was desperately ill in Berlin, hoping every moment to see his family. But my mother felt that she could not take her daughters to the sanatorium without buying us some "smart" clothes. So we spent a week in the dress salons of Paris while my father grew more ill in Germany.

One of the suits my mother bought me in Paris was so striking—strikingly ugly, I thought—that I have never forgotten it. The dress was a bright emerald green with a georgette pleated orange collar and two pleated orange panels falling from the shoulders to the bottom of the dress. The coat was bright orange, with a gray fur collar. It was the creation of a famous Paris dressmaker, especially designed for a growing girl—but alas, I loathed it. People turned to stare at me as I passed and my mother lost her temper with me completely when I refused to wear it in public places.

When we arrived in Berlin my father had passed the most serious stage in his illness and was pronounced, to our great relief, on the road to recovery. So we had time for frivolity and the first thing we did was to have our hair bobbed, a thrilling adventure. Berlin was still recovering from the war. Although the sanatorium where we stayed was a very expensive place, the bedsheets were only changed once a month. The food was frightful. The people on the streets were said to wear shoes of paper but they did not look more ragged than the people of Madrid so they made little impression on me.

In fact, I spent most of my time in Berlin with the children of the attachés in the Spanish embassy, learning how to ice skate. Or I should say trying to learn. Ice was foreign to a *Madrileña* and I never was able to cross ten feet of the slippery stuff without falling.

Christmas was a great event at the West Sanatorium. The food was no less bad than on any other day, but chants arose from the chapel all day long, and every one of the sick rooms was decorated with a Christmas tree. At midnight the procession started. The Mother Superior led the solemn little parade, carrying in her arms a doll dressed in a blue knitted frock and cap, which was supposed to represent the infant Jesus. In Spain the child Jesus was usually naked, with His legs crossed, His toes playfully in the air, and His hands and eyes pointed toward heaven. If He ever wore a dress, it was a silk tunic. The German version paraded that night from sick room to sick room shocked me considerably. Fancy the child Jesus as an ordinary doll dressed in an ordinary baby's knitted suit! These Germans!

On New Year's Eve, we were invited to a party in a big restaurant and my mother reluctantly agreed to chaperon us. We had a hilarious time, for we had never seen a drunken person before and the antics of the Germans who drank schnapps and heavy wine amused us vastly. The next day we went shopping and were hailed with familiarity by a girl in a sweet shop—she had been sitting at the table next to us during the party. This made me thoughtful. In Spain girls who sell sweets did not go to the same restaurants as people who buy them.

Berlin in those days seethed with unrest. We lived in the middle of riots, of political murders, of desperate people trying to win economic freedom. But, even as in Spain, these events did not touch my family. Rosa Luxemburg died and my father dismissed that tragic murder with a shrug. "A well-meaning woman, but a fanatic," he said carelessly, and the name was forgotten. Anti-semites broke heads and windows in the streets and now and then our chauffeur had to take back streets to drive us out shopping. Communists and Socialists fought Monarchists and reactionaries and men died and the streets were red with their blood and we lived serenely in the middle of all this, too indifferent even to discuss it.

For Marichu and I had learned not to bother our parents with questions. And besides, we knew their answers. The world was divided into two groups, the *good* and *bad*. The *bad* people made trouble. They rioted, for instance, on the Unter den Linden, thus inconveniencing the *good* people who wanted to go shopping. In the movies it was sometimes difficult to tell just at first who the *good* people were, but eventually that became clear and then of course the *good* people triumphed over the *bad* people and all was well.

I remembered that in the school in Madrid there was a slight variation. It appeared that besides the *good* people and the *bad* people, there were also the *rich* and the *poor*. We were the *good* children and the *rich* children. On our same street in the next building stood one of the few free schools in Madrid. The Institución Libre de Enseñanza was founded by Francisco Giner and cradled a generation of lovers of nature, culture, and simple things. Señor Giner believed and taught in his school that Spain should have "more bread and more schools," and, most important of all, more democracy. He opposed the rule of the Church, the Monarchy, and the illiterate aristocracy.

We could see the children of our neighboring school playing in their courtyard from our convent terrace. The nuns who supervised our brief recreation period used to point to the children playing below, children of under twelve years of age, and say, "These children are bad. They are not taught religion at school. Their parents are all liberals, and they will be condemned to eternal punishment because they do not believe in the King."

On the other side of our school building and beyond the garden there was an old house belonging to the same nuns who owned our own convent. The children of the poor were taught in this decrepit building. This "charity" school had 140 day pupils, as our own school did, but these little girls came in through a different door, and they were never allowed to play in the garden, for it was our garden. They never got any meals, either breakfast after Mass, lunch or early supper, because their parents could not pay for them. Nor were the poor children taught the same courses from the same books that we studied. We were taught history, or what went by its name, languages, sewing, even music. They were taught to read and write, add and subtract and multiply, and that was all—beside religion. There were some people in Spain who thought the nuns pampered the children of the poor—what need have they to read?

Once a year the day pupils at my school were taken to the charity school by the nuns. We paraded over solemnly in our black uniforms, carrying a chocolate bar and a bun each. This was meant as a lesson for the rich children. We were to learn that we must be "charitable." Each year, before this event, the nuns instructed us carefully on our behavior. We were told to be "nice" to the poor children and not, under any circumstances, to play with them.

But I hated this annual ceremony. I did not quite know why, but I felt miserable under the silent looks of the charity children, and I shuddered when they carefully thanked us in the servile words they had been made to learn and say by the nuns. I felt their hostility, but more than that, I felt ashamed. As I grew older, I managed to pretend sickness or some pressing duty on the day of this annual "lesson" in "charity."

We returned from Germany in February, and Marichu and I were sent back to the convent after our long vacation. I had always hated my school, but now, after the jolly Summer and the long freedom, I felt that I could not bear it any longer.

For I had a wonderful dream, a romantic, dazzling objective in life. I wanted to be an English schoolgirl. For years since I was a small child, I had spent all my leisure hours reading books about English schoolgirls, a sort of European equivalent of the Elsie Dinsmore series. I felt that I knew all the customs and habits of life in girls' schools in England. I knew their

slang for I had spoken and read fluent English since the days
of Miss Nora, and although I spoke with a pronounced Irish
brogue, to which the nuns at school violently objected, I could
devour an English boarding school romance at a sitting. I knew
all about the English food which sounded better than I found
afterwards it tasted—but more important—I knew that English
schoolgirls were allowed to wear white blouses and have
friendships.

As the months went on, even my parents began to notice how
unhappy I was at my Madrid school and at last I was allowed
to send away for a directory of girls' schools in England. Then
for weeks my greatest happiness was reading and comparing
the various advantages of the Catholic schools advertised in the
thick book. It had never occurred to me that the exciting books
I had read about school life in England had little in common
with any real school in real life and nothing at all to do with
a convent school. At last I made what I thought was a fine
selection.

I lived the rest of the days of the school year in a trance. The
last day, when the other girls of my age who were also leaving
the convent for good wept good-by to the nuns, thinking of the
dreadful perils that according to our teachers awaited us in the
outside world, I was radiant with joy.

The Mother Superior came across me in the corridor.
"Aren't you at all sorry to leave us after six years?" she asked
somewhat tartly as the other girls sobbed.

I was so beside myself with joy at leaving this dreary prison
that I forgot my manners. "I hate this awful place," I cried out.
That ended my friendship with what had been my part-time
home for six years.

My mother and I left for England at the beginning of July.
We stopped in Paris just barely long enough for my mother to
get some new clothes. On the train we met a Spanish family
whose daughter had also been in school in England. They rec-
ommended highly a school in Cambridge, and so, after all my
poring over the directory, it turned out that I went to a school
in England I had never heard of before, and was not even listed
in my famous directory.

The convent in Cambridge was very small, a large private house surrounded by a garden, separated from the town's Botanical Gardens by a low hedge. Nearby there was another house where the same nuns held a day school for the town's people. As the Reverend Mother, who received us, explained while we walked around the garden, the children of the day school were "low middle class" and never mixed with the boarding school girls, who all came from the "best" Irish, English, and Scotch Catholic families. As she went on to describe the advantages of the school in the way of three-course dinners, games, lectures at the University, my mind went back to the children of the poor school that our nuns taught in Madrid. In Spain there were only rich and poor and I felt a great curiosity to see what "middle-class" children of England would be like. My mother and I liked St. Mary's Convent and when we returned to London I was enrolled for the fall term.

In London we fell into good luck. I met Maria Vallejo, my old school friend, who was bound for the Ryde Yacht Races and my mother allowed me to go with her to the Isle of Wight. Maria was gay, and the races were exciting, and although we had to go to several dull garden parties, including one given by the mother of the Queen of Spain (that was the worst of the lot) we met lots of amusing people. It was my first real taste of grown-up freedom, for our chaperon could not keep up with us and we had what was to us a hilarious time.

When we came back to the capital I had talked Maria into asking permission to attend my school. Her mother's reply was favorable; Maria could stay in England but she was not to share my room in the convent school. Neither of us understood what was at the bottom of that prohibition but Maria had to inform the Reverend Mother. The Reverend Mother—which was why I grew to love her—was just as puzzled as we were, and shook her head over such strange foreign ways. This seemed a far cry from the nuns in Madrid who would not let us speak to each other alone.

There were only six nuns at the school in Cambridge. They all believed in human friendship and gaiety and they gave Maria and me a very good time during the three weeks we were at school alone waiting for the rest of the pupils. When at last the girls began to appear for the school term we found that the majority of the twenty-one pupils were Irish, with four Americans, one Polish Jewess (Catholic by religion), and one other Spanish girl. We were all from fourteen to sixteen years of age, and according to the nuns, we all came from *good* families.

Chela was the only one who paid much attention to her exalted station in life. She had a quite good Spanish title, but my mother did not consider her parents "smart" or "fashionable" and I knew that Chela would not make a grand debut when she returned to Spain. Perhaps because Chela was a bit touchy over her social position she made life miserable for the nuns by insisting on her superiority. She would not, for instance, wipe up water she had spilled on the floor because "a Spanish aristocrat could not be expected to stoop."

Our school was not exactly the place I had pictured from my English books, but it was so infinitely better than the hateful prison-convent in Madrid that I blossomed out in a few weeks and came to love the quiet pleasant gardens and buildings in Cambridge. We could have friends, and indeed, Maria and I and an English girl named Ann Tyrrell, whose father was later to be an ambassador, became fast companions in a few months. We did not have to keep silence except during class hours. We did not have to go to Mass *every* morning—some mornings we could sleep. The food was frightful of course, as nearly all English food is, but we grew accustomed to it and eked out the meager portions with bread and butter.

I do not suppose that the instruction given in that convent school compared very favorably to really good schools of high standards, but after what Maria and I had been taught in Madrid it seemed wildly fascinating. Our powers of persuasion must have been great at that time for we convinced the Reverend Mother that we did not need to study geography or mathematics or such dull stuff. Instead, Maria and I took special courses in English literature, social science, and apologetics—all taught by a nun we adored, Sister Lucy. We all took a course in art, too, and went to a series of lectures by Sir Arthur Quiller-Couch at Cambridge University. Twice a week the whole school marched over to the University "Backs" in a "crocodile" double line with one nun walking at the end of the file. Maria and I became the leaders of the convent house and the leaders of the "crocodile" in a very short time. We had conquered the school, we were young, and we were happy. It seemed very remarkable to me.

I stayed in England from 1920 to 1923 without once returning to Spain. It was the one happy period of my life my parents gave me. I lived quietly, but pleasantly. I grew strong and healthy, playing games in the English manner. I learned to do things for myself, to dress myself without a maid, walk out without a chaperon. I had a pocket allowance and learned to buy things for myself. I read—perhaps the books I read, for after all I lived in a convent school, were not very important, but I would never have even read them had I stayed in Madrid. I learned that men and women can talk and walk and go to the movies and drink tea together without committing "mortal sin." I learned all the simple things that girls learn everywhere, I suppose—everywhere except in Madrid.

The nuns of St. Mary's Convent believed in giving girls a certain limited freedom, and although I suppose the rules at our convent were much stricter than at most girls' schools, Maria and I found them remarkably liberal. We never wrote home that we were allowed to go alone to London in the daytime—for we knew that our parents would have come post haste from Madrid to remove us from the care of persons who did not send a chaperon tagging at the footsteps of every pupil. Actually we were so proud of the freedom we were allowed that we never behaved so circumspectly as on those shopping trips in London. We weighed every step realizing the trust placed in us, determined not to betray with even so much as a gesture the confidence the nuns had given us.

During my three years in England, my parents came over to see me every Summer and sometimes also at Easter. While they were there, we traveled all over England and Scotland. My father was keenly fond of traveling—the only real interest we had in common. He knew some history, was passably fond of reading, and had a certain curiosity to see and learn new things. Tall, handsome, very manly in appearance, with a slight black mustache, thick black hair, thicker eyebrows, beautiful black eyes, large shapely nose, I was proud to walk with him and be taken more often for his wife than for his daughter. I am sure my father liked it too.

If I had been less proud and less sure already of what I thought was right and wrong, I could have gotten anything I wanted from my father. Everybody knew that I was his favorite daughter. But I would not "sell" my independence. I think my mother was slightly jealous. She pretended to herself that I too was her favorite daughter, but she appeared to love in me all the qualities that I did not have. My mother would have liked me to be soft, feminine, and subdued. She would think for days of some plan or of some dress that she wanted for me and I, in two abrupt sentences, would destroy all her schemes. While father and I and sometimes Marichu, as she grew older and less chubby, went sight-seeing, mother remained at the hotel reading her endless yellow-bound French novels. Or she would go out to do some shopping if the town we were visiting had any shop worth mentioning. We took this as a matter of course. Hairdressers also took some of her time when we were traveling, not to mention the inevitable Swedish massage which at one time obsessed her.

For my mother's life was one long attempt to reduce. Slender as a young girl, she grew stouter in middle age—or rather would have grown stouter except for her heroic attempts to stay within the limits set by fashion. She was capable of any sacrifice for her figure. She took endless pills, went on long hunger diets, and her health suffered. Her temper, too. For all her trouble she managed to look smart, but her face had a tired look not at all indicative of the easy life she had always led. She was not beautiful when I remember her, but she could look very attractive, and she was always fashionable.

In the summer of 1922 my two best friends, Maria Isabel and Maria, left the school for good. I was only sixteen and my parents thought I was too young to return home and make my debut in society. But at St. Mary's Convent I was considered much more grown up than the other children. So the Reverend

Mother moved me into the lay teachers' quarters, and I shared a room with my sports teacher, Josie O'Neil. Josie was 21. She had permission to stay out until nine o'clock at night—and, in the course of time, so did I. I took two courses at the boarding school and spent the rest of the time learning painting at the Arts and Crafts School. I am afraid I was lazy and undisciplined, not by temperament, but because of the bad training I had received since my childhood. Even Cambridge with all its advantages could not correct these defects.

Once a week I was yanked out of the serene Cambridge life and for a half an hour lived again in dour Spain—through my parent's letters. I knew that Josie O'Neil and I led the most innocent and blameless lives—yet I would never have dared to report to my father and mother the pleasant hours I spent in this old English town. I knew it did not fit into the pattern my parents had planned for my future life. As the time grew nearer for my final return to Spain, I became more and more gloomy. I felt like a prisoner going to his execution rather than a young girl preparing for her debut.

One day I met a Mexican lady whose relatives were quite as distinguished in Spain as the de la Moras. To my surprise she kept a small dress shop in Cambridge. I turned the idea over in my mind for weeks and finally I persuaded her to let me live with her, and pay me a small salary for my work in the shop. She agreed, and I took all my courage in my hands and wrote a long letter to my parents in Madrid. It was a very dramatic letter, I am afraid, and I think now it was a very sad letter. I told them I was grateful for my English education, but that what I had learned in Cambridge made it impossible for me to lead an idle, useless life. Many of the women of the best families in England were going into business. I had no special training so I would serve as an apprentice to my Mexican friend and return in a few years to Spain prepared for a definite career.

I mailed the letter. Then for a week I hardly slept, thinking of the answer. Sometimes my hopes would run high and I built castles in the air thinking of the new work in front of me, of freedom. Other times I would fall into the most gloomy depths and think of my grandmother and me sitting beside her in the horse-drawn carriage, or reading aloud the *Lives of the Saints*.

The reply should not have surprised me. I could read through the lines that my mother had shed bitter tears and my father had been cruelly disappointed with my appeal for freedom. He answered first and two days later my mother's reply came. My father wrote that he was astonished that I did not long to return to my mother's side to help her in her tasks in the world.

"I can see there is very little else for you to do in England," my father wrote. "You must return very soon for your mother is lonely for her dear eldest daughter and longs to take her out into the world."

My father added that I should thank the Almighty God that I did not have to go into business, make my living, or keep a dress shop.

My mother's letter was very bitter. "Your English education has not produced the results we had hoped for. Intead of training you to be a lady, it has bred discontent."

My mother's letter carried the ultimatum: she would call for me in April of that year, 1923, and on our way back to Spain we would stop in Paris to buy the clothes for my debut.

I could not fight my parent's decision. I was seventeen, absolutely unfitted to make my living, untrained, unaccustomed to freedom. I could not run away, for I would obviously be running away to starvation. All the nuns, even Josie O'Neil, tried to convince me that my parents had made the only possible decision for me. But I was afraid to go home. I dreaded my mother's temper, I dreaded the stiff formal life of Spain with its hopeless restrictions.

But just as I hovered on the edge of utter despair Maria Isabel wrote me a letter too—she wanted me to spend the summer at her beautiful new palace near Bilbao. Her letter was gay and happy—she said we would have a fine time.

My heart jumped a beat. The dress shop in Cambridge seemed less exciting. After all, I was young and what the world, or rather my own world, had best to offer was being laid at my feet.

I began to wait for my mother with impatience.

II. MARRIAGE: THE LIFE OF A SPANISH WOMAN

(1923-1931)

MY MOTHER brought me from my quiet Cambridge convent school to a restless, brooding Spain.

It was 1923. The whole country still smarted from the dreadful disaster of Annual and Monte Arruit. The generals, the noblemen, the rich and powerful could not forget the Morocco defeat—the humiliation went deep. The workers did not forget the bloody battle of 1921 either—for they still mourned their 8,000 dead.

The reactionary government, backed by King Alfonso, tried to flick off the infamous Moroccan campaign, a thing of little importance. But Spain knew the facts, Spain shouted for the punishment of the inept and cowardly. The first word I heard as I crossed the Spanish border was the famous phrase of the hour: *responsabilidades*. Find the responsible ones! Revenge on the responsible ones!

The *responsabilidades* were at once easy and difficult to find. The corrupt, decadent ruling classes of Spain were quite obviously responsible for the hopeless mess the country had made of its pitiful colonial empire. But Spaniards were not allowed to think this, let alone say it. The crime must be fixed on the shoulders of some specific general or politician—and that wasn't easy, for apparently the whole political system had been party to the debacle in Morocco.

General Berenguer, military commander of the Spanish protectorate and indeed of all the Spanish territory in North Africa, was the most obvious scapegoat. In 1921 he had ruled over two separate slices of the Spanish colonial holdings. Between these two docile colonies lay a stretch of wild desert country held by native chieftains. In December, he decided on a great operation to clear up this hostile territory for once and for all. Marshaling his troops on one side of the enemy territory, he directed General Silvestre to start from the other side. The ill-armed, primitive natives were to be burned between two fires of civilization and forcibly deprived of their liberty or lives, or both.

But the plan of the two generals went remarkably wrong. For one thing, neither General Silvestre, who commanded Spanish troops conscripted by force from the slums of Madrid and Barcelona, nor General Berenguer, who directed foreign legion and native regiments, could exactly count on the morale or temper of their men. The Spanish soldiers hated their officers, hated the system that brought them far from home to shoot men defending their liberty. The native troops regarded their Spanish officers with something more than a jaundiced eye.

For Morocco had long been the happy hunting ground for the miserably paid Army officers. Officers in Morocco got double or triple the pay received by men of equal rank in Spain proper. They had better lodgings in the colonies, quicker promotion, an easier life. The Spanish officer spent six years in Morocco and came back to Madrid with savings, his career assured, his trunks filled with Moorish drapings, furniture, and souvenir bric-a-brac. Life for the officers in Morocco was made easy by a grateful government.

Which was strange, considering that the officers of Spain's armed forces in her protectorate were a liability to the colonies rather than an asset. Unlike the officers of the British and French colonial armies, the Spanish majors and generals and lieutenants did absolutely nothing in Morocco except infuriate the natives, seduce the women, and get drunk in cafés. Spanish officers did not learn the native dialect. They disdained the native customs. They took proud pleasure in snubbing native rulers. They left Morocco as they found it: dirty, backward, hungry, wretched. The British and the Americans, shrewd imperialists, install bathtubs wherever their greedy appetites lead them. The French cultivate native chieftains and flatter a king out of his kingdom.

But the officers of the Spanish army brought neither bathtubs nor suave words to North Africa. The wily Abd-el-krim, a native chieftain, got his training from General Silvestre as he later got guns from Germany. Working in the central office for native affairs in Melilla, Abd-el-krim went to the proud Spanish general one day with a request. General Silvestre heard his native assistant out. Then he did not bother to reply with words— for does one waste words on a native? Instead, he drew his sword and thrashed Abd-el-krim with its flat shining side.

"You must learn about Spain and Spaniards," General Silvestre told Abd-el-krim as he sheathed his beautiful sword.

Abd-el-krim learned.

The campaign to "pacify" the hostile strip of country between the two halves of the Spanish protectorate got under way in December of 1921 with a few minor victories for General Berenguer and General Silvestre. At last the commander of the territory suggested that General Silvestre start moving across the strip to lay the planned-for trap. But General Silvestre was a favorite of the King's. Alfonso, who liked to put pins in maps, ordered his pet general to take a few more towns before he proceeded to the rather dull business of acting as a beater for General Berenguer's hunting.

General Silvestre took five thousand men out on a sortie into hostile country. The desert sands swirled around the rear guard of his troops as they marched off to take a native town or two—and that was the last ever seen of General Silvestre or his five thousand men.

Abd-el-krim had learned about Spaniards from General Silvestre. He commanded the native troops who wiped out his teacher and every one of his unfortunate soldiers.

General Berenguer rushed to pick up the pieces of his campaign. But town after town fell to Abd-el-krim. The Spanish Army all but collapsed before men who wanted freedom more than life. More generals rushed out from Spain—but they were surrounded and had to surrender. Fresh troops, hastily called from the narrow crowded streets of Barcelona and Madrid, sailed for Morocco. Badly trained, sullen, they were no match for Abd-el-krim who had learned about Spaniards from the flat of a sword on his bowed back.

Spain seethed as the disastrous news leaked back. And then came a final blow. General Navarro, especially sent from Spain to help clean up the mess, occupied an important strategic position at Monte Arruit with two thousand men. Surrounded, General Berenguer advised him to surrender. Thirty Moorish chieftains, under a white flag, came into the little walled city to negotiate. The details were settled, the surrender papers all but signed when somebody—they never found out who—yelled, "treason." The Spanish officers fell upon the thirty Moors and slaughtered them where they stood.

Night fell. The delegation did not return. A spy brought the terrible story of the death of the negotiators. Abd-el-krim moved on Monte Arruit. The Moors took only a few prisoners of war. Most of General Navarro's men died that night.

Monte Arruit aroused all Spain. Eight thousand men had fallen in a campaign which had proved worse than useless. A handful of Moors had defeated a Spanish army of fifty thousand. Catalonia, Spain's industrial area, rose. The workers of Barcelona demonstrated against conscription, against the venal and inept army, against the adventure of the Madrid Government. Alfonso, charged with the whole Morocco defeat, would brook no interference from his subjects. The Army sent General Martinez Anido, famous even among Spanish generals for his cruelty, to Barcelona.

Two hundred and twenty-eight assaults on persons, resulting in death, were committed in the streets of Barcelona under the regime of General Anido.

And still Alfonso could not convince Spain that Morocco had been an accident. All the General Martinez Anidos in the world could not "pacify" the "natives" of Catalonia. The Army had lost face. The Liberals came into power.

The new regime did what it could to calm the outraged people of Madrid and Barcelona. Civilian politicians were placed at the head of the Navy and War Departments. A civilian high commissioner was sent to Morocco to replace the Army commandant. Even the Church was gently tapped on the wrist. The clergy was forbidden to sell the works of art found in churches and monasteries. For years the Spanish Bishops and Cardinals had enriched themselves by selling the priceless paintings and embroideries they found in dark corners of old chapels and churches. Much of Spain's great art heritage had been sold to American, British, and French museums, or to private collections. The Liberal government ended this practice.

Indeed, the new regime went so far as tentatively to suggest religious freedom for Spain. Catholicism was the only religion allowed under law and a Liberal Cabinet Member offered an amendment to the Constitution allowing freedom of conscience.

"You are returning to Madrid," my mother began. "Spain is not England for which I, at least, am grateful. Your father and I bitterly regret your English education. Only too apparently it has not fitted you for life in Spain."

I tried to interrupt. "But, mother, you don't understand, you don't see that . . ."

"Your father has asked me to inform you of these matters," my mother went on, firmly ignoring me. "In Madrid, at least, you will behave as a lady should. Your father and I expect you to obey us."

My face must have betrayed my dismay.

"Constancia!" my mother said, irritation playing in her voice. "How can you look so dismal? You are going into society, it will be gay, you will find your husband—yet you act as though you were going to prison."

She hesitated on the word, seeing my gesture. "No nice girl wants the kind of 'freedom' you talk about," she said passionately. "I never found it tiresome to behave like a Spanish lady, and I never thought my home was a prison."

I could find no words to reply to her.

"Why do you want to go on the streets alone?" my mother cried. "Have you forgotten everything the good nuns of Madrid taught you? Your father and I want to protect you—but you— must have some wild plan in your mind, perhaps you . . ."

"Mother!" I replied bitterly. She stopped then, but this was the first of our disputes. After three years in England I find the old customs of Madrid humiliating. To be followed on the streets like a child with her governess! Never to have a word alone with anyone!

And when we drove home from the station in Madrid I had the final blow. My mother had engaged a young English girl, a Miss Merriden, who was to watch over me on those rare occasions when my mother was ill or having her hair dressed and could not go driving or walking with me in the park. The very presence of Miss Merriden infuriated and humiliated me—but in this case at least I triumphed over my mother.

For a few weeks after I came home, Miss Merriden was discovered to be the mistress of a count whose daughters she had been chaperoning. It appeared that all of Madrid, except my mother, had heard this interesting bit of gossip. Miss Merriden was sent packing hurriedly and my mother, quite dashed, had to look for a chaperon rather more fitted to guard the morals of a young lady.

I made a sensation in my family that day I returned from England. They all remembered me three years before, a tall, lanky, overgrown youngster with long, thin, bony legs, thin shoulders, a long neck, and a small head. My eyes were always big, black, and soft. I had an olive complexion with hardly any color and in those days my large white teeth were hidden behind steel dentist's braces. My eyebrows were nearly as thick as my father's and my straight black hair, braided in two thin pigtails, did not enhance my childish beauty.

Jaws dropped and eyes bulged in the Maura family when I stepped out of the limousine door that June day in 1923. My legs and shoulders had filled in. My hair had been cut and softly waved. The Institut de Beauté in Paris and expensive, nice clothes had done the rest. My family hardly recognized me. My eyebrows had been carefully shaped and my olive complexion was a good background for the new tinges of pink and red on my cheekbones and lips. For nearly a year I never washed my face with soap and water. The Institut de Beauté had sold me a lettuce cream which was supposed to work "marvels" and stuck to it grimly. I used bottle after bottle of rose wate wash my eyes. All the family welcomed back home a young who could more or less obviously hold her own in the fi competition among the daughters of the leading families o Madrid. The rejoicing was universal from my grandfather and grandmother down to the house servants. The ugly duckling had turned out successfully. My marriage was assured. I was an asset, not a liability.

I was touched when my mother showed me to my old room. She had transformed the plain schoolgirl's bedroo into a fashionable, luxuriously furnished bed-sitting room where I could entertain my old friends and read or study. For a moment I was quite overwhelmed—and then I felt a wave of irritation. In 1923, red-lacquered furniture and paper walls were the rage of fashionable Madrid. So my mother had papered the walls of my bed-sitting room in a design I immediately disliked and my dressing table and looking glass were red lacquer. And I did not like red lacquer.

The new furniture was not the only innovation. My mother brought in the ill-starred Miss Merriden, and then as they were leaving me to unpack, my mother rang for Julia. Julia upset me much more than the red lacquer and Miss Merriden put together. For as children at the convent school, my sisters and I had had a maid—a country girl who pressed our white collars, braided our pigtails, washed our faces, and made our beds. But Julia was no successor to these cheerful, amiable, rather uncouth peasant girls. Julia was a fashionable ladies' maid, haughty, proud, talkative, middle-aged, the sister of a parish priest.

From the moment I set eyes on Julia I felt profoundly uncomfortable. After my mother and Miss Merriden left, Julia knelt down before me to take off my shoes and stockings. I had often enough seen my mother's maids kneel before her to dress her, but my very soul turned over in me as Julia slipped off my shoes. I endured it as long as I could, but a few days later I told Julia I could not have her kneeling before me or putting on my stockings either. After that she used to fumble around in the corners of my room while I dressed hurriedly, both of us miserable and embarrassed.

I was hardly unpacked before my mother marshaled her forces and led me out into Madrid society. In those days balls or big parties were of two different varieties. An "evening" ball began after Madrid's very late dinner hour of ten or eleven and continued until very late indeed. An "afternoon" ball began at six o'clock and lasted until ten or eleven when dinner was served. Madrid society had only five or six of the evening balls a year, usually held in the same big palaces and foreign embassies.

I went to my first party in June, a party given by a baroness famous for her afternoon dances and her wig. If her parties were not really extraordinary, her wig was. I never found out whether it covered a bald head or a gray one—in any case it was jet black, surmounted by a bias curl which at her parties was fastened on by a diamond brooch. Most of her parties were given for her grandchildren, almost never for her contemporaries. She used to sit with the Infanta Isabel, the King's aunt, another elderly crone, in a sort of a balcony built in the ballroom, watching the young people amuse themselves.

I wore black taffeta for my first party. My mother had her way with its design and my dress had a square neck, puffed sleeves, a tight bodice, a full skirt, and at the bottom of it, bands of red and blue velvet. I wore a huge brimmed golden straw hat also trimmed with blue and red velvet and carried the inevitable gloves. My mother and I arrived at the party in a new car of American make my father had just bought. White-wigged, long-stockinged, short-trousered lackeys ushered my mother and me into a large drawing room just off the ballroom. There I was presented to my hostess who in turn presented me to the assembled guests—and there I curtseyed to the Infanta Isabel who represented the Queen and King at these informal afternoon parties.

The Infanta Isabel was an institution at Madrid society affairs. The King and Queen only went to evening balls and few of these—so the Infanta was delegated to give the needed distinguished touch to afternoon social affairs. If you met the old Infanta in her home, surrounded by all the objects of bad taste that she cherished, sitting in an uncomfortable Victorian armchair, dressed in gray silk and pretending to knit or read, but really only dozing, you would easily have taken her for an ordinary middle class grandma. She liked everything that was ugly. Perhaps in her youth she had loved some of the beautiful things of life—I don't know. But she always reminded me of Doña Ramona, our steward's wife. They had the same red patches on their faces, the same apoplectic look. But Doña Ramona had become old through hard work and suffering while the Infanta looked as if she had grown old and fat through eating too much and never doing anything. She confined her flowing flesh in a tight corset—clearly discernible through the gray silk. Perhaps the tight corset was to blame for the old lady's tendency to doze into sound sleep on every possible occasion.

I have always wondered why she was popular with the people in the street. Driving in an open carriage or motor car, she would be cheered as no other member of the Royal family was ever cheered in Spain. Perhaps the simple life she led, the fact that she never mixed in politics and that none of the dark happenings in the Spanish history of the century could be blamed on her, were enough to make her popular with the people if only in comparison with the rest of her family. Besides, for some intangible reason *she* was Spanish. The Queen Mother was a German, the King's wife was English, and there was nothing Spanish about the Royal household. The ancient Infanta lived in an old palace in one of the old streets of Madrid and spent the summer in the Palace at La Granja built by her ancestor Philip V. For many years the Palace with its beautiful cool gardens had remained empty. The Royal family had preferred other more lively and amusing places for the summer. But it suited the old Infanta's taste and I suppose the people were grateful to her for it. Not that the old lady between her dozing sleeps was able to think out measures to make her popular with the Spanish people. There were few other brains in Spain known to work as slowly as hers. Everything about her was just a coincidence. She fitted perfectly in the picture of the afternoon dance where I made my debut in Madrid society— for the other people I met were young in years but no less archaic in spirit than the good old Infanta Isabel.

And indeed, for all my English education, I began my life in Madrid society with a gesture popular the century before I was born. Coming home from school, I found my grandmother more ill than usual. I was a devout Catholic in the Spanish tradition—and I made a vow not to dance for two years if God would grant my grandmother's recovery. There was very little merit attached to my vow, considering that if my grandmother had died I would have been forced, according to Spanish custom, to go into deep mourning and not dance or appear in public for over a year at least. When the first young men came up to me to ask my mother's permission for me to dance, I explained my vow. They stayed by me, talking to this strange young thing—and the mothers of the other debutantes of the season sensed a dangerous rival for their daughter's brilliant marriages in the young de la Mora who combined the exotic results of a "modern" English education with the demure devoutness of old Spain.

I went home from my first party in Madrid bitterly disappointed. I had met, my mother told me, the very flower of the young men of Madrid. And I thought they were terrible. I had never seen such a group of boring and silly young gentlemen in my life. My mother bit her lips in annoyance. A few days later she took me to the Sunday horse races in the Madrid Hippodrome—the great gathering place of Madrid society, young and middle aged. My mother sat with friends in her box. I was invited to walk up and down, as is the custom, with a group of young men and girls. I will never forget that afternoon's walk. In ten minutes I found the conversation and behavior of my contemporaries in Madrid society so unbearable that I ran away and hid under the grandstand, where, in full sight of ticket vendors and program boys, I burst into wild tears. My mother finally found me and listened impatiently while I tried to explain that the thought of having to marry one of those stupid, dull, decadent human beings terrified me. She took me home with hardly a word—and I think that I decided then and there that afternoon that I would not, at no matter what cost, make a "brilliant" marriage.

The horse races and the afternoon balls were the beginning. Every day I went out to lunches, tennis parties, dances (although I steadfastly refused to dance). My cousins had a tennis court in the garden of their Madrid house. These girls, the daughters of my uncle the Duke of Maura and his rich Cuban wife, had made their debuts the same year I had made mine. They gave frequent tennis parties where I met most of the people who went about in Madrid society at that time. And I never recovered from the deep feeling of oppression which made me burst into tears at the Hippodrome. I managed to make myself popular in society, because my mother insisted on this. I smiled and played tennis and learned to gabble about nothing. But I never felt comfortable or happy, surrounded by the great and famous names and titles of Spain.

Indeed, even my mother admitted after a time that the young men of the Madrid aristocracy were a pallid, lifeless, senseless lot. Once I overheard her say to a friend that she hardly knew a normal young man in the whole group. And yet she expected me to marry from this narrow circle.

The late season—my first in society—drew to a close. I could hardly wait for the last evening ball. For I had invited Ann Tyrrell to spend the summer at La Mata with us. Her father was now Permanent Under-Secretary of the British Foreign Office. I had often spent week-ends and vacations at her house in England and now my mother wished to repay this hospitality.

After the long dreary days spent chattering with girls just out of a Spanish convent, I was wild with impatience to see an English schoolmate again. I drove up to La Mata feeling happy, the first time in weeks.

Ann came on the express from Hendaye and we met her at Segovia, two hours before the train arrives in Madrid. We drove her directly to La Mata—and the beautiful countryside around our summer home was the first thing she saw in Spain.

The next morning I had the steward bring out my pony cart and I drove Ann around our estate, stopping at the two villages just outside its borders. The villages perhaps do not deserve that name—each numbered about ninety inhabitants and a church. Ann thought they had been abandoned.

"People don't live there!" she cried. I stared at Ann's pointing finger in surprise. She was indicating one of the tumbled-down piles of stones and mud, the color of the earth itself, where nearly a dozen peasants, as I very well knew, did indeed live, and had always lived. For the peasants, all of them, even the babies who are carried in wrapped-up bundles, go to the fields to work in the daytime, returning only at nightfall. The two little villages were deserted and empty.

Ann Tyrrell had traveled widely before she came to Spain— but La Mata shocked her. Usually foreigners see the big cities first. They behold the great cathedrals, the fine paintings, the lovely buildings with admiration—and they forget everything else. For a foreigner to visit a Spanish village like the two near

La Mata first before the cities is very rare—and Ann's astonishment opened my eyes.

I had gone into the peasants' houses from childhood on and I had thought it was perfectly natural that they should live in poverty, dirt, and darkness. Now Ann's horror found reflection in my own heart. Next morning we got up early. I suggested a walk. We took one of the loveliest strolls in La Mata, past the ruins of a fifteenth-century monastery, back through the village. Then I led Ann to the house of a peasant who had worked for us nearly all my life.

Higinia, the wife, still bore the marks of Spanish beauty. But at thirty-five, work in the fields, eight children, poor food and little rest had made her old. She looked past fifty. I am sure Higinia had never in her life washed any part of her body except her hands and face, and this last only in Summer when she dipped her dishes in the stream that went through the village. But the little stream was frozen in the Winter and dried by the sun for many months during the Summer. The drinking water in her village trickled from a corner in the churchyard. Townspeople would say that drinking water from a graveyard was dangerous, but Higinia and her fellow villagers had no choice.

Higinia's husband had served in the army—and once that had taken him as far as Madrid. This gave him considerable authority in the village—he was a well-traveled man, a citizen of the great world. In addition, Román could read, and almost—but not quite—write. This learning made him the village seer. His reputation for knowledge had spread over the whole countryside after the famous incident of the white pigeon.

For Román had been dragged away by army officers just after Higinia announced herself pregnant with her first child. Lonely and frightened, Higinia called the village midwife when her time came. The young woman suffered terribly and the midwife, afraid for her patient's life, put a white pigeon on her belly, to cure what she thought was puerperal fever. Román returned just in time to save his young wife from the dangers of a squawking pigeon strapped for two days to her stomach, and from other practices of the ignorant midwife.

The villagers were amazed to hear that a white pigeon not

only would not cure childbirth fever, but might even cause it. No one had ever told them before that the bed of a woman in labor and all her linens should be kept carefully clean. The priest, observing Román's considerable influence with his fellows, grew suspicious of a man who disdained the ancient ways of treating illness. But the peasants saw logic in Román's point of view. The white pigeon method of treating childbirth fever disappeared in spite of the priest.

Román was a man of many talents. Beside his learning and medical knowledge, he also knew music. He was a one-man band and played for the village feasts around the whole countryside. This made him a man of means—he often earned as much as five *pesetas* a day, double the amount he could earn working from sunrise to sunset in the fields. And even with this comparative wealth, Román's family of five usually had too little to eat, not enough warm clothing for winter.

I took Ann into Higinia and Román's house that morning. The house was identical with all the others in the village. The entrance opened into a little corridor with three doors. One led to the kitchen, the second to the bedroom, the third to the stable. The men, women, children and animals came in and out the same door. In the Summer, the flies from the stable made the little house very nearly impossible to live in. The only way to endure the pests was to keep the house in absolute darkness—and in winter the house was also dark because the two square openings in the kitchen and bedroom were too small to give much light and in any case were boarded over, in lieu of the glass these peasants had never seen, to keep out the cold. The coolest place in the house in the summer was the corridor—furnished with a wooden chest, a couple of benches, and a drinking water stand. The floor was of hard earth, naturally, sprinkled every day with water.

Ann and I were honored guests, so Román led us into his bedroom where, as a special treat, we were allowed to sit on an old straight-backed sofa, the pride of his life. But our visit began very badly. I explained that Ann was from a distant country and could not speak Spanish. But alas, this met with no response at all. Not speak Spanish? The lady must be deaf.

Román and Higinia shrieked at Ann who grew red with embarrassment. And then I realized with a sudden wave of shame,
that Román and Higinia, the two leading savants of their village, had never heard that there were other countries in the
world beside Spain, had never been taught that men spoke
other languages than Spanish. Until that day I had not really
understood the terrible ignorance of the illiterate peasants who
worked on my father's estate. And although I did not know
quite why, I felt that my family and I were somehow responsible for this tragic ignorance.

Román and Higinia, unconscious of their error, began to
feel sorry for the poor young lady, my friend, so young but so
unfortunate. Deaf, at such an age! They opened their family
chest, and carefully lifting aside the beautiful holiday clothes,
passed from father to son and worn only on state occasions, drew
out the finest present they had to offer us—sausages from last
year's pig, kept in fresh lard. Ann's face betrayed her feelings
about eating raw sausage and lard and so I had to gulp an extra
portion, explaining that she felt ill. But the old grandma, deaf
herself, seeing Ann refuse the sausage, rose to the family occasion. From the depth of her apron pocket she drew a piece of
hard cod, put aside for the winter when for days there would
be nothing but onions and bread. We struggled for five minutes
trying to explain to the old woman why Ann would not eat
hard cod—even after a morning's walk.

Ann and I walked away from the little village back to the
manor house in a solemn mood. All my life I had lived around
peasants and taken their ignorance, their poverty, their misery
as a matter of course. My uncles used to make jokes about the
peasants—jokes repeated over the dinner table. They never
spoke to a peasant without asking him questions which would
confuse him—so that they, the overlords, could have a hearty
laugh. Now suddenly, I saw these peasants as people, human
beings, and in a rush of feeling, I understood their sorrow, their
universal melancholy. I felt ashamed, deeply ashamed.

But I was seventeen and my friend from England was eighteen, and it was summer, and we forgot the peasants working
endlessly in the fields. Life was gay. La Mata was twelve miles

from the old palace at La Granja where the Infanta had gone for the summer. A few families, preferring the mountains to the seashore, had taken up summer quarters under the wing of the King's old aunt, and Marichu, Ann, and I became overnight the belles of this summer circle. Every day we played tennis at the exclusive tennis club at La Granja—nearly every night my mother had a party or dance for us. And then in September my father held La Mata's first big shooting party.

A Spanish shooting party, unlike the English who manage to make the hunting of a fox or shooting of grouse a solemn, ritualistic affair, is attended with the maximum of trouble, accidents, and excited talk. My father had invited twenty guests— some of the best shots of Spain—and their arrival was the big event of the decade in the peasant villages. No sooner had the sensation of seeing twenty strangers bump over the country roads subsided when the hunting dogs arrived. The Duke of Medinaceli had loaned father his *jauria,* his pack of trained dogs, and they traveled all the way from the South of Spain in the care of a majordomo. The majordomo was nearly as picturesque as his canine charges. He wore a wide brimmed hat, short jacket, leather trousers—and a vastly worried expression.

The morning of the great day all the hunters assembled in the courtyard for instructions. The dogs had already gone out with their keepers to the mountains where the big game hid in the hot summer. They would drive the deer, foxes, and boar down the mountain trails into the thickets of the plains. And there, assigned to likely spots, would stand the hunters, armed to the teeth, ready to pick off the fleeing game as it passed.

But there were, with the wives and daughters of the shooters and our household, more hunters than good shooting stations. So each hunter was assigned a lady companion who was to help him while away the time until the dogs sent the boar crashing into the forests. My mother, with a careful eye on me, assigned me to an elderly, dull old fellow, a good friend of my father's. But I had other plans. For among our shooting party guests was a young diplomat soon to be sent on his first post abroad by the Government. His father, a marquis, owned Spain's most absurd newspaper—an aristocratic gossip sheet never sold on the streets but only mailed to subscribers. My mother read it faithfully, as indeed, all Spanish society women did. I wasn't much impressed by the newspaper, but I was exceedingly impressed by the young man who seemed to me, in my naïveté, gay, intelligent, and romantic.

So when the hunting party left the manor house, I managed to make a hasty shift in partners, and while all day long the others shot boar I flirted with my gallant cavalier. When night fell we finally returned home to find the rest of the hunters celebrating many a kill. They greeted us with jeers.

That night, as we undressed for bed, I told Ann I had fallen in love. She looked at me in amazement.

"How could you possibly be in love so quickly?" Ann asked, looking very shocked and very English.

I laughed and tried to explain, but Ann only shook her head. She found the Spanish people excitable, mercurial, temperamental, gay one moment, hysterical the next, and somber the third. England was never like this, she said, and grinned.

The shooting party ended the season at La Mata. My parents took Ann back to England and with them went Marichu to spend another year at my school in Cambridge. My mother no longer felt that an English education was a good preparation for the life of a Spanish girl of good society, but my father would not deny to one daughter what he had given the other.

I left at the same time as my parents, but for Arriluce, not England. My brand new beau went back to Madrid—to borrow money, I think, to follow me. I set out, lightheadedly with Maria Isabel, my school girl friend, for the fun at a seaside resort.

And I ran into history in the making.

I arrived at Arriluce two days before General Primo de Rivera, violating his oath, announced a rebellion and with the King's approval set up a military dictatorship under which Spain was to groan for many long years.

Maria Isabel and I missed seeing an important page in history the night after I arrived. The whole family, and I with them, was invited to a ball given by the Dowager Queen at the Palace

of Miramar. But alas, we knew those state balls of old. Maria
Isabel and I declined to spend the evening being bored by stiff
formality. So Maria Isabel's parents went alone, grumbling at
the carefree spirit of the younger generation.

They returned in great excitement. General Primo de Rivera
had rebelled—and they had seen the King receive the news with
a pleased smile in full view of all his court. Political friends
filled Arriluce all the next day, for the word had spread that
Maria Isabel's father, the Marquis, had spoken to the King only
the night before.

"I think he knew of the uprising in advance," the Marquis
kept saying, pleased to be the center of attention for once, "he
didn't seem at all surprised, only filled with satisfaction."

For there were exciting question marks in this rebellion of
Primo de Rivera's. Of course, it was perfectly obvious why
King Alfonso was pleased by a military dictatorship—no doubt
he had a good deal to do with planning the coup, and certainly
without his approval the doughty General would never have
dared violate his oath to the Constitution of Spain. For every
die-hard reactionary in Spain was annoyed and even frightened
by the Liberal Cabinet in power. Not that the Liberals had
really accomplished any reforms in the corrupt monarchy, or
even that they talked of doing so. But the mild suggestions the
Liberal Ministers timidly put forward to make Spain's government slightly more efficient outraged the Army, the King, the
landowners, and the industrialists.

But much more important—the weak Liberal Government
began to make people think. It was rather like offering a starving man a plate of very thin soup. He drinks the soup. But it
doesn't satisfy his hunger—it only makes him think of steaks and
chops and good white bread. So the people of Spain, long oppressed by a backward and vicious monarchy, found the thin
soup of the Liberal Government an unsatisfying meal. They
began to want more.

Naturally, the restlessness of the Spanish people found its
greatest expression in Catalonia, the one place, outside of Bilbao, which was really industrialized. Here, where modern ideas
had come in with the new factories and electric light plants, the

reactionaries found it hardest to keep the people in darkness and ignorance. Here the industrialists began to be afraid that the constitutional monarchy was not enough to keep wages low and hours long. A sterner government was needed, they thought. And General Primo de Rivera was the military governor of Catalonia. What could be more natural than the choice of this local military man to stop in its tracks the growing popular movement for a more democratic form of government—by making him a military dictator?

Yes, the reason for the General's rebellion was clear enough to the people who sat all day at the Marquis's fine house discussing it. But two questions remained. What would my grandfather, the head of the Conservative party, the leader, after a fashion, of the feudal land-owning aristocrats think of this dictatorship put forward by the rising industrialists of Spain? And what part did foreign capital play in the General's coup?

The second question was answered by time—the General himself soon began to distribute large portions of Spain's internal resources to the foreign "friends" who helped him to power. As for my grandfather—the worried Marquis, who had echoed Don Antonio's political views for a lifetime, could never get a very explicit answer from him. It was quite clear that my grandfather, and indeed all his land-holding followers, disliked the dictatorship. My grandfather had personally fought the military all his life, and in our family generals and lesser army officers were openly despised. Still it appeared that my grandfather had at least acquiesced in the Rivera rebellion. For we all learned that after the first excitement died down that the King had long ago asked Don Antonio's advice—and my grandfather had replied guardedly that perhaps it would be better to let "those who refuse to let others govern, govern themselves." Give the Army rope to hang itself, my grandfather had said in his roundabout polite Spanish fashion. And with the aristocratic land holders it was much the same—not a case of loving the dictatorship more but liking the liberal government less.

So the King had made his choice, and as it turned out, it was a very bad choice for the Bourbon rulers of Spain. For from the moment that Alfonso welcomed the news of the Primo de

Rivera uprising with a pleased smile, the Monarchy and the dictatorship were tied together forever. The dictatorship could not last without the Crown, and the Crown could no longer exist without the dictatorship. The King thought he had made a wise move for himself and his children, and indeed, all of us who sat idly chattering at Arriluce thought so too. As the days passed, in fact, the subject grew tiresome. The dictatorship was in the saddle, nothing would change for the people who owned lovely villas and could give their daughters dances and parties and fine clothes and rich husbands. Politics, after the first flurry, seemed dull. Maria Isabel and I settled down to have a fine time.

Arriluce was the perfect setting for two seventeen-year-old girls who wanted nothing more, at the moment, from life except fun. The great house stood on a cliff overlooking the beautiful sea. Far away from the smoke and dust of the industrial town of Bilbao, Arriluce was one of a little colony of enormous mansions built by the rich and titled folk of the neighborhood. Nowhere else in Spain, not even in Madrid, did the rich live in such luxury and comfort as in this suburb of Bilbao—for Maria Isabel's family, like the others of the group, had made fortunes trading with England during the war and had learned its habits of living from Mayfair, not Castile. The traditional Spanish aristocracy lived in great pomp and greater discomfort, but the Bilbao upper classes had plumbing and electric toasters and wonderful bathrooms and interior decorators who scorned ugly Victorian furniture.

I liked the life at Arriluce. Maria Isabel had two brothers who were quite young but very jolly—and the Marchioness herself was famous for her gaiety. Perhaps a little too famous. My mother, who was fashionable but very strait-laced, raised her eyebrows at the very mention of the Marchioness's name. But the Marchioness was not concerned with what my mother or anyone else thought of her. All she cared was to have the Royal family and the "smart set" staying at *her* place. She had lost her youthful slimness and was spreading loosely in alarming proportions. But unlike my mother, she was no martyr to her figure—she worried much more about having a good time. She enjoyed brilliant spicy conversation and at that time when there was no danger of leftism in Spain, she enjoyed reading books that I am sure in later years she would have fed to a bonfire. It was fashionable in Spain in those days of the Weimar Republic to be left-intellectual. The liberals of Britain's post-war days had a considerable influence on the minds of those Spanish aristocrats who boasted a superficial western culture.

But the Marchioness's intellectual daring was hardly shared by her husband. He was the president of as many boards of directors as was humanly possible for any one man. He came home from work exhausted every day to sit down to an enormous meal served by four butlers and cooked by the very best French chefs. The Marquis was also a Deputy for my grandfather's party and before Primo de Rivera stopped all political activity he went once a year to Madrid to sit at the Cortes. It was his only vacation.

I came to know the Marquis and his gay wife very well, for I spent two months with Maria Isabel every year until I was married and for many seasons after that. I always had the same room—a blue suite with a blue bath. Maria Isabel had her own bedroom, sitting room, dressing room, and bath near her mother's rooms. We had breakfast in bed every morning, sometimes together, and then we started out for the day. Usually our program began with golf and we played on beautiful links overlooking the sea. Then we took Maria Isabel's motor boat, an exact copy of the King's, out for a jaunt. In the afternoon, we went to the club for dancing, drinking, and a little mild gambling. In the evenings, the Marchioness usually took us back to the club for more dancing.

After a few weeks by the seashore that summer, I began to think twice about my pallid, sick-looking beau from the shooting party at La Mata. I hardly knew him, after all, and the rumors I picked up about his habits and way of life hardly seemed reassuring. In the meantime, however, he had told his family about me and they gave him their enthusiastic approval of his choice. I was quite a catch, wealthy, the granddaughter of Spain's most famous political leader—and on top of that—

considered quite a beauty in Madrid. Maria Isabel and I spent hours discussing the problem. I began to feel more and more dubious. My mother did not yet know of this flirtation, but later she too gave her approval—a fact which afterwards caused some bitterness between us. For when my beau turned up unexpectedly in Bilbao to make arrangements for the formal announcement of our engagement, I discovered something most unpleasant and terrible about him. He was sick. Obviously, he had no right to make plans for marriage. It appeared that my mother knew all about this, for it was quite obvious to anyone except a young, ignorant girl brought up in a convent. But in spite of this defect, my mother at least, was willing to marry me to this young man because he came from a good family and would one day inherit a title.

My beau pressed me for an immediate answer to his suit. But armed with my new knowledge, I told him very plainly why I would not marry him. He never forgave me for such a frank answer. It was unheard-of in Spain in 1923 that a well-brought-up young girl of seventeen should think, let alone know, about such things. Everyone attributed my freakishness to my English education.

I had to settle down in Madrid after a gay summer. My parents disapproved of my friendship with the Arriluce family although they had nothing against Maria Isabel herself. Still, they welcomed me back to Madrid with stern warnings that I must adjust myself again to the formal, dignified, prison-like life of the capital. I was restless and unhappy. I yearned for something to do, some outlet for my energy. I had nothing definite to plan for—I just could not be satisfied with the life my mother had arranged for me. I was to go shopping in the mornings, driving in the park in the afternoons, to parties, theatre, cinemas in the evenings with an occasional evening in our box at the opera. Idle moments, my mother said, should be used for embroidery and sometimes a nice, decent book. What else did a well-educated, well-brought-up girl need to make her happy? But I found my life empty. Religion, the great solace of Spanish upper-class women, no longer sufficed for me. As for marriage, I had been semi-engaged once, and since then could find no other suitor that pleased me or ever interested me. I was bored—although I hardly knew it. My father and mother discussed my revolt endlessly, trying to decide what I should do while waiting for a suitable husband. For finding a husband was the real aim of my existence and I was never allowed to forget it.

Finally my parents came to a decision. I should spend my time in "good works" if society life was not enough for me. Ordinarily, a woman of the Madrid upper classes does not take to "good works" until she is a matron or a definite old maid. But if I was bored by the "gay" life of Spanish society, I might begin my charitable activities early. My mother had neglected some of her "good works" during the last two years in preparation for launching me into society, but now she would go back into charity activities and take me with her.

I began my "good works" with great enthusiasm and no misgivings. I had been taught all my life that the rich and religious had a duty to perform in life—the succoring of the poor and helpless. True, my actual training in such work had been the annual bun I had been made to hand to the charity pupils at the convent school. But I discounted that miserable experience. I was grown up now. I would throw myself into "good works" with all my heart, and perhaps then I would be happy and useful.

Unfortunately my first experience in "good works" was a major disappointment, for my mother and I started off in the *Marias del Sagrario*. This was a Jesuit enterprise designed to quell the growing restlessness among the village clergy. The parish priests in most of Spain's country churches lived in no such luxury as the city priests and bishops and cardinals. The frightful poverty of the villages was reflected in the comparative poverty of the village priest. The bishops did nothing to remedy the miserable conditions of the parish priests. Indeed, they added fuel to the flame by driving at high speed along the dusty country roads in huge foreign limousines. In some of the past elections the village priest, who was supposed to hold his flock in line for the landlord, had been known to talk and vote against the local absentee owners. The Society of Jesus was alarmed. The situation must be immediately remedied.

The poorer villages were each assigned a lady upon whom was bestowed the sonorous title, *Maria del Sagrario,* literally, a "Mary of the Sanctuary."

My mother was one of those ladies, and now I was to help her. We started off one morning to visit the parish priest to whom she had been assigned by the Jesuits. It was a fine day and our chauffeur covered the roads from Madrid to the little country village in record time. We arrived before noon, two handsomely dressed, rich ladies, to find the parish priest pruning his fruit trees in the small garden behind his house. He had not expected us, for we had not bothered to tell him of our plans. He had not shaved for several days and he wore a weatherbeaten cassock turned the color of flies' wings, soiled and buttonless. My mother stood, sweetly gracious and condescending, while the poor priest scraped and bowed and asked our apologies.

"My parish is so poor, Madam," he said, with a certain cunning.

My mother brightened.

"This is what we have come to see you about," she began. The priest listened, wide-eyed, while she told him about the group of pious ladies in Madrid under the spiritual direction of the Jesuit Fathers who thought and worried about the poor parishes where the Lord did not always have a light burning in the sanctuary because the parish was too poor even to buy oil for the lamps.

"And we have thought, too," my mother continued graciously while I stood uncomfortably by her in that little orchard, "of the saintly priests who do not always have money to buy wine for the consecration in the Mass and are forced to add water again and again to the nearly empty bottle."

The priest cast down his eyes and I wondered if my mother would also tell him about the last elections and the priests voting against the landlords.

"It is the bishops," the priest finally began, when my mother grew silent. "Only two weeks ago our bishop came to the village and you could hear his motor car for miles away and all the peasants came and saw him descending from his rich limousine, and if he can afford such a rich motor car, then surely there should be money for the lamp and the wine, and . . ."

My mother held up her gloved hand. She spoke sweetly, for the Jesuit Father had instructed us to be kind and charitable. But she spoke firmly. For we had been told very carefully how to reply if the parish priests blamed the bishops for their poverty. The parish priest stood quietly under her gracious rebuke, bobbing his head up and down on his dirty cassock as my mother described the hard life the bishops had, and how they needed speedy motor cars to visit their far-flung flocks.

"And now," said my mother when the priest offered no argument, "will you show us the church?"

I was astounded to see that church. It was dirty, barren, and decrepit. The floor needed a carpet. The altar needed a new cloth. The images in the church were few and very old. My mother looked the place over and then promised the priest a complete new carpet and all the other decorations the church needed.

The priest beamed. On the way home my mother said to me, "He will never vote again against the Conservatives."

I felt uneasy after the first trip, but when we returned a month or so later I grew downright uncomfortable. It was a pleasant Autumn day. As our limousine passed through the narrow streets of the village, I found the peasants staring at us with blank hostility. Had the *Marias del Sagrario* taken any interest in the material welfare of the parishioners? Had we bothered to find out if the village had a school or a doctor? Had we paid any attention to the fact that in this village of our charity work all the children under three years of age had died the winter before in a diphtheria epidemic? No. Our "good work" was to win the parish priest from his suspected liberal views.

We arrived at the church to find the priest waiting for us, this time dressed in a clean cassock, shaved, and very servile. The new carpets and altar cloth and the large image of the Sacred Heart we had sent had already been installed. A reception committee, composed of the wives of the few rich farmers of the village, was on hand to thank us for our gift. We climbed the steps to the little chapel. Although we had found it decrepit, I discovered that we were to leave it ugly. The carpet was cheap and hideous. The image of the Sacred Heart was in the worst possible taste. The altar cloth was garish.

We had rather expected to find the entire grateful peasantry of the village assembled in our honor. The reception committee and the priest were apologetic. For it appeared that the peasants were sullen. The diphtheria epidemic had left them heartbroken. They felt that a doctor—for the village, it developed, had none—might have saved a few of their children. My mother passed over this situation tactfully. It was enough that we had obviously won the heart and devotion of the parish priest. He would take care of the political views of his parishioners. But I was so horrified I could take no interest in the proceedings.

Driving back to Madrid in our car, my mother asked me harshly why I had been so unresponsive, so lacking in enthusiasm.

"You took absolutely no interest in the whole thing. And, after all, you are to take over my work in this parish!"

My eyes filled with tears. I could not explain to my mother why I found this "good work" so horrible—because I hardly knew myself. But I felt that it was wrong. There was a silence in our car. And then my mother spoke again—on a different subject. She had decided, apparently, that supplying new altar cloths to poor parish priests was not a suitable charity for a young restless girl. Next day I started a new "good work." This time I was to work among children—the sons and daughters of the Madrid poor.

My mother belonged to an association of Catholic women, also directed by the Jesuits, which was responsible for Catholic education in Madrid. My own school life had seemed so inevitable that I honestly had never even thought of how the children of the poor learned to read and write and do sums in the great modern city of Madrid. Now I learned that under the Primo de Rivera dictatorship, as always before, there were almost no free schools in Madrid. Some ninety thousand children of school age in Madrid had absolutely no school facilities of any kind. The Catholic ladies who belonged to the association each paid for the upkeep of one small school somewhere in the city. Naturally, these few charity schools hardly made a dent in the appalling illiteracy of the population but still, my mother said, the work of the association was of the greatest importance.

So, feeling eager to do something to help the poor children, I went with my mother to visit the school her funds paid for. We drove away from our great house into the dirty, narrow, cobblestone streets of the poor quarters of Madrid. The women and children crowded the narrow sidewalks and our chauffeur had to honk impatiently to get them out of the way, for they lived all day in the streets and went to their dark ill-smelling little rooms only when it rained. The car stopped at the door of one of these ancient houses. We climbed up three flights of dirty wooden stairs and knocked at a door that had not been painted for at least a quarter of a century.

A young, tubercular-looking woman opened the door. Her pale, sad face stood out in the dark gloom of the hallway. She was the schoolteacher of my mother's school. We walked behind her into the narrow rooms—the class rooms for forty youngsters. As we entered, the children jumped up.

"How-are-you-Madame? We-are-very-well-thank-you-and-thanks-to-God-and-to-you-Madame." Their sing-song monotonous voices hit me in the face like a slap. The pale teacher smiled. She was proud of her achievement. Not a child had forgotten the words of the melancholy chant.

I looked around the dreary tenement rooms which had been whitewashed two years before when my mother had converted the dilapidated flat into a school. The only thing on the cracking walls was a crucifix. There was not a single picture, or drawing, not a pot of flowers or a carpet, not a cheerful thing in the whole room. The school curriculum was almost as scanty as the interior decoration. The children learned the catechism, with its questions and answers—and that was all. Perhaps it was all they could be expected to learn from the thin little teacher.

My mother paid her six dollars a month to teach this school. Obviously it was not enough to keep her well and strong. The school made me feel almost faint with shame. And yet, bad as it was, had it not been for the association of Catholic women these children would be out playing on the pavements, entirely without schooling.

I found the school a challenge and I began to lay plans for its improvement immediately. I doubled the salary of the school-teacher to start with, for I thought if she were better fed and more cheerful she might make the children happier. Then I decided to hang some pictures, bring some potted flowers, supply the children with crayons and paper to draw on, and a few story books to read from. But gradually my interest in the miserable school died. For all my plans met with failure. The association felt that if I had more money to spend or could collect money from my friends for my school, it should go to the establishment of other schools. Story books were all very well for the children of the rich, but the children of the poor should not be distracted from their study of the catechism. I found no answer to these arguments and it did not occur to me that I could do anything else for these pale, sad little children. I visited them twice a month, paid the salary of the teacher, and looked about for more "good works" to keep me busy.

A friend of mine brought me to the Sisters of Charity. My mother belonged to this same charity institution, so she approved my new work which brought me very directly this time into contact with the poverty-stricken population of Madrid. The Sisters of Charity, with their aristocratic helpers, visited poor families once a week, bringing their miserable, half-starved members a paper bag of food, a few copper pieces, and good advice—sometimes even a job for the man of the household if he promised to join the Catholic trade unions. Many of the households on the list were of men and women living in sin with illegitimate children—usually because they lacked the money for the marriage fee. But young ladies were not supposed to know of even the existence of such evil conditions. We only visited poor households made up of young widows and their children. We made our visits accompanied by the Sister

of Charity. Our weekly food package consisted of a half pound
of lentils, a half pound of rice, a half pound of beans, one hundred grams of sugar, and fifty grams of coffee. This had to keep
the family alive until our next visit!

I had never seen, nor even dreamt of, such sordid poverty
as I saw that Winter in Madrid. Nothing in my sheltered
existence had prepared me for the frightful scenes that met my
eyes regularly once a week. The other girls who made visits
with the Sisters of Charity seemed to get some satisfaction, even
pleasure out of their weekly rounds. But it filled me with enormous depression. I had enough sense to realize the scanty package of food we brought could do little good for people so far
gone in hunger, disease and poverty.

The Sisters of Charity questioned the young widows every
week. "Did you go to Mass last Sunday? Have you gone to confession this month?"

Sometimes the answer was sullen, or, worse, in the negative.
Then the young widow was scratched from our list and we left
her to shift for herself without our beans and lentils and hundred grams of sugar.

And the sharp eyes of the Sisters of Charity missed no tell-
tale signs in the crowded smelly rooms where our charity clients
lived. Did it appear that the young widow was consoling herself
with a suitor? Did gossip in the hallways indicate she now and
then went out dancing? For these sins, too, she was crossed off
the list.

All that Winter I was swept by passionate feelings of shame
and remorse—remorse for I knew not what crime. I felt bitterly
ashamed of my own empty and luxurious life. But I was taught
by my mother, by the Sisters of Charity, in fact by everyone I
saw or talked to, to find justification in it by the few hours a
week I gave to works of charity. Indeed I was subtly made to
think by my mother that the people I met on my weekly visits
were not the same kind of people we were, that the unfortunate
poor were the products of something unknown, for which we
were not in the least to blame. But I could not find this explanation really satisfying. "The poor we have always with us,"

the Sisters of Charity said, and my mother echoed, "God's ways are inscrutable."

And yet the poor I visited seemed no different from the people I had always known, except for the poverty, the dirt, and lack of education. Surely these young widows also wanted happiness and security for their children? Surely they too needed only the opportunity to lead quiet and decent lives? Sometimes I made some comment, or sometimes I could not help the tears coming into my eyes at the injustice I saw.

"She has a heart of gold," my parents said.

Golf, polo, and pigeon shooting were the three favorite sports of Madrid society. The King rode his polo ponies and shot pigeons inside the enclosure of the beautiful park called La Casa de Campo. The royal park was naturally closed to the public but a selected few of Madrid society, my family among them, had cards to admit them to the royal playground.

I met King Alfonso for the first time at the pigeon-shooting club. The King used to spend much of his time there, arriving early in the afternoon and staying until quite late. He sat in one of the boxes overlooking the shooting field, surrounded by a group of men, all of them dressed in loose shooting jackets, drinking and laughing. Now and then the name of the King would be called in his turn to come out on the shooting field. He was a very good shot and seldom missed his mark. The King obviously reveled in the easy applause he got from his group of friends as he swaggered back from the field to the clubhouse. One of my uncles, also a very good shot, was always with Alfonso in the box—I often saw him leaning over to tell the King some new joke which always brought uproarious laughter.

I used to go often, with a group of girls my age and our inevitable mothers or chaperones, to watch the shooting. It never seemed very sporting to me. The pigeons, freed for a moment from their traps, were easy marks. Even if the pigeon managed to escape the first time, it was picked up inside the enclosure and used again. We sat around all afternoon with drinks and the typical fried sausage and potatoes watching the King shoot the fluttering birds. Sometimes after the shooting was over there would be dancing. It was all very informal but very snobbish because only a chosen few were admitted to the club. I do not remember ever seeing the Queen at the pigeon-shooting afternoons. The King always danced freely with the women he liked. He did not even bother to keep up appearances. Some good-looking woman new in Madrid, a foreigner perhaps, or a Spaniard from outside the capital, sometimes just a social climber who had at last attained the goal of admission to the inner circles, caught the King's eye. He did not care much for names or pedigrees; so long as a woman was beautiful, it was enough to please him. I remember watching him one afternoon make advances to a beautiful young matron, one of the nouveaux riches who had fought her way into high society. The girl, for she was little more than that, was obviously thrilled by the Royal attention. I myself had a feeling of nausea, watching the beautiful young woman dancing so close to the King with his evil-looking nose and famous bad breath. Everyone in Spain knew about the King's disease. Even young girls like myself, who were supposed to know nothing of life, spoke about it. And still that social climber, that beautiful girl, became the King's mistress as did many others, before and after. And it was hardly a secret—the whole society world discussed it very freely.

The polo ground was just as exclusive as the shooting club, but more formal. Foreign diplomats were never seen at the pigeon-shooting, but they usually appeared for polo. The Queen, surrounded by her guests, usually sat in her special stand, watching the game. Her appearance brought a certain decorum. The King was inclined to mistake vulgarity for popularity and bonhomie.

Primo de Rivera went well with the King's plebeian tastes. He, too, found vulgarity reassuring. Nobody knew what Primo de Rivera's dead wife had been like, but all Madrid knew the type of woman the Dictator admired on the stage. Indeed, he made it exceedingly obvious. For whenever a review or musical comedy came to Madrid which featured an undressed chorus or the like, the Dictator reserved a box as near as possible to the stage.

Nor did he admire the beautiful ladies on the stage silently, from afar. Whenever he saw something to excite his interest, he did not attempt to control his emotion but spoke loudly and frankly to the woman or women on the stage, informing them of exactly what was on his mind. But he was the Dictator of Spain and therefore free—the only man in the country— to do as he liked. Curiously enough he would invite a group of friends to his box and more than once among these guests was his future bride. Her admiration for the General was so great, however, that she was incapable of jealousy. All she wanted was to give him the nice home that only her personal fortune could provide. For Primo de Rivera was not a rich man. It is true that during his lifetime a "voluntary collection" was made to which all trade union workers and government employees and the Army were asked to contribute "voluntarily," with a decided risk to their jobs or freedom if they did not. These "voluntary contributions" amounted to four million *pesetas*—the fortune left by the Dictator to his children.

But at the time he was engaged to our maiden lady friend, it was thought that she, and not the workers of the nation, would provide for the Rivera children. But alas, the Dictator pushed his luck too far. His fiancée suddenly started speculating on the stock market—an unheard-of venture—for her fortune was in sound, solid investments. She made an enormous sum of money overnight and retired from her flurry of investment activity. Tongues began to wag. Perhaps she had a special sort of tip? Who but the Dictator or some close friend of his could give such sound advice for speculating on the stock market? The affair became a national scandal. Primo de Rivera was forced to choose. The rich wife or the country? He wisely chose the country and shortly afterwards began his "voluntary contributions."

Primo de Rivera's attitude towards women, as all this indicates, was a very curious one. He called himself a feminist, but his feminism was of a very strange nature. He looked to the traditional Catholicism of the Spanish women to provide him with a strong bulwark of conservative support against the liberalism of their menfolk. The granting of a few just measures to women, and very few indeed, they were, was not intended as a measure of liberalism, but as a means of preserving Spain's old Catholic and conservative traditions. He invited thirteen women to his National Assembly, two of whom declined. He would often be seen having tea with the remaining eleven, so unexpectedly risen into public life.

He publicly made known his disappointment at feminine ungratefulness when in 1929 the women students joined the University riots against the dictatorship and the monarchy. In one of his typical "official statements" that all the newspapers were forced to publish, he said: "It is with deep pain that I learn from police reports that the women students, not only did not try to calm the excitement, but, on the contrary, on some occasions helped to fan the unrest. . . . I have taken pains to give women participation in the privileges of citizenship, but I shall now have to reflect carefully as to whether it would not be better to prohibit the admission of women to official careers." Primo could only understand two classes of women: beautiful girls to whom he could throw a compliment and have an interchange of spicy conversations, if nothing else; and staid matrons with large families and Catholic and conservative ideals.

In 1926 I was twenty—and not married. I began to worry. Of course I had plenty of beaux—what we called "flirts." But the kind of man who has money and social position and health, and who loves you and whom you love in return, and who asks your hand in marriage from your father—this kind of a man was slow in turning up in my life. And I was becoming more and more bored. Life had absolutely no meaning. I was tired of parties and tired of "good works." My mother and I quarreled more every day. In this state of mind, uneasy, restless, almost desperate, I met the young man whom I was to marry.

It was the end of a Summer we had spent at St. Jean-de-Luz. It had been a difficult and unhappy vacation. I was twenty, looking for a husband, waiting for marriage, and yet only half

awake to the meaning of life. My mother never spoke to me of
sex, or of the problems of love and birth. It was a sin to think
about these things—a sin I faithfully confessed every time I
could not help committing it. I was supposed to learn intui-
tively. I was no different from most Spanish girls. Sex education
was not tolerated in Catholic schools. The mere thought of
such a thing would have made my family frown. Girls left
school at fifteen or sixteen and their mothers themselves were
not clear on the simplest problems of biology. As the times
changed in Spain the mothers came to have the idea that girls
coming out of the convent somehow knew more about life and
sex than they themselves did after many years of marriage. The
invisible barrier which this created was caused mainly by the
lack of information on both sides. I never knew a girl whose
mother ever even dared to speak to her of sex problems.

With Spanish boys it was very different. They learned nothing
at school—except what the older boys taught the younger. But
traditionally the first money Spanish boys received from their
fathers went always to the same place: the house of prostitu-
tion. It was always so in Spain, and people said it always would
be. Spanish girls were ignorant, and Spanish boys grew up
brutalized.

And then I met Bolin, whom I was to marry.

It happened very simply. My sisters and I were staying alone
at our villa in the seaside resort. Mother had gone to Paris to
buy clothes and father had returned to Madrid. We had the
inevitable chaperone-companion with us, of course, and the
servants, but we had a good deal of unexpected and delightful
freedom. Every evening my sisters and I walked down to the
pier and every morning we went to the beach and later to the
Pergola, a resort club. I was rather glum those last days of the
Summer—I kept thinking of my return to Madrid and the parties and the "good works" and the unasked question always
around me: "Why has she not married? A girl of twenty!"

I have forgotten whose casual introduction led to my first
bow to Manuel Bolin. I was standing on the veranda of the
club, moody and bored, when I looked up to see a young man
nearly seven feet tall. Now I was tall for a Spanish girl—most

Spanish men were shorter than I. I was sensitive about what I considered my great height and I thought one of the reasons I could not fall in love with any of my suitors was my great tallness and their shortness. So I looked twice at Bolin. Two days later we were engaged.

And then came the deluge that really led to my marriage. For I think if everyone I knew, my family and friends, had received Bolin with shouts of joy I would have been wary and examined my future husband with some care. Instead, I was greeted on all sides with loud expressions of dismay, and this long before my family knew of the informal engagement.

"Constancia," girls I knew from school said to me, "it can't be that you are *really* thinking of marrying that Bolin?"

I felt the anger rise in my throat. These stupid silly girls with their false set of standards! I began to feel very heroic. I was marrying for love, and not for money or a title or social position.

People who had known Bolin in his native town of Málaga were especially insistent. But alas, they were never specific in their objections and they only made me more determined to marry the man with whom I now decided I was madly in love.

Bolin took me to meet his mother. Her two maiden sisters and her brother, who was the Catholic Bishop of London, owned an old-fashioned villa, an ugly convent-like structure on the sea front at St. Jean-de-Luz. Bolin's half-English mother impressed me as a very prim and proper lady of foreign manners. She was very nice to me and so were her two maiden sisters, a peculiar mixture of English and French spinsterhood. Looking back on it now, I realize that they thought me a magnificent match, an unexpected piece of good fortune for their Manuel. The Bolin household exuded a certain shabby air of gentility, which perhaps, because it was new to me, I did not know how to interpret.

Indeed, I was so excited at the idea of getting married and leaving my parents' home that I forgot to study the man who was to be my husband. In my excited daydreams he played a very small part. I planned even then that I would have no children, and since I had really no idea of what marriage meant, I was never troubled by thoughts of my fiancé as a companion or friend.

It was rather difficult for me to find out about Bolin or his family either. He seemed to be fascinated by the simplest details of my life. He was twenty-two and had always lived in Málaga, going for the Summer months to the south of France. I did not know Málaga then but the name sounded very romantic. My friends asked me, "Will you be a provincial?" But I tossed my head. I was tired of Madrid. Málaga sounded beautiful.

One day, walking along the pier with Bolin talking of our future, the question of money arose. I knew that Bolin worked in his father's brokerage office in Málaga. Now I discovered that his father had not yet assigned him any definite salary. I naturally expected that we would be independent after we were married, so, feeling very matronly and grown-up, I asked him what his father would give us monthly. I had no idea, when I was twenty, of how much money it took to live on the scale of luxury my parents did. Bolin was not very helpful either. I did know something of the amounts my mother spent to run her household, for during the past year my father had insisted that I should learn how to manage the family accounts. But the sums I mentioned seemed enormous to my fiancé—he assured me that his father would pay him more than enough in salary to live very comfortably in Málaga.

I had no idea of the value of money. I did not know how difficult it is to earn money. I never dreamed that I would not always have enough to buy anything that I might need, or thought I needed. Until my marriage I had the impression that when one belonged to a certain group of human beings, such as my family and my friends, money was endless. Of course, there were certain very expensive things like diamond necklaces or sable furs which naturally one did not buy—at least not without much talk and excitement. But the other things—the servants, the governesses, the special food, the foreign schools, the clothes from Paris, the automobiles, the elaborate Summer vacations, the two houses, one in Madrid, one in La Mata, completely furnished and staffed with servants and stewards—

these things one had because it was only natural to have them. People like my parents and my sisters and myself possessed such things—an unwritten law said so. Our kind never wanted for any of these "necessities" of life.

Bolin and I spent a lovely fortnight at St. Jean-de-Luz. We went about together as foreign couples did, arm in arm, on the pier. We danced and swam and talked together while our chaperon gnawed her teeth and rolled her eyes in fear. But as the time for my mother's return grew near, I began to worry a little myself. I didn't want my mother to hear that Bolin and I had actually been seen alone together, even if it was in broad daylight on the beach. Such behavior would be a terrible scandal in the family and I knew my mother would be horribly humiliated at the thought of her daughter behaving like an English girl. So I packed up my sisters and the six servants we had brought from La Mata and put us all on the train for Spain. Bolin was very gallant and helpful, and we parted with many romantic promises.

I met my parents at La Mata and spent the evening telling them of my engagement. They were bitterly disappointed. The name Bolin meant nothing to them. Málaga was a distant provincial town. I was their eldest daughter, their favorite. They had planned a brilliant marriage for me. Even if I was twenty, they felt that I should wait for another kind of bridegroom, one more suitable in money and social position.

This kind of objection was all that was needed to make me believe that I was really and madly in love with Bolin.

"I don't want to make a brilliant match," I told my father. "I am in love. I want to marry for love. I want to be happy."

"Bah!" my father growled. He could hardly bear to discuss Bolin—it made him so angry.

"Why can't you fall in love with the right kind of man?" my mother asked me plaintively, but I found her arguments unimpressive. I knew that she thought of the effects of my undistinguished marriage on her social position. All fashionable Madrid would raise its eyebrows at a de la Mora girl marrying some shabby provincial.

Bolin had gone back to Málaga. After two months in which

my love for him grew out of all proportions in my heated imagination, he came to Madrid to see me and meet my family and formally ask my hand in marriage. I was worried about the hotel he would choose, as I knew it would make a great difference in my family. I breathed a sigh of relief when he telephoned from the Savoy.

My mother asked him to lunch that first day and I watched everybody's face nervously to see what success he was having. The final test was after lunch when we went down to my grandmother's apartment and he was introduced to the whole clan. Bolin made a rather good impression, if a tepid one. I never heard either strong criticism or great praise of him. My family thought his manners pleasant and his appearance rather foreign—which was not strange for his mother was half-English and his father of Swedish descent. No one thought Bolin either particularly intelligent or brilliant, but that caused no great worry.

What really agitated the family was the financial position of the Bolin clan. Since there was no title, no great Spanish name to consider, the great problem was money. But it was not easy to discover my fiancé's financial circumstances. Málaga was a distant provincial town, unknown to people of Madrid at that time. Only crazy English people, sailing directly from England to Gibraltar, would think of going there. Madrid society only went south to Seville; traveling in Spain was unheard of and vulgar. My father made inquiries about the Bolin family in Málaga but he met a blank wall everywhere. Nobody seemed to know if the Bolins were rich, or only middle class; whether they had money, or only seemed to have it.

My grandfather inadvertently really made my engagement possible. I was so worked up by that time against what I considered "social injustice" that nothing could have prevented me from marrying Bolin. While he was still visiting me in Madrid one Sunday, as we came from a game of golf, we were met by a frightened servant.

"Your grandfather is very ill and the Señora [my mother] has rushed out in the car to the place he was stricken!"

My grandfather had gone out that Sunday as usual to paint.

He had chosen a lovely spot—the house of an old friend of his, built on the solid rock and facing the Guadarrama Mountains. Dressed in his loose country jacket, sitting on the great terrace with his easel before him, he had been staring intently at the beautiful mountains of Spain, when death found him, suddenly, unexpectedly.

A servant saw his straight lean body, always held so proudly, topple from his little painting chair. A moment later the beautiful haughty face with its perfectly shaped nose, its carefully trimmed white beard, was empty. His heart had failed. He had died, as I know he would have chosen to die, painting the heart-moving mountains of the country he loved so well.

When my mother came in her car, thinking to bring a sick man home, she found a corpse. The drive back to Madrid with my grandfather's body sitting upright in a corner so that all judicial proceedings could be avoided was a terrible shock for my mother.

The news of Don Antonio's death came as we were eating lunch. I remember that the dessert had been placed before us when someone called me on the telephone with the dreadful words, "He is dead." I came back to the table to find an enormous tangerine on my plate. The tangerine was cut like a basket and inside there was a filling of ice cream covered with Chantilly. I was very fond of that particular sweet. I stared at it for a moment and then I began to gulp it down. It was not greediness—but shock. Whenever I am nervous or excited food seems to quiet me. It is almost a necessity at such moments.

But I remember feeling a wave of shame—thinking how indecent it was to enjoy my ice cream when in a moment I had to tell my sisters and fiancé of my grandfather's death. I can still see that tangerine after all these years when other pictures have faded in my mind.

My grandfather's death was a nation-wide event. Spain mourned with great pomp and formality for her most famous statesman. Our family went on public view from the moment that the news was told. The large white-and-gold drawing room, so much unused, was turned into a mortuary chapel. We watched silently while a firm of undertakers transformed its usual hideousness into something even worse. Black draperies on the walls, wreaths of flowers—with that peculiar death-smell only wreaths can have—candles, prayer benches filled the room.

For three days my grandfather's body, dressed in a monk's habit, the beautiful face shriveled in size but tense, a wax face framed by his white beard and hair, lay exposed in the opened coffin. Incessant processions came up the stairs to see him and sign their names on sheets of paper placed on a table in the hall for this purpose. The number of signatures was a record. The King and Queen came the first day to pray before my grandfather's body and to present their condolences to my grandmother and the rest of the family. Primo de Rivera did not come, which was something of a scandal, but he sent a general to represent the government at the funeral. I remember how stupidly I giggled when I saw the general going up to present his condolences to a stout weeping lady who was praying and crying. He had taken her for my grandmother but she was only a very distant friend of the family—one of those ghouls who turn up at funerals and weep more loudly for the deceased than the intimate family. I suppose it was not very funny, really, but after three days of constant vigil around the coffin, listening to the stereotyped condolences from everyone, with the drugging smell of death and flowers and constant tension of hushed conversation, my nerves felt ready to snap. Our real sorrow seemed forgotten in the deluge of artificial pomp. The funeral was followed by big crowds, not as big as those that had followed Pablo Iglesias, the Socialist leader, a few days before, and not the same kind of crowd either.

When the funeral was over, everyone in the family sighed with relief—and then began to realize that during the strain and confusion Bolin had become almost one of us. Always helpful and sympathetic, he had been at everyone's elbow. He rose to the emergency and really won his bride at a funeral.

With the funeral over, the following nine days of continual prayer for my grandfather's soul, with Mass being said from dawn to midday in my grandmother's private chapel and rosary being said in the afternoon, were like an anti-climax. About the fourth day of these ceremonies, conversation began to wander to other subjects: to the King's and Queen's faces, and the words they had used, how long they remained beside the coffin, who was the unimportant general Primo de Rivera had sent in his place, and so on.

And then I realized with a shock that nobody really mourned for my grandfather. Even my grandmother took his death rather calmly—and I could see that really, deep in our hearts, we did not and would not miss the handsome old man, so taciturn, so withdrawn, so famous. Our prayers were an artificial and tiresome ritual. I longed for the nine days to be over.

At the end of the nine days my mother took me aside and said, "My child, your Manuel has behaved like a son to me. I shall never forget it."

Our formal engagement was set for March, and the wedding date was to be fixed then. Bolin returned to Málaga and we settled down to a Winter of deep Spanish mourning. The women all wore complete and hideous black. We went nowhere except to church and sometimes a discreet walk in the park. Day after day my mother, my sisters and I stayed in the house, bored and annoyed. We were all glad to see the Bolins when they arrived in March, for we put off some of the mourning then and came back into life.

My fiancé arrived, as is the Spanish custom, with his parents. It was the first time our families had met and the first dinner went off rather well. In fact, my future parents-in-law seemed a distinguished old couple, as cultured as my parents at least, and certainly less frivolous than my mother. I made up my mind to like them. They spoke proudly of a son they had in England in the Spanish embassy who was also a correspondent for the *ABC,* the leading Madrid newspaper of the time. All these foreign contacts sounded very interesting to me.

Bolin brought me engagement gifts—a perfect black pearl ring surrounded by diamonds, set in platinum, and a tiny diamond-studded wrist watch. My family were impressed by the gifts but my father took Bolin aside and bluntly talked finance. My father was prepared, he said, to give me a substantial monthly allowance—what would my bridegroom have? But

Bolin as usual was very vague. His father would give him a comfortable salary. My parents found this vagueness on financial matters alarming but the affair had gone too far now to stop. The date of my marriage was fixed for the month of May and the Bolins returned to Málaga.

"Of course, you must buy your trousseau in Paris," my mother said after the Bolins were safely gone.

We spent three hectic weeks in Paris, selecting an enormous wardrobe. Besides all the lingerie and day and evening clothes my parents bought me, I also selected the clothes which were to be gifts of my bridegroom. It is a Spanish custom that the bride receives her wedding dress and part of her trousseau from her fiancé. Smart clothes were difficult to buy in Málaga so I was given the money to make my choice in Paris. My mother and I rushed madly during those weeks in Paris from one great dressmaker to another. Everything we bought had to be of the finest.

And while I stood being endlessly fitted in the dress salons of the Rue de la Paix, my linens were being prepared in Spain. I had marvelous bridal chests. My parents gave me enough linen to last for fifty years—and more—much more. I had embroidered sheets of the finest Irish linen, towels for an enormous household, blankets, tapestries and dishes and silver and furniture, all of the finest and most expensive. My silver, for instance, was a complete set for twenty-four, with every imaginable kind of extra piece included beside the usual knives, forks, and spoons. I had silver platters and silver serving dishes, fine old china, and priceless vases. And besides my parents' gifts, I received over four hundred wedding presents from friends of my rich and powerful family. Bolin gave me a pearl necklace which matched the necklace my father had given me at my debut. I had them strung together and the result was a beautiful double row pearl necklace. My parents gave me besides my trousseau a diamond necklace and Bolin a new Buick roadster.

I was wild with excitement at choosing all the clothes and dishes and linens and furniture and silver for my new household. Every day some new present came to the house. My sisters stood around open mouthed watching me enviously as I prepared for my wedding day. In all this confusion I had very little time to think of what marriage meant—or what sort of person Bolin was. After all, I had seen him very little. Except for the few days at St. Jean-de-Luz, nine months before, I had seen him only as a Spanish girl sees her fiancé—always with my mother or a chaperone near us. I had been carefully brought up to fear and despise the sex relationship between men and women. Now I was to be legally married, and presumably everything would change in my life. When I stopped to think, in the middle of the fittings, in the middle of packing fine lamps and oriental rugs for shipment to Málaga, I felt frightened.

One day, my mother came into my room, now much disordered by tissue paper and half-sewn clothes. The maid left at her gesture and we were alone—uncomfortably so. My wedding was four days off. My mother had obviously come to speak to me of my new life. She stood awkwardly, her face red with embarrassment. Finally she blurted, "I suppose I should talk to you about the new life you are going into, but I don't know what I could tell you about marriage that girls of your generation don't already know better than I do."

I could not reply. I had nothing to say. I wanted to ask her questions, to beg for some quite elementary information—but she seemed so forbidding and so embarrassed that I could not speak. The moment passed, and we never again discussed marriage.

As my wedding day approached we began to worry about my grandmother's health. She seemed to grow worse daily and now that my grandfather was dead, she seemed not to want to live. But we could not postpone the wedding for she might linger in this condition for months.

I could not sleep the night before my wedding. I was nervous and frightened. I got up feeling quite ill and could eat no breakfast. By noon I was dressed. I wore a very simple white satin gown, like a tunic. My veil was a beautiful old lace heirloom, which belonged to the Bolins, held on my black hair by a wreath of flowers. My father found me waiting for him in our drawing room.

"You are very beautiful," he said gravely, and I was pleased.

My father took me to the church and there we found the bridegroom with his family and all my family assembled. The old Gothic church, restored in the nineties, had seen many famous weddings, the King and Queen's among them. For my marriage, it was beautifully decorated with white flowers and green garlands. A great rich carpet stretched from the steps to the street—the finer of the two carpets put down for weddings at the church, according to the sum of money paid. I don't wonder I walked on the finest carpet—I found out later my mother paid a thousand dollars as my wedding fees.

I hesitated at the great Gothic church doors. The organ began to play. I walked slowly up the aisle with the music throbbing and the light falling dimly through the stained-glass windows. I knelt at the altar on a pillow beside my bridegroom, with my father on my right hand and Bolin's mother on his left hand and twelve male witnesses in a semi-circle around the altar. Facing us was the Bishop of Segovia who had come to Madrid for the ceremony. A little behind me on two low stools sat the page boys, two of my little cousins, who were supposed to hold my beautiful lace train. But instead they pulled so at my veil I could hardly keep it on my head.

"Remember the virtues of your ancestors," the Bishop boomed.

And then suddenly a messenger appeared at the doors of the church. The Bishop's voice rolled out in the dimness of the ancient building. The messenger whispered in the ears of two of my uncles. They left the semi-circle of witnesses and hurriedly left by a side door. My grandmother was dying. If they were to see her in life, they must hurry. All the wedding guests stirred. The Bishop faltered and then went on, much flustered. Faces changed. Death instead of life breathed on my wedding ceremony.

Bolin and I rose, to walk again down the aisle, man and wife. And before we left the altar, I absently slipped off my wedding ring. I had no special reason for doing it—only nervousness. But some of the old crones whispered. I was an unlucky bride.

We returned to what should have been a gay buffet party.

But all the guests knew that my grandmother lay dying in her room, her last agonies colored by the sound of the wedding guests above her. I ran up the stairs, in my lovely white gown and lace veil. A group of press photographers tried to bar my way but I cried that I was on my way to my dying grandmother. The old lady lay in her familiar bed, her ugly face contorted with pain. She opened her eyes as I joined the circle around her bed.

"Constancia," she murmured, and my uncles sighed, for I was the only one of her family she had recognized that day.

She raised a feeble hand and touched my veil. "Beautiful," she murmured, whether of me or the veil I never knew. Suddenly she seemed a little stronger.

"Good fortune, my child," she said, "I wish you good fortune. We will meet again in another world."

I went to my room with my eyes filled with tears. My maid helped me to dress in my going-away outfit, a pearl-gray suit with hat to match, very smart at the time. Our new roadster was at the door. We were to drive to La Mata to spend our first night.

Bolin and I walked through the drawing room greeting our friends. Then his brother, the same distinguished brother who lived in London, added what he thought was to be an English touch to the wedding—but it proved to be a most macabre one. After the English custom he threw handfuls of rice and an old soft slipper after us as we ran down the stairs.

But the rice did not fall on our shoulders. It pelted the parish priest from the very same church where I had been married an hour or so before. He stood, in his vestments of death, followed by two bell boys, ready to carry the last sacraments to my dying grandmother.

The hilarious shouts died away. The astonished priest soberly brushed the rice from his black vestments. The pious young people of my wedding party sank to their knees and began to pray. Bolin and I knelt in the cold marble hall. The priest moved slowly to my grandmother's apartment and with the murmured prayers of my friends for the soul of my grandmother in my ears, my new husband and I finally set out on our wedding trip.

Our roadster covered the miles to La Mata and the beautiful mountains in very quick time. I suppose I should have been filled with joy to be at last alone with my husband, the man that I thought I loved. But I felt no joy. I was not sad at my grandmother's approaching death for she was very old and she had been sick for twenty years and more. But the terrible confusion of the last few weeks, the hysteria that had surrounded the preparations for my marriage, the exhausting hours without sleep I had spent before my wedding day—all this left me numbed.

The steward welcomed me with warmth and tenderness at La Mata. A little apartment with three bedrooms, a living room, a bath, and an enclosed veranda had been prepared for us, so that we would not be alone in the great large house. A fire blazed in the stone fireplace. A specially fine supper was laid out for us. The steward's wife, who loved me dearly, hovered over me as we ate, trying to get me to taste the food. But I could not swallow the fine dishes and sweets she had prepared. She stayed for a long time, chatting with us. Finally her husband called her harshly.

"Leave them alone," he said abruptly. She kissed me and wished me happiness, and then we were really alone.

I felt sorry when she was gone. I was afraid. This man seemed a stranger, suddenly.

And in the great silence and quietness of La Mata my marriage proved to be very different from what I had expected. I knew before morning that I did not, and never would, love my husband.

Next morning, we were to get on the Paris express at Segovia. My parents' chauffeur came on the train to pick up our car and take it back to Madrid.

He handed me a letter as he arrived at La Mata. My grandmother had died in the night. But my mother asked us not to return for the funeral. "You are starting to live now. Take advantage of your happiness."

Bolin and I had planned to spend a few days in Paris and then go on to Italy—a wedding trip of two months in all. After the first few days, I felt so lonely I told my new husband I wanted a pet dog to keep me company. He paid no attention to this at first—and I soon discovered, indeed, that we had nothing at all in common. I wanted to show him the Paris I knew and loved, but although he had never visited the beautiful city before, he was not in the least interested in sight-seeing. He didn't care about the lovely churches, or the famous restaurants. He found walks along the Seine boring, and pictures stupid. In fact, he didn't seem to be interested in anything at all.

One afternoon we returned in a taxicab from the races at Longchamps. We were a fine prosperous-looking couple. I wore a very smart suit with a hat so much in fashion I had won approving glances from the women in the stands that afternoon— quite a feat. Bolin was handsome and well dressed. We drove down the Champs Elysées—and suddenly I burst into tears. In all my life I had never been so bitterly lonely and so completely unhappy.

Next morning we bought a pedigreed bulldog—an expensive if handsome creature. The dog really wasn't much of a companion but at least he gave me something to think of during the rest of my wedding trip. For the poor beast developed distemper shortly after we bought it and at each new Italian resort we visited our first stop was at the veterinarian's.

Before we left Paris, we had spent all the money Bolin had for our wedding trip. Of course, I knew nothing about this— I had to find it out much later from my mother-in-law. Bolin had wired his father to send him money and long before I arrived in Málaga, Bolin's whole family considered me a wastrel and a spendthrift. This was most unfair, for I had no idea how little money Bolin had for his wedding trip and besides my new husband spent most of his funds, as I was to learn much, much later, at the race tracks we visited.

We spent a month in Italy, at Rome, Venice, Naples, the usual honeymoon trip. Every day, almost every hour, was a new disappointment. We went to the Palatine hill overlooking the

Roman Forum. I tried to revive history and enjoy the beautiful sight. But Bolin said he had a toothache and sat sullenly with his back to the view.

Italy made little impression on me. Mussolini was just then consolidating his grip on the country and shots rang out in the night under our hotel windows. The country seethed with unrest. But we knew nothing of this. Bolin was too stupid to be interested in politics and I was too ignorant, too young, and too miserable.

We chugged away from Italy on a wretched little boat which landed us in Barcelona and there we boarded a fine recently built Spanish transatlantic liner which called at Málaga. My family connections brought us the largest and most beautiful suite on the ship. I have no idea what my husband's thoughts were as we approached his home, but I know that I was filled with fear and stayed inside my cabin, weeping. At last the stewardess called me to the deck. Málaga lay in the distance.

It was very beautiful.

The little city lay under the bright July sun, a lovely pattern of rich flowers, great green palm trees, chalk-red cliffs, striking buildings, and, framing it all, the blue harbor. Málaga, seen from a ship slowly approaching it, had form and grace. On the left towered the great cathedral, dwarfing the cream-colored houses clustered around it. On the hills above the center of the city lay the ruins of the old Moorish fortress, very simple in line, pure dazzling white in color. On the right were the houses of the rich, perched on the red cliffs, surrounded by luxuriant foliage. And even from a distance, the rich, tropical, bright flowers and very green palm trees of Málaga made the whole city seem one great garden arising out of the sea. I am sure that many travelers must have found its intoxicating colors, its rich cliffs, its lovely ruins an invitation to happiness. And perhaps I might have done so too—if I had not been an unhappy bride coming home with an unloved husband.

Bolin's family met us at the dock. Even my parents-in-law seemed less cordial to me than they had been in Madrid. We drove to their comfortable, rather middle-class house, and there I had a terrible shock. I had sent two shipments of furniture and rugs and china and silver, all my wedding things, to Málaga, expecting that Bolin and I would have a home of our own. I found all my household gear unpacked and crowded into two rooms in his parents' house. It appeared that we were to live permanently with my husband's parents. None of the Bolins, either my husband or his parents, had even bothered to ask me if this arrangement suited me or would make me happy. When I spoke to my husband that night about my surprise, he was amazed in turn. Did I take him for a millionaire?

I settled down to life in Málaga—a dreary, hopeless, forbidding life. It was very hot during the day. During the Summer months, the *Malagueño* upper classes did absolutely nothing but rest or sleep inside their cool houses.

In the evenings, the whole family would assemble at my parents-in-law's house and remain there for hours talking. Without exception, my relatives struck me as the dullest people I had ever met. They were interested in absolutely nothing but themselves and their money and they spoke constantly about these two unique subjects. The men sat on one side of the garden and the women on the other. I should have stayed with the women, my mother-in-law, her daughters, the aunts and cousins of my husband. But after a few nights I found I had absolutely nothing to say to them. Their conversation was one long complaint about the servants and the price of food.

So I moved over to the men's side—while the women glared at me. But the men were no better. With the typical hatred of the Spanish middle classes for those of their same kind who manage to make a few hundred more than themselves or attain a certain degree of security through a government position, the men of the Bolin family, for the greatest part idle and living on their incomes, directed all their diatribes against their friends in municipal positions. My father-in-law was the only one in the family who worked, and he was the least wealthy of the group.

And then gradually I discovered something which shocked me horribly, something which kept me from sleep for many nights. It appeared from the conversation of these idle, dull, stupid men that most of them lived off their *wives'* fortunes. The Bolins themselves had little—except a knack for marrying rich women. In fact, marrying a rich girl seemed the most natural, sensible way of making a living the Bolins knew.

From this discovery it was only a step to the truth about my own marriage. Bolin soon let me know he expected to live off the allowance my father made me—his father could not be expected to pay him a very large salary. I was too shocked and miserable to reply to him. I was married. I believed that a good Catholic girl could never undo her marriage. This was to be my life and my husband until I died. I decided to try to like it—I felt I must—or I would go mad.

But I could never adjust myself to life in Málaga with my husband's family. It was not that I had been accustomed to much more luxury. If the Bolins had been simple and unpretentious I would not have minded their household. But the life was not simple—it was exactly the opposite. It was pretentious and mean. The marble floors were considered grand and Bolin's prim English mother thought herself very aristocratic. But on the other hand the servants were wretchedly underpaid and the price of everything we ate and wore was discussed constantly at the table.

I stood the Bolin household as long as I could. Then at the end of the summer, I gathered up my courage and insisted that my husband and I should have a house of our own, no matter how small and inexpensive. There was a great battle, but I won—for I would not take no for an answer. Bolin and I decided on Torremolinos, a beautiful part of the coast where many foreigners lived. We took a lovely bungalow much too large for us and much too expensive, as I soon discovered. But I still had no notion of money nor of our budget—and I still believed in spite of everything that my husband's father would pay him some salary.

The house had belonged to an English major who after his wife's death had retired to a small cottage in the garden. Our bungalow stood in a large garden on the cliff overlooking the Mediterranean. An old castle, turned into a sort of strange

rooming house for retired British officers or middle-class English people, was at another end of our garden, and nearer to
us lived the gardeners and another English couple in a third
small cottage. We all shared the same tennis court and the same
path down to the rocks where the water was clear and trans-
parent and you could dive and bathe from the beach.

It was very good to get away from the Bolins and their many
relatives and live by ourselves facing the blue sea, surrounded
by low white walls and bright red geraniums. I soon found out
that the majority of our neighbors were quite mad—but perfectly harmless.

These people all amused me, after the Bolins. We knew few
of the Spanish families who had houses in this section. Bolin
went to work every day and came home rather early in the
afternoon to bathe and play tennis and go for walks in the
country. The life at the sea was enough for me after I finished
my housekeeping duties and I felt happy for the first time in
many months. For I was expecting a child, a child which I
hoped would fill my life, perhaps somehow solve the problems
of my marriage.

And while I waited for the baby, I kept house for the first
time in my life. I had three servants and I felt quite simple and
heroic overseeing their work. The parlor maid I had brought
from Madrid, my personal maid was from Málaga, but the cook
was from the countryside and quite primitive. I used to get very
excited baking cakes and making pastries from recipe books
my English friends lent me. Once the Bolins came from Málaga
to call and I proudly served my best cakes and cookies which I
had made with great care that morning. But they hardly tasted
my confections—they were too busy scolding me for my extravagance.

Those months by the seashore might have been very lovely—
except that we had constant money troubles. The only sure
source of income was my father's allowance. Living as we did
that could not stretch very far. After I had paid the rent, the
servants' wages, the auto expenses, and the light and water,
there was hardly anything left. Food was very cheap but even
so the cook had to have a few *pesetas* every morning to go to

the market, or to buy from the men on donkeys who came around to the house selling vegetables, fruit, fish, eggs, and fowl. After the tenth of the month, I never had any cash and so I had to ask my husband to get his salary or allowance from his father.

But Bolin was very hard to deal with. He would never give me a lump sum for the household. After my most heartfelt pleas he would gingerly hand me fifty *pesetas*—less than eight dollars. It appeared gradually that his father saw no reason to pay his son any sum of money—was he not married to a rich woman? And Bolin was not interested in our household. When he had money—and he often had it—he did not care to contribute it to household expenses. He had other uses for it. He was not very ethical about the way he got money either. I discovered later that he had borrowed from everyone in our small garden community—borrowed and never repaid.

I am afraid that my husband was no novelty in his family. Before our child's birth I was looking for baby carriages in Málaga. They were hard to find, so I suggested that one of Bolin's aunts, who had several left over from the time her children were babies, would perhaps lend me one. My husband delivered the message to his aunt, but there was no reply. Finally the matter became pressing and I tackled the Bolin lady myself. Her reply upset me for days.

"I would not mind," said this haughty lady, "giving you one of the prams as a present if I were sure that when your child grows out of it you would not give it to any poor fisherman's family. I could not stand the sight of a dirty child in the pram my children rode in as babies. That is why I never give my children's old clothes to the poor. I would rather burn them than see them worn by street children."

I declined her amiable offer.

As the hour of my child's birth approached, I grew nervous about the medical facilities in Málaga. All the babies in the "best" families were brought into the world by three or four old crones—midwives, who gossiped ferociously, dressed in black, and seemed always dirty. I suppose I could have asked them to wear white coats and wash their hands, but instead I brought a trained nurse all the way from Ireland to be with me when I had my baby and take care of the child afterwards.

I was not afraid of childbirth—I even welcomed it eagerly, for I longed for my child who was to comfort me in my loneliness and give my life purpose and happiness. I dreamed of a girl—Bolin when he mentioned it, which was seldom, seemed confidently to expect a boy.

But I was right. My child was born in February and we christened her Constancia Maria de Lourdes—Luli for short.

My parents came down for the christening of their first grandchild and Bolin welcomed them eagerly. For he wanted my father to get him a job on the Madrid stock exchange. He said he could not get on with his father. But my parents refused him. I think they had already discussed the matter with his parents and decided that life in the capital had too many temptations for a young, and as it now appeared, impoverished couple. I was quite content in my lovely house by the seashore and the baby enchanted me completely. But Bolin insisted that he could no longer work with his father. I thought then that he was sincere and I considered it my duty to help in the career of my husband.

So against everyone's advice we went to Madrid. But the reception my parents gave us was one of the greatest shocks of my life. I had expected, naturally, to stay at my old home. I knew there was plenty of room for a dozen families our size. But my mother and father informed me they had only room for the nurse and the child—Bolin and I must go to a hotel. With tears of pride in my eyes, I dragged Bolin off.

Madrid without funds was very different from the Madrid I had known before. Bolin and I soon had no money to pay our hotel bill. We could go no place, see no one, only sit glumly in the hotel wondering what to do next. Finally my pride broke. I went to my father and begged for help. My parents decided the "lesson" they intended to teach us—for what reason I never knew—had taken effect. My father got Bolin a job on the Madrid stock exchange. It was Summer and with a sigh of relief I left with my baby and her nurse for La Mata. Bolin stayed in town with his work.

I was not very happy that Summer and yet my time was filled with the baby and the old familiar life at La Mata. Luli was a long, thin baby, just as I had been and the nurse and I struggled with her that first Summer, for she was not very well. Bolin came to La Mata week-ends. He was never very communicative. I asked him questions. How was his work? Did he like it? Was it interesting? Did it have a good future? Yes, he answered to all these questions—yes, and nothing more. We had even less in common that Summer than when we were first married. Bolin never cared for Luli, found all news about her dull and hardly bothered even to look at her. My family was very cool to my husband—I was always on edge during the week-ends.

When Autumn came, Bolin arrived at La Mata one Saturday just before our return to Madrid. "You know," he said in a very offhand way, "after three months of hard work at my job they have paid me nothing. I have had to pawn your pearl necklace."

I was simply amazed. I went to my father with this sad story and I could not tell whether he was as surprised as I to find my pearl necklace gone to the pawnbroker or not. I believed Bolin and his story, of being cheated out of his pay, for I knew nothing of his peculiar habits.

But this was the beginning of a long succession of such incidents. My friends got Bolin a variety of jobs. My husband always began each one with great enthusiasm, followed by a long period of indifference. After six months, he came to me with the same story: his employers had cheated him or misused him. That first Winter in Madrid I spent quite peacefully, however, for Bolin's newest job was traveling in Spain for General Motors. I brought my things from Málaga and furnished a pleasant apartment very attractively. Little by little I began to see my old friends again and in a few weeks I was moving in the same circle I had known all my life. Bolin was nearly always out of town and for a time I felt mildly happy.

The Bolin family back in Málaga was quite overcome with joy to find out that their son had a good job in the capital. Sud-

denly I was restored to their favor. They invited me to come
and visit them in Málaga and they even took me on an ex-
tended tour of French and Spanish Morocco—a trip that fascinated me.

But when I returned to Madrid I had a great shock. My husband had been in a motor car accident. It developed he was not
very badly hurt, to my relief, but when he recovered he did not
go back to work. I could not get the truth out of him. He had
plenty of excuses, more and more fantastic as the time passed,
but it appeared that he had no intention of going back to
his job.

The inevitable money troubles began again. I was ashamed
to go to my father again. One day it struck me as a great novelty—a sort of revelation—that I might try to make a little
money myself. I would get a job! I knew the American wife of
an official in the General Motors Company. It was she, who,
knowing my troubles with my "unstable" husband—to use a
kind word—first gave me the idea of working. Once I had di-
gested the notion, I fell upon the plan with great energy.

My first attempts to earn money were not very successful.
Without saying a word to Bolin or my family—who would have
been very shocked—I answered in person an advertisement of
the Singer Sewing Machine Company, asking for a secretary
who spoke English. I almost got the job, although the faces of
the two men who interviewed me grew red with amusement
when I gave them my name. And then I made a terrible mistake. I knew absolutely nothing about applying for a job, and
nothing at all about conditions of work for women in Spain.

"Are you married?" one of the men asked, his pencil poised
over my application blank.

"Certainly," I replied calmly—and that was the end of my
hopes. Married women were not employed by reactionary firms
in Spain.

And then Zenobia crossed my path—not to leave it for many
years. I had heard about Zenobia from my American friends in
Madrid. She had furnished apartments to rent and whenever
any new American couples arrived in Madrid they inevitably
started by looking at her flats. She also had a shop where she

sold Spanish peasant shawls and linens and pottery and the like
to American tourists. Her mother had been half American and
her father Catalan—and Zenobia herself was the wife of one of
Spain's greatest poets, Juan Ramón Jimenez.

The stories about Zenobia fascinated me. I determined to go
and see her and put my problem before her. I made an appointment with her over the telephone. Curiously enough, she
seemed to know all about me—I had not realized until then
that Bolin and I were the target for much gossip in Madrid.

I arrived at Zenobia's home expecting something strange and
exotic. I found a very respectable house with old-fashioned furniture arranged with dignity and simplicity. Zenobia was not in
yet. Her poet-husband came to welcome me. It has been repeated too often by too many people that Juan Ramón's head
could have come out from one of the Greco paintings, but not
because things are more obvious are they less true. His manner
to me was charming.

I needed understanding and now I found it. For the first time
somebody thought it was quite natural and sensible that I
should want to work. I was very grateful to her for not asking
me too many indiscreet questions about my husband. I had become very conscious of his strange character but I was convinced that it was my duty both religious and moral to stand by
him and lead him back into the right path. In other words,
what God had united could not be broken by us. I would just
have to put up with it for the rest of my life, making the best
of it I could.

I did not lack courage. In fact, it required much more courage to follow the path I had set for myself than to break away
and start life anew. The second way out had not even occurred
to me at the time. My parents had vaguely hinted on different
occasions, every time that we found ourselves deep in some new
trouble and they heard about it, that I could always return to
their home and live there with my child, once again as a daughter of the family. This was hardly enticing after all the efforts
I had previously made to leave my parents. Now to return home
with a child and after an unsuccessful marriage—I could not
think of it.

A legal separation would not help matters in any way because there was no divorce and I could not marry again. I was a Catholic and to marry again, my first marriage would have to be annulled by the Pope. It was just at that time that two or three scandalous cases of annulment took place in Madrid. They shocked public opinion and me.

No, it was my duty to carry on and to make a good citizen and husband of the father of my child. All I was asking Zenobia was to help me do so. She told me she was leaving for a tour the next day, but before that she would put me in touch with some American people who wished to take Spanish lessons. Also, she said, while she was away I could perhaps look after her furnished apartments. She could only afford to pay me 1.50 *pesetas* (about ten cents) an hour for that kind of work; she knew it was very little and she was ashamed to offer it to me. But, she said, she could do no more. She gave me a fifty *peseta* note for my expenses and, more important than anything else, she offered on her return to have me help her and her partner in their Spanish peasant industry shop.

I was very pleased. I knew it was absurd to think that her 1.50 *pesetas* an hour and even the 150 *pesetas* a month I would get from each of my American pupils was going to solve my financial troubles. In all, I would hardly get enough to pay the rent of the apartment where we lived. But I had the sense to realize that it was an opening.

I could have spent that Summer at La Mata with Luli but I remained in Madrid. It was the first time in my life I lived in the city during the hot months and I found it very strange. I walked every morning to my two American pupils. One was a very charming intelligent woman who had been in Mexico and knew some Spanish. The other was a most uninteresting and vulgar German-American girl. They were both wives of newspaper men.

I stuck to my job all during that Summer. And then in August, I had an invitation I could not find the courage to refuse. An English friend, passing through Madrid, wanted to take me with her to London. My only expense would be my fare back to Bilbao, where as usual, I had been invited to stay at Arriluce.

I had already planned to visit Maria Isabel, and this time I intended to combine business with pleasure. I had a stock of fine peasant linens Zenobia had suggested I take with me, and I hoped to get many orders from my rich friends at Arriluce.

The Summer had been long and hot, and I was tired. I longed to see England again—I had not been back since my school days. Bolin did not object. He could hardly do so, as a matter of fact, after he had sat idly for two months watching me work with what I thought was zeal and energy. And so in high good spirits I packed my bags and started off for a London holiday.

I came back quite excited and pleased with myself, having had a wonderful time in London and Arriluce and having also made a good profit, to find that Zenobia's partner was away and I could have her job in the shop, temporarily at least.

A de la Mora, the granddaughter of Maura, a clerk in a shop! Even a fine shop, owned by two society women! I accepted the job first and thought about this situation only afterwards when my parents sternly called it to my attention. For I had slipped gradually into my new work—now I took up my duties in the little shop as a matter of course, with enthusiasm and pleasure. The hours were long and the pay very little, but I found having a real job for the first time in my life entirely absorbing.

My parents found it horrifying. The scandal was terrific. "Arte Popular" was a shop similar to the ones English and American women of good society had been running for years. But in Spain a girl of a decent family going into business was unheard of. Madrid society turned up its collective nose in positive horror. My family argued with me endlessly. But I replied that I intended to stick to my husband whom they knew I disliked by this time, although I never spoke of it. I told them I considered it my duty to do what I could to hold his life together and make him a home. If he would not foot the bills, I would.

In the Autumn before starting my new job, we had moved into a less expensive apartment. I still kept two servants and a Swiss nursemaid for Luli, to replace the more expensive trained nurse. Of course, we could have lived most comfortably in Madrid on my salary plus my father's allowance—which he carefully placed for me in a bank account Bolin could not touch. But before I went to work I made a final effort to straighten out my husband. We saw each other little by this time and had little to say when we were together. Yet I prevailed upon the Marquis of Arriluce to give Bolin another chance. He started to work for the Chrysler Motor Car Company the same month I went to work in Zenobia's shop.

The shop was very little known when I first went to work there. But my appearance as a clerk was a sensation. All my old friends and plenty of other people came to buy from the granddaughter of Maura. The sales that year reached a record.

That Winter, while I worked furiously hard in the shop and Bolin, nominally, at least, had a job too, I made a new dear friend. Ana was a new kind of friend for me. Her mother was Italian, and her family was distinctly lower middle class. Ana however had extraordinary feminine charm, a natural fineness. She had no intellectual pretensions and still she was clever, bright, quick-minded and generous. Like myself, she was unhappily married, and although we seldom spoke of our husbands, our unhappiness was a bond between us. That Winter her husband died very suddenly. She was alone. Zenobia gave her a job in the shop, too, and she came to live in our apartment.

Spring came in our household that year with a terrible explosion. Bolin had left his work—for what reason he sullenly refused to say. Ana with her good nature smoothed over what would have been a very violent scene. But from that time on, the breach between Bolin and myself grew wider and deeper. I despaired of my hopes of making of him a good citizen and father for my child.

The tension at home and the hard work at the shop left me exhausted. Suddenly a very welcome invitation came from my family to visit a great international exhibition held that year in Barcelona and to go from there to Mallorca to witness the unveiling of a statue of my grandfather in his native province. I was delighted and set off eagerly. Bolin, of course, was not invited, for my family now ignored him completely. But I was anxious for the holiday.

The trip to Don Antonio's ancient home was quite an affair.

The whole family, my uncles and sisters and parents, sailed for Mallorca where my grandfather had been born.

My uncle, who had taken the title of Duke of Maura after my grandfather's death, headed the family party crossing to the island. We landed at seven in the morning. Even at that early hour the islanders gave us a marvelous reception, partly because our family there was very numerous and partly because feeling against the Primo de Rivera dictatorship was already running so high the people seized any opportunity, even a demonstration in honor of a dead political leader, to show it.

The overlord of the island, Juan March, frowned on the Maura demonstration for he was already an implacable enemy of all Mauras, living or dead. The dictatorship had brought him spoils and besides, March felt there was only room for one great man, dead or alive, on his native island.

This Juan March was a most remarkable character. He started political and business life with a fine "importing" business. When the dictatorship observed that the government could not seem to stop his "importing" tobacco into the peninsula and Morocco, Primo de Rivera bought him off by giving him the tobacco monopoly in Africa. This brought in great riches—which March used to buy all the Mallorca land he could get his hands on. Then he sold it back to the peasants, on pain of dispossession, at what he called "fair" prices. Sometimes, if the peasant had no cash, the "fair" price was a vote in the next election. And so March became a political leader by roundabout but most interesting methods.

Our visit was a triumph. Some of the islanders who failed to discern that my oldest uncle lacked his father's strength and intelligence, hailed him as a direct heir to Don Antonio's political prestige. My uncle had plenty of ambition if not enough brains, and he rallied these island followers around the slogan of the "anti-dynastic monarchy." It was the first time I heard this famous slogan shouted openly and I took some pains to discover its meaning. Put simply, the idea of my uncle and his friends was this: a monarchy is necessary for Spain. But Alfonso cannot survive the inevitable fall of the Primo de Rivera dictatorship. His sons cannot inherit the throne for they are all tainted, one

way or another, with the dreadful hemophilia, the disease the
Queen had brought from England to doom the reigning family
in Spain. So Spain needed another King—a King chosen from
some new family. Just which family remained to be decided.

The whole scheme sounded a little fantastic to me, but my
uncle had a fine time conspiring at Palma and the rest of the
family had an even better time seeing the sights in great style.
The richest Maura followers put cars and chauffeurs at our disposal and we did all the sight-seeing we could in a few days.
And although we caught only fleeting views of Mallorca, the
unusual beauty of the island made a deep impression on us all.

But if our knowledge of the physical aspects of the island
was casual, we learned even less about the people. I caught only
one glimpse of the olive pickers—at a big estate owned by an
island aristocrat. My family watched them sing and dance at a
special entertainment in our honor and I asked our host about
where the pickers came from and how they lived. For the olive
crop is the great wealth of Mallorca and the peasants who work
their own bits of land during the year come at the olive-picking
season to work for the landlords. Usually the conditions under
which the peasants work during the picking season are frightful. Our host boasted of his modern dormitories for his workers
where, although the peasants slept on the straw-covered ground,
men and women were separated for the night.

We made the inevitable visit to the famous stalactite grotto
of the Drach in Manacor. The Maura followers had decorated
the grotto in our honor with colored lights and while we sailed
in boats in and out of the strange caves, we heard soft violin
music coming from behind the rocks. Afterwards we congratu-
lated the solemn islanders on the lights and the music—for they
were obviously very proud of their arrangements.

We left Mallorca regretfully. It had touched our hearts, and
we had been moved when we found centuries-old traces of
Mauras in old houses and tombs. This lovely faraway spot had
been our homeland once, when our family was simpler and not
so famous. Even the many Mauras we met on the island gave us
pleasure and pride. We had a feeling of finding our roots, good
roots, in this ancient and beautiful place.

The Summer of 1930 approached. The shop would close in July, as always. Bolin was out of a job again and I had exhausted the list of my friends who would help him. I felt I had nearly come to the end of my rope with my moody, irresponsible husband, and I told him frankly that in the Fall I expected him to go back to Málaga and work with his father, since he had made such a failure in Madrid.

Bolin refused to take any blame for his queer failures in the capital, but he agreed that we should spend the Summer with his family at their villa in St. Jean-de-Luz. I dismissed my servants, even my nursemaid for Luli, and determined to save money and live simply at the seashore. We arrived at the seaside just as the Bolins went into mourning for the Catholic Bishop of London who had just died. I heaved a sigh of relief, as I thought that the strict rules of Spanish mourning would prevent Bolin from wasting money at the various clubs.

We had two rooms at the old-fashioned villa—one for Luli and myself, another for Bolin. For the first time, I realized that I had a child. Luli was only three but until then she had lived, as I had when a child, with nurses. Now I grew to know her—and I discovered that although she was hardly more than a baby she realized I was unhappy and tried to comfort me. After the long restraint of the Winter, the tiring job, the long hours, I am afraid I often wept in my room, with Luli standing beside me, trying to cheer me. As the weeks passed, I began to think of the future in a different fashion than I had ever done before. Bolin was not at all interested in his child and Luli did not seem to care for him. This helped me make my plans.

Bolin himself soon left me to his family and the strict rules of Spanish mourning. His aunts from England reprimanded him often but he paid no attention. He went constantly to the Yacht Club, the smartest place that season. When I objected to the expense, he replied that a friend had invited him to sail his yacht in the races and he had to train every day. His lies were no less convincing than before, I suppose, but now I could be taken in no longer.

My feast day was the nineteenth of September, and a very miserable feast day it was too until Maria Isabel and her mother arrived unexpectedly at St. Jean-de-Luz and begged me to return that very day with them for my annual stay in Arriluce.

Suddenly I was very anxious to go. The long dreary Summer was over at last. My life seemed to lie ahead of me. Luli I left for a few more days with her maiden great-aunts who adored her. Bolin was away as usual. It hardly seemed worth while to waste time waiting to say good-by to him.

I sat quietly in the car driving back to Spain. And all at once I knew I was finished forever with the absurd and painful life I had been leading. All my childish ideas of staying with Bolin no matter how miserable and unhappy he made me, evaporated. I was a woman, a woman of energy and with, I had begun to think, at least enough brains to make her own living. I had no thought of divorce and remarriage for I was a Catholic and besides, divorce was illegal in Spain. I only wanted to live my own life with my child, free of the man who had made me so unhappy for the last three years.

From Arriluce I wrote Bolin a long letter, explaining myself. I suggested that he go to Paris to try his fortune and return to Spain only when he had proved he could hold a job. I asked him to face the situation between us with courage and sincerity. The letter was not exactly a definite break, for after all I was a Spanish woman brought up to believe a husband and wife could never sever their matrimonial bonds. Still it was quite clear that I no longer wanted to live with Bolin.

What effect the entire letter had on my husband I never knew—but one thing I suggested he did with great alacrity. Some money had been sent to me at St. Jean-de-Luz. Instead of forwarding it, he took the money and hurriedly departed for Paris.

I sighed with relief to hear he had gone, and settled down to enjoy myself at Arriluce. I had brought my linens and in a few days had made quite a good sum of money. I stopped worrying about my future. I felt able to support Luli myself. After the long strain of the years just passed I felt a heavy load fall from my heart. The Autumn was beautiful at Bilbao. I meant to have a good time.

When I returned to Madrid, my parents-in-law were arriving for a visit and since I had not heard from them since my husband had departed for France, I was worried and nervous. I made my apartment ready to receive them—and then they telephoned me from a hotel after their arrival.

We had a very sentimental session that morning. The Bolins wept. They begged me to forgive them for their son's behavior. They threw themselves on my mercy. An open separation would mean a scandal which would rock their provincial lives. They quite understood how badly their son had behaved—but still, would I not from that moment forward be their daughter and come live with them in Málaga? Their tears won me over, quite against my better instincts. With many misgivings I rented my apartment, went to fetch Luli from St. Jean-de-Luz, said goodby to my dear friend Ana with whom I had spent some weeks, and left Madrid for Málaga at Christmas time.

I hated to return to that empty life and those dreary days with the women of the Bolin clan. My own family disapproved —they wanted me to return to my home and be *their* daughter again. But I arrived at Málaga feeling a little cheerful anyway, for I had arranged to be a saleswoman for a Barcelona silk factory in Málaga and the surrounding territory. I thought it would give me something to do, a chance to escape from the Bolins when they got too tiresome, and to earn a little money. But my mother-in-law, much less cordial than she was in Madrid, showed little interest in my plans. The Bolins had no real interest in me. They only wanted me in Málaga to stop the scandal. They told everyone my husband was in France with a very good job, and I would join him presently after he had arranged a house for Luli and me. It was the most outrageous lie, but it served to quell gossiping tongues and that satisfied the Bolins.

I had gone away for a week-end when the news of Ana's death reached me. She was ill only a day or so and died, a very young and a very lovely woman. I was deeply shocked by Ana's death. I had really loved her and I realized as I settled down sadly in Málaga that I had built most of my plans for the future around her. Now life seemed empty.

I had been so much taken up with my personal troubles that I had hardly noticed the acute political situation. Even at the house of the Bolins not everyone agreed. My brother-in-law, the same one who had once been in England, came from Seville to spend the Christmas with his parents and in his violent fashion he fanned the flames of discussion. Trying to forget my own worries I became interested in what was said around me. I started to read the newspapers carefully and found that the *ABC,* which was the only Madrid paper read in the house of my in-laws, contained the most crude insults against anything and anybody not in sympathy with the Monarchy. I went as far as to join the queue before the only book shop in Málaga where the *Heraldo de Madrid* was sold. It was not an extremist newspaper by any means, merely liberal and objective, but when the Bolin family saw me reading it in the house, they were frankly alarmed and shocked.

I hardly cared what the Bolins said to me. True, I had bowed to their wishes Christmas Eve and had gone to confession, but it was not a real change of heart on my part. For gradually, in the past years, I had been growing away from the Church in which I had been born and educated. I still went to Mass every Sunday, and even had had more than one squabble with Ana who although born a Catholic had lost her faith.

But something had happened to my pious heart, something which I suppose had been brewing inside of me for years. For it is impossible to live in Spain as I did, in a wealthy family, and not see what the Church means to the rich as a weapon against the poor. I had no political theories of life, but I had a keen sense of justice. I remembered the bun we took to the charity pupils at my convent school; I remembered the village where we gave an altar cloth while the people died for want of a doctor; and above all, I remembered the peasants at La Mata.

These things might never have made me more than uneasy, but the month after Luli was born my mother insisted on taking me to confession at the Jesuit Fathers' residence in Málaga. I had spent half of my life around them, but I had always resented their prying questions, their keen interest in what seemed to me purely personal affairs.

Then, as I knelt before the Jesuit Father in Málaga, replying to his questions, I began to feel more and more indignant.
Softly but implacably he inquired into my most intimate relations with my husband. Finally he asked me a question which
so deeply offended my strong sense of modesty that I refused to
answer. I resolved, as I walked from that confessional, never
again to make a confession or take the sacraments of my
Church.

The Bolins had forced me to comply with my religious duties
on Christmas. But I had given only lip service to the Church.
I would never again believe, as the Bolins wanted me to believe.

Life in Málaga was dreary and sad. I took long walks with
Luli, while the Bolins became every day colder and less cordial.
My silk business did not work out well—I felt trapped. My own
family was completely estranged from me—they resented my
staying with the Bolins instead of with them.

Suddenly the situation changed. Overnight the Bolins became
downright hostile. I could see that something new had occurred,
just what, they would not tell me. My mother-in-law shut herself up in her room; my father-in-law avoided me.

Then at last they were forced to speak. Bolin was penniless in
France. He had written a letter full of apologies, placing the
blame for his peculiar conduct more or less on my shoulders.
He wanted to come home. My father-in-law put it up to me
squarely: either I lived with Bolin as his wife, or I left for good.

The Bolins thought they were being very cunning. They
knew I had broken with my own family. They thought I would
be forced to stay with them and start life anew with their son—
forced by sheer economic necessity. They had a strong card to
play. Most women of Spain in similar circumstances in those
days would have been forced to swallow the bitter pill. What
else could they do?

I thought it over carefully, with a certain sensation of fear.
And then I knew my mind was made up. I did not love my husband; indeed I regarded him with contempt. Even more, I had
discovered that work gave me much more satisfaction than idle
amusement. I valued my independence, I decided, more than
anything else except my child. I was not afraid of the future. I

knew that I was violating every canon of the society I had been brought up in—Spanish women of my class accepted sorrow submissively, as the will of God. To break free of the family was a profoundly terrible act.

But I was ready, at long last, to burn my bridges.

I wired my father, who was a lawyer, and he arranged the legal papers for my separation. The Bolins were forced to allow me my child, rather than risk the scandal of a lawsuit.

So finally I packed up my clothes, took my Luli, and departed for Madrid—and freedom. I was twenty-five years old, and ready to begin my life once again.

As my train came into the station at Madrid, I was filled with a sensation of strength and happiness.

III. SPANISH AWAKENING
(1931-1936)

I CAME back to Madrid in March, 1931, to begin a new life. And I found my country embarking on exactly the same high adventure.

The word "found" is precise. I was twenty-five years old, the granddaughter of Spain's most famous politician of the War period and niece of two indifferently expert modern political leaders. And yet until that March day when Luli and I arrived in Madrid, bound bag and baggage for a life of independence, I knew almost nothing about the contemporary history of my country. This sounds strange, and yet I was no different from most Spanish women of my background. I had lived in the home of political intrigues and never once heard politics discussed at the dinner table. I had kissed the hand of Spain's great Conservative leader every day of my life until he died—and never heard him utter one word about state affairs.

Perhaps I might have slowly developed an interest in my country after my marriage if I had not been so bitterly unhappy. But for three long years my life had been turned in on itself. The great events of the rise and fall of the Primo de Rivera dictatorship stirred the whole nation—but not me. Sometimes I glanced at the newspapers. But I was so engrossed in the tragic drama of my marriage that I never made an effort to separate the lies from the truth and to try to understand.

And now suddenly, everything was changed. Overnight I became a citizen of Spain. I think I could not have had four political discussions in my entire life until I returned to Madrid in March—and a week later I was talking nothing else.

For all Spain was in a ferment. The dictatorship had fallen. Great events hovered in the balance. History lay around every corner. And I was free and happy, and suddenly I wanted passionately to know about the world I lived in.

Zenobia and Inés, her partner at "Arte Popular," gave me my start. They listened to my stories of Málaga and the definite break with my husband—but I could see they were impatient.

"But, Constancia," Zenobia finally said breathlessly. "What do *you* think will happen to the prisoners?"

And Inés broke in: "What are they saying about the revolt in the provinces? Are they for the monarchy in Málaga?"

"Why—uh . . ."

I had to stop. I didn't have the slightest idea what the provinces were saying about the King. And I was afraid to ask them *what* prisoners, *what* revolt. It was apparently like asking what Atlantic Ocean, what Spanish peninsula.

And then in the next week, as I encountered the same question all over Madrid, heard the same anxious talk, I began slowly to piece together the story of my country for the past six years or so. The truth was not easy for me to find. I had to ask many questions, remember snatches of my uncles' conversation, listen to the current conversations of my friends with a careful ear and try to bring them all together in a pattern. But gradually the story of the decade just closed began to come clear in my mind.

The Primo de Rivera dictatorship had been unpopular from almost the moment of its declaration in 1923. The General himself had early proved to be too stupid, too inept, and too awkward to keep even his natural supporters in line. His whole rule had been one long series of attempted revolts, underground intrigue, and open defiance. His frequent statements in the papers offended the Spanish sense of dignity—for they always displayed the colossal stupidity of their author. The press censorship, quixotic from the beginning, got worse as time passed. The open corruption of government officials made the Primo de Rivera rule a constant, steady smell to the heavens.

Much more important, Primo de Rivera, brought to power by Spain's industrialists, had to depend on them to consolidate his wobbly position. A combination of Catalonian capitalists and foreign investors supported Primo de Rivera and kept him going. The dictator paid for this favor by offering the big manufacturers unlimited power and the foreign investors important concessions in Spanish mines, electric power, and the like.

But still the General teetered on his public perch. Across the Mediterranean, Benito Mussolini appeared to be making a dictatorship successful. Spain's General decided to go forth to learn. He returned from his trip to Italy with two new ideas: fine roads, and a Fascist party.

The roads he eventually built with the help of foreign capital—although the terrible scandals which followed the completion of each new road shook the dictatorship over and over again. The contracting firms who supervised the work stole millions from Spain's treasury.

The Fascist party Primo de Rivera never achieved. The corrupt political bosses of the countryside joined forces with Primo but the people could never be induced to form a mass following for the nearly illiterate General. As the months and years passed Primo de Rivera and the King grew more and more troubled over the growing hostility of the public to the dictatorship. Finally the General took drastic steps. He set up what he called a "National Assembly"—a sort of appointed legislature which was supposed to rubber stamp his political action. He tried to induce the labor unions to participate in this National Assembly, with the hope of making one great "company union" out of Spain's labor movement. But the unions indignantly refused despite the strong pressure for collaboration from Largo Caballero, Socialist trade union leader. Primo de Rivera was left with his dummy "assembly" no more popular than before.

Then gradually the people began to organize resistance against Primo de Rivera. For if you lived in wealth and security in Madrid, as I had done for so many years, the dictatorship seemed like a comic opera affair. The General himself was the butt of so many jokes—sophisticated people were inclined to laugh a little at Spain's "strong man." But actually there was nothing comic opera about Primo de Rivera and the Bourbon King who ruled with him. Under the fanfare of the government in Madrid lay bleak suffering. The whole country groaned under a vicious and oppressive government. During the dictatorship, real wages fell and hours rose in the mines and factories—Primo de Rivera's gift in kind to the industrialists and Spanish and foreign bankers. During the dictatorship, the peasants saw their wretchedness increase even though that hardly seemed possible, so wretched had they been before.

More, the whole country shuddered under heavy-handed repression. Newapspers were mercilessly censored. Men went to jail for a whispered word against the King or Dictator. Hundreds were driven into exile. The universities languished—many were ordered to shut down for months or even years as a punishment for an outspoken professor. Spain, backward after the War, turned back the clock with Primo de Rivera. The roads were new, but the Government seemed medieval, not even Victorian.

But Spain did not grow silent and hopeless under the heel of the Dictator. As early as 1926, there were uprisings. The conservative landed gentry, uneasy under the rule of a military dictatorship that favored the industrialists rather than the landowners, tried a coup against Rivera. But the country would never rally again to the slogan of a constitutional monarchy—the people connected Alfonso and Primo de Rivera, the Siamese twins of reaction. So the conservative revolt failed.

A group of Republicans tried that same year of 1926, too, but the revolt was badly planned and executed and came to nothing. These uprisings were only the beginning. Year after year the Republicans, the Constitutional Monarchists, even dissatisfied militarists, tried coup after coup. Each of these early attempts failed, and each was followed by a wave of reprisals.

But the people of Spain could not be beaten into subservience to a dictator. Primo de Rivera might send patriots to prison by the hundreds; drive decent men into exile; close the universities; put a police spy on every street corner of Madrid and Barcelona—and still Spain lay like a pile of sticks soaked with kerosene, waiting for the match.

The dictatorship had never been on too solid ground. In 1929 it began to wobble dangerously. A new university "reform" order infuriated the intellectuals—it provided that university degrees were to be handed out by religious schools, so as a result the university degree would no longer have meaning.

Primo de Rivera's remarkable financial operations began to catch up with him. With an announced "surplus," the government found itself unable to borrow cash to finance its day-to-day activities—a strange sort of "surplus." The finance minister, a faithful Primo de Rivera man, finally revolted and resigned, unable to make head or tail of an upside-down budget that seemed to show surpluses while the whole world sold the *peseta* short on foreign markets.

Even the King began to grumble. He no longer spoke proudly of his "Mussolini." A terrible scandal over money paid to the French newspaper *Le Temps* to stop a campaign against the dictatorship in the foreign press hardly improved matters. Primo de Rivera began to grow hysterical under the steady opposition pressure.

And then, a year later, Primo de Rivera fell from office, almost as an anti-climax. The Army unseated the General—although Primo de Rivera helped to destroy himself by one of the stupidest moves in Spanish history. A provincial general, the military governor of Cadiz, had prepared to rise against the Dictator. General Goded, a young and ambitious officer, had no particular political principles behind his revolt—except his own self-interest. But he interested a few civilians in his plot, among them my uncle, Miguel Maura, a tepid Republican.

Primo de Rivera heard of the coming revolt. Hemmed in on all sides, he made a major mistake. The King still believed Primo de Rivera had the backing of most of the Army. And Primo obligingly proved that he did not—all the King wanted to know. For the stupid old General sent a circular telegram to the ten captains-general in command of the different military zones, asking them whether or not he should stay in office. Only two replied with enthusiastic yeas—the rest cautiously wired they would support "the King and the Crown under all circumstances." King Alfonso dismissed Primo de Rivera the next day.

The dictatorship had fallen. What next? With the news that Primo de Rivera had fled to Paris and the King had installed General Berenguer of Morocco fame as head of the government, a great wind swept Spain. The exiles poured back into Madrid and Barcelona—often greeted by General Berenguer's police, to be sure, but still they came back. And the great question in Spain was: Will the Monarchy last?

The people thought it would not. In fact, they were determined it would not. Alfonso must follow his "Mussolini" to Paris. The frightened Monarchists, churchmen, and landholders hoped for the best. General elections were inevitable. The King must summon the Cortes—even though he dreaded this as the beginning of the end of his reign.

"Summon the Cortes?" Alfonso said one day. "That amounts to bringing the Republic in on a silver tray."

Still, there were those Monarchists so near-sighted and optimistic as to believe that a general election would give Alfonso a majority. And there were those other Monarchists, more realistic, who believed that an election might be manipulated to show the desired majority.

And while the King and his supporters hesitated and refused to call for the elections, the people acted. On August 17, 1930, representatives of all Republican groups and UGT (Socialist Trade Unions) met secretly at the seaside resort of San Sebastian to consider the condition of their country.

So long as the various Republican parties were divided and quarreling among themselves, the Monarchists would win the elections the King *must* call. So on that August day in San Sebastian, the Socialist, Catalonian national parties, Republicans, trade unions, and a dozen other smaller parties decided on a pact of unity—and a simple program. The program was for a democratic Republic, land reform, and freedom. The pact resulted in the selection of a Committee, many of whom were to become afterwards famous in the Republic: Alcalá Zamora; Azaña, who was to be president; Casares; Prieto who would be War Minister in darker hours than this. An alternate group, selected in case of the arrest of the first, included, among others, my uncle Miguel.

The committee had planned to function in the hoped-for elections. But months passed. The King hid behind General Berenguer. It appeared he had no intention of calling the Cortes. Finally the Republicans became desperate—were they to wait while another dictator grew under their very eyes?

On December 15, the Republicans tried to revolt against the Monarchy. The plans had been made very carefully. The Air Force, which unlike most of the Army was officered by many Republicans, was to back up the trade unions. The planes were to rise over Madrid as the trade unions declared a general strike.

As the morning of December 15 broke, the Air Force revolted according to plan. The Republicans in the force gave the Monarchists a choice: either they joined the revolt or submitted to being locked up. Ignacio Hidalgo de Cisneros, a young man born to the purple of Spain who had long since left the comfortable confines of his family's opinions, was one of the leaders of the Air Force uprising.

He went from barracks to barracks that morning saying: "We are rising against the Monarchy. The King has betrayed our country. Our only hope is the Republic. Those who wish to join us come out. The others will be locked up—no harm will come to them. We wish to give them an excuse for not having prevented our uprising should it fail."

Most of the men threw in their lot with the Republic. The Monarchist officers went quietly to their improvised jails. The motors roared on the landing field. The planes took the air.

But the plans had miscarried. From the air above Madrid, the revolting pilots looked down and saw a city at work. The general strike had somehow, for some reason, not been called. The pilots were trapped. Monarchist soldiers occupied the barracks on the air field. The Republican aviators, praying they had enough gas, flew across the Spanish borders to exile.

And in Madrid the entire Republican Committee elected in August was betrayed by police spies and arrested. Even worse, two young officers from a northern garrison, mistaking the plans, had taken their men out from their barracks prematurely, and on the road to Huesca were met by Monarchist forces, arrested, and immediately shot. Galán and Garcia Hernandez became the heroes of Republican Spain, martyrs to liberty.

And when I arrived in Madrid in the beginning of March, the whole city was alive with talk about the Republican Committee, who were soon to be tried in court for their crime against the Monarchy. For Alfonso's position had become less secure rather than the opposite with the miscarriage of the Republican plans. The whole country openly mourned Galán and Garcia Hernandez. The people rallied around the imprisoned Republican leaders.

The aristocracy tried to build a protective wall around the Royal family. Alfonso and his wife and children must not feel the cold breath of the people's hate. If any member of the Royal family went to the theatre, members of the aristocratic fraternity would rush to the same auditorium to applaud madly the Infantas or the King. But alas, their cheers would bring a deluge of catcalls and hisses from the galleries—often the King had to leave hastily in the second act while the actors tried to be heard above the din of cheers and counter demonstrations from the cheap seats.

Feeling ran high on both sides, Republican and Monarchist, as I was soon to learn. Shortly after I returned to Madrid I went to call on my old friends, the Arriluce family. Maria Isabel had married and was living in Bilbao, but her parents still had their large apartment in the capital. Now I rang their doorbell, eager to see the Marchioness and tell her of my definite separation from Bolin.

The butler answered. For years this butler had bowed low to see me, and then ushered me directly down the long corridor to the Marchioness's private sitting room. For years the Marchioness had greeted me with loud cries of pleasure.

But something strange and bewildering happened this day. The butler greeted me with frigid formality and led me into the large, empty state drawing room.

"Please wait, Madam," the butler said in his most formal tones.

I sat uncomfortably on the edge of one of the Louis XV chairs staring at the tapestries covering the walls. Finally I decided the butler could not have recognized me. I got to my feet, intending to walk back to the Marchioness's sitting room and explain the mistake, but Miss Wall, the Irish governess, appeared in the door. Miss Wall had been with the Arriluce family for twenty-five years and I knew her almost as well as I knew the steward at La Mata.

"Miss Wall!" I cried cheerfully. "I was beginning to think I was in the wrong house; I am afraid the butler didn't know who I was, and . . ."

"Good afternoon, Constancia," Miss Wall said coldly.

I stopped for a moment. Surely I was wrong? Surely Miss Wall was not snubbing me? But then, perhaps she had a headache, perhaps she wasn't feeling well. "I must tell you what has happened," I began eagerly. "You'll be glad to hear about it. I'm definitely through with Bolin, Luli and I . . ."

Miss Wall rose. "Here is the Marchioness," she said stiffly.

I turned to the doorway of the formal drawing room. The Marchioness, dressed to go out, stood looking at me. I rushed to greet her—how many times had we not embraced as we met after a long absence. But she held up a gloved hand.

"I was just telling Miss Wall," I stammered, "that I have come back to Madrid for good, and I am going to support Luli and myself and be independent and never have to live with Bolin again, and . . ."

I could not talk to this stone wall, these frigid faces. I fell silent, my heart beating painfully.

The Marchioness stood, examining me with great care, as though she had never seen me before. Finally she spoke, choosing her words carefully, "I have to know if what I have heard about you is true. Are you a Republican?"

"Repub . . ." I choked on the word. I had never been so completely astonished in my life. The Marchioness of Arriluce had been a second mother to me since I was sixteen. She had been more than a friend, for she had drawn me into her family circle. Now she stood before me, drawn up to her most regal height, demanding an answer to her question. Was I a Republican?

For a moment I couldn't answer. For gossip had stated my views quite wrongly. A Madrid shocked at my separation from my husband had apparently decided that independence and Republicanism went hand in hand.

"Can you not answer, Constancia?" Miss Wall said sternly.

And then suddenly I was swept with a wave of hot anger.

"I can indeed," I heard myself saying—almost shouting. "If being a Republican means to sweep away all the corruption of my country, then I am a Republican. If being a Republican means justice for those who have never tasted justice, then I am indeed a Republican. If . . ."

"Please spare us speeches," the Marchioness said.

But I did not feel like sparing the Marchioness speeches. I

had just, at that very moment, found out that I was a Republican and the discovery was most exciting.

"If being a Republican means food for peasants who starve while they grow food for others, then I am. . . ."

"Indeed," the Marchioness said, her voice rising in shrill anger. "Good day, Constancia."

The butler appeared suddenly—I am afraid he had been listening. The doors opened before me. The Marchioness followed me into the corridor.

"You are a traitor to everything your grandfather stood for and defended all his life," she cried. "We can never again have anything to do with you."

The butler swung open the street door, I marched out, my head high and the tears stinging my eyes, and as the door to the Arriluce apartment closed behind me I stood still in the street, angry and excited, full of my new political ideals, and full of a terrible rage. The Arriluce family! I had lived among them and similar people all my life. These were—or had been—my friends. How could I have ever liked or even tolerated such mean, servile, cowardly, stupid human beings? They were through with me—and suddenly I realized that I was through with them and their kind forever.

I swung down the street of Madrid, walking briskly.

The Marchioness lost no time spreading the great scandal that Constancia de la Mora—Madame Bolin—was a Republican. All of aristocratic Madrid shuddered to hear the tale, although of course everyone could say, "I told you so." For had I not actually held a job in a shop? Had I not left my husband? One thing leads to another. A woman who wants to be "independent" will sooner or later end up as that lowest of all things, a Republican, a traitor to the Monarchy. And in a fortnight I had lost all the friends I had known since my childhood.

My parents returned to Madrid from a journey a week or so after Luli and I came to the capital. And they had a series of shocks to digest. First of all, I was not coming home to live as a disappointed matron for the rest of my natural life. I had decided to live alone with my child in Madrid and work to support her.

No sooner had my father and mother swallowed that terrible story than they heard I had also turned Republican. This, combined with the fact that my uncle Miguel was in jail charged with treason to the King and participation in the Republican revolt, put a shadow on the family. My fashionable mother had to over-protest her own Monarchist opinions to convince her suspicious friends. Only the memory of my dead grandfather, so orthodox and famous a supporter of the Crown, saved my mother from social decline.

Still, my parents were much less hostile to Republican theories than the rest of the clan. Uncle Miguel's fame, plus the fact that I was their favorite daughter, made them try to be tactful. We never discussed politics at my parents' table and they had apparently decided on a policy of sympathetic understanding to try to win me over. My mother discussed household problems with me and for a time my parents were so successful in their treatment of me that I came to dine with them often and I allowed Luli to stay with her grandparents very frequently.

I had plenty of household problems to discuss with my mother. While I was still in Málaga, I had rented the apartment through Zenobia to an American newspaperman, Jay Allen, and his wife and small son. Now when I returned to Madrid I found the paper hangers and painters busily making the apartment ready for the Americans. The Allens were impatiently waiting for the paint to dry while they stayed at a hotel. With my heart in my mouth I went to call on them to beg them to let me have the apartment back for myself.

Jay Allen was in bed when I arrived—sick, he explained cheerfully. His counterpane was covered with newspapers, books, and typing paper. His small son, dressed in long blue pants, occupied a corner of the room where he played an intricate and exceedingly noisy game with himself.

Mrs. Allen, a young and charming woman, moved around the room, answering the telephone, finding books for her energetic husband, and bringing order out of the confusion that began afresh the moment she relaxed her efforts.

"I hope you will forgive me," I stammered.

The Allens listened to my story and then all three, including the grave child, assured me that it was no trouble at all, of course I should have my own apartment, they would start immediately to look for another, I shouldn't waste a moment of worry for disturbing their plans—it was nothing.

I backed out of the door with the Allens waving cheerfully. Three days later an English friend told me that I had an American accent—horrors! It wasn't really true then but as soon as I began to know Americans I did indeed speak American. I had been brought up on Irish brogue and Oxford English, but the vivid and colorful language my American friends spoke blotted out my former accent. English had always seemed a rather cold and distant tongue, not like the warm and graceful Spanish of my own country. But American seemed quite different, a living, sharp, precise, and staccato speech. I took to it like a duck to water and a few months later an Englishman told me he was sure I learned English in Kansas.

Luli and I had hardly settled down in our redecorated apartment when a new political crisis hit Madrid. General Berenguer was forced out of office. The King hesitated. He went so far as to ask Sanchez Guerra, the old ex-Prime Minister, to form a cabinet including some of the Republicans held in jail. But at the last moment Alfonso balked and formed one of those conservative coalition cabinets which had saved the Monarchy in 1917 and 1921 and which he hoped would save his dynasty once again.

My uncle, the Duke of Maura, was made Minister of Labor in the new Cabinet—a choice which rocked all Madrid, for he was undoubtedly the first Cabinet Minister of Spain whose brother languished in jail, charged with treason to the King. I went to dinner at the Duke of Maura's house a few nights after he took office and sat quietly listening while my uncle and his friends talked feverishly of how to save the Monarchy. They were all of the opinion—in fact my uncle said so loudly—that the Coalition Cabinet would preserve Spain for the Crown. My uncle still controlled the "League of Young Maurists," an organization formed years ago to support my grandfather. Now the "Young Maurists" were all comfortably middle-aged—but they still kept their title. The Duke hoped to build this somewhat faltering organization into a solid bloc of support for the King in the coming elections. For long before my uncle had given up his "anti-dynastic" slogan. The first act of the Coalition Cabinet was to promise elections: municipal elections first, then provincial elections, and finally elections for the Constituent Cortes.

The plan was very clever. The King could test his strength twice before the crucial Cortes election and if he found weakness in the municipal elections, he could take whatever steps were necessary, even to canceling the Cortes elections, to keep himself in power. I heard my uncle explain all this not without side glances at me, the notorious Republican. I kept my peace, but I could not help thinking that this uncle was reckoning without the people of Spain.

And while my mother's eldest brother worked hard to preserve the Monarchy, her youngest brother prepared for his trial. The "Provisional Government of the Republic," as they called themselves, was ordered to appear before the Supreme Council of the Army and Navy on a charge of encouraging military sedition. The trial was set for March 21. All Madrid hummed with excitement. Even at my parents' table, the trial had to be discussed. My mother had visited her black sheep brother in jail with the hope of affecting a reconciliation between the Duke who was serving the King and Miguel who was trying to overthrow him. Nothing had come of my mother's attempt to bring her brothers together, and now that Miguel was to go on trial for his life, the whole family hoped that somehow, some way, the Duke might find it in his heart to save his brother.

I had dinner with my parents on March 20, the day before the trial. One of the Duke of Maura's daughters was seated near me, and as I talked with her I suddenly had a brilliant idea. I was determined to go to the trial. I did not understand yet why men obviously living in comfort, with good homes, good positions, had sacrificed everything and gone to jail when they could have been political leaders if they had only been ready to declare themselves supporters of the Monarchy. I wanted to find out why men were ready to give up everything, even their liberty and lives if need be, for the Republic.

But I had discovered that all the passes for the trial had long since been given out. I had no way of getting in to hear the proceedings. I looked at my timid cousin across the table. And then I suggested, casually, that she take her father's official motor car the next morning and drive down to the trial. My cousin was an innocent; she had no idea of the sensation she might cause by turning up at the trial of the Republicans in the Duke of Maura's official government car.

Promptly at eleven the next morning my cousin and I swept up to the main entrance with the police clearing a way for the official government car. Press photographers, electrified by a cabinet minister's car appearing at the Republican trial, trained their cameras on the limousine door as the chauffeur helped us out. All Madrid saw our pictures in the paper that night and the family correctly decided that I had led my poor innocent cousin badly astray.

I didn't care about the newspapers. I wanted to get inside that trial, and not only for the first day, either. I found an usher at the trial who had been an old servant of my grandfather's. He told everyone I was my uncle Miguel's daughter and I was led to a front row seat, which I occupied for the entire trial.

The trial started and ended as a political meeting. The speeches of the defense lawyers were greeted with wild applause. The defendants bore themselves with great dignity and courage and every time they spoke the tense audience cried encouraging words.

My uncle Miguel's wife and daughter and I were the only members of the whole Maura family at the trial and the spectators, knowing the division in the clan, seemed to feel that I showed great courage in defying my powerful uncle, the Duke, by appearing at Miguel's trial and obviously favoring his cause.

And as the trial went on, it became clear that the government would not dare punish the "Provisional Government of the Republic" with death or even a severe prison sentence. For all Madrid cheered the defendants. Great crowds gathered every night to watch the prisoners go back to their cells. The admirals and generals began to get more and more nervous as the trial dragged on, the defense counsel more and more confident.

The verdict was not unexpected: "Guilty but with extenuating circumstances, six months and one day prison sentence. Sentence suspended." For since the Constitution had been destroyed by the Dictatorship it was not possible to rise against Constituted Authority.

The Republicans were free. I was one of the hysterically shouting crowd that moved out of the court room to the street with the triumphant defendants. Now the Republicans were free to prepare for the coming elections. I went home that night feeling that Spain would soon be a Republic.

The municipal elections, the first of the three scheduled Spanish elections, were set for April 12. On April 11, the Monarchists made a last desperate effort to convince the voters that Alfonso should rule Spain. The last cries of the reactionaries were heard everywhere—they were the cries of a dying man. For all the taxicabs and even many private cars in Madrid carried Republican flags that exciting day, flags bearing the words: "Vote for the Republican-Socialist Coalition."

I had lunch with my parents that day before the elections— a violent and exciting lunch—as it turned out. My sister Marichu's husband, a very moderately intelligent young man, arrived late, after we had gone into the dining room.

"You know why I am late?" this gentleman cried as he came in breathless and sat down before his soup.

The family listened, all ears, while Marichu's husband related his tale. Arriving at the house in a taxicab, he had refused to pay the driver, unless the man removed the Republican flag and the slogan "Vote for the Republican-Socialist Coalition" from his cab.

"At first he threatened to call the police," my brother-in-law said, his cheeks flushed with triumph, "but when I reminded him that the police might have a cure for a taxicab driver who refused to take down a Republican flag, he muttered something about the police being in the pay of the King, and drove away. He'll think twice about putting up Republican flags again when his company makes him pay up for my fare which showed on the meter—it was a big fare, too."

"Well done," Marichu cried. The rest of the family kept silent, knowing that my esteemed brother-in-law's story was sure to provoke a violent controversy.

"You cowardly swine!" I yelled at him. "What a fine gentleman you are, stealing pennies from the poor because you disagree with their political opinions. I hope you will enjoy the thought that the driver's wife and child will have nothing to eat tonight. That should improve your own appetite. . . ."

"Constancia!" my father began hastily.

"Traitor!" my brother-in-law shouted, but I cut him short.

"You with your seat on the stock market, you should steal *pesetas* from taxicab drivers, you . . ."

My mother broke in. "I will not have this vulgar quarreling at my table," she said somewhat unsteadily.

My brother-in-law and I sank into sullen silence. But I never sat down at the table with him again. And all over Spain on April 11 similar scenes were occurring. Brother against brother and father against child—all Spain divided to the right and left, the King or the Republic, which would it be?

Next morning dawned quiet and fine. Inés, Zenobia, and I drove around in Zenobia's Ford to watch the balloting at the polls. Women, of course, had no vote—but we had a most lively interest. Madrid seemed very still. We noticed that the Monarchist posters had all but disappeared, while the Republican slogans plastered every wall in the city.

We had lunch at a quiet restaurant. As we were having coffee, my uncle Miguel came in with a group of Republican candidates.

"How does it go?" I asked, rushing over to his table.

"We are winning everywhere," he said solemnly.

Inés, Zenobia, and I were profoundly excited. We went back to Inés's little flat over our shop and discussed the future. What would the Republic mean to Spain? We talked for hours. We saw a new Spain, a beautiful country where justice was the rule, not the exception. We saw a backward country suddenly blossoming out into a modern state. We saw the peasants living like decent human beings. We saw men allowed freedom of conscience. We saw schools, schools for everyone. We saw an end to the decadent corruption. We saw life, instead of death, in Spain.

Spain was accustomed to elections being won by the party in office—did they not control the counting of the ballots? But corruption cannot dam a flood. Late on the night of April 12, Count Romanones, speaking for the Cabinet, said, "The result of the elections could not be more deplorable for us Monarchists." And he knew it better than anyone else. For the peasants in his own district, defying the vigilance of the political bosses, risking unemployment and hunger, defying the Church, had marched to the polls and defeated their landlord and ancient ruler, Count Romanones himself.

Monday found Madrid restless and excited. The few newspapers allowed on Mondays as a result of the Sunday Rest Act confirmed the Republican Socialist Coalition triumph. Everyone felt something must happen now, happen fast and fiercely. The Prime Minister himself agreed with Madrid. The newspapermen dogged his heels as he walked to the Palace to present the Government's resignation.

"What more news do you want?" he snapped to the reporters. "Spain went to bed a Monarchy and got up a Republic."

The day dragged on, full of rumors. The King and his advisers were panic-stricken, torn with indecision. Even my uncle, that staunch Monarchist, felt that it was no use to counter the wave of popular opinion with armed repression. The Army could only slaughter—the Army could not win for Alfonso.

The "Provisional Government of the Republic" issued a manifesto: "In the name of Spain, which has now come of age, we declare publicly that we are bound to act quickly and with energy to satisfy the nation's desire for establishing the Republic."

The Palace replied to the manifesto. Elections for a Constituent Cortes would be held at once.

But the people went faster than the King's promises or even the declarations of their leaders. Madrid was awake that night with harmless crowds cheering and singing improvised songs, asking the King to leave. Even the police and the people fraternized in the Puerta del Sol, the great center of Madrid where all demonstrations took place. A group of Civil Guards fired a few shots against the holiday crowds. One man was killed and another wounded. But even this reminder of the Monarchy was not enough to dampen the exhilaration of that evening.

The morning of April 14 brought the news that in the small industrial town of Eibar in the Basque country, the victorious candidates had seized the City Hall and proclaimed the Republic. The Royal family, abandoned at that moment by the Spanish nobility and many of their personal friends, shuddered within the Palace. But their fear was not justified. Revolution exploded in the streets, but there was not a single shot fired by the people, not a single building put to flames, no assaults, no violence, no bloodshed. The Republican and Socialist youth formed a chain around the Royal Palace, not because they were afraid of any violence, but because they wished to prevent the noise of cheering and singing to reach those inside.

About midday, the news reached Madrid that Barcelona had also proclaimed the Republic. At three o'clock I was in a taxicab passing the General Post Office on one of the main squares of Madrid, when the driver suddenly slammed on the brakes.

"Look!" he shouted, his voice breaking with excitement. I craned my neck. On the flagstaff above the Post Office the flag of Monarchist Spain was fluttering down and as I stared, feeling a lump come in my throat and tears sting my eyes, I saw the flag of the Republic rise above the Post Office.

The taxicab driver and I jumped out of the automobile. Arm in arm we marched into the dense, cheering, wildly excited crowds. The great buildings of the government rose all about us, and one by one we saw the Monarchist flags go down over the War Ministry and the Bank of Spain—and one by one the beautiful new flags of the Republic, of the new Spain, go swiftly up the flagpoles.

I tore myself away from the madly happy crowd to rush home to my telephone. I sat with a group of friends. First we rang up uncle Miguel; then the homes of some of the members of the late Cabinet, including my uncle, the Duke; and then some of the newspapers. The Monarchist newspapers would either not answer the phone, or their staff members pretended they did not know what was happening. The telephones of the liberal newspapers and the Republican leaders were constantly busy—but when we finally got uncle Miguel, the information he had astonished us.

The King had left Madrid. He had fled from the Palace that afternoon, just as I had seen the flag go up over the Post Office. A motor car had taken him direct to Cartagena where a destroyer awaited him. Before leaving the Palace he had signed a temporary renunciation of the Crown of Spain. My Monarchist uncle, the Duke, had written the famous document in its entirety and the King had hastily signed it. Had the good-natured people of Spain been more politically acute they would have considered that document a provocative gesture.

For uncle Gabriel had written a document in which the King insisted that he had a perfect right to the throne of Spain; the document clearly stated that the King did not renounce a single one of his rights, privileges, properties, nor did he renounce anything whatsoever for his family. The Republicans decided to keep that document secret until all the members of the Royal family crossed the frontier.

The next morning the Queen, left behind by her husband, gathered her family at the old Escorial station near Madrid, and surrounded by a scattered handful of aristocrats, took the train for Paris.

The Queen's railroad car was not across the frontier before it met another official train, coming from France. The exiles from Monarchist Spain—the pilots of the Air Force who had flown to safety across the border when the uprising failed, the other members of the Republican Committee who escaped the police spies—were returning in triumph. Among those who hung out the train windows, waving and cheering as the dense crowds assembled in the railroad stations, was Ignacio Hidalgo de Cisneros, one of the leaders of the Air Force revolt.

The returning exiles were Spanish gentlemen, trained in traditions of gallantry. They arranged with the engineer of the

Queen's train to route that lady's engine through the backyards of the towns the train passed, so that she would not need to see the great crowds assembled to welcome the returning heroes of exile.

The streets of Madrid were filled with gala crowds for nearly three days. The Republican Government took control, finding office very difficult at first—for the administration of the state was in the hands of the same civil servants who had for years faithfully served the Monarchy. Alcalá Zamora was elected Premier of the first Republican Government of Spain; my uncle Miguel became the Minister of the Interior. Spain had become a Republic without disorder or bloodshed.

Zenobia, Inés, and I tried to settle down to our business, but we spent most of our time in the little shop talking politics— like every other Spaniard in those days. And to tell the truth we had very little business anyway. Few of the society women who had come the year before to sec the granddaughter of Antonio Maura working as a saleswoman returned that Spring of the Republic. One of the first reactions of the aristocracy of Madrid to the new Republic was to withhold money from circulation—a very effective way of sabotaging the democratic government. And as time went on and they had to buy food and such necessities, they decided that at least they could go without glass, pottery and embroideries, rather than buy them in a shop run by Republicans!

But although we did not do much business Inés, Zenobia, and I met every morning in the shop to discuss the news of the day. I remember one morning Zenobia arrived with a newspaper in her hand, wildly excited.

"But look," she said, and then dragged the paper away from us so that she could read the item again herself. "The Republican Government plans to establish free non-religious schools in such numbers as to provide at least an elementary school education for every Spanish child—and this within the next five years," Zenobia read. "Illiteracy must go, is the new slogan."

We cheered her on. "I could kiss every Cabinet Minister," Zenobia cried. "I am happy, Spain will live again!"

And we felt the same way. Imagine Spain with thousands of free schools! For almost the only free schools in Spain under the Monarchy were those few miserable ones run by various Catholic aid societies and Religious orders. I thought of the school my mother had paid for—and I thought of the new, free schools for every Spanish child. Then I felt like Zenobia—I must kiss every Cabinet Minister! The Republicans planned to build as many schools in a year as the Monarchy had built in a quarter of a century!

Zenobia, Inés, and I didn't much care if our shop failed or not, in this new Republic. We felt we would have plenty of opportunities to use our energy in helping to build our country. And indeed, I thought of a service I could do the new Republic almost immediately. I applied for a government post in the P.N.T.—although I would never have dreamed of applying for such a post under the Monarchy.

The P.N.T. was a national board, organized and financed by the state, to foster travel in Spain. New maps were printed for tourists, pamphlets published describing the beauties of Spain. Hotels or rest houses were built along the roads for motoring tourists. The promotion of travel in Spain, not only by foreigners but by Spaniards as well, was supposed to be one of the main aims of the P.N.T., which had been organized by Primo de Rivera.

I had heard that the P.N.T. was in serious difficulties under the Republic. The aristocrats whom Primo de Rivera had placed in charge of the organization had fled abroad. I spoke two foreign languages, and I felt I could be of service. I saw great importance in attracting foreigners to our country to see with their own eyes what the Republic was doing for Spain and to dispel the evil stories that Monarchist propaganda spread abroad about the Republic. Then, too, I wanted to help promote travel in Spain by Spaniards. Even I had traveled much more abroad than in Spain and I felt that many of the regional incompatibilities and natural distrust of the Spanish people would be dispelled if they grew to know their own country. But to accomplish this, traveling would have to be cheap and convenient enough for all Spaniards, not only the rich few.

Full of enthusiasm, I went to visit Rafael Sanchez Guerra, who was secretary to the Prime Minister. I had known his father, the ex-Prime Minister, many years. I had visited the family in Paris while old Sanchez Guerra was a voluntary exile under the dictatorship. So Rafael received me very graciously and promised me a job in the P.N.T. But I left his office quite crestfallen. I was sure he had mistaken my enthusiasm for the Republic for a need for a job and salary—which I didn't really need at all. I still had my allowance, which was quite enough for Luli and me. But I brushed aside the momentary disappointment and waited eagerly for my job to begin.

After some delay I went to work in one of the government buildings. My colleagues were a sharp disappointment. Some were rich men, the owners of watering places and the like—others the brothers, relatives, and friends of Republican politicians. They had no idea of building the P.N.T. into an organization of real use to Spain and the Republic. Along with the civil service employees left over from the Monarchy, their one ambition was to do no work at all for their generous salaries.

I felt I must not allow myself to be demoralized. I made such a fuss that I was finally given some work to do. I wrote a pamphlet on the castles of Spain which was never published. I was sent on a trip to inspect one of the hotels the P.N.T. owned. I found it was a huge, fabulously expensive luxury hotel situated in a most remote and out-of-the-way place. It had almost never been used except for shooting parties given by one of the aristocrats Primo de Rivera had appointed to the P.N.T. I returned anxious to make a detailed report on this scandal. I felt the hotel must either be closed, for it was an expense to maintain, or turned into a cheaper hotel for less distinguished but more numerous guests.

But I found no one to be in the least interested in this "white elephant." The chief civil servants had undoubtedly been part of the plot to buy and maintain this luxury hotel and the new Republican officials were too indifferent to the P.N.T. to care one way or the other.

My experience in one department of the Republic must have been duplicated in a dozen places. In the majority of government offices the people who did the administrative work for the Republic had once loyally served the King. The spirit of the Republic was never allowed really to penetrate the Government. It was not enough to change the heads of the Government, something much more drastic should have been done. But we were all worried about legality—we wanted no shadow of "force" to fall over the infant Republic. As a result, the people of Spain paid for the "legality" of the first Republican Government in a bitter coin in the years to come.

But while the Republic lagged in administrative matters, it plunged boldly ahead into its legislative program. The first item on the long overdue reform was the separation of Church and State. Democracy had brought such a policy to every other European and nearly every other American country years—a hundred years in most cases—before, and the Church had benefitted. Now Spaniards were to be allowed freedom of conscience: a man was to be given the right to worship as he pleased, or not at all if he so chose. The Catholic religion was not attacked. On the contrary, those who wished to be Catholic could continue to practice their religion in the same way as before, but there were to be no penalties for those who did not choose to be Catholics. The faithful would have to support the Church, instead of it being supported by the Government, but the Church was not to be suddenly cut off from the state treasury; the gradual scale would give it a chance to get its income from other sources as it does in all other countries—from its own faithful.

But even before these measures were taken, the Church had already sided with the Monarchy. From the pulpits the priests had asked the faithful to vote against the Republican-Socialist Coalition, threatening eternal damnation to their flock if they did not support King Alfonso. For the Church knew the Republic would mean free public schools; some civil marriages; burial without compulsory Catholic funerals. And these were three important sources of revenue to the Church. But it appeared that the majority of people in Catholic Spain wanted the Church to stay out of politics and content itself with spiritual rather than material affairs—for the Republican vote was overwhelming.

The Republic had brought me new work and new enthusiasm. Now it was to bring me other new interests of a much more personal kind. For one day at the end of April, my younger sister Regina asked me if I would chaperon her at a lunch given by the pilots of a flying school near Madrid. I agreed reluctantly—chaperoning young girls seemed a little dull. But I made a condition: some one of the pilots should take me up in his plane. I had never flown and if I was to be bored at a silly luncheon I meant to be paid with a flight.

I met Regina that lovely Spring day in Madrid in an open-air restaurant in the Retiro park. Her beau had already arrived. We sat sipping drinks waiting for the officer who was to drive us out to the air field for the luncheon and my first airplane trip. I was quite frankly bored until Regina and her beau began to talk about the major for whom we were waiting. He was a famous man in the Air Force, this officer, commandant of the air field we were to visit and counted one of the finest fliers in Spain. His comrades had nicknamed him "the Prince" because his generosity and gallantry were proverbial.

He was a descendant of the Admiral bearing his same name who helped to lose the battle of Trafalgar and his father had been an aide-de-camp to Don Carlos, the pretender to the Spanish Crown—but he was enthusiastically Republican. He had been one of the leaders of the Air Force revolt against the dictatorial Monarchy, the last to fly across the border after taking many of his friends to safety. During his exile his brother-in-law, who had been a friend of King Alfonso's, had made him all sorts of promises if only he would return home and swear loyalty to the King. But this aviator, son of the landed gentry of Spain, preferred penniless exile to serving the Bourbon ruler.

"You will fall in love with him, Constancia," Regina said, giggling. "Everyone does. His men worship him and so do all the women he has ever met."

I sniffed.

Regina's beau was very earnest. "Your sister is silly," he said solemnly. "You are very honored to meet my superior officer. He is only thirty-five, but he has just been made commander of the air school, and they say he could have had any job he wanted in the Republic—the Republican leaders know how much they owe to him."

I raised my eyebrows. "You make it difficult for him," I said coldly. "No one could be so great a hero."

"There he is!" Regina giggled again and I turned to watch a tall, slim man in civilian clothes threading his way through the tables. As he came closer, I could see he had a few gray hairs at his temples. His face was rather long, his eyes dark, he wore a small mustache. Without doubt, he was a very handsome man.

"This is my sister," Regina said. "Constancia, this is Ignacio Hidalgo de Cisneros."

We bowed with careful formality. Major Hidalgo de Cisneros piloted us through the restaurant to his car. Regina and her beau got in the back seat of the little Ford. The chaperon of this luncheon party sat in front.

At the air field Major Cisneros drove us to his little house. Luncheon began with Regina talking intently to her officer while the major and I exchanged polite chit-chat. I feared the hero was bored. I could hear him telling his friends how he had entertained young ladies of polite society at his house.

"I always look after the chaperon," I could hear him saying.

Regina's beau began to explain Republican politics to my young sister who, I am afraid, was more interested in the personnel of the Republic than in its principles.

I broke into the conversation. "Yes, but at the trial I heard Alcalá Zamora say . . ." I began.

"You were at the trial?" the commandant asked me.

"In the front row every day."

"So," Major Cisneros said.

Two hours later, the orderly was hovering around the table. Regina and her beau had wandered off, and the commandant and I were still talking, quite lost to the world.

With a start I remembered my responsibilities. "Come, Regina!" I said, jumping up.

The officers drove us to the air field. It was quite against the rules for civilians, especially women, to fly in Army planes, but the commandant gave me a flying kit, put me in an open two-seater, warmed up the motor, and then raced off the landing field. I looked down to see the gold, reds, and greens of the province of Guadalajara spread out before me. I felt the wind in my hair, and my heart beat with excitement and joy. From that day I have loved flying—and I never fail to have that marvelous sensation of power and exaltation every time I step into an airplane and soar away from the ground.

We did not fly far that first day. The plane, like every other the Republic of Spain owned, was an old crate, rusty and about as safe in the air as a broken-down sewing machine.

The commandant turned now and then in his seat to ask me with a gesture: "Do you like it?"

He couldn't hear my voice but I think he understood how I felt, for he grinned and took the plane up higher.

At last the motor stopped. We slid back to the earth. The mechanics on the field helped us out and I had a chance then to see what this officer meant to his enlisted men. For they obviously adored him. Nobody was servile, but the commandant's wishes were anticipated before he said them aloud.

Driving back to Madrid the commandant turned to me and asked, "You are married?"

"I am separated from my husband," I said stiffly.

There was a pause. "You live with your parents, I presume?"

"No." I hesitated, for my way of life was strange to most Spanish men. Then I said quietly, "I am working. I live alone with my little girl and my maid and nurse."

The commandant nodded. "Is it difficult?"

"I would rather be independent than live in security." I waited, for in Spain this was a daring thing for a woman to say, even in the Republic.

Ignacio turned to me, grinned, and said, "Good for you! I admire you!"

And the next day I ran to answer my telephone myself, while

my maid looked surprised. But it was not Ignacio, nor the next day, nor the day after that. And after a week I sighed and let the maid answer the doorbell and stopped ruffling anxiously through my mail in the mornings. The commandant apparently had other friends.

Spain was a Republic. For a few weeks the aristocrats trembled in their boots, waiting to see if the new Government would seize their lands, imprison their leaders, and drive them into exile. No Republican had been safe in Spain during the Monarchy. Surely Monarchists would not be welcome in the Republic?

But the leaders of the Republic were legal-minded. They knew history, for many of them were college professors. They knew that the American Revolution, to name only one, had ruthlessly weeded out the followers of George III. But surely such measures would not be necessary in Spain in the enlightened year of 1931? Democracy should mean an opportunity for all to express their opinions, should it not? A few Republicans urged that democracy should mean an opportunity for all who believed in democracy to express themselves—and something less than freedom for those who wished to overthrow it. Must democracy watch itself being destroyed, these realists asked?

But the legalists won out. The Monarchists, who still had the power of wealth in the new Republic, owned the largest newspaper in Madrid, the famous *ABC*. Every day the *ABC* predicted the overthrow of the infant Republic. Every day the *ABC* printed long, tender interviews with the hero, King Alfonso. Every day the *ABC* wrote stirring accounts of the activities of the Monarchists at home and abroad.

The Monarchists grew more arrogant as they grew more sure of the leniency of the Republic. They rented luxurious headquarters in a main street of Madrid. They held meetings, printed pamphlets, put up posters, all urging the overthrow of the Republic. "Bring Alfonso back!" they cried.

On Sunday, May 10, the generous, legalistic policy of the new Republic bore bitter fruit. A group of the young aristocrats— fine, polished gentlemen with canes and carefully trimmed mustaches and beautifully tailored clothes—met to make plans for a major demonstration. The King's birthday fell on May 17. The Monarchists would go into the streets of Madrid and make a riot, in honor of their King. That Sunday might have passed off harmlessly, but for the enthusiasm of the young dandies. The plans for the next week's meeting intoxicated them. They came swaggering out of their luxurious headquarters, cheering Alfonso, shouting, "Down with the Republic!"

The taxicabs were lined up in front of the Monarchist building, the drivers were waiting for business. Now the taxicab drivers of Madrid were among the staunchest Republicans in the city.

"Down with the Republic!" shouted the young aristocrats.

"Down with Alfonso!" the taxicab drivers yelled back. "Viva the Republic! Viva Liberty!"

The aristocrats looked black. The editor of the newspaper *ABC* walked out of the building, swinging his cane. He singled out a little cab driver.

"What do you say, my man?" the editor asked.

"Viva the Republic!" the driver yelled. "Down with the Monarchists!"

The editor swung his cane sharply. The cab driver gasped and slumped behind his wheel, the blood flowing from his head.

But the Monarchists had reckoned without the people of Madrid. A crowd had gathered, a muttering, sullen crowd. The editor started to walk away, leaving his victim unconscious.

Somebody shouted, "They killed him! The Monarchists killed a Republican!"

The cab driver was not fatally injured, but the mistaken rumor spread like wildfire. I was driving home from the country that Sunday afternoon, and we passed the crowd and saw two fine limousines, the motor cars of the Monarchists, going up in flames.

I arrived home full of anxiety. The Monarchists had mistaken the peaceful nature of the Spanish people. The Republic had come without a shot being fired. The aristocrats had not even been threatened. So, since the people apparently did not intend to destroy their former rulers, the aristocrats apparently had decided to destroy *them*. The Monarchists took good nature for weakness. It was an error.

The crowd grew outside the Monarchists' headquarters. The aristocrats retreated to their club rooms. The Civil Guard arrived and tried to hold back the sullen Republicans. And then suddenly shots rang out, shots fired directly into the crowd.

A man fell, screaming, and died while the crowd bent over him. Two children, hardly more than babies, sobbed in the gutters, blood flowing from their legs and arms.

Who had fired those fatal shots? Some said they had come from inside the Monarchists' headquarters. Others said they came from behind two trees where the Miralles brothers, young Monarchist enthusiasts, were posted.

Madrid boiled with indignation. Tram cars stopped. Taxis drove back to their garages. A general strike was declared for the next day. Monday's newspapers brought further rage. General Berenguer, the King's Prime Minister—who had been arrested and charged with the death of Galan and Garcia Hernandez—had been set free by the Republican leaders. But legality again had superseded caution. The General's counsel was persuasive and the Republic freed its enemy.

By noon on Monday, the Socialist trade unions had called off the demonstration strike and asked their members to go back to work. But not all of Madrid came under the discipline of the workers' organizations. Trade unionists kept order, but angry crowds still roamed the streets. A large and passive crowd, quite silent, watched a little group of men, not more than a hundred, set fire to the Jesuit Fathers' residence at Calle de la Flor, where I had made my first confession. Most of the thousands who watched the fire took no part in lighting it—they watched quietly and grimly. And after the fire had burned away, the *Madrileños* went home, their angry feelings somewhat soothed. There were no works of art within the Jesuit residence and the money and valuables were saved and deposited with a small watchmaker in the neighborhood. All the Jesuit Fathers had fled before the building was set on fire.

I did not witness this or any of the other fires which spread through Spain. I spent that day at Inés's flat over the shop, thinking in anguish of the consequences of these terrible moments. The people of Spain had been tormented into these fires—they turned against the provocateurs who sought to destroy their liberty. The Republican leaders could not stop the aroused people except with armed force, and the Government of the new democracy could not and would not fire into the crowds. The Spanish people were more than just, they were merciful to the aristocrats who had so long oppressed them. But when the Monarchists threatened to overthrow the Republic, the people acted.

I knew that the fires lighted that Monday in Spain were the inevitable result of the arrogance of the Monarchists. But I also knew the consequences. The next day I went to visit my uncle Miguel at his home, and found him grave and fearful. For we knew that people like my parents, reactionaries at heart, but somewhat undecided when the Republic came to power, had now made up their minds. So long as the Republic did not change anything in Spain, so long as the Republic allowed them all of their old privileges, they were ready to give it lukewarm support. But now that the issue had been made clear, they were ready to fight the Republic to the death.

From that day, Spain was openly divided in two. The cleavage split families, brothers and sisters, fathers and sons, mothers and daughters, and even husbands and wives. Politics could no longer be a subject for polite dinner-table conversation. People *lived* as Monarchists or Republicans, reactionaries or progressives. Men decided for freedom, or against it. Most of Spain, the peasants, the workers, part of the small middle class, stood for the Republic. And all of rich and privileged Spain, the big industrialists, the landowners, the titled nobility, the church dignitaries (though not all the village priests), stood against it.

Going home that night from uncle Miguel's, I knew my lot was cast with liberty. And I felt then, as I feel now, that freedom would eventually win in Spain. The Spanish people could not and would not be defeated.

But I knew the next years would be hard.

The flames died down. Quiet was restored in all the Spanish provinces. People went back to work. The Constituent Cortes was called, and, as everyone expected, the Republican-Socialist Coalition had a big majority. The Republicans filled their benches with intellectuals, many of whom were to prove their complete uselessness in politics. But the people had made a rather touching gesture to culture, so long despised in Spain. The Monarchy had ruthlessly oppressed the universities; the Republic honored college professors with election to offices they could not fill very well.

The first article of the new Constitution drafted by the Cortes read: "Spain is a democratic Republic of workers of every class, organized in a regime of Freedom and Justice. The powers of all its organs originate with the people." These were brave words but unfortunately not very true when they were written, for the peasants had still to be emancipated from the landlords and the workers had yet to obtain even the most elemental labor reforms. Still, Spain's Constitution was meant to herald a new day for the ancient country.

The main problems facing the country were the agrarian conditions, the Army, the Church, and regionalism in Catalonia. The brand new Constitution solved all these problems beautifully on paper—but practice was another matter.

Agrarian conditions in Spain in 1931 were very nearly feudal. For the first time, as the Cortes debated the agricultural problem and I talked politics every night with my friends, I came to know something about peasants and how they lived; I remembered La Mata—and now I learned that all Spain was one great La Mata. Fifteen million Spaniards lived on the land in 1931. Of these, sixty per cent owned only six and three-tenths per cent of the land, while four per cent owned sixty per cent of the land. A few, in other words, owned nearly everything, while the peasants owned almost nothing.

It was hard for me at first to understand what these figures meant in human terms. I had grown up among the people who owned the land; now I began to know something about the people who did not. I discovered, for instance, that seventy per cent of Spain's entire population lived on the land—this was indeed an agricultural country. I read in the newspapers, with a real sense of shock, that the Duke of Medinaceli, for instance, owned 79,146 hectares of land, while two and a half million Galician peasants owned only 2.9 million hectares—a little more than a hectare per family (a hectare is two and a half acres). My own father owned parcel after parcel of land in the provinces of Salamanca and Segovia—and he was not primarily a landowner but rather a Madrid business man. And the peasants who worked my father's estates did not own so much as space for a fruit tree to grow.

Spain was not a poor country. But Spain's lands, owned by rich gentry, were impoverished by deforestation and cultivation by backward and futile methods. Spain's peasants were underfed. Living on the land, they starved. Vast regions were held by cattle owners who, rather than raise fodder, turned their expensive beasts out into fields that might have raised food for thousands.

The Agrarian Reform Bill tried to solve some of these problems. Uncultivated land and enclosed common land was to go to the peasants—while the Republic compensated the aristocratic owners with generous payments. Then, rich landowners were prohibited from exporting grain and other agricultural products beyond certain quotas. Thus, prices for food in Spain would be kept low enough for workers to buy and Spain would not export food while its peasants and city workers went hungry. Finally, the "parish" law was passed, to prevent the hiring of outside workers while local men were unemployed. This law, if enforced, would prohibit landlords from starving peasants who voted for the Republic by hiring cheap labor from Portugal. A peasant was entitled to a job working on the landlord's fields if the landlord needed farm hands.

The Agrarian Reform Bill painted a rosy future for Spain. Peasant families were to be settled on the lands the Republic bought from the aristocrats. The few who owned sixty per cent of the land were to be replaced by the many. But reform cannot take place on paper alone. In 1931 the peasants were filled with hope—a few years later they were, most of them, still waiting for the Republic to give them food and land. Agrarian reform moved so slowly that I could not help wondering whether it was not being administered by the very people who wished to prevent it.

The Army question was neatly solved in the Constitution, too. But Manuel Azaña was made the first Minister of War of the Republic. A cold, careful intellectual, he had been interested in theoretical military problems for many years. He was an expert on military textbooks and could win battles on paper better than any other intellectual in Spain. How often had Azaña not sat at a café with his friends, discussing the problems of the Spanish Army? How many times had he not expounded his neat simple plans for reforming the Spanish Army to hosts of admiring friends? How often had he not explained, over a coffee, that the Spanish Army had over eight hundred generals, one officer for every six men, and was still the most inefficient Army in Europe?

But now he was Minister of War, in fact, not in after-dinner conversation.

Now he had to deal with the most corrupt, tough-minded, self-seeking military caste in the world. He had to make an efficient Army out of officers whose first principle was hatred for the Republic they were supposed to serve. In short, he had to create a Republican Army out of a Monarchist Army. Azaña's first move was to retire on full pay any general who wished to leave the service—and this move was such a major mistake that it all but destroyed the Republic itself.

For Azaña knew nothing of the Army in life. The officer caste identified itself with the feudal landowners and the biggest feudal landowner of all—the Church. The Spanish Army was not supposed to be "political." That is to say, it never questioned the authority of either King or Church. But the Army had always reserved its right to "pronounce" on any situation which it considered did not benefit its specific policies or privileges. The "pronunciamientos" never stated a positive policy, only disapproval of some challenge to the Army's power.

Azaña knew the Army was pro-Monarchist—but he didn't know what to do about it. Instead of taking drastic steps, he hesitated. Everyone knew the Army should be completely dissolved and built up again with Republican officers trained in new schools and selected from the ranks. A new Republic needs a completely loyal Army. But Azaña shuddered at the opposition such a move might bring. He decided to cut the number of officers by simply retiring all those who would leave on full pay. The result was that the few Republicans in the Army, disgusted at Azaña's tactics, retired. The more or less indifferent officers also left. The Monarchists engaged in active conspiracies against the Republic naturally stayed. Azaña, in other words, weeded out most of the loyal or semi-loyal army officers and built the Army into a completely pro-Monarchist, conspiratorial organization. And those Monarchist officers who also left the service, keeping their full pay and their uniforms were able to remain in close touch with the Army.

The separation of the Church and State brought more opposition from the reactionaries than any other step the new Republic took. In fact, the Monarchists managed to create the impression abroad that the new Republic was anti-religious, godless, seeking to destroy religious worship. Nothing could have been less true. The United States Government was not considered godless when it separated the Church from the State during the occupation of the Philippine Islands. Enlightened democracies universally consider that a citizen of a free state should have a right to worship as he pleases and the choice of contributing money to a church treasury or not. The Catholic Church of the United States does not ask the American Congress to subsidize it with millions of dollars annually.

But when the Cortes decided to make freedom of conscience a law in Spain, the whole world trembled with the cries of the outraged Monarchists. The Church was powerful. Out of the whole population, 168,762 men and women served the Church —a larger number of persons than was employed by the Government with its police forces and all its administrative officials. The Church was the largest landowner and the most merciless landlord in Spain. Whole villages of peasants were reduced from independent landowners to church tenants. The Church was a great capitalist in Spain. The Jesuits alone owned hundreds of mines, steamship companies, electric light plants, banks, hotels, newspapers, telephone companies, radio stations, and railroads. The Church, as a big capitalist, offered fierce competition to secular Spanish business men. My father's electric light company, for instance, was nearly driven to the wall by the rival Jesuit company in Madrid—until my father wisely entered a combine with the Jesuits.

The Church was wealthy and powerful and so it exerted enormous influence. The State Agrarian Bank, for instance, owned by the Jesuits, supplied credit to over two million small business and farmer families. Do you want a mortgage on your little orange crop? Good. How do you vote in the elections? Are you a Republican? Then the bank is very sorry, but it cannot extend credit.

Or the Catholic National Agrarian Federation—a group designed to prevent the peasants from organizing. The Federation owned seventy magazines and five daily newspapers. Their presses ran day and night flooding the country with propaganda from the Federation. And the Federation was owned and controlled by the Jesuits.

Again, the Jesuits nearly controlled the educational system of Spain. True, the Republic promised free non-religious schools. But they were still to be built and their teachers still to be trained. In the meantime, do you want to send your son or daughter to school? Where else, then, can you send the child but to the religious schools? And suppose the boy or girl comes home and says, Do you vote Republican? The teacher told the other children not to talk to me because I am wicked—she says you vote Republican.

The Church was powerful. In the Cortes, Gil Robles was the leader of the Confederation of Spanish Right Parties—the "Ceda." The Ceda's chief task was to preserve the privileges and power of the Church and the other big landowners.

The new Republic solved the problem of the Church on paper—but time was to show whether it had solved it in reality.

The problem of Catalonian independence was the least knotty of the questions the Cortes had to solve. For generations, the Catalonians had dreamed of a separate political state—but these dreams had often been fostered by men who hoped to manipulate the people of Barcelona for reaction. Now, under the Republic, the Catalonian language and flag were made legal. Catalonia was granted its autonomy with separate administrative officials—something like a state in the United States. All Barcelona turned out to welcome the Madrid Republicans when they arrived to sign the Catalonian agreement. Progressive Spain was to remain united.

A month in the new Spain passed faster than a week under the Monarchy—for me at least. I worked in the mornings at the Government office, in the afternoons at the shop. At night I sat talking politics—feverishly—with friends. Life seemed free and good and happy. I was twenty-five. I was beginning to understand myself and my country. Every Spaniard faced great problems and grew, I think, in trying to solve them. Those days in Madrid were absorbing.

And so when my phone rang one afternoon in June, I had to think quickly a moment before I remembered the name the voice announced, "Ignacio Hidalgo de Cisneros."

"Yes?" I said finally, remembering with a little twinge the week I had spent hoping—just a little—that the hero commandant would call me.

"I have been away," Ignacio said eagerly. "I had to go the day after I saw you at the air field. I am wondering—I have been hoping—that you would remember me well enough to go with me tonight to a reception at the air field."

"Well . . ." I began doubtfully.

"Do come," Ignacio said, full of enthusiasm, "it's for Ramón Franco. He's just been made head of the Air Force and we're having a celebration for him." Ramón Franco was then very much in the limelight, having taken an important part in the Republican Air Force uprising, while his brother Francisco was still an unknown general.

I found myself dressing more carefully for that reception than I had dressed for years. Not since the days when I went to my first parties had I taken such pains with my hair and the folds of my skirt. And suddenly I felt very young again—not like a woman whose life is over, whose fate is forever settled. I kissed Luli good-by and ran down the steps as I heard Ignacio ring.

We had a wonderful time. It was a gay party. I laughed to see all the other Air Force officers swaggering around in their uniforms while Ignacio, who, next to Ramón Franco, was probably Spain's most famous aviator, sat quietly in his civilian clothes, telling me little jokes and pointing out the famous people. That night as he brought me to my door, I noticed his voice waver a little (although he pretended to be casual) as he said: "Will you go driving tomorrow?"

I went driving. And not only "tomorrow" but almost every day. We used to start out, sometimes with Luli between us on the front seat, sometimes alone, after my work at the shop was finished. It was hot that Summer, and we used to go for picnics to the mountains just outside of Madrid. Sometimes we stopped at a little café near the air field, where the proprietor was a good Republican, and many nights we used to join in the conversation that went on day and night among the airmen who sipped drinks on the café terrace.

One morning I went into the shop still giggling to myself over a blow-out we had had on our drive the day before. I was dressed in one of my nicest Summer frocks, for Ignacio was calling for me after work to take me to dinner—as usual. I suppose I must have been singing a little to myself—either that, or the look on my face and in my eyes must have betrayed me.

"You are seeing him again tonight?" Zenobia said suddenly.

"Who?" I asked, very innocent.

"Constancia!" Zenobia's voice was near tears. I looked up from the peasant linens I was sorting to see Inés and Zenobia, my two dearest friends, regarding me with sorrow and alarm.

I was still a married woman, they told me, Republic or no Republic. All Madrid was gossiping about me. Ignacio was famous; I, too, was a well-known figure, the daughter of a distinguished family. They knew my friendship for Ignacio was harmless—but Madrid didn't know. Economic emancipation was all very well. I could work for my living. But going out

unescorted—going out with a man at all, when I was married—
this was a very different matter!

Married! I had hardly thought of Bolin for months. We had
a legal separation and it was not my fault we did not have a
divorce. The Republic promised divorce laws, but the Cortes
moved slowly. In the meantime, I was violating all the conventions of conventional Spain.

But I realized, as Zenobia talked to me, that I could not and
would not give up Ignacio, conventions or no conventions. I
hardly knew what Ignacio thought of all this—he had never
mentioned Bolin after our first discussion. But I was determined to win Zenobia over. So I arranged a meeting between
Ignacio and Zenobia—we went driving in Zenobia's little car,
for now at last I was learning to be more discreet. I wanted
Zenobia on my side when at last the gossip filtered back to my
family and they confronted me with the same question my own
friends had. Ignacio liked Zenobia immediately and she in turn
became a fast friend of his. And now things became easier, for
Zenobia agreed to go with us on our picnics and excursions,
and some of the gossip died away as Ignacio and I went everywhere with the equivalent of a chaperon between us.

The Summer grew hotter in Madrid. We three, Ignacio,
Zenobia, and I planned a vacation together. I was afraid to go
to La Mata for my holidays, because my family was already
aware of Ignacio, I felt, and waiting for an opportunity to discuss him with me. So the three of us decided to take Zenobia's
little car and tour the province of Salamanca. But at the last
moment, Ignacio was kept on duty. He sent a young soldier to
drive us, and Zenobia and I started out to see our country. We
were both filled with the new patriotism we had learned with
the Republic and we wanted to know our country better.

The afternoon of the second day out of Madrid we arrived
at the village of La Alberca—where the women wear beautiful
black cloth skirts cut in a flare and barbaric gold and silver
ornaments. But we were not interested in the picturesque. We
wanted to see the changes the Republic had brought to these
remote sections of Spain. But La Alberca had not changed—at
least we could mark no break with the past in this ancient

Spanish village. The houses looked just as decrepit; the women sitting on their thresholds looked just as weatherbeaten and worn. We could not help but realize how long it would take Spain to change the habits and customs of fifteen million Spanish peasants, scattered over the remote and ancient country.

But even La Alberca had benefited from a few changes. The jail, a stinking hole not fit for beasts, had been abolished. A young woman who could answer the telehone and run the typewriter at the same time, a major feat for these parts, acted as an information bureau for travelers. And she sent us on our way down a steep mountain road to the Monastery of Las Batuecas.

Las Batuecas was the site of an old Carmelite Hermitage, built three centuries before in a rich narrow valley, but abandoned later by the friars who objected to such solitude. In the last twenty years the Order had tried to make the ruined, decayed Monastery habitable again. But the place was too lonely. A small group of friars had offered to remain, but one by one they had all given up until now Brother Joaquín alone represented the Order in their old domain.

The few habitable rooms in the Monastery had been turned into a hostelry where guests were welcomed in the same manner as were the traveling gentry of the Middle Ages. Beside Brother Joaquín, the cook and her sweet daughter Carmencita lived in the solitude of the Monastery. The child was fair-haired, a pretty little thing, dressed in a tight calico bodice held in with tucks, long sleeves, and full long skirts like the clothes little Castilian villagers wear. She took us up to our rooms which were much better than we had expected. The wooden floor was not very clean and there were cobwebs in the corridor and in the four corners of the room, but the mattresses had been recently made, Carmencita proudly told us. Her mother had washed the wool in the river and made the mattresses herself. The little girl also showed us a room containing a bathtub with a cold water tap, but shyly she explained that it had never been quite possible to use the bathtub since the monks had somehow forgotten to install the pipes.

We were up at six the next morning and the old Monastery

garden was lovely and cool at that hour. A smooth slab of slate placed under a tree in front of the house served the purpose of a table for the hostelry. There Carmencita had already laid breakfast for us. They did not bake bread in this valley because no wheat grew here; now and then a peasant would come down from La Alberca to sell bread or to bring the delicious flat rye pancakes which we had for breakfast that lovely morning.

Brother Joaquín offered to drive us into the part of Spain known as Las Hurdes, of which the narrow, rich, and beautiful valley of Las Batuecas is the deceptive threshold. The small valley is luxuriant. Trees and flowers grow in wild profusion. Birds and small animals break the mountain quiet. Even Zenobia and I, who knew nothing about farming, could see that the soil was good and might have grown wheat and food. But the valley belonged to a rich merchant, later to a Duke who lived in Madrid. They kept the road from La Alberca and the old Monastery open for a rare tourist—and for themselves.

From the Monastery to the first river, a rather shallow, empty river with sandy banks, like most rivers of Spain, we saw a complete desert. Not a desert of vegetation, for the trees were green and the grass was tall, but a desert of human beings. The landlords from Madrid did not care to farm the rich soil.

Zenobia and I were not entirely unprepared for what Brother Joaquín showed us in Las Hurdes. For once, long ago, my grandfather had as Prime Minister ridden on horseback to visit the people he governed in this remote part of Spain. I had often heard the tale, as a child, and then it seemed like one of the English fairy stories Miss Nora had told my sister and me.

For my grandfather had ridden all day long on horseback. At nightfall, he came to the first village of Las Hurdes. Tired and hungry, he asked a little old woman he saw sitting by a tiny hut for a piece of bread and shelter for the night. But the woman only gaped in surprise. Bread? She had no bread. Lodging? Could he sleep in her hut?

But the hut was too small for a grown man, my grandfather complained—and was there not a piece of bread in the whole village to feed a hungry man—to feed the Prime Minister of Spain?

The woman cackled. Did the Prime Minister of Spain not know that thousands of Spaniards lived, or rather tried not to die, in a region that produced nothing, on a land that gave nothing, in villages where nothing came from the outside because there were no roads, no mail, no telephones, and no grass or hay to feed cattle that might lead them through the mountain paths to the outside world? And did the Prime Minister of Spain not know that in Las Hurdes the only bread ever seen was brought by the "bread seller" who trotted down on a mule from the other side of the mountain, bringing sacks filled with dried up crumbs?

The story I was told as a child stopped there—I always thought that perhaps then my grandfather waved a magic wand and produced three beautiful loaves of bread for the old woman. I remembered only one other detail of the story—that my grandfather could hardly enter the old woman's hut, even bending over. For it seemed that the people of Las Hurdes, undernourished for so many generations, had been stunted by their hard life. They never grew to the size of normal men, and so their little stone and mud huts were not tall enough for the Prime Minister of Spain.

My grandfather's tale had stuck in my mind, and I am afraid it seemed strange and enchanted. Certainly the story had not prepared me for the frightful reality that Brother Joaquín showed us without comment.

The first village we saw in Las Hurdes was nearly abandoned. "The people have died of goiter or malaria," Brother Joaquín said briefly. "A medical expedition came here once to study and cure the malaria, but there is not much you can do for people who get so hungry they eat the earth, sprinkled with a little water to help them choke it down."

Zenobia and I felt faint—such a picture of human desolation we had never seen or even imagined. "Why don't the people leave?" Zenobia asked finally.

Brother Joaquín considered and then answered slowly, "Once some of the strongest and cleverest of the men—and that is not very strong or clever—walked over the mountains to Salamanca. But when they came to the villages of the province, they found

they were different in size and looks from the rest of their countrymen. The other peasants laughed at them, or shied away
from them in fear. And this made the travelers very bitter and
unhappy and at last they came home to Las Hurdes and since
then nobody has ever gone away."

Zenobia and I fell silent. We drove along the barren road
and at last we came to the priest's house in the second village.
His dwelling was not exactly luxurious, but compared to the
other huts in the village, he lived like a king. He even had a
real bed with a mattress and a rocking chair. He sat on the
veranda surrounded by potted flowers, with his view of the
village carefully screened off by clinging vines.

The moment the priest saw us he began to tell us his woes.
"Imagine how it is," he said, "to have to live among such ignorant, starving peasants! They are idiots, imbeciles, every one of
them!"

Zenobia, usually so calm, flared up. "Idiots! And if they had
something to eat, would they be so stupid? Suppose the landlord of the valley allowed them to farm the fertile land instead
of forcing them to live on the barren side?"

The priest looked frightened. We were well-dressed ladies—
gentry, he supposed.

"Pardon," he said nervously, "let me show you our church."

But the church infuriated us even further. For, besides the
priest's house, it was the only dwelling not made of mud in the
village. Its spire rose fine and high, built of brick and stone and
inside the church were bright altar cloths and images. A flight
of stone steps led to the church, rising from the thick mire of
the village street. Lolling on the church steps were half a dozen
pot-bellied, languid children, each wearing only a ragged loin-
cloth, their hair matted and full of burrs, their bodies covered
with mud and filth. They played with a thin little pig, the only
animal the villagers owned.

Zenobia and I had no further strength left to argue with the
fat comfortable priest. We took a few steps through the thick
mud of the village street. We spoke to a woman sitting before
her tiny hut. She stood up as we addressed her—she was hardly
more than four feet tall. She wore a few rags tied around her

waist and hugged a baby to her lean breast. The child's head was covered with thick yellow scabs, one of his eyes was swollen shut and oozing pus.

"Good morning," I stammered.

The woman stared at us blankly.

"Is the child sick?" Zenobia asked.

The woman's face began to work—I thought she was going to cry. But it was fear. With a kind of animal groan, she disappeared into her dark and odorous hut.

Brother Joaquín saw our distress. But he would not drive us back to the Monastery until we had seen the hero of the village. He was a doctor and teacher all in one. He kept the only school and he did what he could to prevent the villagers dying of goiter or malaria. He had been offered other posts—but he stayed in Las Hurdes.

"Someone must stay," he said very cheerfully, as we talked to him, "and now that the Republic has come, perhaps the people will be settled on fertile land, and then they will grow and prosper. There is nothing wrong with these people. They are not congenital idiots, as some comfortable scientists have written. They are just hungry."

Zenobia bit her lips.

"Hungry," the doctor said reflectively. "Yes. They have been hungry for nearly three hundred years. This is what hunger will do."

"What can we do for you?" I asked—and I felt that we should lay medals at his feet. But all he wanted was books on science. We made a list of what he needed and the first thing Zenobia and I did in Madrid when we returned was to visit a bookshop and send him a small library of scientific treatises. I think the bookseller was amazed to see two women buying books on medicine and finding tears in their eyes as they spelled out the address.

We met Ignacio a few days later and the three of us, with our soldier-chauffeur, drove North this time to Galicia and the Asturias. I was beginning to know my own country and I fell in love with it. We had only a few days—only enough to see the green vineyards built like terraces on the green mountains, the barefoot women, the miserable villages, and the beautiful manor houses, the peaceful Galician fjords. We saw it, but we could not know it in the few days we had left of the vacation. At Santiago de Compostela we spent hours rambling around the lovely cathedral, and on the drive back to Madrid I told Zenobia and Ignacio, with deep emotion, that I was beginning to feel that I was a Spaniard, at long last. For I had been brought up to believe that Spain was vulgar, beneath the notice of fine and fashionable people. Everything in my life—from the language I used to the food that I ate and the clothes that I wore—had been copied from the English, French, and Germans. And now I felt a deep pride in my beautiful country with its courageous people, its lovely monuments to the past, and its deep belief in the future.

Ignacio and I made up our minds on that lovely summer trip that our lives could not be lived separately. Zenobia sensed that we had made a decision. Now that she knew Ignacio, she could not advise me to give him up. Back in Madrid, Ignacio and I decided to be married as soon as the Cortes passed the divorce bill. It was not a decision I made lightly—and yet I could not yield to the opinions of my old friends and family. I knew they would consider my second marriage, when it took place, as a sin against God and an offense against morality. My parents believed that a woman must suffer from a first unhappy marriage to the end of her days. But I could not face the future so hopelessly. I felt sure Ignacio would make me happy; and I was determined to marry him.

But the passage of the divorce law took time. Ignacio and I began to get more and more impatient as the Autumn passed into the Winter, Christmas came and went, and still the Cortes debated Agrarian Reform. And then at last, in early February, 1932, the Speaker of the Cortes read the proposed Marriage Reform Bill and the debate began.

Our shop was very near the Cortes building. I used to beg off from work early and rush across the street and down a block to the government hall. Ignacio and I had friends who got us permanent press seats, and we used to meet in the reporters' gallery nearly every night to listen to the debate. In the stately hall of the Cortes the Catholic opposition would often be speaking as I arrived. Puff-faced, unhealthy-looking Gil Robles, leader of the reactionaries, would be scribbling notes at his desk while some Monarchist deputy would hold the floor, thundering against divorce, trumpeting that what God had joined man could not put asunder!

The deputies on the floor of the Cortes all knew Ignacio and they came to know me. As the weeks passed, we became famous spectators, easily the persons most intimately interested in the bill up for debate. As I took my seat every night, the Republican-Socialist deputies would wave and bow to me, sometimes send up notes assuring me that they planned to make a big speech soon to confound the opposition. I suppose I will never in my life again have such an impatient interest in a piece of legislation. I came to know fine points of parliamentary law. I cheered the advances of the Republicans and mourned the triumphs of the Monarchist-Catholic bloc. And sometimes Ignacio and I would anxiously hold hands while one of the Republican leaders held the floor and argued for haste in the passage of this Marriage Reform Bill.

But divorce laws are not passed in a day. The Catholic opposition fought bitterly, every step of the way, blocking on the most minor points, arguing footnotes and punctuation marks for days and whole weeks. Their policy was obstruction. The law was sure to pass, for the Republican-Socialist Coalition had a majority. But Ignacio and I sometimes despaired of the divorce law passing while we were young and in love. We used to make sad little jokes as we went to dinner after the Cortes session—the law would be passed when we were old and gray, bent and crippled.

Madrid is a large city, but small in a certain way. A few weeks after Ignacio and I had begun to attend the sessions at the Cortes together, the whole world knew that we would be the first couple in Spain to marry after one of the pair was divorced. Ignacio's sister announced well in advance of the passage of the law that she would never speak to a woman so "loose" as to be divorced.

My own parents heard the story rather later than most of Madrid who knew me. But hear it they did, and my father was apparently assigned to interview me and argue me back to my senses. He asked me to come to the house to speak with him. I arrived in the late Spring, after my mother and sisters had already left for La Mata. The house was empty, the furniture covered with white slip covers, the pictures and lamps wrapped with colored netting. The whole place had a dusty and solemn and ghost-like look. I came before my father, and the porter let me into his study, where I sat, nervous and fidgety, on a chair draped with white linen, staring at pictures wrapped in paper.

The strangeness of the setting, the deep quiet of the deserted house, the feeling of loneliness made that interview with my father the only frank talk I ever had with him in my life. Never before and never again did I dare to tell him what I really thought.

He began quietly. "Is it true?"

"Yes, father, I intend divorcing Bolin and marrying Ignacio the very first moment the law allows it."

My father's face darkened. "Constancia! Is one mistake not enough?"

I heard Ignacio described as a Republican without a fortune of his own, whose family, aristocratic enough, had long since washed their hands of him; an Army officer who was a friend of Socialists.

I kept staring at the picture covered with paper, trembling with anger.

"A divorce is a dishonor the de la Moras cannot bear," my father went on. "Must you destroy your mother's life as well as your own?"

I pulled at my fingers, trying to control my rage.

"But if you *must* marry again," my father went on, "please do it without dishonor. Let me give you the thirty thousand *pesetas* (about $3,000) for an annulment, so that you can marry again in the Church."

"Church!" I cried, my face getting dark with anger. "I have too much respect for the Church you speak of to perjure my-

self before its laws. I'd have to take an oath that my first marriage was forced on me—wouldn't I?"

My father looked uncomfortable. "Be reasonable, Constancia, you . . ."

"Reasonable! You ask me to take a false oath before God,
so that I can 'marry within the Church.' Who respects religion
more, you or I? Who would suggest a perjured oath to keep up
appearances, you or I?"

My father bit his lips in annoyance. Then he dropped the
subject and went back to speak of Ignacio again, with rising
fury. And now I began to understand. He had thought I would
accept the offer of the annulment instead of the divorce—that
had not really worried him. What tormented my father was the
possibility of my marriage to a Republican, perhaps even a
Socialist. For I realized in this interview that father had never
taken my political opinions very seriously. I was a woman—
women's political views were of no importance. But, he felt, if
I married Ignacio then indeed I would be given over to the
side of his enemies. All this he could not quite say, for fear of
uttering the words and making them final, but I understood.

And then as he fell silent, I began to speak; I was very cruel,
so cruel that I wept bitter tears of regret afterwards. And yet
I spoke the truth.

"We are already enemies, father," I said, "whether you will
admit this or not. And now I have definitely made up my
mind."

He made a gesture of denial, but I swept on.

"You have never done anything to make your children happy,
least of all me. I have never known what it meant to be happy
until now. My whole education was a lie. You sent me out into
the world to choose a husband without giving me any knowledge with which to make my choice. You very nearly ruined
my life by teaching me fake prudery, false standards of wealth
and position. You taught me to be idle and vicious and arrogant. I had to learn through bitter years of suffering how to
unlearn everything you taught me!"

"Constancia!" My father's eyes were full of tears, but I could
not stop now that I had begun.

"My whole education was to make me dependent, not independent. You never taught me how to earn my living, and so I could only lean on my husband or on the money you might give me. My sisters have never had a single chance to be happy —do you think they are happy with the husbands you chose for them?"

My father turned away from the sting of my words. But now I nearly shouted. "You call me here to ask me to give up my whole life. Instead, you should be proud, you should rejoice that at least one daughter of yours has been able to see clearly, at least one daughter has made herself independent, at least one daughter has learned enough to choose a husband with whom she will be really happy."

I stopped then, seeing the drooping shoulders, the bowed head of my father. He had no answer to me, and I could not speak again. We kissed each other and I went away.

I picked up the paper on August 10, as I went to work, scanning the type eagerly, as usual, for some new news of the divorce law. Instead, black headlines met my eye. A Monarchist uprising had failed the night before. General Sanjurjo, once a close friend of Primo de Rivera, had led the abortive revolt. He was seized in Seville, on his way to Portugal.

The Spanish people raged at this startling news. General Sanjurjo had pledged his fealty to the Republican Government only a few months before. He led the Monarchists in revolt against the legally constituted Republic. And yet his death sentence was commuted to life imprisonment.

Ignacio and I drove out to see Indalecio Prieto, Minister of Finance, the Sunday after the uprising and all the talk at the luncheon table was about the leniency shown to the hated General Sanjurjo. This was the first time I had met Prieto. He seemed very fond of Ignacio, indeed they had lived in the same boarding house in Paris during the exile. His two daughters welcomed me very cordially, and we all settled down to discuss the danger of handling Monarchist conspiracies with kid gloves. Prieto hardly spoke. He sat like a Buddha, with his small eyes half closed, his hands resting on his prominent abdomen. Now and then he threw a phrase into the conversation, which indicated that he had heard everything said. I was a little irritated to find that Prieto did not take Ignacio's political opinions very seriously; in fact, he almost patronized Ignacio.

One morning while the divorce law was still being discussed in the Cortes, my maid came running into my bedroom, her eyes all but popping, her voice trembling with fear.

"Madam," she quavered, "your husband—he's outside, with some other gentlemen. Oh, dear!" And she burst into tears.

I couldn't help giggling. I am sure it was the first time in his life Bolin had ever frightened anybody. Still, I dressed quickly, with a beating heart. For Bolin undoubtedly had followed the passage of the divorce law in the Cortes as closely as I had. He knew I planned to divorce him and get the custody of my child. At that time in Spain a widowed mother did not have full control of her own children, and I was about to get full control of Luli, thanks to the new laws. Bolin had apparently come to withdraw the document he had signed giving me my child when I left him. In the interval before the passage of the law, he planned, no doubt, to take Luli away from me. And once my child was in his family's home, I would be unable to get her back. And Bolin, who had never shown the slightest interest in my Luli, would have the income from the child's little fortune.

"So!" I said to myself. "We shall see!"

I walked slowly into the living room. Bolin was flanked by two lawyers, imposing-looking gentlemen.

"In the name of the law," said the first lawyer in loud, pompous tones, "your husband wishes you to resume married life under the same roof with him."

He repeated this phrase three times—and three times I calmly refused. Then the lawyer announced the withdrawal of the document authorizing me to take full charge of the child and her education, permitting me to sign documents, undertake business, rent the apartment under my own name, dispose of my bank account, ask for a passport and to travel abroad. With this withdrawal I would be at his mercy until the law of divorce was finally approved and even after that, until my divorce was granted.

The next request was made by the lawyer in even more solemn tones. "My client, Señor Bolin, requests that his child should live under the same roof with him, and that you should at this very moment turn her over to him."

Here again, I would have been at his mercy if my lawyer, a woman, had not been cleverer than Bolin's. I had placed Luli under the care and tutelage of a special court, created in Spain a few years before for the care of minors. The child had been deposited with my parents until the court should determine whether Bolin or I should have custody of her.

When I announced this to my early morning visitors, their faces fell, and they left my small house, single file and crestfallen, while my maid, a warm-hearted, intelligent peasant girl from Castile, and I cried in each other's arms with unrestrained emotion and delight.

Soon after, Luli's case came before the Court for Tutelage of Minors. Few changes had been introduced in this branch of justice under the Republic. The Duchess of Infantado, fit wife to the "noble gentleman" who had chosen the industrial field during the World War rather than remain haughtily distant from the riches streaming into the country, was president of the jury. All the other members were either magistrates or judges, specialists on the question of minors. While I waited for the case to be called before the jury, Bolin was ushered into the same anteroom and sat on a seat opposite me.

I could not speak to him. I just stared at him and wondered how he could afford such expensive shoes and such smart clothes. This small question turned round and round in my mind during the hour we waited to be called into the Court. At last we filed into the courtroom and were asked to sit on two chairs side by side in front of the tribunal. No lawyer could represent us. We had to state our own cases. I tried to put forward, in as few words as possible, the fact that for two years Luli had lived with me and I had received nothing whatever towards her support from Bolin or any other member of his family. In fact, neither Luli nor I had heard from him at all during these two years. Now that I would soon be able to ask for a divorce—the moment the law was definitely approved—Bolin tried to oppose my petition of divorce by depriving me of the child he knew I would never be willing to give up.

Bolin made a long speech. I was sure that he had memorized something written by his lawyers. He accused me of giving the child a "Masonic education"—what he meant by that I was never able to discover. He seemed to think that the child's nurse was still the old German woman I had engaged in Málaga. Actually, a few months after my arrival in Madrid I had engaged the young German girl who had since then looked after Luli. She happened to be a Roman Catholic. I knew that until the law of divorce was approved and some fundamental Spanish laws were changed, if anyone accused me of giving an anti-religious education to Luli it would be enough cause for her to be taken away from me. I was very careful that no such accusations could ever be made.

The Court dismissed Bolin's charges—but my child was made the legal ward of my parents. I could not have custody of Luli because, the Court stated, "I was working and could not take proper care of my child."

I knew perfectly well that the Court gave Luli to my parents because its members, all die-hard reactionaries, believed that Luli would be brought up much more "safely" by my parents than myself. But in the Spanish Republic of 1932 it was still legally possible to take a child from its mother because the woman was working to support it!

I could not help thinking that if I, who appeared before the Court well-dressed, speaking the language of the well-educated, was treated with such violent injustice, what must not happen to the women of the poor who usually had to bring their troubles to that tribunal!

And indeed, I soon learned that my conjectures were correct. After Luli's case was heard, the Court heard the case of a woman whose son, thirteen years old, had been caught for petty thievery. The child had been placed for a time in a reformatory and afterwards the Court had decided to keep him in a special institution for delinquent children whose home environment was bad. The mother was expected to pay for her son's pension, but she had not yet paid anything because she said she could not afford to do so.

The woman came to the court wearing *alpargatas* torn at the toes, an old calico skirt, and a short woolen shawl over her shoulders. Bare-headed, her youngish face lined and wrinkled with work and tears, she stood in front of the jury where I had been seated.

The Duchess of Infantado addressed the woman. "How much do you earn per day?"

"Two *pesetas* fifty a day on the days that I work, which is twice or three times a week. I have two other children to look after at home and my husband is dead these last six years. I cannot afford to pay the 0.75 *pesetas* pension for my child."

It was fascinating and monstrous to hear the Duchess answer the woman, to tell her how, on an income of an average of 7.50 to 10 *pesetas* a week ($1 to $1.50), she could afford to sustain her family and pay the pension for her boy.

The mother did not reply to the Duchess. She stood quietly, staring at the beautifully dressed lady who told her, in sweet cultured tones, how to feed, dress, clothe and shelter her family and still pay the boy's board bill. When the Duchess had finished her homily, the mother gave the Court a long look, filled with dignity, and left the room, her head high.

The Duchess and the other magistrates were removed by the Republic shortly after I lost Luli to my parents. I asked for a revision of my case immediately. And this time, before a more impartial justice, I was awarded the custody of my child, and a few days later I had Luli safely back with me.

The Cortes finally passed the divorce bill and my woman lawyer filed my petition for divorce immediately. My case was one of the first to be heard in Spain. Bolin decided to fight me; first he wrote a long letter to my father declaring he could not accept divorce because of his religious scruples. It was the first time I had known him to be even faintly interested in religion. My father ignored the letter, knowing my mind to be made up.

Next, Bolin engaged young José Antonio Primo de Rivera, the dictator's son and already known as the incipient leader of the Falangist movement in Spain, to be his lawyer. But the young Primo was shrewd; he asked my father whether I was a bad and dangerous woman from whom Luli should be snatched at any cost. My father replied that he thought not—and young Primo withdrew from the case. Bolin had the same luck with two or three other lawyers, all of whom started the case with enthusiasm and withdrew when they saw how little chance Bolin had.

Finally, four months after I had filed my petition, the case was heard. I sat alone in the courtroom—Bolin did not come from Málaga. The trial took little time, my case was very clear. The court gave me full custody of Luli until she came of age— but added that I could not remarry for a stipulated period of time after the decree was granted. My lawyer felt that stipulation was illegal; she advised me I could be married at once.

Ignacio and I saw no reason for delay and we set our wedding date for January 16, 1933. My parents ignored my wedding day, but two Cabinet ministers of the Republic, Prieto and Marcelino Domingo, agreed to be witnesses at our wedding. We asked a whole party of our friends to go with us for the ceremony, too, including Zenobia and Inés, of course, and we all set out very gaily for Alcalá de Henares, the little town near Ignacio's flying field.

I couldn't help laughing on the way out to the field. I felt wonderfully gay and happy, unlike the miserable morning I had dressed for my first wedding. I wore a simple, tailored dress, very different from the elaborate white satin I had worn as I marched down the aisle of the Church of San Jerónimo so many years before.

Our wedding turned out to be rather more eventful than we had expected—it was a sign of the times in Spain. For the reactionary authorities of the little town of Alcalá, spotting two Republican Cabinet ministers in our group of witnesses, proved balky. Monarchists through and through, they were determined not to perform Spain's first marriage ceremony for a couple one of whom had Spain's first divorce. We waited in the dusty municipal building, Ignacio fuming with rage, Prieto and Domingo purple at the insult offered them by a nasty little provincial reactionary town clerk. But our cause was not lost in the end. News spread through Alcalá like wildfire—the Republicans rose as one man to see that Ignacio and I were married.

We were somewhat disconcerted to be made a political issue on our wedding day, but in the end the marriage was very jolly indeed with all our partisans lined up outside the courthouse and cheering furiously as the hastily drafted Republican substitute for the Monarchist town clerk pronounced us man and wife. The whole wedding party finally drove away in magnificent triumph with the defeated town clerk and his friends looking dismal and all the workers of the little town waving and shouting good wishes.

I had already moved into a new apartment with Luli and when we arrived home my little Castilian maid and Luli's German nurse had quite outdone themselves—our wedding guests sat down to an excellent lunch and a very gay party.

And afterwards, when everyone had gone home, Ignacio and I sat down on our new sofa, which we had just bought with great pride and enormous care, and watched Luli playing dolls on the carpet in front of us—and suddenly we both began to laugh. For at last Luli was safely ours, and all the dreary months of waiting for the Cortes to pass the divorce bill were over, and we were sitting in a home of our own, married—and so very happy.

I was twenty-six years old. And I had just begun to live.

We had spent all our money on the divorce and the new sofa and the new pictures and the other things we had bought for our new home, and so we were, as I was later to hear my American friends say, "flat broke." Ignacio had decided that my father's allowance was to go directly into a bank account for Luli the moment I received it—we planned to live on Ignacio's small military pay and whatever extra I earned at the shop. This was a revolutionary idea, for Spain. Most Spanish gentlemen expected to supplement their own incomes with allowances paid by their fathers-in-law, and plenty of Spanish men, like my first husband, lived as a matter of course on their wife's money. Naturally I was very pleased by Ignacio's decision, and we both agreed that the money, which would amount to a considerable sum by the time Luli was grown up, would provide my daughter with the finest education possible.

My family, like all the friends I had once known, refused to acknowledge that Ignacio and I were married. We were living "in sin." This meant, of course, that I could never call upon my father or mother, nor introduce them to Ignacio. They thought of me, and treated me, exactly as though I were party to an illicit relationship with a disreputable man.

This might not have troubled me too much but for Luli. For she visited her grandparents once a week and I did not feel that I could change this custom. And my parents tried to question Luli, on every visit, about the kind of life Ignacio and I led. The child, who was only five, began to sense that something was wrong. These constant questions! Returning from her grandparents, she would ask me, "Mommie, grandma always asks me about daddy. Why does she ask me about him? Doesn't daddy go to see grandma too?"

Alas, Ignacio was not invited—nor was I—to my parents' home, and we began to realize that as long as we lived in Madrid, Luli's life would be far from normal. One of our main concerns was to surround Luli with an affectionate, normal, matter-of-fact family life, something which she had never experienced before. After much discussion, we agreed that we must move out of Madrid, perhaps out of Spain for a few years at least, until Luli had grown accustomed to a perfectly normal sort of home life. Then she could adjust herself to the peculiar circumstances of my family relationships.

Ignacio, one of the most self-effacing of men, hated the idea of asking the Republican leaders whom he had helped in exile and in revolt for any favor at all. Because Prieto was a close friend of his, Ignacio felt he could never ask the Minister of Finance for anything. Finally, after much soul-searching, Ignacio decided to ask Marcelino Domingo to send him to Mexico as a military attaché to the embassy.

There was no answer at all for a few weeks and then unexpectedly Ignacio was called to Prieto's office and told that the Council of Ministers had decided to create the post of air attaché in the Berlin and Rome embassies. Ignacio was offered the post.

We were much disappointed, for we wanted to visit the Americas, and Fascist Italy and Germany did not interest us at all. Ignacio made another bid for Mexico, this time with more courage since he had already been offered one Government post, but Prieto told him that the Government very much needed an entirely reliable man as air attaché in the native haunts of our natural enemies—and put that way, we both agreed that Ignacio's duty lay in Rome and Berlin.

Before we left for Rome, we were entertained at dinner in both the German and Italian embassies in Madrid. Not that I met any of my former friends at these embassy parties. The foreign diplomats were careful not to mix the fowl and the flesh with the good red herring. They entertained the Republicans because they had to—and they never invited Government leaders to the parties at which they entertained their personal friends, the reactionaries and Monarchists of Madrid.

We were soon to discover that the first Republican Government of Spain also had many difficulties with its own diplomats. The Republican Ambassador to Italy, for instance, suffered from an appalling inferiority complex. He had to live in the famous and beautiful Spanish embassy in Rome, the Palazzo Barberini—and he always acted as though he were camping out in the midst of the magnificent marble and glorious pictures. Indeed, he had the air of a caretaker—I always thought he walked through the marble corridors with the hushed step of a custodian illicitly sneaking up the stairs reserved for the gentry.

Ignacio only smiled at his superior's obvious discomfort in the palace—what really annoyed him was the Spanish Ambassador's political behavior. For this college professor, instead of being proud of the new Republic, carried his inferiority complex over to his professional duties. Because he represented the new Republic of Spain, he apparently expected to be kicked constantly. When he was merely ignored, he was as pleased as a child, and counted it a great victory.

And we soon found out, at our new post, that the Ambassador to Rome was not unique. The new Republic suffered many a diplomatic defeat because its representatives abroad were inclined to apologize rather than boast of their new Government. Of course, the Republican Ambassadors had a hard row to hoe. They were surrounded by "career" diplomats, whose political sympathies had not changed with the overthrow of the Monarchy and who kept their reactionary opinions to themselves— although they soon discovered that the Government in Madrid was tolerant of its dissident civil servants, at home and abroad. But these fine gentlemen, who were received as personal friends by the other diplomats, sneered at the Republican Government behind the Ambassador's back, sabotaged his shy efforts to make friends for the Republic, laughed at the Madrid Government at every opportunity, and made it perfectly clear to the rest of the diplomats that their sympathies were distinctly not with the Government they were supposed to represent.

Ignacio and I were simply infuriated by this state of affairs. We hated the "career" diplomats who sabotaged the Republic— but we were also more than irritated at the Republican Ambassador who was so grateful for a few Fascist crumbs and constantly apologized for his fatherland. We were proud to represent our country, proud to represent the Republic—and we never lost an opportunity to make this perfectly clear.

After a few days at one of the expensive hotels of Rome, Ignacio and I came face to face with the problem every young couple on their first diplomatic post wrestles with—money. For a diplomat's pay does not start to come in regularly for two months or more after he arrives at his post. In the meantime, he has to buy clothes—uniforms if he is a military attaché as Ignacio was, evening clothes of the most expensive kind for his wife. We decided that we simply could not afford to stay at the proper hotel during the months while we waited for Ignacio's first salary check. So while all the rest of the embassy staff raised its collective eyebrows, we took a deep breath and moved into

a little flat with an American newspaperman we knew, Bob
Stunz. I suppose that we violated all the rules for young diplomats, but we didn't care, we were perfectly happy.

We took a studio in the Via Marguta—we had a large room
with dilapidated furniture, a big window overlooking a charming court filled with wistaria, rickety steps leading up to a low-
ceilinged bedroom. Bob slept in another cubbyhole of a room
next to the kitchen, and we all shared a primitive bath.

Somebody sent us a Spanish girl to come in mornings to do
the cleaning and cooking. She was a great mystery. She was
fanatically religious and, when we were forced to dismiss her
because her cooking was frightful and her cleaning worse, she
wrote us a letter threatening me with eternal damnation and
informing Bob that but for her vigilance, I would long ago
have succeeded in poisoning him!

I hunted houses while we lived in this Bohemian dwelling
and finally just as Luli, her nurse, and our furniture arrived
from Madrid I found a little apartment in a small villa and
managed to get my household settled permanently. Since we
were to live six months in Berlin and six months in Rome, we
decided on small quarters in Italy. But Ignacio and I had fun
arranging our possessions in our new little apartment and I was
so busy, I hardly had time to reflect how happy I was in a city
where I had once spent the most miserable days of my life,
with my first husband.

Our new apartment wasn't settled without a certain amount
of excitement. We had to install electric light fixtures and our
landlord sent us a gentleman impressively clad in a black shirt
covered with Fascist medals. We were so struck by such splendor that we hardly dared to ask him for an estimate on the job—
surely a Fascist of such distinction could not be dishonest. But
this important personage sent us a bill for eight hundred lire
after the task was done—easily four times what the job was
worth.

Ignacio advised caution. Fascists were not to be trifled with
by accredited diplomats to Rome. Let us avoid an "incident,"
he said over the dinner table. But the next morning, when the
fine Fascist came to collect his outrageous bill, I lost my temper,

and in the few words of Italian I knew then, mingled with my somewhat similar native tongue, I gave him a dressing down such as I am sure he had never heard before. And to my surprise, all his arrogance crumbled. He reduced the bill to three hundred lire on the spot and retreated bowing, mumbling thanks, and mopping his brow. It was my first experience with Fascist servility and bluster and I have always thought since that cowards' hearts beat behind those arrogant brown and black shirts.

One of the newer residential sections of the town lay just off the street where we lived in Rome. But there were still some of the old tenements not yet pulled down to make way for the homes of the rich and middle class. Across from our villa, for instance, forty families lived in a crumbling, blackened, ancient old tenement house. Rosa, our cook, had a tiny apartment in that house where she lived with her little boy.

Rosa was a widow; her husband had died the year before. Since he owned a tiny vineyard in Abruzzi, he could not die in the hospital free of charge. His young widow had to work as servant to pay off the hospital bill or lose the little vineyard. She estimated it would take three years for her, living on the barest, most meager standard of living, to save enough to pay that hospital bill—it had taken her husband four days to die in a crowded ward.

"Why don't you sell the vineyard, Rosa?" I asked her one day.

She looked at me for a moment, her steady black eyes filled with sorrow. "*Ma, Signora,* the dead one had three brothers all married and with children, and they all have to live on that little vineyard which is hardly enough to keep the body and soul together for two people."

Rosa's little boy played all day long in the gutter while she watched him from our kitchen window.

"Doesn't he go to school?" I said once, leaning out to see the pretty youngster scooping mud for mud pies into a broken old dish.

And again Rosa looked at me with the resignation I saw so often in Italian peasants. "*Ma, Signora,* there aren't enough

schools and I would have to wait years before I could get my
little boy into the one in this neighborhood."

In this very simple way, the very first weeks we lived in
Rome, we began to know Fascist Italy. We began to understand
what lay beneath the blatant "prosperity." Ignacio and I saw
the fine new roads Mussolini had built, but we were Spaniards
and fine new roads seemed a little suspicious. We remembered
Primo de Rivera's roads. We discovered gradually that the
grandeur of Fascist Italy was built on the blood and tears of
the peasants and working people. Men starved so that tourists
could admire the dictator's beautiful roads. Women went hungry so that Mussolini could build fast engines to bring his trains
in on time. Children grew up illiterate so that the dictator
could buy guns for his enormous army. And sometimes today
when I hear people say, "Well, but Mussolini gets things done,"
I think of Rosa, whose little boy played in the gutters, whose
life was one long epic of starvation—Rosa, one of the millions
of sacrifices to "getting things done."

As for the society which we necessarily had to frequent, it
was one of the most corrupt and evil I had ever seen. The
Spanish aristocracy was stupid and dull and wasteful and infinitely boring—but religious prejudices made it extremely
prudish. Fascist Italy was anything but prudish. The Italian
aristocracy, as well as the Fascist government officials, made a
parlor game of adultery. The ladies of "good society" quite
openly violated their marriage vows. No man could stop his
car on the Via Veneto or any of the other great Roman streets
without being approached by a smiling lady who suggested a
drive. Foreigners in Rome soon learned that the price they had
to pay for the favors of these accommodating sirens was not
measured in coin of the realm; these ladies were far more interested in securing for themselves certain social advantages.
The Italian prostitutes were rigidly confined to restricted districts—the ladies who took the place of the Parisian street-
walker belonged to the "best" society. I am not easily shocked,
but the behavior of the Italian aristocrats and their Fascist
masters was downright revolting.

In the first few weeks after our arrival, the Italian people were being exhorted to hate the Jugoslavs—for reasons which even the editorial writers seemed to find obscure. Next, everybody was ordered to hate the French because they had "stupid democratic ideals." After that, all Italy was informed that every man of honor should hate the English, because they were interfering with the conquest of Abyssinia. It was my private opinion that these campaigns bore little fruit. A few silly college students dutifully rioted in front of the various embassies, but the Italian peasants and the Italian worker, men of reason and good will, shrugged off the "hate" campaigns as just another example of the madness of the people in power.

In fact, the only genuine dislike for another government I saw in Italy was a profound hatred for the Third Reich. The Italians disdained the Germans, and the German embassy lost no opportunity to make sport of Mussolini and his bombast. The Italian editorial writers even allowed this dislike for the arrogant Germans to creep into their papers, off and on. In a backhanded way, they managed to imply, for instance, that an air-raid rehearsal was a precaution taken against Germany.

Indeed, Ignacio discovered to his surprise that this distrust of the two Fascisms for each other even permeated official circles. The German air attaché had to ask Ignacio for information about Italian planes given to Ignacio as a matter of course by his "friends" at the Italian Air Ministry. In exchange, the German attaché brought Ignacio statistical information which after study proved what Ignacio had already guessed—that the boastful Italians had an Air Force far inferior to the Germans.

Ignacio and I hated the feverish, corrupt atmosphere in Rome and although we made a few friends there, we were always glad to leave for our holidays, which we mostly spent in the beautiful Italian or Austrian Alps. After one such holiday, in the Summer of 1933 when Ignacio and I had been married and away from Spain about six months, I received a telegram from my father. My mother was critically ill in a Frankfurt sanatorium—would I come at once? She asked for me day and night.

I took the morning plane from Rome and arrived that same

afternoon. My parents were terribly touched. Although my father had sent for my other two sisters, they were staying at amusing resorts and neither of them cared to make the trip. My mother seemed overjoyed to see me and began to recover almost the moment I arrived.

While we waited for my mother to recover completely, my father and I went for long walks in the lovely German country-side. We talked idly of politics. I wanted to take up the discussion we had had in Madrid, but we were both too shy and reserved with each other. I did manage to tell my father how happy I was; he did not reply but changed the subject, tact-fully, I am sure he thought.

My father's remarks on the political question puzzled and worried me. He was a rich industrialist, not a feudal land-owner. And yet he spoke of organizing opposition to the mild Republican reforms through strong employers' associations. I listened to his confident flow of talk and wondered.

When I returned to Rome after my mother's recovery, Ignacio and I talked with a sense of dark foreboding of what my father had told me. Obviously things were not going too well with the young Republic. Besieged on all sides, the Republican leaders suffered from timidity rather than courage. Alcalá Zamora, who had withdrawn from the first Cabinet because the majority favored the separation of Church and State, had just been made president of the Republic. He was white-haired, gentle-looking, a great orator, something of a mystic. He had been a Monarchist most of his life and turned Republican during the dictatorship. Now, pressed hard by the reactionaries, he signed a decree dissolving the Cortes and ordering new elections. The powerful, rich reactionaries set great hopes by these elections. My father had intimated in Frankfurt that he had knowledge of elaborate plans—if not plots—to put the country back into the hands of the reaction-aries at the next general election.

As the time approached for the November election, Ignacio and I began to get more and more nervous. The newspapers seemed to make no sense. *El Socialista,* official organ of the Socialist Party and the UGT (General Union of Workers) in

Madrid, one of the few Spanish papers reaching us regularly, certainly gave no idea of the danger the country faced. My father's confident words struck a cold chill in my heart every time I thought of them. Surely the Republicans sensed the dangerous offensive?

On November 19th, Ignacio and I waited for news impatiently. And when at last the wires began to pour into the embassy we realized how complete the first Republican Government had failed. The reactionaries had won—completely.

"I can't say I'm surprised," Ignacio said gloomily.

And I wasn't either. For the first Republican Government, timid, weak, legalistic, had promised general reform—and accomplished almost nothing. Where was the land the peasants were to be given? Still in the hands of the reactionaries. Where were the better working conditions for the city masses? The only time the Republican Government was really ruthless was when they sent armed forces to crush strike disturbances.

The reactionaries had presented a united, bold, and determined front in the elections. They presented thousands of mattresses, and other gifts to the workers, buying votes where they could not intimidate.

And the Republicans—they were split in a dozen parts. The two big trade union federations, the UGT and the CNT, fought each other while the reactionaries smiled. Largo Caballero, head of the UGT, was Minister of Labor in the Republican Government—a reasonable man, my father said. The CNT, Anarcho-Syndicalist Trade Union Federation, refused to vote. The timid, weak policy of the Republicans—the reforms made on paper but never in fact—plus the split in the labor movement gave the reactionaries a clear majority in the new Cortes. True, the total number of progressive votes cast was larger. But the Ceda, the organization of the Spanish right, controlled the Cortes. Black days lay ahead for Spain.

The first immediate results of the election, as far as Ignacio and I were concerned, were very surprising. Ever since we arrived in Italy, Ignacio had worked very hard to keep the Spanish General Staff informed on facts about the Italian Air Force. I worked hard with him, helping him in the translation of

Italian publications and technical articles in the daily press. He visited factory after factory, inspected planes, talked to engineers, we made friends with people in the Air Ministry. Ignacio's weekly reports were models of information and had been, until shortly after the elections, received with great enthusiasm in Spain.

Now the General Staff suddenly grew bored by Ignacio's efforts. We knew that new people, hostile to Ignacio politically, had been immediately appointed to the General Staff. But we were surprised and puzzled to find that these military men, reactionary or not, no longer cared to get precise information on Italian military affairs. It almost seemed to us then as though they had other and better sources of information on the Italian Air Force than what their military attaché could find out. Our mystification has, of course, since been cleared up; treason takes time and careful planning.

When the Lerroux government, which rose to power in Spain after the November elections, sent a new Ambassador to negotiate a concordat with the Pope, Il Duce decided to pay a little attention to the Spanish embassy which had been notoriously neglected by Fascist authorities since the proclamation of the Republic. The appointment of the Ambassador to the Vatican was followed immediately by the naming of a new head of the embassy in Rome to replace the unfortunate old professor sent by the first Republican Government. The new Ambassador was a reactionary—but he was the son of a hat maker and the aristocrats in the old Spanish diplomatic corps treated him so badly that I think he sometimes toyed with the notion of becoming a Republican, in revenge.

Of course, he was no more help to Ignacio than the professor —we had to establish our own contacts in Rome. Ignacio got some help from General Liotta of the Italian Air Ministry who seemed to be fond of us in spite of our notorious dislike of Fascism. But the famous Colonel Longo gave Ignacio most of his leads. Colonel Longo had been in Spain for many years, first training pilots for the Spanish Air Force, and later as air attaché in the Italian embassy. Every Spanish pilot knew Longo

—and so did every lady who lived in a house of ill repute and every bartender in Spain.

Colonel Longo returned to Italy shortly after we arrived in Rome. He was ordered home to help prepare for the flight General Balbo planned to make to the United States. He was one of the leaders of the squadron of planes that crossed the Atlantic and when he returned he was placed in the Air Ministry to supervise the work of foreign air attachés. His job, of course, was to show the foreigners just enough to impress them and not too much to give them any real information.

But Ignacio, who had to conceal his contempt and dislike for the lady-loving, dashing Colonel, soon had the handsome Longo telling him all sorts of official "secrets." The Colonel doubtlessly thought that Spain was much too unimportant and Ignacio too innocuous for him to have to hide anything from his Madrid "friend." In any case, Ignacio was in a much better position than any of the other foreign air attachés and if the Government at home had cared at all, they would have realized that his reports were much more complete than the ordinary work of an air attaché.

We had an opportunity, twice, to shake hands with Il Duce, the author of the Fascist system which cost so dearly in hunger and blood—and both times we turned it down. The first time was at a dinner Mussolini gave to the Spanish embassies at the Quirinale and at the Vatican. We politely declined, although our Ambassadress called us angrily several times on the phone to insist on our presence. After the dinner we had a good chance to laugh at the people who attended. For Mussolini marched into the dining room, waved aside introductions, sat down and gulped his meal and departed—leaving a group of very shamefaced people.

The other opportunity was at a reception given for Chancellor Dollfuss. We did not attend, as our mild and personal protest against two dictators making merry together.

Later on that same Winter, I saw Mussolini at the big ball given by the Brazilian Embassy to celebrate its elevation from the rank of a legation. I happened to stand a few feet from the dictator and observed—with some satisfaction, I must say—that he is not really a very tall or very imposing man. Until he pulls out his jaw and rests his hands on his hips, putting his right foot forward, he remains an obscure, stodgy, heavily built individual, without much character or personality.

Ignacio's appointment as air attaché was for Germany as well as Italy, but the General Staff had not yet asked him to report in Berlin. Still, we welcomed the invitation of a friend of ours, a German girl of rich parents and mildly anti-Nazi sentiments, to spend a fortnight with her parents in their country place near Munich. Liselotte's father was a very rich manufacturer— he had a factory near their lovely house. The family longed to be given some decoration or title by the Fuehrer and thus made all possible efforts to please him. They only forgave their Liselotte's lack of sympathy for the Nazi regime because she had once been married to a Hungarian count.

We arrived in Bavaria shortly after the Nazi purge of June, 1934—everyone was still whispering of it. The Spanish Consul at Munich told us gruesome tales of the bloody business and some of Liselotte's neighbors mentioned the affair in muted voices. But at the family table no mention of Hitler's behavior was allowed—only the greatest respect for the Fuehrer was tolerated.

During our stay, Hindenburg, the feeble old man who had betrayed the Republic by turning the government over to the Fascists, died. The whole family went into immediate, deep mourning and Liselotte's aunt, who had planned on dancing a tango with Ignacio, a real Spaniard, had to give up her wishes. The whole household, maids, butlers, cooks, gardeners, uncles, aunts, children, was expected to listen in on the radio to the long funeral.

While we were staying at Neuburg-am-Donau, Ignacio, Liselotte, and I motored up to see the musical festival at Bayreuth. I was sadly disappointed. I thought the music only second-rate, the staging very poor, the crowds pompous and affected, and the whole atmosphere dull and even rather silly. The sight of Wagner's villa inhabited by Hitler and guarded by cordons of S.A. men was enough to disgust any lover of German culture.

Liselotte gave us a chance to observe the German upper classes at home. It was a most revealing fortnight. I have often been surprised to read in the foreign press that Hitler has ruined "business." True, the Nazi regime in Germany has nearly wiped out small business, but, as we could see with our own eyes, it is the perfect handmaiden for the great trusts of Germany. Liselotte's father supported Hitler because the moment the Fuehrer came to power he could—and did—cut wages and lengthen hours in his factory. Moreover, nearly all the small competitors were taxed out of existence, bullied by Nazi party people, ruined by fascist demands. But Liselotte's father, who owned a really big business, made more money under Hitler than he had ever done before in his life.

We were glad to leave Germany, which seemed more oppressive every moment, to spend the rest of our holidays in Austria, then a pleasant country, Venice, and the Dalmatian coast. The lovely port-towns of Jugoslavia, the blue sky, the charming people, made us happy. Everywhere we went, of course, we observed the trouble Mussolini was stirring up between the Serbs and Croats—and yet the fierce dignity of the people, their pride and love of independence, made us feel more secure.

We returned to Rome, tanned and refreshed, feeling happy—and in a day were overwhelmed with anxiety. For the news from our country was bad—very bad. Often when Ignacio went to the embassy to pick up his mail—he was afraid to do his work there for we knew the place was full of Fascist spies—the secretaries and clerks, seeing him coming, would fall silent in the midst of an animated conversation. For by now, Ignacio was the only loyal Republican at the embassy. Prieto wrote us a few short letters which filled us with worry. But they gave us no information and only hinted at a coming disaster.

My uncle, the Duke of Maura, another uncle's brother-in-law, the Count of Los Andes, and dozens of other Monarchists, came to Rome under the guise of pilgrims and conspired with Alfonso at the Grand Hotel for a restoration of the Monarchy. Later on, we learned that Alfonso and his Monarchist friends had been promised guns and money by Mussolini to support a successful coup in Spain—a coup that this particular group could not arrange.

But while Alfonso plotted in Rome, reactionaries in Spain were moving briskly ahead with their plans to put the clock of the nation back a hundred years. The land and other reforms of the first Republican Government had been made mostly on paper. But the Ceda, the organization of Spanish right parties, was determined to wipe out even the theory of land for the peasants, wages and unions for the workers. After the disastrous elections, Alejandro Lerroux, the traitor-radical, had been made head of a moderately reactionary cabinet.

Now, on October 4, as Ignacio and I waited at the telephone for the dreadful news, the Ceda rose to power without the need of Mussolini's intervention. Lerroux, betraying the Republic much as Hindenburg had once done in Germany, gave the Ceda three seats in his Cabinet, the posts of Justice, Public Works, and Agriculture. Thus a party that had declared as its program the abolition of progressive social laws, restitution of all Church property, and revision of the Constitution, was given control of the three crucial departments in the Government.

When Ignacio and I heard the news, our hearts sank. The people of Spain could not and would not tolerate the sudden end of what had begun with such promise only two years and a few months before. Nobody could turn back the clock in Spain without reckoning with the determined will of the Spanish people.

On October 5 came the news that we expected. We heard it with a thrill of hope. The Republic was not yet lost. The workers of Madrid had declared a general strike!

And in Barcelona, Republican leaders proclaimed the Catalan Republic—not as a separatist movement, but to save Catalonia from the rule of the reactionary-fascists in Madrid.

All of Spain, as well as we could make out from the faulty news we got in Rome, rallied to the Madrid strike call. Half hoping, half fearing, Ignacio and I recalled that an ill-timed agrarian strike in the provinces of Extremadura and Andalucia during the Summer had wasted the strength and lives of thousands and thousands of peasants. Could these peasants, the victims of months of starvation, respond now to the Madrid call for action? Ignacio and I didn't know—we could only hope.

One thing we knew for sure. The miners of Asturias, those brave and determined workers, would respond to the general strike call. They would fight reaction until their last breath—we knew it!

Then it happened. On the night of October 6, Ignacio turned from the telephone and sank heavily into a chair.

"Barcelona fell," I said, gulping back the tears.

"Surrendered," Ignacio replied bitterly.

We couldn't understand, then, how a great, rich city like Barcelona whose people, almost to the last man, wanted to defend their Republic against Gil Robles and the Ceda—we could not understand how it surrendered. Surrendered? Impossible! Months later, we had time to discover that the leaders, lacking faith in the people, became frightened. We learned that Barcelona had no arms, no slogans against the Ceda—but more than anything else, we learned that Barcelona surrendered because the Republicans, split in a dozen different ways, could not agree among themselves what to do.

The general strike was called off in Barcelona on October 9. In Madrid, the workers, disheartened by the collapse of resistance in Barcelona, began to trickle back to work. The miners in Asturias alone were holding out.

"I can't stand it here in Rome any more," Ignacio said that night. "Maybe I could be of some use in Madrid."

I hesitated. I knew that Ignacio returning to Madrid just at this time, without the orders of his superiors, was in great danger. The Republican leaders were already in flight to France. The Ceda was not, like its Republican opposition, merciful to enemies. But I could not ask Ignacio to stay in Rome. I decided then, and I never changed my mind, that I would be a poor wife indeed if I expected Ignacio to do less than his duty because of me.

"You go," I said, and tried to smile.

Ignacio grinned. "It's perfectly safe," he said, and I tried to believe that.

Ignacio borrowed a plane. I did not go with him to the flying field for fear of making his departure conspicuous. We both felt that the staff of the embassy was much too busy sending telegrams of congratulation to the Ceda, the Civil Guards, and the Army for having crushed the general strike, to notice Ignacio's absence.

"Well, Connie," Ignacio said, when he had buttoned his overcoat and packed an overnight bag.

Be careful, be careful, be careful, I kept saying in my mind—but not aloud.

"It won't be long," Ignacio said gently and in a moment he was gone.

I was alone in the apartment with Luli. "His diplomatic passport will keep him safe enough," I told Luli, who didn't understand much about passports.

Three days passed, long, endless days. No news from Ignacio. Almost no news at all from Spain. What was happening? Where was my husband? Had he arrived in Madrid at all? Had he been arrested?

The suspense began to eat into my heart. And then I had a very welcome diversion. Maria Teresa and Rafael Alberti, both most distinguished writers, arrived in Italy on their way back from Moscow to Madrid. They had been attending a writers' conference and just as they were about to sail for home from Italy they received a wire from Maria Teresa's mother telling them that their apartment in Madrid had been searched several times and the police were waiting to arrest them the moment they set foot on Spanish soil.

They were penniless—all their money was in Madrid. They appealed to another writer, a friend of Ignacio's and mine, for help, and he suggested that I meet them and discuss their situation. I liked the Albertis the moment I saw them. Our apartment was small but they moved in that very night and slept on a made-up bed in the living room. It was easier to wait for news of Ignacio with the Albertis, such firm sympathizers with democracy in Spain, at my side.

Ten days passed. My self-control was slipping. I couldn't sleep at night. And then, on the evening of the tenth day, came a telegram signed by a friend of Ignacio's. My husband was safe across the French border. I slept for the first time in a week.

Two days later the Albertis and I motored up to Ostia, the Roman sea base, to meet Ignacio. On the way up, I kept think-ing of how we should live now, with Ignacio presumably an exile and of course our diplomatic career over. But when I saw my husband I felt so happy that I didn't care if we starved —at least it would be together.

Going back to Rome, Ignacio told us his story. He had arrived in Madrid to find the strike over. He had gone directly to Prieto's house and found his two daughters terribly worried. The police were searching for their father—he had been one of the leaders of the general strike. Ignacio volunteered to help Prieto across the French border. The Civil Guards were watch-ing for the Republican leader all over Spain—a dozen fat, bearded gentlemen had been erroneously arrested already.

Ignacio devised a clever plan. He borrowed a car with a French license tag. He donned his Air Force uniform and drove alone in the front seat. Hidden in the rear luggage compart-ment of the car lay Prieto. The plan worked splendidly at first. The Civil Guards saluted as they saw an Air Force major pass-ing. Prieto, one of the best-known figures in Spain, was out of sight.

But half way to the border, Prieto exploded. The cramped quarters were killing him. He straightened up and rode on the back seat. Next, he got hungry, and insisted on stopping at the house of a friend whom he described as absolutely reliable, for dinner. Ignacio's nerves have always been cast iron. Flying in the Spanish Army crates leaves a man no room for hysteria. But even Ignacio got nervous before he spotted the French border—with Prieto in plain sight for all Spain to see, riding along in the back seat of his car.

At San Sebastian, Ignacio got out, changed his uniform, and after dark Prieto was driven by a French chauffeur safely into France.

"What's happening in Spain?" I asked.

Ignacio sketched the situation briefly. The Asturians were

still holding out. The Government troops were not considered reliable—the slaughter of Spanish miners could not be carried out by Spanish conscript troops. The revolt was not yet over.

The Ambassador seemed vaguely surprised to see Ignacio the next morning, but only showed signs of anger when Ignacio refused to sign a telegram congratulating the Ceda for crushing the general strike or contributing to funds being raised by the *ABC* for the Civil Guards.

"We'll be out of a job in a week," Ignacio said cheerfully that night.

It was almost the only joke we had those days. The news of Asturias began to leak through from Spain. The Italian newspapers printed almost nothing of the truth but the escaping Spanish exiles told us the whole dreadful story.

For Gil Robles and his Ceda had turned Spain into a bloody prison. The brave Asturian miners holding out for democracy were slaughtered in their tracks by Moorish troops brought in by a government afraid of its own conscripts. The new Chief of Staff, General Francisco Franco, brought Moorish troops into the Spanish mainland on their first mission of war in Spanish history. Raping, looting, slaughtering, they went through Asturias like a dreadful fire.

Ignacio, who expected to be recalled to Spain momentarily by the Ceda, decided to make a perfectly open trip back to Spain. He stopped in Barcelona to visit Azaña—arrested and sent to the prison ship in the harbor—and then went on to Madrid where he was received at the War Ministry with icy coldness. His superiors intimated that he would not be recalled—unless he wished to leave the Army, of course. General Franco was trying, just then, to get all the Republicans in the armed forces to leave.

"That's exactly what I won't do, Connie," Ignacio told me later, "and leave the way open for a completely fascist army? Never."

Back in Rome, Ignacio told me the terrible story of the Asturian miners. Franco had brought a whole army of Moors— the miners were overwhelmed by enormous numbers, arms, bombs. Some of the Army officers bringing the Moors over had revolted, some of the Air Force pilots ordered to bomb the women and children of Asturias had refused to obey commands. But it was not enough. The struggle for freedom was over.

And now the violent and bloody repression. Few stories in history are so terrible as the dreadful happenings in the Asturias after the Moors had conquered. We heard the stories first-hand from the refugees who fled for their lives across the border. An inoffensive journalist who had seen too much was murdered; children and women were arrested and tortured with fire and steel whips until they told where their fathers and husbands were hiding. Thirty thousand were put in prison. Thousands of others hid in the hills.

Ignacio and I began to feel we could stay in Rome no longer while our brave countrymen were tortured to death in Spain. There was nothing we could do—and yet . . . Then we made a quick decision. The men lucky enough to escape were pouring into Paris, cold, hungry, penniless. We had an excellent salary. We didn't know how long it would last, but as long as we had a penny we meant to share it with the Spanish exiles. So we packed up, bag and baggage, and set off hastily for France.

The Asturian people were united against the reactionary Ceda. They watched their men being led out to the firing squad; they brought their women home from the prisons, crippled and bent by torture. But no terror could break their spirit. They smuggled men out of the country and out of their terrible poverty they sent money abroad to help them. The Asturians we found in Paris were living on almost nothing, scattered about the suburbs, reporting with a sense of almost military discipline to their leaders.

We only wished that we had found the rest of the Spanish exiles living with such firm determination to conquer the future. Prieto stayed in a modest apartment, answering letters and seeing friends. He made no attempt to rouse the French Socialist Party to the gravity of the situation in Spain. He was filled with bleak pessimism. He blamed the failure of the general strike in Madrid on Caballero, who had led it—while Caballero blamed the debacle on Prieto, who was supposed to have led the Army in revolt against the Ceda. The Army most certainly had not risen—whose fault it was nobody quite knew. Caballero was in prison, but Alvarez del Vayo, his good friend, came to Paris to patch up the feud between the two Socialist leaders and try to interest the French Socialist Party in Spain's future. Del Vayo understood that the world must be rallied to stop the terrible reprisals in the Asturias and all over Spain. He felt that democracy could not win in Spain unless all the parties supporting the Republic were united.

"We *must* unite," Del Vayo said—but Prieto, lost in pessimism, could not answer.

While we were still in Paris, Ignacio received the unexpected order to go to Berlin. For over two years we had been waiting to be sent to Germany and now, when we expected at any moment to be recalled, we were at last given our orders!

We flew from Paris to Berlin in a Lufthansa plane; for the first time I flew "blind" over the clouds to come down right over the Templehof Airfield, with a precision that astonished us. It proved how well the Lufthansa pilots knew the way from Paris to Berlin, how carefully the Nazis trained their potential army of bombing pilots. Others have since noted the eagerness with which Lufthansa has flown the Berlin-London route in fog and clouds, relying entirely on instruments.

At Templehof we were met by an imposing-looking gentleman in a bowler hat and astrakhan collar, smoking a fat cigar: the general manager of the Lufthansa who took us to the hotel. An hour later two officers from the German Air Ministry, both of whom spoke correct Spanish learned in Latin America, came to offer their services. They told us we would have a car at our disposal for the length of our stay and that they would alternately come every morning to accompany Ignacio in his visits to officials, factories, and airfields. We knew the ambassador had told the Air Ministry of our arrival, but the reception we received was certainly much more than we expected.

As the days went on, we were increasingly surprised. Ignacio was received by the Chief of the German Air Forces, General Milch, and we were both entertained by him and his wife, to-

gether with an important group of Air Force officials in one of
Berlin's most exclusive restaurants. I was presented with a gold
pin bearing the insignia of the Aero Club at a special dinner
in the club quarters at which we were guests of honor. A special
Junker 52 plane was put at our disposal to take us to Bremen
where I was shown the town by a polite German officer, while
Ignacio visited the factory of the Focke-Wulf Aircraft Company. Later we were entertained at a very elaborate dinner in
the Club inside the "Hag" town (a small town within Bremen
of Kaffee Hag fame). The head engineer of the Focke-Wulf
plant invited us to his home, in one of the smartest residential
quarters of Berlin, a few days later. All these attentions entirely
bewildered us.

At last the Nazis made themselves clear. What they wanted,
they said, or what they "generously" offered Spain and were
hoping Ignacio would convey to the Spanish War Ministry, was
this: Germany was ready to provide Spain with a powerful Air
Force for which Spain need not worry about payment. Some
foodstuffs, abundant in Spain and very much needed by the
Reich, and a "few concessions," such as the permission to establish in Spanish territory a wide network of powerful radio stations to help direct German Lufthansa planes and Zeppelins
en route to South America, would be all that the Reich expected in return. Of course, the sale to Spain of many German
airplanes would entail sending technicians and instructors to
the Spanish Army.

We could not understand then what the Nazi aim was, but
Ignacio realized quickly how dangerous it would be to
strengthen the Spanish Air Force with German help at a moment when the control of all the Army was in the hands of a
most reactionary Government with General Francisco Franco
as Chief of Staff. He obviously did not say this to the Germans,
but instead continued to accept their hospitality, anxious to see
how long it would last. What we were never able to understand
was how the Gestapo could have been so uninformed about our
political opinions. They had doubtlessly taken it for granted
that the Spanish air attaché must be in full agreement with the
new Government's policy. We were careful not to show them

anything to the contrary, feeling that all the information we could get about their designs would be very valuable. But when we informed Prieto later of all that had taken place during our visit to Berlin, he did not take it seriously, and neither did any of the other Republican leaders. Forewarned might have been— but alas, was not—forearmed.

Berlin was very different from the town I had visited in 1919. The smart restaurants in the Unter den Linden and the Kurfurstendam where we were taken to dinner by the Air Ministry officials were always crowded with men in uniform and richly, if tastelessly, dressed women—the wives and mistresses of the Nazi bureaucracy and the business men. But walking along other parts of the town and looking into the cheap eating places or traveling in the subway or at the cinemas, the people's faces seemed apathetic and remote. Many times we were approached by poorly, but decently, dressed men who asked for money as if they were asking for directions to some street. The big department stores were by no means as crowded as I remembered them years before, and the merchandise was much less varied and of a lower quality than anything sold in the Paris or even Italian department stores. Berlin was not a happy city.

The German Air Ministry remained polite to the end. We were bowed out of Berlin with the same courtesy as we had been welcomed. The all-seeing eye of the Gestapo slipped badly on Ignacio and me—we departed with information on Nazi airplane factories and Nazi plans for penetration of Spain which might have been invaluable to Republican leaders. It was not Ignacio's fault that his country was not prepared when the time came to resist a Nazi invasion.

"Don't get so excited," Prieto said in Paris the day after we left Berlin.

Ignacio bit his lips—but he said nothing. We left immediately for Rome, surprised that the orders for our recall had not met us in Paris.

We enjoyed the last months we spent in Italy. The staff at the embassy shunned us with careful horror—you could almost hear them saying as we passed, "Beware! Republicans!" Ignacio

SPANISH AWAKENING   201

worked hard, and the information he learned about Italian airplane factories afterwards proved valuable indeed.

It was the early Spring of 1935 and Italy was preparing for her Abyssinian campaign. Everywhere we drove in our car we found camps of blackshirts training and the roads leading towards Naples were crowded with men in uniform and military convoys. The Fascist press drummed up volunteers for the "holy cause." Restrictions were growing and the military and air attachés in other embassies complained of the increasing difficulties the Italian War and Air Ministries made on their visits to factories and military camps. Ignacio, through his "friendship" with Colonel Longo—who had not yet left on his new assignment to South America where he was made air attaché-at-large—still managed to get just the information he wanted.

When the Italian press, for instance, blustered that a new type of Savoia bomber had entered mass production, Ignacio could smile up his sleeve. For he knew that the Savoia factory had produced exactly one such plane so far—and that one defective. Indeed, when the Fascist papers, trying to bluff England and France, announced that a whole squadron of these mythical airplanes had been sent to Abyssinia, Ignacio laughed out loud. We knew the engineers who worked desperately to improve the experimental model. We were rather irritated, however, to see Mussolini's childish game of "Boo!" work so well. For the English and French air attachés spent their days playing bridge with Italian princesses and polo with Italian princes, taking time off in the mornings to send home translations of the airplane boasts made in the Rome newspapers.

We spent the first hot weeks of the Italian summer in Rome waiting patiently for the inevitable recall. News of Spain reached us regularly and we were eager to be back in Madrid. The unity of the democratic forces in Spain was growing— growing slowly—but surely. The Ceda had not been able to turn our country back to feudalism. The reactionaries were running into thick weather. Ignacio and I itched to be home, to play a part in the building of resistance to fascism. But Ignacio couldn't resign. He had to stay in the Army—it was essential.

The Republic needed Republican army officers. So we had to sit in Rome, waiting.

Finally, as we sat at breakfast on July 28, the Ambassador's secretary telephoned Ignacio. "Come at once!"

We returned to a sullen, powder-box Spain. All Catalonia was suspicious, on tenter-hooks. The Catalonian leaders were still in prison. The people of Barcelona smoldered with rage.

In Asturias the terrible repression still went on. The whole world knew now of the atrocities the generals and the Civil Guards had committed in this rich mining area. Even conservatives and some reactionaries began to turn sick as they learned the details of the terrible terror in the Asturias. Gil Robles and the Government tried to cover up the truth—but the story of the Asturian miners could not be suppressed.

Ignacio was naturally not welcomed with cheers by the War Ministry. Indeed, he was promptly sent to Seville, almost in exile, for he could not be forced out or thrown out of the Army. I knew he would be in Seville for only a few weeks or months at the most, so with Luli I settled down in Madrid. Ignacio came up very often to see us.

Inés and Zenobia were still running the little shop and I decided to go back, and put in the little money I had—to expand the business. But none of us was very interested in selling peasant linens and potteries to tourists. We had a feeling of suspense, a conviction that something must happen soon to change the state of affairs. The corruption in Government circles could not be concealed. A Dutchman who had been granted a concession to establish legal gambling again in Spain paid large sums to Government officials, and then, considering himself cheated, made the whole plot public. The newspapers revealed new and far-reaching examples of bribery and theft in official Government departments daily. The Asturian tragedy lay heavy on the people's hearts. Madrid workers still suffered the reprisals of the general strike and could stand it no longer. The peasants saw their food growing more scanty daily. Something must happen—soon!

On October 20, over four hundred thousand Spaniards came

from all parts of the country, some on foot, many riding donkeys, to hear Azaña speak in an open-air meeting ground outside of Madrid. The Government and the police hoped to provoke disorders. Mounted troops harassed the thickly packed crowds as they crossed the bridge over the Manzanares. Agents provocateurs, mingling with the people, tried to start riots. Machine guns mounted on trucks menaced the slow-moving thousands. But the Spanish people had learned discipline. It took me and the hundreds of thousands of others nearly two hours on foot to cross the bridge and reach the meeting grounds, but the day passed without a single incident.

The meeting put hope and determination in the hearts of every man and woman who stood listening to Azaña that Sunday morning. Four hundred thousand strong, the Spanish people thundered after the speaker, as he led them, the slogan of the day—and the times: "For a general amnesty! For the release of the thirty thousand prisoners, victims of the terror!"

Early in November, as Ignacio and I sat quietly home one night, we got an urgent telephone call. We drove over to the designated house and found Prieto, smuggled back into Spain from the French border. The crisis, he said, was coming to a head. He was needed in Spain. Pessimistic and sad in France, Prieto seemed now full of energy. The great meeting of October 20 had apparently revived his faith in the Spanish people. The reactionary Government must fall. We must all work, work hard!

At first we planned to hide Prieto in our house but Luli who was going to school was a seven-year-old chatterbox, to whom politics was a mystery. I knew she could keep a secret—but I could also hear her, in my mind's ear, telling her friends, "Daddy and mommy have a secret! We have a man hidden in our house, only it's a secret and I can't tell you his name!"

So we settled Prieto in a household without children and he began to direct the work of the right-wing Socialists. The left-wing group in the Socialist Party, headed by Largo Caballero, was also intensifying its agitation and although much more unity was still needed, the two groups worked hard that late Fall.

Early in December of 1935, the inevitable political crisis broke. Scandal and corruption overwhelmed the Ceda. The reactionaries tried to patch things up with a makeshift, newly formed "Center" party but the trick didn't work. The interim Government, weak as it was, did do one good deed. Nuñez de Prado, a Republican general and one of the most promising of the younger men in the Army, was named chief of the Air Force. He promptly recalled Ignacio from Seville and made him his chief adviser. Naturally, Nuñez de Prado and Ignacio did not have a free hand, with General Franco still Chief of Staff, but they did transfer some of the Monarchist and Nazi-minded traitors in the Air Force to remote districts and promote Republicans to important posts.

Even the Monarchists and fascists were dissatisfied with the "Center" Government. President Alcalá Zamora could not stand up under the pressure of the people.

On January 8, 1936, President Alcalá Zamora dissolved the Cortes and called for general elections on February 16.

With this announcement the State of Alarm, declared by the Ceda on October 6, 1934, came to an end. The censorship was lifted and the left press promptly began to publish documentary evidence of the Asturian repression. Exiles came back from Paris. The election race was on.

I thought, during the days between January 8 and February 16, that I would never again live through such weeks of terrible suspense. Time proved me wrong, but I still remember those Winter days with a sort of catch in my throat.

For we all knew that this election would decide Spain's fate— fascist or democratic, the Middle Ages or the World of Tomorrow, tyranny or justice—which would it be? The existence of the Republic was at stake, the existence of liberty, the very existence of a free Spain, trembled in the balance.

On the one side was lined up all the wealth and power of Spain. The big industrialists, the landowners, the powerful Religious orders, the Church hierarchy (but not all the priests), the Army caste, they stood on one side.

And on the other side were the people of Spain.

The parties of the right made a compact. The Ceda, and their twin party, the Agrarians, were the largest and most powerful parties of the reaction. The Monarchist Party could not run candidates in a Republican election, but they supported the other two parties with few votes and much money. The utterly discredited "Radicals" of Lerroux, covered with the mire of corruption, sided with the Ceda and the Agrarians. The Falangist Party was small, rowdy, and murderous rather than powerful or numerous. The Falange, an exact copy of Italian and German fascist organizations, was well armed and fairly well organized in Madrid, Seville, Barcelona, Valencia, and Vigo. They were used as shock troops by the Ceda and they made no pretense—they were frankly paid mercenaries (ten *pesetas* a day) in the Ceda ranks. The Traditionalists or Carlists, although they disagreed with the Monarchists on who should be king, agreed on almost everything else. They had some strength in Navarre, where the peasants who lived in the mountains, isolated from the rest of Spain, were brought up on the memories of the two Carlist wars of the last century. A few scattered independent parties of Catalan nationalists, mostly representing Catalan business men, voted with the Ceda.

This was the formal line-up of the reactionaries. But this was only the beginning of the story. For behind these formal parties lay money, and more money. The Ceda leaders demanded—and got—enormous contributions from banks, business men, landowners. The reactionaries fought their election battle with the biggest "slush fund," as they say in America, ever even dreamed of in Spain.

The people fought the election not with money but with— and this for the first time—unity. For the tragic events in the Asturias, the bloody repression, the censorship, the specter of fascism in Germany and Italy, the knowledge that this election was the turning point for Spain as a nation—these at last brought the Republican and Socialist leaders to realize that inter-party squabbles were unimportant compared to the necessity of fighting fascism in Spain.

For the first time, all the political parties in Spain which counted themselves anti-fascist and pro-democratic united in a

great pact called the Popular Front. It is important to understand—and all of Spain did understand then—that the Popular
Front was not a revolutionary organization.

In fact, the formal Popular Front program began with these
words: "The Republic conceived by the Popular Front parties
is not a Republic directed by social or economic class motives
but a regime of democratic liberty inspired by reasons of public
interest and social progress."

The first point on the Popular Front program was a general
amnesty for all political prisoners. "Free the thirty thousand!"

The second point was a program of public works similar to
the Roosevelt PWA plan.

Third, the power of the Bank of Spain was to be curtailed.

Fourth, schools were to be placed again under state control,
and a big new educational program was outlined.

Fifth, peasants were to be given various forms of assistance,
as outlined in the original Agrarian Reform Bill.

Sixth, workers were to be given social legislation, minimum
wages and the like.

This very mild document could not be considered a threat
to capitalism in Spain. It rejected nationalization of the banks,
land, or factories. The social legislation it proposed did not
compare with laws governing wages or working conditions in
other democratic countries. It did not even propose direct help
to the unemployed. The Popular Front program, in essence,
proposed continuing the reforms begun by the first Republican
Government and interrupted by the two black years of the Ceda
and Gil Robles. The Popular Front parties envisioned a free
Spain, with civil liberties and progress for all.

Backing this Popular Front program were a group of Republican and anti-fascist parties consisting of Azaña's Left Republican Party, Martinez Barrio's Republican Union, Sanchez
Roman's National Republican Party, and Luis Companys's
Catalonian Left Party. All these parties gave the Popular Front
its middle-class representation.

Also supporting the Popular Front were the working-class
parties, the Socialists, including the Prieto and Caballero
groups, the Communists, and the small Syndicalist Party. The

CNT, Anarcho-Syndicalist Trade Union Federation, and the FAI, the Iberian Anarchist Federation, would not sign the Popular Front pact since in theory they did not approve of political action within a capitalist state; but even they promised their support and participation in the elections.

This was the line-up. The reactionaries with their frank program of fascism and back to the Middle Ages, the people with the Popular Front program of democracy and mild liberal reform.

The election battle was hot and furious. The Ceda, backed with unlimited funds, went into the contest with their backs to the wall. Frightened by the daily exposures of the Asturian terror made in the newspapers, Gil Robles took a bold step. Dubbing himself *Jefe,* the Spanish equivalent of "Il Duce" or "Fuehrer," he frankly made a fascist campaign. His unhealthy, fat face was exhibited in huge photographs covering a whole block of windows in the Puerta del Sol, the main center of Madrid. The ladies of his party offered blankets and mattresses to the poor Spanish peasants and to the unemployed in exchange for votes. Every apartment house in Madrid was covered by the Gil Robles forces—the good ladies of the Ceda offered fifty *pesetas* a vote. My own little Andalusian maid collected twenty-five *pesetas* from a Ceda man canvassing our apartment house and got a free ride to the polls with a generous lady who made up a little party of eleven servant girls. Each girl got another twenty-five *pesetas*—as my maid told me afterwards, they each kindly thanked the lady for the ride and the money and then they each went into the polls and voted the Popular Front ticket!

Outside of Madrid, the election was fought with equal bitterness. The reactionaries, inundated by the tide of popular indignation, tried every trick in their bag. Bishops threatened damnation to church goers should they vote the Popular Front ticket. Children were taught that voting the Popular Front ticket was a mortal sin. Peasants were threatened with starvation by their landlords, workers with loss of their jobs by employers.

The morning of February 16, Ignacio and I got up with a

feeling of terrible suspense. We knew that the people were for the Popular Front, but could the poor peasants and half-starved workers stand up under the threats and the money offered them for their votes? Blankets and mattresses are a rare luxury —the *Jefe* had passed out hundreds and thousands of them.

Ignacio and I voted early. I went to the polls for the first time in my life. Our neighborhood was not a smart, fashionable district and most of the people standing in the long line at the schoolhouse voting booth were clerks and small middle-class people. The voters understood each other. We were unanimously for the Popular Front. We didn't talk much. We stood quietly, waiting to vote Spain democratic.

Ignacio and I went home after we had cast our votes. We sat by the radio and the telephone, waiting, waiting for the news. We heard that in the working-class districts, the men and women marched singing to the polls, full of enthusiasm. We dreaded riots—but the day passed peacefully in Madrid, in spite of the armed Falangists.

By lunch time our apartment was crowded—people came and went all day, asking for news, repeating rumors, or just coming to be near us. All of us who loved democracy spent February 16 in a sort of wild suspense that drove us to each other.

At six o'clock that evening, the first groups of cheering, madly excited people rushed out into the streets of Madrid to celebrate victory.

We could hardly believe the news, at first. But as the reports began to come in from the provinces that night, the victory was confirmed. The Popular Front had won a great victory all over Spain. The Popular Front candidates rolled up enormous majorities.

The reactionaries, seeing that all was lost, tried last desperate tricks all over Spain. Reactionary Army officers tried to lead their men out of the barracks to fire on crowds. General Franco, who was still Chief of Staff, began handing out guns to civilian Ceda sympathizers. The Falangist groups tried murder.

But the people would not be bullied out of what they had just won. Angry crowds met the Army officers. The Falangists were met with force. Monarchist headquarters were attacked—

after Popular Front candidates, victorious in the elections, were arrested by the Civil Guards acting under orders of fascist mayors.

The people suspected a plot. Were they to be shot down by a Ceda military uprising? The Prime Minister resigned. Azaña took his place, with a purely Republican Cabinet, excluding the Popular Front representatives. But the reactionaries subsided, the military plot was postponed, and Spain sank into an uneasy sort of quiet.

For from the morning of February 17, all democratic Spain remained on the alert, in a real state of alarm. The people had suffered too much to rely entirely on the Republican Cabinet of Azaña. Our home, like that of every other democrat in Spain, was in a constant state of excitement for months. I do not remember a night or day we were not hurriedly told of some secret plot against the Republic. The reactionaries, having lost at the elections, obviously intended to win at the point of the bayonet.

But the Republic had not yet learned how to defend itself. Much had happened since Alfonso fled in 1931. The Asturian miners had died for freedom—died and been tortured. Censorship, terror, repression had made Spain a slaughterhouse only yesterday. Constant alarms, news of conspiracies, exposures of plots, made it plain that the fascists intended to overthrow the Republic by force tomorrow.

And yet Azaña and his cabinet still worshiped legality, still believed in making haste slowly. Azaña would not demote an Army officer, for instance, until it could be proved at trial that he was actually plotting to overthrow the Government. Ignacio used to rage with despair. He knew the group of officers preparing the coup against the Republic—everyone in the Army knew them—still the new Minister of War, Santiago Casares Quiroga, to whom Ignacio was aide-de-camp, would take no definite measures against them.

My husband, however, is a man of determination. Balked on all sides by the really criminal carelessness and lethargy of the Government, Ignacio nevertheless took some steps to fight the coming rebellion. Although he was aide-de-camp to the War

Minister, he insisted on keeping his post as second-in-command of the Air Force, even though it meant working day and night. From this strategic post, he painfully, day after day, selected the most reliable Republican aviators from all over the country and had them transferred to Madrid. The traitors under his command were transferred to unimportant districts, or pensioned out of the force. He assembled the best planes in the Spanish Army—and they were very bad—at the Madrid air fields. After weeks of painstaking effort, he came home quite exhausted one night and told me, "Well, the capital is protected by a one hundred per cent loyal air contingent. Now if the Republicans do not begin to feel sorry for some of the traitors I transferred we can feel fairly safe, as far as the air is concerned. I don't think the old crates I left in Seville and León can bomb anything, let alone Madrid."

And he was right—they couldn't. But in March, 1936, neither Ignacio nor I envisioned invading planes from foreign countries bringing a deadly cargo of bombs to Madrid.

The preparations for the military revolt against the Republic that went on day and night after the February 16 elections were only part of the reactionary plans. Business slowed in Madrid. The rich sent their money abroad and many Monarchists and landowners followed their gold to Paris. In our little shop Inés and I watched our business slowly disappear. We didn't care much—once again all our thoughts were with the Republic.

Zenobia, however, felt differently. Her first enthusiasm for the Republic had cooled. Her furnished apartments remained empty. The slack business annoyed her. She had made new friends while I was in Rome and when I came back I found her much changed. During the elections she had stubbornly refused to "take sides," as she called it, and in spite of Inés's attempts and my own to convince her, she was "neutral" on election day and did not vote. Now, as the March days passed, she became more and more irritated with the Government, and more and more indifferent to the success of the Popular Front. Politics had become life in Spain—friends could not differ on the really important broad ideas. My friendship with Zenobia quietly began to cool.

I found many changes in personal relationships when I returned that Winter to Spain. My parents, for instance, broke their long silence concerning Ignacio. We were invited, together, to dinner—a great concession. Ignacio would have much preferred to stay away but I felt that since they had decided to "forgive" me, I should do the same. So we trotted off, once a fortnight, to a stately dinner at the new apartment I had just decorated for my mother. For our shop had turned to interior decoration as the trade in peasant linens grew slack, and my mother's spacious and charming new home was one of our first orders. My young brother, whom we met now and then at my parents', had just returned from Germany where he had been sent to school for a year. I tried to discover whether the Third Reich had made any impression on him but he was much more interested in boxing and girls than politics—a healthy sign in such a family.

I never met my two married sisters at my parents'—my youngest sister was an invalid. I gathered that Marichu and Regina and their husbands did not care to break bread with two such notorious supporters of the Popular Front. Marichu, I knew, was most unhappy with her husband. She had become a famous poker player in Madrid society circles, and the money she made gambling made up in part for her stockbroker husband's stinginess. But the latest news about Marichu was more disturbing than her poker playing—she had become very active in the Falangist Party, together with one of my cousins, a daughter of the Duke of Maura. My parents were very worried about Marichu. They would have liked her to have been a ladylike supporter of the Ceda or the Monarchist Party—but to work for the Falangists when everyone knew they were paid gunmen! My mother said that Marichu's unhappiness with her husband and her "crush" on young Primo de Rivera, the handsome, heartbreaking leader of the Falange, drove her into this vicious organization. I could not help but add that I knew the pattern well, I had seen it abroad: a wealthy, idle, ignorant young woman, married for money to a man she dislikes, seeking sensation, any antidote to boredom—this was the ideal fascist.

Regina, whom I had always liked better than any of my sisters, was nearly as remote from me as Marichu. She had married an agricultural engineer who bore a great name of Spain, but still had to work for a living. Since my divorce and remarriage to Ignacio, Regina had not seen me—I was tabu, a woman living under the badge of shame. Even though my parents finally decided to lift the ban on my second marriage, Regina would not change her mind. Her husband had once held mild Republican opinions—he had been given a post in the Department of Agriculture under the first Republican Government, but later on, during the reaction, he was one of the most active in sabotaging land reform.

Ignacio and I never found it easy to see my parents. We all carefully avoided topics of any real interest and I think I discussed more weather that Winter with my mother and father than any other time in my life. Still, in spite of the victory of the Popular Front, we managed to keep peace with them, mostly for Luli's sake, until one evening my father shattered the whole flimsy fabric of our relations.

My father had taken a great liking to Ignacio. In spite of Ignacio's "dreadful political opinions," in spite of our "living in sin," my father told me that he wished he had more sons-in-law of Ignacio's mettle.

So on this fatal evening, Ignacio was invited to be present at our family conference. My father offered us brandy and coffee after dinner. Ignacio smoked a wonderful cigar. My mother moved quietly in the background. I began to feel nervous. My father was obviously working himself up to some important family pronouncement. We waited. Then my father began:

"You know, Constancia, I am getting on in years."

I was amazed. My father was quite young, vigorous, expanding his business every day. I had never heard him mention the possibility of his death before.

"I must think of my children."

Ignacio turned red in the face. He hated to be reminded that

I was the daughter of a very rich business man and a great land-owner. We made it plain to everyone we knew by our simple way of living that Ignacio's Army pay provided our household.

"You know," my father went on rapidly, "under the Agri-cultural Reform Bill a number of parcels of my land will have to be sold to the peasants. But if I divided it up now between my children, the separate parcels would not be great enough to bring the land under the provisions of the law."

"Father," I interrupted, "you don't have to consult us about your land. You know Ignacio and I do not want land. We are not farmers. We cannot live on the land or work it; we work in Madrid. We don't wish to be absentee landlords—do what you like with the land."

My father coughed. "You haven't quite understood. Marichu and Regina understood immediately."

My mother looked embarrassed. My father hesitated and went on, "It would just be a matter of your signature on the papers. I would still—well, ah—it would be a matter of con-venience, you understand, the law, you know. Everybody is doing it. . . ."

I jumped up. "In other words you want us to be your accom-plices in circumventing the Agricultural Reform Law?"

My father's eyes darkened with anger as he turned to Igna-cio: "Eventually, on my death, this is Constancia's inheritance. Do you want your wife's land to be sold to some wretched beg-gars? And if you don't care, consider what you are doing to Regina and Marichu. Constancia's parcel must be included in the distribution, otherwise the law will still affect us."

Ignacio moved towards the door. "This is a private matter between you and Connie," he said stiffly. "I have no part in it. You must discuss it with her."

But I followed Ignacio to the door. "You know my opinion without asking, father," I said coldly, and Ignacio and I left together, feeling cold inside with anger.

After this episode, we saw my parents rarely and always under a great strain. My father had forgiven me my marriage, even tolerated my outrageous political opinions, so long as they were theories. But when my husband and I put our opinions into practice, my father was outraged. He could understand—or try to—some silly woman wanting the peasants to be better off. That was humanitarian nonsense. But to refuse to preserve your own inheritance—a matter of property—this was sheer, perverted madness.

In spite of the growing tension in Madrid, Ignacio and I now and then had some little joke that amused us. Our shop designed some furniture for Prieto, for instance, and the stout Socialist orator was so worried by the light modern tables and chairs of simple design that he consulted all his friends with the greatest anxiety, anxious to get their approval. Dr. Juan Negrin, whom I had met at dinner parties before, finally came around to our shop and examined all the furniture before it was moved into Prieto's flat. He was an amiable, pleasant sort, a professor of physiology at the University—Ignacio and I liked him immensely. I waited for his verdict on the furniture with some anxiety for even Prieto, whose taste ran to heavy and ugly furniture adorned with curlycues, respected his judgment.

"It's splendid," Dr. Negrin declared when he had looked it all over—and we were much relieved for now Prieto would like it, we knew.

We had little time that anxious Spring, however, for such pleasant thoughts as interior decoration. Spain was in a steady ferment. Alcalá Zamora, the President who had sold the Republic in 1933 and tried to sell it again in 1935, was about to be impeached. There were rumors that the projected military coup would take place as the Cortes displaced Zamora. But although the President refused to meet the committee from the Cortes, the impeachment went off on schedule without incident. Soon after, Premier Azaña was elected President. His Government had so far accomplished nothing, it had displayed only weakness and leniency, but he was the official Republican candidate and elected without opposition.

For the fascists had abandoned voting for violence. On April 14, the anniversary of the Republic, the war of street murder, provocation, and riot began on the streets of Madrid. It continued, almost unabated, for months, as the fascists, working on

a careful schedule, operated to shake the nerves of the democrats and give Republican Spain a bad name in the world.

The Falangists, the paid gunmen, were the shock troops of
reaction. My father and his friends gave money and stood by
to watch the results. Professors, lawyers, magistrates, and political personalities were shot at by Falangist assassins who lay
in wait for the marked victims at their own doorsteps. Sometimes a group of them, wearing the Army uniforms they were
permitted to keep although no longer in service, would precipi-
tate a riot during a parade.

All over the city, vendors of Popular Front newspapers were
found murdered in lonely streets and severe beatings were frequent. If a man killed his assailant in sheer self-defense, the
Falangists staged a huge funeral which served as an excuse for
more rioting.

And after every such incident—and hardly a day went by without at least one—the *ABC* and the other fascist newspapers
would trumpet: "Popular Front anarchy and violence rages!"

Many Socialists and Republicans fell in the streets of Madrid
that Spring. The Popular Front forces held no great public
funerals. Their dead were buried quietly with bitter tears.
Struck down in the night, done to death by a gang of paid ruffians, the democrats of Madrid were carried silently to their
graves while the fascists clamored: "Restore law and order!"

A Republican officer, Carlos Faraudo, fell, shot in the back
by a paid mercenary. His only crime was serving the Republic
loyally.

The Government, slow moving, legalistic, took alarm at the
death of the Army officer. They decided to protect well-known
Republicans by assigning secret police to guard their lives.
Ignacio was constantly followed by a miserable little police
officer who was much more worried about saving his own life
than protecting Ignacio from the murderers who threatened
him. Largo Caballero and others were shot at on the streets of
Madrid that Spring, in spite of the Government secret police—
and the only answer from the Republican Cabinet was more
little men to follow more Republican officials around.

Ignacio sometimes came home from the Government offices gray with frustration.

"Connie," he would say. "Why don't they *stop* this? Why don't they outlaw the Falangists? Why don't they break up these street attacks by arresting the men who are paying for them? Why, in heaven's name why, don't they stop the coming rebellion by purifying the Army?"

We couldn't understand why not. The people demanded it. Caution necessitated it. And yet the Republican Cabinet, declaring it would not act "illegally" or "unfairly" did little more than transfer a few generals out of Madrid to strategic spots in Morocco or the provinces.

Madrid was on tenterhooks. Twice a week we got word that the revolt was scheduled for that night or the next. We sat up many a night beside the telephone, waiting for the terrible news that the Madrid garrison, or some other garrison, had risen against the Republic. And every morning, after such a sleepless night, Ignacio would go off to the War Ministry and beg his immediate superior, the War Minister and Premier since Azaña's election to the Presidency, Casares Quiroga, to act.

But Casares would laugh. "You're an alarmist, Cisneros," he would tell Ignacio, "I have everything under control. I consult with the other Ministers. We consider we have taken the steps to insure the safety of the Republic."

"But the street fighting!"

"Gangs of toughs," Casares would reply; "the police can handle them."

Once Ignacio went with some other friends, who agreed with him that the Republic must act swiftly to preserve itself, to visit Azaña—to beg him to use his influence with the Cabinet.

Ignacio had expected to find the man who made the great speech of 1935, the man who had been imprisoned by Gil Robles. But Azaña had changed. Secure in his beautiful little presidential palace, once the King's property, Azaña had lost touch with the people. Remote, disinterested, he had already sunk into the lethargy that was later to overcome him completely.

"The Republic is sufficiently protected," Azaña told Ignacio
coldly.

"But the generals who have been transferred to the islands,
like Francisco Franco and Goded, still command troops. The
only effect of transferring them is to make them think they are
regarded as traitors and to force them to act quickly!"

"The Cabinet is in full control of the situation." It was
Azaña's last word on the matter.

In the Cortes, the reactionaries pressed their advantage. After
every Falangist attack, the fascist deputies demanded a regime
of "law and order." The Popular Front majority voted solidly
in a bloc to defeat the traitors, but the Cabinet, solidly Republican instead of Popular Front, moved too slowly for the Popular Front forces. The people had voted for reform. Where was
the reform? Months had passed and still the Republican Cabinet hesitated. The people had won the election but the representatives of the people in the Cabinet apparently expected to
take a decade instead of a month to give peasants food and
workers a living wage.

For example, the Popular Front pact had included as a plank
in the platform a provision that all the workers who had been
thrown out of jobs after the 1934 General Strike should be re-
employed. My father, for instance, had hundreds of workers
starving in the slums of Madrid whom he would not re-employ.
"The working class must be taught a lesson," he said.

And now, although this problem was very pressing in Madrid, with unemployment mounting and employers closing
plants in a kind of "capitalist sitdown" against the Popular
Front, the Republican Cabinet hesitated to use force or the
threat of force to enforce the decree. The locked-out workers
did not get their jobs back—even though February 16 was
weeks and months ago.

Faced with so many problems, worried by the sabotage and
obstruction of the reactionaries, the Cortes slackened its pace.
Not one of the measures of the Popular Front had been yet
carried out by the Cabinet. Why pass laws when the Republican
Cabinet took forever to enforce them?

The anarchists, with their theory of non-political action,

took advantage of the government lethargy. Every trade had an anarchist strike. But the Socialists and Communists—who since the lifting of the censorship published their own paper, the *Mundo Obrero*—urged the people to be patient.

"Don't play into the hands of the fascists," the Communists cautioned.

"The fascists are just waiting for the chance to crush what they will call a 'revolutionary' strike. Be patient," the Socialists said.

But the left wing of the Socialist party, led by Caballero and the Anarchists, could not see the wisdom of this policy. They added to the confusion of the situation by a series of ill-timed strikes.

And as the Spring deepened into the hot Spanish Summer, the city and the nation grew more and more tense. Sometimes, walking through the streets, it seemed to me that the whole country was holding its breath, waiting, waiting, for the inevitable catastrophe.

Once we thought the rebellion was upon us. In Yeste, near Toledo, the Civil Guards slaughtered eighteen peasants who had been slow to leave land a private reservoir company had illegally purchased. The peasants were hastily buried by the Civil Guards—one still had his pack on his back when his body was dug up by his frantic wife. The whole nation stirred. The workers in Madrid hesitated. The fascists prepared to smash down when the sympathy strike they expected broke over Madrid.

"Stay at work," the Socialists and Communists begged, "stay calm for the sake of the Republic. Preserve democracy by forebearance!"

The plot did not work. The eighteen peasants died as victims of a plot that did not quite—by a hair's breadth—come off.

Now the tension grew nearly unbearable. I never heard the telephone ring without feeling sick with fear. A long building strike, complicated by employers' sabotage, government weakness, and anarchist disruption, put Madrid in a state of alarm. The debates in the Cortes grew more acrimonious.

And now suddenly the plans of the long-expected revolt were prematurely discovered. The news spread through Spain like wildfire. The Falangists showed their hand too soon by seizing the Valencia radio station and then, embarrassed at getting their dates mixed, retreating. Documents proving the participation of many generals in the plot to overthrow the Republic were found in the offices of a Falangist military organization.

All Spain knew of the plans for the revolt. Ignacio and I felt almost relieved. Now the Government *must* act. Now it was plain as a fly on the nose. Now the whole world had exact information on the plot to overthrow the Republic.

But Ignacio came home the night of July 12 in a perfect rage of despair. "No."

I had not needed to ask the question. Then he broke out into a torrent of angry speech. "Any idiot would know what to do. Arrest Franco. Arrest Mola. Arrest the whole dirty lot of them. Act now and explain later. Try them six months from now if you must—but arrest them now, *now*, while there is still time!"

I wrung my hands. "What's the matter with the Government? Why don't they *do* anything?"

Ignacio imitated his superior, his voice breaking in anger. "Be calm—these are just bogey men you have conjured up. We are democrats. We must preserve freedom of speech and civil liberties for all."

"That includes the fascists," I said bitterly. Ignacio nodded.

"And traitors. I don't care how much they talk, but these men are planning a military revolt and we have the proof and still they won't arrest them. Heaven preserve us all!"

We had just fallen into an uneasy sleep that night when our phone rang. Ignacio jumped out of bed. I sat up in alarm, the light blinding my eyes.

"Dead?" I heard Ignacio say. He came back into the bedroom heavily to begin dressing.

"They shot José Castillo."

Castillo was the commander of a specially picked group of Assault Guards, known to be one of the few completely reliable

police units in Madrid. They had their barracks in a little
house not far from our apartment and Castillo used to drop in
sometimes at our home on his way to and from his work.

On this terrible July night he had gone for a little walk with
his wife—to breathe a bit of fresh air in the stifling Summer
evening. The fascists shot him in the back.

Ignacio left in the middle of the night. All next day the
people waited for the Government to arrest and punish Castillo's murderers. Everyone in Madrid knew the fascists had shot
the police officer in the back. Around midnight Castillo's
Assault Guards arrived from their barracks down the streets
of Madrid. They had waited for the government and the
government had not acted. Now they would take justice into
their own hands, for the men had loved their commander
dearly.

A few hours later the men returned to their barracks. Calvo
Sotelo, the fascist leader recently risen to prominence over Gil
Robles, lay dead.

Madrid held its breath. Could the Government delay a moment longer? The people had acted to protect the Republic.
Now the Government *must* act.

Ignacio came home, exhausted, late that night.

"Now the Government will try to do in two days what should
have been started the same day we won the elections. And even
now they will not dare to take serious measures. Franco, Goded,
Mola, all of them are sure to start something before we have
time to stop them."

He fell across the bed and slept, after twenty-four hours at
the War Office.

I remember those words of Ignacio's now. But then I thought
that he was terribly tired, nervous, perhaps over-excited. We
had spent a dreadful Winter and Spring with one alarm after
another. Perhaps he was too pessimistic.

Next day passed quietly. I breathed a sigh of relief. Our
Summer plans were all made. Luli was already at a camp in
the Escorial. We were invited to Ibiza to stay with the Albertis.
The shop had closed as usual on July 1. Inés had already left
to visit her family in the United States. We were packed up.

But before we left Madrid, I had decided to move nearer to the
War Office and the shop. I had selected a charming terrace
apartment, hired painters and electricians. Ignacio could not
leave immediately and I wanted to stay to see our furniture
safely installed, the curtains hung, and so on. Freddie Bauer,
member of a prominent Madrid banking family, asked us to
stay with him during the week or so before our new apartment
was in order and we were ready to leave for our vacation. We
moved over to his pleasant little house gratefully.

The funeral of Calvo Sotelo was a fascist demonstration. In
the Cortes next day Gil Robles, back in the limelight again,
declared, "His blood is on the heads of those people who support the Popular Front." He added, "The country is already
fascist—we shall perhaps have few more words to say to each
other in the Cortes. The day is not far off when the violence
you have unleashed will turn back on you." The Government
called his speech a declaration of civil war. Truth-loving people
could only be amazed at a fascist blaming violence on the Popular Front. The violence had not come from the people. Calvo
Sotelo paid with his one life for the lives of a hundred Spaniards fallen in the last few months at the hands of Falangist
gunmen. Why should the Spanish people mourn Calvo Sotelo,
the new fascist *Jefe,* when Castillo and so many more lay dead?

The next two days passed in ominous expectation. Ignacio
worked day and night, giving orders to his reliable pilots to
stand by for action. I tried to rest at home but found it impossible. It was too hot to go down to the new apartment and
watch the painters; besides, for the first time, I couldn't get
interested in moving. In the evening Ignacio and I and a few
friends sat talking idly, nervous and on edge. One girl burst
out on the second night, "I wish it would start. I can't stand
the waiting."

But I still didn't believe it—quite. I went on with the plans
to go to Ibiza. I tried to convince Ignacio he should come with
me for a rest but he was so worried and absent-minded I don't
believe he even knew what I was talking about.

Then came July 17, 1936.

The morning began as any other. Ignacio left early for the

War Ministry. I stayed home, reading in the cool drawing room. Ignacio came home to lunch, pale, utterly worn out. He said Casares had sent him home for a nap.

The telephone rang as we were having coffee in the drawing room.

"I'll come over if you want me," I heard Ignacio saying, "but I'm very tired and need sleep. Can't you manage at the Ministry without me?"

Then there was a pause. Then I heard Ignacio's voice. It had a crisp, precise, not excited but very tense sound.

"Very well, I will be there at once." Another pause. "At once, I said."

He came to the door of the drawing room. "The Army uprising has taken place in Morocco," he said to me. "All communications are cut with the African side. Some posts in Spain seem to be revolting."

I stood up, feeling my throat tighten. "When?"

"Early this morning. Casares knew soon after ten o'clock but he went to a Cabinet meeting and only told the other Ministers casually at the end of the meeting. Now he thinks it might be of some importance. And the man sent me home to take a nap!"

The tone was bitter—I had never heard Ignacio speak so before.

"Important . . ." I stammered.

"This is the uprising. We shall see whether Spain will be fascist."

Ignacio left at three o'clock in the afternoon of July 17, 1936.

IV. "WIDOWS OF HEROES RATHER THAN WIVES OF COWARDS"

(1936-1939)

JULY 17, 1936. Three o'clock.

A military uprising in Morocco. Ignacio had gone to the War Ministry. I was alone in the house. It was very hot. I pulled aside the blind and looked into the street. Down the block a little peddler pushed his cart. Otherwise nothing. The sun beat on the pavements. Madrid was quiet.

July 17, 1936. Four o'clock.

Ignacio would call very soon. He would say: "It is nothing. The traitors are all under arrest." Then we would leave day after tomorrow or the day after that for the seashore, to lie under the sun and watch the breakers foam over the rocks.

July 17, 1936. Five o'clock.

The house is so quiet, so empty. Now surely Ignacio will call very soon. A military uprising in Morocco. But suppose it was part of a great plot? Ignacio had expected it. Suppose the garrison in Madrid revolts? The people will defend the Republic. Spain will never be fascist—not while the people live.

July 17, 1936. Eight o'clock.

The heat hangs on. My face is damp with the hot winds. In the street there is more movement now, people passing quickly, talking. I can hear their voices, but no words. Are they talking of the uprising? What do they say?

Nine o'clock.

Our host, Freddie Bauer, returns. He has been making the rounds of the cafés. The best-known leaders of the Ceda and the Monarchist party are sitting in the Molinero restaurant, their usual meeting place. Freddie thinks this is a good sign. Surely the Government would have arrested the fascists if the uprising were serious?

I look at him across the supper table. "You think so?" I ask him.

Freddie stares at his plate. "Well, they were looking very jubilant," he says bitterly; "they were ordering champagne and making toasts. They acted as though they were celebrating something."

We eat in silence. Finally Freddie bursts out. "The people will defend themselves—if only the Government gives them a chance."

July 17, 1936. Midnight.

How can it be that Ignacio has not called? He must know that I am sitting at home in the empty, quiet house, waiting for his voice to reassure me. He would have called, I know he would—if he had the chance. So he must be working furiously. Then the uprising is serious.

July 18, 1936. Four o'clock in the morning.

I sit beside the window in the drawing room, staring into the empty streets. Freddie comes home again.

"Ignacio has not returned," I say.

"Go to bed, Connie," Freddie replies. "There is no news."

I lie in bed, but I cannot sleep. When the light comes I get up and bathe and dress and drink coffee. The little maid brings in the early morning newspapers. The headlines are black—but meaningless. The uprising in Morocco is not serious. The Government has the situation under control. The Government has taken precautions.

Taken precautions. I sit beside the window again, dizzy with fatigue, watching the people go out to work. Do they seem strange this morning? Are they talking of the revolt?

July 18, 1936. Eleven o'clock.

The empty house trembles with the blatant loud ring of the telephone.

"Ignacio! Are you all right? What is happening? Are you not coming home? Is the uprising . . ."

His voice, sharp and staccato, cuts me off. "I am at the War Ministry now. I have been at the airport most of the night. I must keep all my loyal pilots standing by for orders."

"But what's . . ."

"Connie!" Ignacio's voice was loud. "I want you to promise me something."

"Yes, but . . ."

"I want you to absolutely promise to stay inside the house. Do you understand? Do not go out, under any circumstances."

I was bewildered. "Ignacio, why not, what's going on?"

But Ignacio hung up. I was furious. I had yet to learn that commonplace of wartime: that there are times when one cannot speak over the telephone.

July 18, 1936. Four o'clock.

I slept a little, awaking still fatigued. The heat grew. The radio in the house was broken. We could not find a mechanic to repair it. But the Government ordered all radios turned on permanently, and loud enough for neighbors to hear. Through our open windows floated the magnified voice of the Government announcer. *"People of Spain! Keep tuned in! Keep tuned in! Do not turn your radios off! Rumors are being circulated by traitors. Wild stories are causing panic and fear. The Government will broadcast day and night—learn the truth from this station. Keep tuned in! Keep tuned in!"*

Across the street from Freddie's house, a little soft drink and sandwich stand installed a radio. People sat sipping cool drinks at the small painted tables in the diminutive garden—listening. Crowds stood around the counter—listening.

Freddie and I could not sit in the empty house. We needed people around us. We walked out into the evening and sat quietly at one of the tables, listening to the blaring voice from the radio and listening to the talk of the people.

"The Republic has the situation in hand," the Government announcer said.

"Ha!" a little man sitting next to me told his stout, good-natured-looking wife. "This time we'll really give it to those vermin! The Army! Every general, every last one of them, ought to be shot." His wife nodded.

"President Azaña has moved from his residence at El Pardo to the National Palace in Madrid."

A tall, immaculately dressed dandy standing just in back of me snorted. "So! The Government has things in hand! But Azaña has to move. So!"

My neighbor stood up. "Say it again, you dirty Monarchist." The crowd turned from the loud speaker. "Where's the king-lover?" somebody yelled. The well-dressed man slipped discreetly away.

"I can't make head or tail of it," Freddie said. "What in heaven's name is going on?"

I shook my head. If only Ignacio would come.

At midnight Freddie left me and I went home to bed. I fell

asleep with the voice of the announcer still pounding at my ears.

Next morning I woke with a start. It was very early. Through my open windows floated the voice from my neighbor's radio.

"Attention! People of Spain! The Government will now briefly review the military situation."

I sat up in bed, wide awake. *"The rebellion against the Republic, led by a handful of traitorous generals, began with the Moorish troops. They persuaded their soldiers, by the use of the most vicious lies, to rise against the Republic. Some of the Moorish troops have been transported to the peninsula, where they are attacking—unsuccessfully—Republican troops.*

"In the meantime, other members of this conspiracy against liberty have incited isolated regiments in the north and south to rise against the Republic. Fighting is still going on in these cities but we feel sure of the outcome. Málaga has been attacked and is in flames. Government forces and rebels are fighting in the streets of Barcelona."

I began dressing hastily. The news made more sense now. The plot had been carefully laid. Garrisons all over Spain apparently were to rise at the signal of the rebellion in Morocco. But the Rebels had not taken the Republicans completely by surprise. Comparatively few garrisons had risen. The Republican troops, barring accidents, would be able to handle the situation.

I ate my breakfast reading the headlines, feeling more confident by the moment. For I did not know, nor did Ignacio at the War Office, nor did the people of Spain know, that even as we all awoke and went to work that morning of July 19, 1936, in Berlin and Rome two dictators were giving the orders for the invasion of Spain by fascist troops, airplanes, cruisers, transports, technicians, Army officers, ammunition, guns, and money. The unequal battle—Spain against Germany and Italy, with England and France and the United States handcuffing my country's fighting arms—had already begun. But we did not know it.

About ten o'clock, the Government broadcast the news that General Francisco Franco, the hated general who sent the

Moors to rape and kill in the Asturias, had flown to Morocco from the Canary Islands where he had been stationed after his removal as Chief of Staff. Now the pieces of the plot were beginning to fit together. Ignacio had always said that Franco was a very ambitious man—General Goded was more intelligent; General Mola a better soldier; but Franco was the most ambitious.

Ignacio came home Sunday morning at five o'clock. He had not slept or eaten a proper meal since he left the house Thursday afternoon. He looked haggard, thin, and so tired that I took pity on him and put him to bed without a single question.

A few hours later I woke again to the sound of the radio. I closed our windows hastily. Ignacio must sleep. But I stole out into the street and listened. The Government of Casares had resigned. *"Martinez Barrios will head a new Government. Listen in! Keep tuned in! The names of the new Cabinet Ministers will be announced shortly."*

Ignacio woke in an hour. At breakfast, Freddie and I bombarded him with questions. Ignacio talked fast as he ate. The revolt was much more serious than anyone had expected at first—anyone except himself and most of the Republican Army officers in Spain. The plot was a careful one, designed to bring all the converging Rebel troops from the provinces into an attack on Madrid. The Government must stop this converging process. But the only forces which could be used with complete trust were the workers belonging to trade unions and Popular Front parties. The Republican Government, however, did not wish to arm the people. Therefore it had resigned, to be replaced by a more moderate government which intended to make peace with the Rebels.

"Peace?" I cried, jumping up from the table. "But that means fascism? And the people will never . . ."

Ignacio grinned. "Don't get so excited, Connie," he said, gulping coffee. "I don't think it's all over yet—not by a long sight. Martinez Barrios doesn't realize the situation. He can't make peace with the fascists. He doesn't know it yet, but he can't. You should see the crowds outside the War Ministry. Thousands of them. They've been there since Thursday night.

Just standing quietly, or sleeping in the garden and on the curbs, holding their trade union cards in their hands. Waiting for arms. Just waiting."

We listening in for almost an hour, but the Government announcer had nothing else to say about the Martinez Barrios government. Ignacio prepared to leave for the Ministry. But before he went he made me promise I would not go out on the streets. Fascist snipers had been picking off workers, known Republicans or mere passers-by. He could not have a moment's peace while he worked at the War Ministry if he thought I was in danger of being shot in the back.

The details of the plot had been outlined by Ignacio over breakfast. The Rebels had declared a State of War in all the towns where the garrisons had risen. In reply, the Government of Casares before it resigned had issued an order relieving all soldiers under Rebel officers from military discipline and asking them either to return to their homes or join the Army forces which had remained loyal to the Government. The workers had answered the Rebel generals by a nationwide strike—a somewhat inadequate defense against bombs and artillery, but at least an indication of their temper.

The Rebels had started with two groups of soldiers—the Moors, who had been told (falsely, of course) that the Republican Government planned to murder them in revenge for their atrocities in Asturias, and the Navarre Carlists, the isolated fanatics, always ready to take arms for "God and King"—*their* God and *their* King. General Mola, military commander of Navarre, was to lead the Carlists to Madrid, conquering on the way several Basque provinces which the unfortunate men of Navarre had been taught to hate. General Goded, the author of the whole military plan of the Rebels, was to storm Barcelona and conquer Catalonia and the Balearic Islands. General Cabanellas, commander in Saragossa, was to lead another column to Madrid, taking the principal towns along the way. In Seville, Queipo de Llano, the loud-mouthed general, counted on the garrison and the rich ranchers' sons, the Andalusian *señoritos*.

This was the main outline of the plot against the legal Government of Spain. The Civil Guards were expected to do their share, especially in the rural countryside. The city police in various large towns were also counted on to co-operate with the fascists. The Air Force and Naval officers were considered doubtful by the Rebels, but they supposed they could count on at least neutrality from these two branches of the service. Madrid was to fall in a week or so, ten days at the most. The Government set up was to be a military dictatorship.

The plan hit some snags immediately. The situation in Saragossa seemed confused. General Nuñez de Prado, head of the Air Force, was sent by the Casares Government to talk to General Cabanellas, an old friend of his. Ignacio was to fly with his chief, but at the last moment work at the War Ministry kept him from leaving. General Nuñez de Prado took three of his best staff officers. The plane landed at Saragossa. The staff officers were promptly shot and General Nuñez de Prado waited two months for the bullet from his "friend."

But the Air Force gave the Rebels their most unpleasant surprise. Ignacio and Nuñez de Prado had worked together for months. Now, when the crisis came, a solid block of forewarned pilots, mechanics, radio operators met the Rebel officers and arrested them. The Government did not save all its planes—a tragedy at Seville cost Air Force lives and planes. The loyal pilots in all African bases had been ordered by the Government to refuel and land at Seville. In the meantime in Seville the loyal Air Force people fought a pitched battle with the Rebels —a battle which they lost when they were hopelessly outnumbered by infantry attackers. As the loyal planes from Africa landed at Seville their pilots were dragged from the cockpits and shot.

In the Navy, the sailors revolted against their Rebel officers and seized the ships being used to transport Moors to the mainland.

After Ignacio left that morning, the house seemed very quiet again. The radio was still silent—no news of the Martinez Barrios Government.

Freddie offered to go and find out what was being said in

town. About three o'clock he rang me up from a public telephone. "There's a huge demonstration against surrendering!"
His voice was so excited I could hardly make out the words.
"The people of Madrid say they won't have a Martinez Barrios
Government. They want a Popular Front Government, and
arms to fight the Rebels. Connie, you should see it! It's wonderful!"

For the plain people of Madrid, thousands upon thousands
strong, had marched to the Puerta del Sol, the heart of the city.
Their ranks were orderly. Their air was full of dignity. They
were very determined. No surrender to fascism! Arms for the
people!

While many a Republican leader still saw the four-day-old
revolt as a sort of military rumpus, the people of Madrid, the
plain workers, the small clerks, knew better. They were, even
in July, determined to fight fascism to the bitter end—and they
forced the wavering Republicans to bolster the defenses of
Spain. The Government was hastily revamped again. Premier
José Giral took office together with several members of the
previous Casares Cabinet. It was not yet a Popular Front Government for only members of the Republican parties held office.
Nevertheless, the people had won a point.

But while democratic Spain fumbled painfully putting on
its fighting armor, while the people begged for guns and called
general strikes, while Republican leaders suggested peace par-
leys, two fascist dictators and their allies in high places in the
British Government moved swiftly and surely to their objective
—the seizure of the rich Spanish peninsula with its mines and
industrial regions, its prospective Army, Navy, and submarine
bases. Mussolini and Hitler had planned the attack on Spain
for months—now they moved with appalling speed. While we
sat in Madrid those hot July days, debating the calling of a
people's army to the colors, Hitler had already dispatched his
Condor Legion, his planes, his technicians, and his bombs and
bullets. Mussolini had ordered his air force into action and
Italian transports were preparing to carry Italian regiments to
the Spanish fronts.

We didn't know all this in July, 1936—we guessed at some

of it, to be sure. For we knew that our country was rich; we knew that English and other foreign companies already owned its best mines, its most productive enterprises. We could see by looking at a map that Spain would be a rich plum for the fascists. And we knew that the Rebel generals would have no squeamish objections to calling in foreigners to slaughter Spaniards. Fascist papers in Spain had been writing for weeks that two or three million Spaniards "needed to die" before the nation would be "safe" for the generals. But our guesses fell short of the terrible truth. It was to take us weeks and months to realize that we were not fighting a civil war but a fascist invasion.

In the meantime, the wobbling, timid, conservative Republican Government of Spain had already been dubbed "red" by British newspapers. Although it was, and has always been, perfectly clear to anyone with the slightest degree of common sense that the Spanish Government was a mildly liberal democratic Government, England's largest newspapers were already on the fourth day of the revolt calling the Giral Government "Communist." In July we were all amazed at this sudden deluge of lies. Attacked at home by the fascists, we found ourselves betrayed abroad by the newspapers of a friendly democratic Government. Only months later, when we discovered how carefully the plans had been made for the revolt, did we understand how it was that the English newspapers sided so instantly and with such a barrage of cleverly timed falsehoods with the fascists.

Freddie and I spent part of Sunday worrying over the strange pieces of the fascist puzzle-plot. But about four o'clock we were suddenly electrified to get wind of a rising in the Madrid garrison. Freddie dashed out, leaving me alone to pace the floor up and down, to telephone to Prieto's daughters, to curse myself for giving Ignacio my promise to stay in the house.

That night I heard that the people were storming the Montaña barracks. They were unarmed, with only an old cannon which they shifted from spot to spot with lightning speed—

to make the fascists think they had a whole collection of light artillery.

The next morning I was awakened by the sound of bombs—for the first time in my life. I rushed to the terrace and found Freddie already there in his dressing gown, watching two old planes circle the city. While I watched, I saw two puffs of smoke and heard two more rumbles—the sound which I grew to find so familiar, so constant, so unimpressive that a year later I would not look up from work or awaken from sleep, unless a bombardment were remarkably heavy.

But on this July morning, the whole population of Madrid rushed to its windows and roofs to see the bombers, for they were our Government planes attacking the Montaña barracks. All night long the Government loud-speakers had ordered the fascists barricaded inside, to surrender—all night long the people had besieged the troops. Now, with Rebel forces planning a march on Madrid it was obviously impossible to allow hostile troops within the capital limits. The bombers went up to force the fascists to surrender.

We watched the bombers circle three times and then disappear. A few minutes later our phone rang. It was Ignacio, announcing the people's victory. The men and women of Madrid had forced the gates and seized the arms within the Rebel nest! The capital was safe.

That Monday was exciting. We had no sooner finished lunch than the radio announced a further Government victory in Barcelona. The Rebels were crushed in Catalonia. General Goded, their leader, was a prisoner. General Fanjul, another fascist notable, had been arrested in the Montaña barracks in Madrid.

A few hours later, the radio announced the death of General Sanjurjo, who had been killed in an airplane crash as he flew from Portugal to join the Rebels. Foreign newspaper correspondents, prompt to seize on dramatic items, rushed into print with the news that Sanjurjo had been scheduled to lead the revolt. "Leader Dies on Way to Command Rebel Army," some of the items read.

Spaniards, of course, could only smile at this dramatic announcement. The old general, dating from the Primo de Rivera dictatorship, was known to have used all his energy and enterprise in affairs of a purely personal, nay, sentimental kind. Even in 1926, when he was at the "height" of his military career (he once won an engagement with a tribe of practically unarmed Arabs) all Spain knew the doughty General Sanjurjo for the country's most famous "bon vivant," to put it politely. In fact, there was a famous joke to the effect that Sanjurjo might not know Moors but he certainly knew women. After the Republic commuted the death sentence he had so richly deserved when he led the Monarchists in a revolt against the infant democracy, the lady-loving general retreated to Portugal where he acted as liaison man between the Nazis and the Spanish generals. He was probably slated to be some sort of a figurehead in the Government the Rebels had planned to set up.

The next few days in Madrid were a sea of confusing stories. Conflicting news came from nearly every town and province of Spain. Ignacio came home rarely and nearly always dog-tired. Prieto, who had no official Cabinet post as yet, was the unofficial Minister of War and Ignacio was his unofficial assistant. The weak Republican Government still in power was at an absolute loss. Prieto and Ignacio forced the new official Minister of War to arm the people, and the War Office was a madhouse as the Government arranged to arm and supply regiments sent to the various fronts by the trade unions and political parties.

Madrid itself seethed with excitement—and tragedy. Families separated for the Summer months were in many cases separated forever. In some cases wives and children in vacation resorts were killed by fascists as fathers and husbands agonized in Madrid for news of their families. Ramon Sender, the well-known journalist and writer, lost his young and beautiful wife in just such a way. She was alone at a country place near Madrid and the fascists, who had heard that her husband was vaguely left wing in his political sympathies, slaughtered her in front of her two babies as she recited the prayers of the Catholic Church.

At first I had been easy in my mind about my Luli, away at a Summer camp in the Escorial. The radio reports seemed to be clear on Government victory there. But as my friends began to report the terrible tragedies of separation and death, I began to grow uneasy. A report, which I afterwards learned was untrue, hinted that the Escorial region was fascist. Suddenly I became panic-stricken. I rang up a friend and borrowed a car. I called Ignacio and told him I was driving down at once to bring Luli home. "You can't!" he said over the phone. "It's impossible. Wait a little. I'm sure she's all right."

I waited in growing terror. Luli! I began to blame myself for having sent her to a Summer camp at all. If the fascists found out who her foster-father and mother were! Or if they bombed the camp!

And then, in an hour, Ignacio called. Luli was quite safe. The Government controlled the Escorial. The children didn't even know about the revolt. Their camp counselors had decided not to frighten them. Luli was well and happy—and getting very sun-tanned!

I sat down heavily and mopped the tears out of my eyes.

July 23 marked the end of the first week of the rebellion. The fascists were crushed in Madrid. Some thousands of Army officers of extremely doubtful loyalty had been placed under arrest and as a result the sniping on the streets had diminished considerably.

I had been in the house a whole week, while great events had rumbled on all about me. I knew that women were needed, badly needed, in a hundred different ways in Madrid. And so I decided that now at last I could no longer remain idle and that I must help wherever I could be useful. Ignacio was dubious and fearful but I over-rode him.

First, I volunteered by telephone to Madrid military hospital. But my services were politely and correctly declined. I didn't know nursing and had no training for rough work in a hospital. Somewhat crestfallen, I rang up Isabel Palencia, who was a member of the UGT, the trade union federation. "Let's go together and offer our services at the UGT headquarters, the

Casa del Pueblo [People's House]." We arranged to meet at a bus stop.

After lunch I somewhat gingerly stepped out on the street. I knew that snipers were still at work, and although the Government had warned the newly armed militia not to fire in reply, I had heard that cars full of patrolmen roaming the streets were still somewhat careless with their unusual weapons. I walked to the bottom of our block, past an apartment house under construction. The street was nearly empty. Suddenly I heard the terrible sound of a machine gun. My throat closed with tight fear. I stood perfectly still, no doubt presenting a perfect target to the fascist snipers across the street in the half-finished building. But I couldn't walk. My knees trembled too much. The machine gun rat-tat-tatted again. I don't know if the bullets came very near me or not. I know they were aimed at me, for I was the only person anywhere near the building.

I kept thinking that I must run. But I didn't. I turned my head, very slowly, cautiously towards the building with its scaffolds. I saw no one. Suddenly an automobile tore around the corner, just as the machine gun started again. The car was full of militiamen, kneeling on the floor, aiming rifles as they came. The machine gun spit more bullets. The militiamen returned the fire. I heard the whine of bullets.

A few hundred feet down the street I saw a newsstand, overturned in the gutter. Slowly and stiffly, while the rifle and machine gun fire whined and rattled all about me, I walked to the flimsy wooden stand and slowly I bent my knees and crouched behind the little wooden barricade. The machine gun stopped. The militiamen dashed into the half-finished building and returned, without a captive. The fascist had apparently disappeared. After several minutes I stood up again. I saw the bus coming. The bus stopped. Just as the door opened, the machine gun started again. The driver waited until the noise of the bullets stopped, and then put the bus in gear.

The bus was crowded—I immediately spotted my friend Isabel Palencia and her young daughter, Marisa, who had just graduated from the University. They were the center of attention in the friendly, even jocular group on the bus. Everyone knew that Isabel Palencia was a famous Socialist leader and the workers listened attentively while she told them we must all be calm and not answer the provocation of the fascists still not arrested. I thought of my experience of ten minutes before—but I knew she was right.

"The fascists are only trying to provoke panic and alarm with this shooting from terraces and windows," Isabel said.

The last stop on the bus was at the Plaza de la Cibeles, across from the Bank of Spain. We got off to walk the rest of the way to the UGT headquarters. I had just stepped down the bus steps when we saw a crowd of men and women running for the subway entrance. We heard shots all around us. We dived for the subway with everyone else.

It was very crowded underground and more people kept storming in every moment. The trains were not running; the subway had become a place of refuge. I suddenly realized that my heart had not stopped thumping since I left the house—and I knew, all at once, what it must mean to the workers and little clerks and shopkeepers of Madrid to keep going to the office and factory every day, with the fascist snipers keeping up the vicious, cowardly attack on people's bodies and nerves.

A weeping woman came down the subway steps. She seemed to be half fainting. Her hair fell over her contorted face. Two young men, obviously strangers to her, supported her. Isabel had never seen her before, but in that crowded underground station, we were all friends.

"What's the matter?" Isabel asked the woman.

At first the woman could only cry—her sobs were terrible, broken, rasping, from the heart. Then she began to talk. "I was walking with my brother past the Palace Hotel, only a little way from here, when a shot came out from nowhere, and then . . ." She hesitated.

One of the young men said softly, "Dead."

At the word, the woman began to cry again, pitifully.

"He was very young," she said loudly, "very young."

Suddenly she seemed to gain strength. She pulled away from the two men who had brought her to the underground. "I must go back to him." But we kept her beside us for a little while.

The militia were searching the rooms of the Palace Hotel for the sniper. They never found him, of course, for his accomplices had probably already led him by some secret passage out of the building.

After a half hour the woman went back to her brother. Many of the people in the underground went with her, to help her with his body. We saw the procession, silent, some of the women crying, moving down the street to find the body of the brother who was "very young."

Isabel, her daughter, and I went silently to the headquarters of the UGT.

A cordon of policemen and militiamen surrounded the trade union headquarters. Isabel showed her card and we three stepped into a sort of orderly madhouse. The UGT building was crowded to the very doors. Men sat on wooden benches, squatted on the floor, slept in corners. Endless queues waited outside the offices of the masons, the steel workers, the electricians, and all the other member unions of the UGT. We heard a word—new to us—passing as a sort of greeting from one man patiently standing in line to another man leaving. The word went from one group to another, was repeated loudly and softly all around us—"Salud! Salud! Salud!"

"*Salud!*" The greeting of the Popular Front. We heard the word and each of us inwardly rolled it on the tongue and added it to a vocabulary suddenly growing under the pressure of war. "*Salud!*"

Isabel tried to see the leaders she knew personally but the task was quite hopeless. Hundreds were waiting to see every trade union executive. So we settled down on the wooden benches to wait our turn to speak to the official in charge of women volunteers.

The crowds at the Casa del Pueblo were sweaty and disheveled. It was hot, very hot, that July in Madrid and most of the men were wearing the uniform adopted as suddenly as the word "salud"—a sort of overall we called *mono*. Men went out to the front in these *monos* and the first battles were fought between uniformed Rebels on one side and a grim line of overalled men on the other.

But the crowd at the UGT headquarters made me feel proud and self-confident. For although many looked tired and had the same expression of silent worry that Ignacio had worn for many days, they were not hysterical, nor noisy, nor even filled with bravado. These men who had stormed the Montaña barracks, gone without decent food or a full night's sleep for more than a week, waited quietly for orders. The Spanish people began to learn discipline.

I began to learn it, too. For when our turn came, the official who met us was polite and gentle, but quite firm. He would give a job to Isabel if she felt she could not be more useful in another place, but her daughter and me he could not help. The trade union could only send its members to assignments. I was irritated for a moment—and then I saw the justice of the rule. The trade union must not send spies or fascists to man the factories and telephone offices and street cars and buses. They must answer for the women they sent to take men's jobs. As for the hospital jobs—that was a very delicate matter. The hospitals were closely connected with military work. Surely we must understand how cautious the trade union had to be?

We understood. We walked out of the building no less determined to find jobs, but much impressed with the dignity and discipline we had seen in the UGT headquarters.

Our bus back home was filled with men in *monos* riding home to pick up a few things and leave for the front. We talked cheerfully all the way to my corner, and as I stepped off the bus, the men waved, and I ducked the inevitable sniper. At home the little maid handed me a telegram from my parents in Paris—wanting to know if I were safe.

I looked at it bitterly. For some time Ignacio and I had suspected that my father was playing an important role in the preparations for the military plot. His electric company had all kinds of connections with Nazi Germany and he had let enough indiscreet remarks fall to indicate that he played some sort of a role as a go-between in the Spanish-German plot.

Of course, it may have been only a coincidence that he had taken the family abroad just before the rebellion broke out. Still, I answered the telegram with poor grace. I knew that whether my father had played an active role in the rebellion or not, he had most certainly helped to finance it. His money paid for some of the guns the snipers used. I wired him that I was safe—and suggested postponing his return for a few days until the Government had restored order in Spain. He replied that he was bringing my mother and brother back to our country place through Portugal.

This was the last direct word I ever had from my parents. Once, early in the war, a lad escaped from the prison at Segovia told me a little gossip about my father. Another peasant boy from our estate, who had been arrested because the priest in our church told the authorities he had voted for the Popular Front, had told his fellow-prisoners the story. My father, when he returned from Paris, discovered that his cars had been "requisitioned" by the Falangists—perhaps because my sister Marichu told her friends that my father had cars on his estate. At any rate my father was quite infuriated and demanded the automobiles back. The Falangists replied that if he didn't watch out they would "requisition" the whole estate. My father, quite purple with anger, dashed off to Burgos and returned with an order for his cars to be replaced.

The peasant boy from La Mata had laughed merrily at that joke—and then, my friend told me, never laughed again. He was shot the next morning and so his cell mate had no further chance to hear about my father.

The telegram from my parents depressed me. I sat home that night, turning over plans in my mind. I was determined to get a job and be part of the movement of the people to overthrow fascism. But what job? Where?

Next morning early, I rang up Maruja, the wife of Fernando, one of Ignacio's best and most trusted pilots. She was alone all day and night, too, and although she had four children she decided to leave them in the care of her two maids and start out with me looking for something we could do for the Republic. Together we went to call on Teresa Gonzalez Gil.

Teresa had been at my convent school. She was the daughter of a middle-class Madrid family, and she had married a re-

spectable young Army air pilot of the usual political opinions
and family background. But her husband had developed with
the years. He took part in the movement that helped bring
the Republic in 1930 and Teresa had left her respectable family
to go to live in exile with him in Paris.

We found Teresa, who had never much courage in any event,
very depressed. Her husband had left the Army after the Republic had come in and founded a co-operative airplane factory.
He had just won a national prize for the design of one of his
newest planes and the rebellion found the young couple just
beginning to sight prosperity. Now Teresa's husband had left
everything, his factory, his beloved wife, and gone off to the
front with a regiment of men recruited from his workers. He
was in the Guadarrama mountains, defending the outposts of
Madrid against the approaching fascist columns.

We had some difficulty rousing the frightened Teresa from
her profound depression. Her husband was her life, she said.
She felt in her heart he would be killed. Perhaps he was already
dead? What could she do without him?

We urged her to work—it would help her forget and after a
long conversation she declared herself ready. Next we rallied
to our group another pilot's wife, Trini, a very pretty but rather
frivolous and useless girl, and Concha Prieto, the eldest of
Prieto's daughters and the most warm-hearted, self-sacrificing
and intelligent of his children.

With my regiment formed, I next stormed the Republican
officials. I rang up a woman I knew at the Committee for the
Protection of Minors, a department of the Ministry of Justice,
and asked what was being done about the children who until
then had been taken care of by Religious Orders.

These children deserve a little explanation. The charity
foundations for the care of children which had existed under
the Monarchy had been taken over, little by little, by the
Government. Not because the Government wanted to, but because they had to. For one of the first steps the rich Monarchists and fascists took under the Republic was to refuse to support the orphanages and pauper schools they had always kept
up before. Let the Government do it, they said cynically. Why

should we care for the poor? Let the Republic take care of its own.

So the Ministry of Justice had to provide the funds for the maintenance of these pre-Republican orphanages. But curiously enough—and this was only a small example of the hesitancy of the Republican Government—the Minister of Justice in the Republican Cabinets followed a flat rule: the orphanages were supported by the Government but their operation remained in the hands of the people who had administered the establishments before.

I happened to know a little about these wretched homes and schools for the poor children of Madrid. Most of the institutions were housed in buildings without plumbing and hardly fit to shelter animals. I remember particularly one small convent in a suburb of Madrid called La Guindalera, housing eighty boys from six to twelve years of age. I visited it in 1935 with an Austrian journalist who wanted to see "social welfare" work in the Spanish capital.

The boys were the first things we saw. They were covered with scabs and filth. Their ragged clothes hardly covered their dirty bodies as they played on the mud and dirt heaps in the courtyard. We rang the bell. An old nun opened the gate of the garden and led us into the house. The windows of the main room were broken and covered with burlap.

The old, short, fat Mother Superior came to meet us. Her lined and wrinkled face quivered and twitched as she spoke, and her words were hardly distinguishable, for she had no teeth. "This foreign journalist would like to see how the orphan Spanish boys live," I told her, but she did not seem to understand.

We pushed our way into the schoolroom. The walls of the classroom were covered with filth of all colors and kinds, difficult to imagine and impossible to describe in print. The desks were also used as eating tables, and I doubt very much whether they were ever used for much else. In the adjoining kitchen the floor was littered with plates, covered with old, hardened food, garbage, discarded paper, and the like. Cockroaches walked

freely on the floor and climbed the tables. My head swam and
I felt sick.

I wanted to show the journalist the contrast between the old
institutions and a new boys' club which we had recently started,
in the same neighborhood. It was a simple club, typical of the
ones we were opening in all the working-class districts of Madrid, a club where boys could spend their hours after school or
where boys who had no school to go to, could spend the long
hours of the day; under roof during the Winter, playing in the
garden during the Summer. There were books and games in
the club, and boys could learn carpentry or music or painting.
They all worked in the garden, too, and played with a big dog
we had installed as mascot.

I found that the contrast was much more than I needed to
impress the journalist. I felt shocked and ashamed that in
1935 such things could still exist in our country and in the
heart of Madrid. But worse still: the orphanage we had visited
was one of those that the rich threatened to close if it did not
get a Government subsidy. The Ministry of Justice, through
its Committee for the Protection of Minors, paid for the maintenance of the eighty boys. Later, when a terrible scandal took
place in that same orphanage, we heard as an excuse that the
Sisters of Charity, who were in charge of the building and the
boys' "education," were old and senile nuns who could not be
used anywhere else and were sent there as a sort of asylum in
which they could wait for death. But that was hardly an excuse
for what I had seen.

This convent at La Guindalera was not much different from
the places that housed three thousand orphan children in
Madrid alone. Of course, after the Popular Front victory in
February, 1936, a few changes had taken place. Some of the
children had been moved to pleasanter buildings and the nuns
who were still in charge of the youngsters were ordered at least
to teach their charges to read and write.

But with the war the whole situation changed. For some of
the nuns fled and others abandoned their children while they
prayed night and day. The Government itself was finally forced
to take care of the children of the poor.

The nuns left their charges without food because they momentarily expected a Rebel victory—not because they were threatened or feared a people's triumph, for in Madrid the first days of the rebellion the people did not make anti-religious demonstrations. There were instances of churches being burned, yes—but only those where stores of machine guns and rifles were found. The people felt that an altar behind which bullets were hidden to kill the people of Madrid was no longer sacred. Only those priests whose parishioners knew them to be fascists suffered. The people went out of their way to protect honest, truly God-fearing members of the clergy.

I had heard that the nuns were abandoning their orphans. So I took my newly recruited band of women to the office of the Protection of Minors department. The executive secretary, a handsome gray-haired man, received us very graciously—and then forgot all about us. We sat in his office for an hour, while a procession of militiamen in their *monos* marched in to report this or that orphanage abandoned and to ask, "What shall we do with the children?"

The office was in the greatest confusion—as a contrast to the UGT headquarters. The staff of the department, many of them still left over from the days of the Monarchy or the first Republican Government, dashed about madly, doing nothing. The executive secretary, not very sure of himself, tried to impress me, the wife of an Air Force officer—for he owned land and was hated by the peasants of his native Valencia.

Finally I heard the secretary shout in desperation: "I don't know what we can do. We have plenty of empty buildings and hundreds of abandoned children, and nobody with a sense of responsibility to take care of them."

I jumped up in exasperation. "That's what we've been trying to tell you all morning. We came here to offer our services."

"Very nice," he replied, bowing, "but we need women to cook and scrub floors and wash the dishes. All the buildings we have taken over are in a terrible mess. And one of our problems is that we have no money. We have already spent most of this year's budget and this is hardly the moment to ask for a new appropriation."

I tried to interrupt, but he held up his hand. He had a little speech, apparently, that he intended to deliver, willy-nilly.

"Not only," he began, with great precision, "do we have to care for the children abandoned by the nuns, but we must also find homes for the thousands of street urchins who sell papers and lottery tickets and so on. They can't be left at the mercy of the snipers. Many have been killed already, poor children."

His face became a mask of grief. "Yes, but . . ." I began.

But he wasn't finished. "The trade unions people came to see me yesterday. There are thousands of other children whose fathers have gone to war and whose mothers have been drafted to take their places at work. We must find homes for them, too. The trade unions people are planning on starting homes with their own funds. But we are a Government agency. We must supervise everything. We must set the example." He sighed and turned back to his papers, adding, "But how? How? I am very over-worked. I do not know where to turn."

This time I talked. "Look here, we are five strong women. We all have children and know how to care for them. Maruja and Teresa are excellent cooks and it won't be the first time I've scrubbed floors."

The secretary smiled and shook his head. We sat down stubbornly. He made little jokes about the situation. We looked blank—unamused, like the English Queen. The secretary began to worry. He thought we were very influential ladies. Every time he looked at Concha Prieto he trembled. So finally we had our way. A militiaman led us to the Travesía del Fúcar.

We drove to our new job in a delivery van—confiscated when its owner joined the Rebels. We bumped over cobblestones for a few minutes and then the driver opened the van door and we stepped out into the seventeenth century. We stood on a narrow, ancient street, facing a convent built with the dowery of some rich lady of the old court. It was a square, but rather graceful all the same, with two small towers on its front façade, a garden in the back, cloistered by high stone walls.

The convent was a school for middle-class girls, but the

pupils were all home on their Summer vacations when the rebellion broke out, and the nuns had fled.

We hesitated at the doors of the convent—and then suddenly the whole neighborhood surrounded us. People appeared at doors and windows, a dozen women trotted up the block to talk to us.

"Why did the nuns leave? Were they threatened?" I asked.

A stout, good-natured woman in a cotton kimono, chuckled. "Oh, no, *compañera*, nothing happened to them; no one asked them to go. But they heard rumors from their friends and relatives and their chaplain told them to leave."

"What are you coming here for?" a woman sang out from her window. "Maybe you're related to the nuns? Maybe you've come to get what's inside the convent?"

A man on the street took the cry up. "The Government owns everything in there now. Don't touch it!"

We laughed. The militiaman introduced us to the whole block. The women all began to chatter.

"You mean you're going to take care of children without being paid?"

"Can I send my two children who drive me crazy and spend all day playing in the gutter?"

"The girls who went to this school paid for the board; it was not a school for the poor. Will you charge, now?"

And then they all began to say: "We will help. Call on us if you need us."

When we told them that we hoped our new charges would play with their youngsters, we became friends of the whole neighborhood. They could not believe that the convent, so long isolated, was to become part of the block, part of their lives. Ever after that day we had only to appear at the door to get a salvo of "saluds!" and waves and smiles.

The militiaman found the key and we entered the hall of the old convent. After the nuns had left, the place had been searched for arms. There were four ugly chests in the hall and their drawers were all pulled out and the contents spilled on the floor—mostly Catholic journals, dusters, and electric light wires and fixtures. We passed on and found that the building was very spacious but old fashioned and dilapidated. The kitchen was a distressing sight. The nuns had left the remains of their last meal. Three days in the hot month of July was enough to ferment the food left on the dirty plates. The red tiled floor of the kitchen and adjoining pantry were simply carpeted by cockroaches.

I glanced up at the faces of my friends. I could feel myself turning pale as the cockroaches moved in a thick wall towards the corners as we approached.

"Are we not the wives of heroes?" Maruja said, somewhat weakly. And with that, good humoredly, we started to work.

First we had to organize the tasks. Two would attend to the kitchen, two others would clean up the house. I was made *Directora;* I had to see to the accounts and order the meals and plan the lessons and the clothes for the children and the baths and the walks. But all these duties accumulated much later. That day we all had to work and scrub floors and put away the rags that we found all over the place and prepare some kind of meal and beds for the children who would arrive that same night.

An hour after we were inside the building, the executive secretary turned up. "Will you be able to feed the children tonight before putting them to bed?" he asked.

Maruja and Teresa had to be consulted; they were very reluctant to make any promises as the kitchen was in much worse condition than they had expected. The chimney would have to be cleaned before they could light the fire and the plates and kitchen pots and pans scraped with a knife, before soap and water could be of any use. Besides, they did not want black beetles all around when they were cooking food and they had already ordered some powder to spray on the floor. And it would take them more than an hour to scrub the place.

However, when they heard the children had not eaten a proper meal for about a week, since the time the nuns had taken them down to the chapel to pray for the victory of the "men of God"—this being the name given by the nuns to the Rebel generals—Maruja and Teresa forgot all their objections.

There were many beds in the old convent and we soon discovered that we could house as many as eighty children.

That first evening fifty children arrived. The first group of twenty came in a big bus and were brought in by an official from the headquarters of the Institution who had gone to fetch them from a convent in the outskirts of Madrid where the children had spent most of their lives. Most of them looked frightened when they arrived. Some were crying silently and one older girl of about seventeen years was shrieking hysterically. They all wore dirty, cheap, black flannel dresses, ungracefully cut, with long skirts and long sleeves. Their faces bore signs of sleeplessness, tears, and smudges; their lifeless hair looked dirty, colorless, and unkempt; each child carried over her shoulder a white cotton bag containing a few miserable belongings. They moved like sheep and talked among themselves excitedly but in very low subdued tones.

I could not prevent the tears coming to my eyes. I had never seen a more pitiful sight than our first group of children. But it was no time to become sentimental. If we were to calm all those children and cope with their fits of hysterics we had to appear natural, to give them the impression that what was happening was nothing abnormal. We took them into one of the parlors leading from the hall, which must have been used by the nuns to receive their most important visitors. It was a large, square room with two sets of stiff-backed uncomfortable sofas and chairs of flimsy legs and undefined tapestry, a round three-legged table, with a white hand-embroidered doily under a mangy plant. Two large scenes of the Passion of Christ faced each other on the wall.

The children were obviously awed to be in such sumptuous surroundings. I had to say a few words to them. None of my companions would speak; had they not just made me the *Directora*? I swallowed hard and tried to smile at the children, controlling as best I could my inopportune tears. "We hope you are going to be happy here with us," I began, "and there is no need to talk in such low voices, because we are not afraid to hear you talking or laughing. Oh, we hope you will soon laugh and play! We have a lovely garden, you know! And more children will come tomorrow, and you can leave your bags in this room for the time being, until you go to bed tonight. Now you can all wash your hands. And then we will all have some supper."

The children looked dazed. Three or four of the most daring ones began to ask timid questions.

"Are we to live here forever, now?"

"Then it is not true what the Sisters said. . . ."

One little girl began to cry. "Don't tell her what the Sisters said. Don't tell her!"

But a chorus of voices answered. "The Sisters said you would be very cruel to us and beat us and they said the *milicianos* would rape us."

The ugly word sounded strange and horrible coming from these little girls most of whom were not yet twelve. This explained the hysterics of the oldest girl, poor Ana Maria whom Concha Prieto was trying to quiet in the adjoining parlor. The Sisters had departed, leaving their charges without food or care, and with the final warning that within a few days they would be ill-treated and abused by the wicked people of the Popular Front. No wonder our new charges were pale and tear-stained, frightened and nervous!

We felt a sudden wave of anger. Even if the misguided Sisters had believed such ridiculous tales, surely it was unnecessary to leave little children alone with terror.

Our dinner was a great success. It was very simple, we thought, and we had been afraid the children would think we would never give them any better food. But we had a salad—none of them had ever tasted such a thing before, and they were delighted. Then the dinner wound up with a rice pudding with milk and sugar, which they praised endlessly. And above all, we allowed them to talk during their meal—remembering my own convent days, I could understand their delight.

Bathing our girls that night was something none of us ever forgot. The convent had an old-fashioned bathroom in a sort of low-roofed shack attached to the back wall. Two bathtubs stood in the bathroom and twelve foot baths were fastened to the walls. We decided it was possible to bathe all the girls that first day—but we had reckoned without our children.

We called two of the older girls and told them to bathe in the two tubs, while we started to work on the babies in the foot baths. But the two girls stood demurely beside the bathtubs, obviously reluctant to undress. Finally they told us they had never had a bath in their whole lives. We found two screens and hoped for the best.

We never dreamt we would encounter the same difficulty with the younger ones. I picked a sweet, black-haired little girl with great black eyes for my first attempt. I unbuttoned Enriquetita's filthy heavy black flannel pinafore, peeled off her thick black stockings and worn shoes. But then came the battle. As I tried to unfasten her dirt-encrusted chemise, she began to struggle wildly, shouting something I could not quite understand—she lisped. Finally I made it out. "It is a sin against modesty!" she wept. Enriquetita was four years old!

Although the bedrooms were in terrible disorder, with the beds unmade and nuns' habits and lay clothes strewn all over the place, we managed to prepare two large dormitories with enough clean beds for our fifty new pupils. We thought the children would feel less lonely and miserable if they were allowed to choose beds next to their especial friends.

I managed to keep my composure while the little ones timidly began to find their companions, but Concha and Teresa had to go off in a corner to weep. For these children had never in all their lives been allowed friendships. Just as my childhood had been one long search for affection, these youngsters, much worse off, for many of them had no homes but the convents, could hardly believe they were allowed—actually allowed—to have friends. Some of the little girls were so shy they could not bring themselves to speak to the youngster next to whose bed they wanted to sleep.

We had a professional hairdresser by the third day to supervise the job of washing eighty heads of long braided hair which looked as though they had never been washed before. She shook her head. Alas, most of our little girls had to have their hair cropped short and Maruja and I spent all the fourth day delousing some seventy heads with vinegar and another chemical. Only ten of our youngsters did not have vermin in their hair!

And we had to sit down and laugh, for the ten lucky ones were inordinately vain and strutted all day, pointing out that *they* did not have bugs!

After the first flurry of washing and finding clean clothes for our children, we called in a young doctor to examine our youngsters. We breathed a sigh of relief after he left, for of our eighty children, only ten or so had tuberculosis or inherited diseases. The rest, down to the last child, were anemic, some badly so, and to our sorrow, many had trachoma, that terrible disease of the eyes. I shall never forget how our children tried to hold back the tears, which would only have made their red eyelids worse, as they were taken away to the hospital. For they had already come to love us, and we had to explain very carefully to them that trachoma is very contagious and dangerous. And we promised them faithfully they could return as soon as they were cured.

I settled down to work in the convent. Ignacio could come home rarely and on the nights when he could leave his work, he telephoned and I met him at Freddie's house. The other evenings I spent at the convent with Luli. I had sent for my daughter immediately and she arrived, sun-tanned and full of energy, delighted to help me.

For Luli, at nine years, tried to do for the eighty children what none of us women could—she attempted to teach them how to play. These youngsters had spent so many years in convents where speech was almost forbidden that they stood around the garden in timid groups. She thought she could solve the whole sad problem by teaching four or five girls a kind of ball game she had learned at camp. But our children did not know how to play—and they could not, after their bleak childhood, learn so easily.

Death hovered all around us those Summer days. Sudden, bitter tragedy overwhelmed us at the convent when word was brought that Teresa's husband had been killed. Maruja and I could only turn helplessly from her pitiful grief. And I think that like every other Spanish woman who saw those first dreadful scenes of grief, in the early days of war, in 1936, our hearts grew firmer. We had meant to resist fascism to the end—but now when we saw what fascism did, saw the agony of grief, our determination hardened.

I could not guess that for years I would live with death, expecting the touch of its cold hand momentarily, watching dear friends disappear forever. I only knew that I could hardly bear to see the agony death brought—and hardly bear the thought that my own husband would perhaps be next. For Ignacio, bitterly restless in the smoky confusion of the War Ministry, had at last gone to take active command of the Air Force. He was flying the old "pimento cans" of the Spanish Air Force, as we called them—nearly worthless and almost suicidal planes. He never told me, and I never told him that I had found out, that twice he flew back to the airport with a machine riddled with bullets, once with a dead observer in his back seat.

Life at the convent went smoothly for the children who were fortunately too young to know that they lived in days of great tragedy and suspense. They rose early and our neighbors watched them doing their setting-up exercises in the garden. After breakfast they had reading and writing lessons, games, and sometimes a visit to the museums still open. Several times the young men and women from the Cultural Militia came to show them a moving picture film or read poetry and play music. We taught them to sing songs, too, and at night after dinner they used to sing very sweetly the folk-songs of Spain.

In a few weeks an enormous change came over our children. They grew almost strong, tanned with the sun. They had been illiterate when they came—now most of them were reading children's gay-colored books. They were happy for the first time in their lives. As we women grew to live with sorrow, our children, at least, grew to live with happiness. Sometimes relatives came to visit the children—and many an "aunt" tried to fall on her knees and kiss our hands for making her little Conchita happy.

The military situation was serious but not, we felt, really dangerous. Madrid and Barcelona were firmly in the hands of the Republic; the Government also held the whole of southeast Spain and northeast Spain from the coast and a line drawn from half way across the Pyrenees to fifty miles or so northeast of Madrid, besides the isolated territory of the Cantabrian coast in the extreme north. We all felt that the rebellion could not last very long. The people's remarkable response to the Government's call to the colors of democratic Spain was our best guarantee of victory. We had a huge Army—untrained largely and not yet armed, but still a reservoir of manpower. Besides that, we had the greater part of the Navy, the Assault Guards, and even most of the Civil Guard. The big industrial centers of the country and the rich eastern coast, as well as all the harbors on the Mediterranean and the Cantabrian and the French frontiers, were in the hands of the Republic.

It never occurred to us that the legal, democratically elected, recognized Government of Spain would have any difficulty buying the arms and supplies it needed to crush the remaining Rebel forces. We felt that the revolt was nearly over—the Spanish generals had no popular support whatsoever. The people were solidly behind the Government. It was a matter of buying rifles, artillery, supplies, and the like—then the Rebels would probably surrender and the whole thing would be over, with the minimum amount of loss of life.

On July 27, the news broke like a bomb in Madrid. The French Government has refused to sell us arms!

Why? We couldn't understand. We knew the British and the French reactionaries had put pressure on the Popular Front Government of France, but that a Socialist premier should deny a legal, recognized Government the right to buy arms to crush a fascist rebellion! It was monstrous! Worse, it was mad. What were the French thinking of?

On July 31, Ignacio brought me more terrible news: the Italians are invading Spain! Italian airplanes had been sighted flying to Rebel territory, some had been forced down in French Morocco, having lost the way. The orders found on them were dated July 16—the day before the rebellion broke out. Mussolini promptly denied this news, just as Hitler denied he was sending arms, men, and guns. After the war was over, both dictators boasted that they helped prepare the plot and sent supplies and all kinds of aid, from troops to bandages, airplanes to trucks, the moment the traitor generals moved.

But in the early August days, Spaniards tried to convince the world—and especially France, England, and the United States—that our country was being invaded by fascists. The democracies turned a deaf ear to our pleas while the fascists strangled democracy in Spain.

When André Malraux arrived with a group of Frenchmen and some planes too old to be used by the French Air Force, we imagined that France was ready to sell us the planes that we so badly needed. It was common knowledge that Italy had sent and was sending Savoias, Capronis, and Fiats—four Savoias crashed in French Moroccan territory on their way to the Rebels—and that Germany's pocket battleships prevented bombardments of Rebel towns in Spanish Morocco by our Navy. On August 3, for instance, the *Deutschland* together with another German destroyer steamed slowly up and down the harbor of Ceuta, making it impossible for the *Jaime I* and other units of the Spanish Fleet to fire on their objectives.

German bombers and pursuit planes—Junkers 52 and Heinkels manned by German pilots—had already landed in Seville and Cadiz. They were helping to carry officers and troops of the Foreign Legion to the Peninsula, speeding the human cargo of Moors and white mercenaries coming across in great numbers every day.

But we were very innocent in those days. We thought France had realized her own danger and was willing to sell us the things we needed to defend ourselves. We did not know then that certain powerful people in France and England had made up their minds, even before the war had started.

When another German vessel, the *Kameroon,* trying to enter the harbor of Cadiz was stopped and searched by the Spanish Navy in Spanish territorial waters, and found to be taking petrol to the Rebels (the fascists were running very short of gasoline, which might have ended the war then and there), the British not only did not support the Spanish Government in its perfectly legal right to patrol its own harbors, but used the incident to discredit us in the world press.

Instead of accusing the Italians and Germans of their perfectly obvious intervention, the British Foreign Office presented a completely false version of the Spanish rebellion to the world. The legal Government of Spain was painted as a lawless rabble. The invasion by two foreign countries was ignored. The British Government knew that if the people were told the truth about the shocking invasion of Spain, the whole world would rise up to protest. And so the British Foreign Office began its long campaign of slander and lies against the Spanish Government. Mussolini and Hitler never tried to obscure their invasion of Spain—the British attempted to cover their tracks for them!

Only one country in the world printed the truth about Spain, from the beginning and until the end—the Soviet Union. Spaniards who had never heard of the Soviet Union before suddenly awoke in those days in August, when we were being betrayed everywhere else in the world, to realize that at least one nation had not abandoned us in our struggle for democracy. Every Spanish newspaper carried the news in great headlines that the Soviet workers had levied a one per cent tax on their salaries and collected 14,000,000 rubles for the Spanish people within the first month of the rebellion.

The news helped us to bear the loss of Badajoz, a little town on the Portugal frontier. For Badajoz fell on August 13, with the "honor" of being the first Spanish town to be bombarded by Italian and German planes. The people of Badajoz will bear the distinction in history of being the first Spaniards to have been blown to eternity by the conquering bombs of foreign fascists. We grew more accustomed to stories of horror later on in the war—but at that time we could hardly bear to read the eyewitness accounts and see the few photographs of the terrible massacre the Moors and foreign legionnaires had committed in this peaceful town when they entered after the bombardment. The slaughter in the bull ring at Badajoz horrified the whole world.

Badajoz only helped to emphasize how desperately we needed

planes. When the rebellion started we had about seventy old crates, mostly French Breguets XIX. After a month of war, we were forced to remodel hastily the few passenger planes we had, to bombard advancing columns.

The old-fashioned French planes Malraux and his men brought were only a bitter sweet. Three of them crashed before they could be used in the war and the others were not much good.

For a long time we kept hoping that we could buy planes abroad. We would get wires from our air attachés in foreign capitals only to have our hopes dashed the next day. The Rebels, in the meantime, had whole squadrons of the best planes German and Italian factories could produce, planes of all types, pursuit, bombers (many of those), and transport planes. And with the planes they had technicians of all kinds: mechanics, men to build and design airports, radio operators, and pilots—especially pilots!

We had almost nothing. No planes to speak of, very few trained pilots, mechanics, and the like. Malraux arrived with the best will in the world, but he had had little experience with actual aerial warfare. And the only men he had been able to hastily round up to meet the critical situation were either well meaning but mostly without knowledge, or frank mercenaries—they were each paid 50,000 francs a month.

It was not, we knew, the French people who left us to die helplessly under the bombs of German and Italian aviators. For they supported us, solidly. They sat at a great meeting in Paris and cheered the words of Dolores Ibarruri, the great woman deputy to the Cortes, as she said: "You must aid the Spanish people! Beware! Today it is us, but tomorrow your turn will come. We need rifles, aeroplanes, and big guns to fight the fascists at your border!"

As "La Pasionaria" concluded, the whole enormous crowd rose to its feet with the mighty cry, *"Avions et cannons pour l'Espagne!"*

No, it was not the French people—but some of the leaders of the French Socialist Party, Blum among them, who had allowed themselves to be bullied into betraying democracy in Spain.

We were handicapped in other ways besides our lack of planes at the beginning of the war. Curiously, we were badly damaged by our innocence, our good nature, and our attempts to keep on good terms with countries which had long since determined to betray us. Our air fields were overrun with spies and Madrid was full of fascists who had foreign connections.

German transport planes landed at our main civilian airport, and one morning when I went with a friend who was taking off for Asturias, I even saw a man I knew to be a spy boarding one of those German transport planes at our own airport! Indeed, the Germans were so bold they once even landed a military plane with complete bombing and machine gun equipment at Madrid. The pilot took off again suddenly when he saw his mistake but had to land for lack of fuel in a nearby field. Then the German Government protested against the seizure of a neutral plane by the "lawless" Spanish Government!

Incidentally, I had met this spy I saw at the airport at a cocktail party given by an American newspaper man and his wife just before the revolt. The party was attended by a number of foreign journalists—and by a number of Spaniards. To my surprise I was the only Spaniard present who was not a known fascist. The hostess explained that most of the other Spaniards, the fascists, present were friends of another one of her guests, Mr. William Carney of the *New York Times!*

The chinks in our armor had to be remedied. The Giral Government, composed entirely of right-wing Republicans, proved a weak weapon with which to fight a war against two foreign invaders. The trade unions and other political parties in the Popular Front were not represented in the Giral Cabinet and Azaña, himself a Republican, realized that the Government needed a broader popular base. Fascism could only be fought with the weapon of democracy, and because the Spanish people lacked arms and airplanes with which to fight the war, they especially needed to have confidence in their leaders. Only a real Popular Front Government could lead the people of Spain in their fight against fascism.

Giral was glad to resign—he knew nothing of fighting a war. His Cabinet was replaced by a broad Popular Front Government. Two Republicans; a Catalan; a Basque representative; Prieto, from his wing of the Socialist Party; Caballero, representing what he called the "left" wing; two Communists—this was the new Government. Only the anarchists would not participate in the Government.

The new Prime Minister was Largo Caballero—for he was undoubtedly the most popular man in Spain in those early days of the war. He was a curious sort of man, with a much-checkered history behind him. During the Primo de Rivera dictatorship he had collaborated with the militarists, but after the February, 1936, Popular Front victory in the elections he had refused to join the Republican Government, preferring to let the Republicans "ruin themselves alone," as he expressed it. We all thought that if Caballero had allowed his Socialists to join the Government in March, there might have been no rebellion in July.

But that issue was dead now. Caballero was a trade union leader, beloved in Madrid because he had once been a worker in the building trades. Prieto was a petty-bourgeois intellectual and the workers preferred having one of their own in office as the leader. True, when the war actually started, Prieto was invaluable in the War Office, while Caballero lost his head and dashed around in a pair of *monos* having his picture taken with the men at the front.

We all hoped—with some misgivings—that Caballero would make the necessary Popular Front leader to give us victory. True, he surrounded himself with a most doubtful "brain trust." Men like Luis Araquistain, with more ambition than principle, men who always kept aloof from the people. We all knew that old Caballero suffered from almost childish vanity, but we hoped that the terrible times would temper his shortcomings and give him dignity and strength to lead the Spanish people. The September Government needed a man of courage and sincerity, selflessness and power. We hoped—not without fear—that Caballero was our man.

Ignacio and I were asleep at Freddie's house on one of the

rare holidays we had from our twenty-four-hour schedules when the phone rang. It was very late, almost three o'clock in the morning.

Ignacio went sleepily to the telephone. It was Prieto. Ignacio had just been named Chief of the Air Force by the new Cabinet, a post left open for weeks after the tragic death of Nuñez de Prado.

Ignacio came back from the phone irritated and depressed. For weeks he had been in direct charge of the tiny squad of Republican planes, flying with his men. Now he would have to go back behind a desk, to listen all day to the S O S of bombed cities to whom he could send no planes because he had none to send.

"It is nothing to look forward to," he growled, as he tried to sleep again.

Neither of us could guess that one day in his life, as Chief of the Republican Air Forces of the Army and Navy, he would have exactly *one* plane to command!

The military situation grew more grave in September—even in our convent we began to feel the tenseness of the city. For since our western front had collapsed after the merciless slaughter in Badajoz, the Rebel armies, greatly reinforced by Moors and Foreign Legion troops, backed up by the finest fascist airplanes, were marching on Madrid. The truckloads of courageous but untrained and badly armed militia which left Madrid for the front were no longer able to hold the fascists. Swept by machine gun fire, bombed from the air, blown to bits by heavy German and Italian artillery, the raw recruits died in thousands—but the line could not hold. Bravery is not enough in a modern war.

We needed discipline as well as courage. The first group to demonstrate that a disciplined People's Army to fight the war in Spain was a possibility as well as a necessity was the "Fifth Regiment." Organized by the Communists, the regiment was formed by men of all shades of political opinion who wanted to defend their country.

This famous fighting unit was the first to appear on a Spanish front with Political Commissars to strengthen the morale of the men and military officers who knew their business. The bravest troops will run under machine gun fire if their leaders are incompetent or their morale shattered by uncertainty.

The "Fifth Regiment" won its fame because it held its ground, never ran in panic but retreated, if its officers decided retreat was necessary, in good orderly formation. Similarly, the "Fifth Regiment" never indulged in sporadic attacks or useless gallantry. The "Fifth Regiment's" Political Commissars explained the meaning of the war to their men, taught the illiterate to read, held lectures during lulls in the battles, looked after the physical well-being of the soldiers, and acted as democratic leaders of their men.

The example of the "Fifth Regiment" started a ferment in the troops. Spain needed a disciplined Army, needed it badly, and *now*. Many misguided patriots fought against the principle of discipline; especially those at home in office jobs. But at the front the men began to notice that the "Fifth Regiment" suffered fewer losses on the battlefield, and was a Rock of Gibraltar in the badly trained Army.

But the "Fifth Regiment" was only beginning its long story of heroic action in September. The military situation was very grave. And then one night, as all Madrid lay still and quiet, with the strict lights-out rule making the city black, we had our first bombing. I shall never forget how my heart beat. Suppose the bombs fell on my children in that flimsy old convent building? After that I never dared leave them alone at night. And Ignacio told me that the war would be a long one and Madrid constantly in danger. "Take the children to the sea coast," he suggested.

The people at the office of the Protection of Minors department told me it was "defeatist" to ask to have my children evacuated. But a few days later I had wild orders to get my children out of Madrid at once—as soon as possible. I suggested Alicante, the beautiful seashore resort town in the southeast. The secretary scoffed, pessimistic as usual.

When I first arrived in Alicante, I was astonished to find the war had hardly touched the little town. The Republicans had defeated the fascist coup in the early days and then settled down to wait for the end of the rebellion. But when I told my story—homes for the children of Madrid—every hand and heart was opened to me. I selected houses deserted by the fascists to house the 650 children I had now directly under my care, and within two days I was busily ordering beds and linen, little tables for my youngsters to eat at, and making arrangements for food.

When the train pulled in, bearing two hundred car-sick, pale, tired youngsters, the first of my homeless ones from Madrid, we were all amazed to find that the whole town had turned out to welcome them. Perhaps this seems like nothing to a stranger, but *Madrileños* were traditionally aliens to the people of Alicante. Regionalism, narrow sectionalism, had separated the people of Spain for long generations.

And now as the first of my youngsters stepped from the train, a brass band—slightly off key, but so earnest—began to play. From around the corner of the station marched all the school children of Alicante, dressed in white, with new red ribbons tied in the girls' hair and new red ties on the boys' shirts. My convent-bred orphans, worn out from the long ride on the crowded train, began to cry from excitement. In their whole lives, nobody had ever paid any real attention to them—and now here they were, being met at the station with a real brass band and school children singing for them!

The Mayor made a little speech on the platform. "Welcome, little *Madrileños*," he began. "Here you will be happy. Our children are waiting to play with you. You will forget all about the bombs and war, because in a little while our countrymen will drive the foreign invaders from our Spain. In the meantime we hope you will come to love our ocean and our city. You must never be afraid or lonely because all of us in Alicante love you. We think of you as we think of our own children."

At this point the Mayor, who was a lean, tall mechanic elected in the Popular Front victory and not too accustomed to making speeches, quite broke down. "*Viva la República!*" he cried, seizing the nearest one of my children and kissing her soundly. "*Viva Madrid! Viva el Frente Popular.*" Then he mopped the tears out of his eyes.

Our little *Madrileños,* their eyes sparkling, were loaded into cars and buses, and with the school children bringing up the rear we paraded all through Alicante to the suburb of San Juan. The streets were lined with the people of the community —the school children sang and their parents wept a little and the Mayor was sad because he had forgotten to say the rest of his speech. He had meant, he said, to explain that the Republic was fighting for the children of Spain and that no matter what happened to the men at the front and their wives, the new generation would grow up happy, in freedom and dignity.

I told him not to mind—his passionate *Viva la República!* told the whole story.

Of course, as at any well-regulated parade, it began to rain as we neared the end of the route. But nobody seemed to mind much. The school children sang just as loudly, the band played just as vigorously, the people—the people of Alicante, mind you —cried, *"Viva Madrid,"* just as passionately. Many times during the war when food grew scarce and our armies were forced back and the future seemed black, I thought of that little parade in the soft rain of Alicante. Even now, the memory of the passionate cheers, the tears to welcome the little *Madrileños,* gives me courage and strength. A people which so deeply wants dignity and liberty for its children can never be really defeated.

The excitement of the parade quite exhausted our tired children from Madrid. We expected to put them to bed promptly. But we forgot that none of them had ever seen houses like the gaudy ones Alicante's rich lived in. The youngsters from the homes of the Madrid workers tiptoed through the houses in awe, touching the hideously elaborate furniture with pathetic gestures of joy. Our children from the convents were much less easy to handle. They had never been inside any kind of a house before and their teachers had never given them any pride of possession. They were the most destructive children I have ever seen—the new toys we had prepared for them vanished in half an hour. The workers' children were struck dumb with excitement to see the dolls and picture books, while our poor orphans, who had never been taught to play, could only tear up the books and break the dolls, and then relapse into boredom.

It was afternoon before we finally settled the children down in their new beds—and we could all breathe a sigh of exhaustion and take stock of ourselves.

For the news that day of the parade in Alicante was very grave. I had hardly time to think of it while the bands played and the Mayor spoke, but now while the children slept, the young doctor, the four girls helping me, and I, held a conference. The Italian army and the German planes and the Moors were advancing with terrible rapidity on Madrid.

The road to Madrid stretched wide and open on a flat plain with a good pavement all the way. The little villages along the route were being systematically bombed. Their women, if they had not time to escape, were being turned over to the Moors for their pleasure. Their men were being shot wholesale. The refugees were crowding Madrid.

Toledo had fallen, a monument, a tragic memorial to government leniency—humanity if you like. The fascists inside the Alcazar had kidnapped the women and children of the townsfolk and taken their own wives and youngsters inside as well. For weeks the Republican troops hesitated to bombard defenseless women and children—were we barbarians? But as the Rebel troops advanced on Toledo, Caballero finally—too late—gave the order to blow up the fortress. But the inexperienced militia, demoralized by the long delay, failed. And so the fascists took Toledo and they were not so merciful as we were.

We learned about fascism from the war.

I had planned to install my children in Alicante and neighboring San Juan and then return to Madrid to work with Concha Prieto in caring for youngsters of kindergarten age whose mothers were taking the place of men in work and whose fathers had gone to the front.

But now the grave war news changed the whole situation. The Government planned to evacuate not only the homeless orphans of Madrid but every child whose parents would agree to send him out of the besieged city. Food was easier to get in

Alicante and with Madrid being bombarded the children were much safer out of the capital. Concha Prieto wired me that she had been asked to work on this mass children's emigration. I was obviously badly needed to find homes for the children, buy their food, arrange for their care.

Ignacio was in Madrid. I wanted to be with him—how badly I need not say, except to suggest that it was wartime and the separation seemed doubly terrible.

And yet it was perfectly clear that I was needed very much in Alicante. The children must be settled comfortably and made happy. Their food must be wangled out of farmers. Trains must be met, cooks hired, beds ordered, sheets made, dresses sewed, books installed, teachers put to work.

I wired Ignacio that I was staying in Alicante and sent for my Luli. I had quite a struggle with my conscience when she stepped off the train, looking so tanned and healthy and gay. I wanted to have her with me in between my mad dashes around the community to inspect premises and bargain with farmers. But favoritism in a time like that was impossible. The other children were without parents. The other mothers had been asked by the Government to send their children to the "colonies" as we called the homes. So I installed Luli in one of the homes. She thrived, too, and I was always secretly delighted, as what mother is not, to discover that Luli was always the leader of her school class.

I have forgotten just when the food supply began to run short for our children. It came about gradually. One day we could find no eggs, the next day only a few. The people of Alicante gave generously to our children. The sick and undernourished and the children were fed first. But gradually the food supply began to grow meager. The volunteers who helped me get food for the children's colonies began to work longer and longer hours, combing the countryside for a bit of meat or a few potatoes. The young doctor who took care of the children began to worry. Our youngsters developed colds.

And then one day Paco, the head of my food foragers, came running breathlessly to our "colony."

"The ship came! The Soviet ship is in the harbor!"

We all went down to meet the *Neva*. The whole town stood on the quay. Such cheers I have never heard. It wasn't only the food which we needed so badly. It was the idea that at least one nation had not betrayed us.

My children all turned out to welcome the *Neva*. They gave the sailors flowers and cheered the captain. The townspeople decorated the quay with banners—and we all felt most embarrassed to discover that the stevedores loading the ship in Odessa had worked night and day to finish their task, contributing their wages to buy more food for Spain. For alas, the *Neva* was not nearly so speedily unloaded in Alicante. Our Russian friends, it turned out, hearing of our shortage had sent thousands of pounds of butter to Spain. But unfortunately all our refrigerator trucks and railroad cars had fallen into the hands of the fascists and Alicante was hot—very hot. What were we to do with our profusion of riches? Our stevedores rushed the wheat and dryed milk and chocolate and canned meat off the *Neva* and then we all had to wait while the city authorities hastily tried to find a place for our enormous new store of butter. Afterwards we all had a good joke for, since the precious butter could not be moved out of Alicante, Madrid's loss was our gain. We ate butter three meals a day for months.

But the confusion over the butter cast no shadow across the joy of the Alicante people. The night the *Neva* arrived little boys roamed the town writing on the walls of the houses, *"Viva Rusia!"* and *"Viva la U.R.S.S."*

"We need the food," our doctor sighed, as he watched the men unload the *Neva*. "Heaven only knows how we need it. Just the same, I wish they were unloading airplanes."

I sighed and wished the same wish. Everybody did in Spain. And yet we all agreed with the policy of the Soviet Union. The Non-intervention Pact set up by England and France was supposed to stop the armed invasion of Spain by Italy and Germany. The whole world knew that Italian troops were advancing on Madrid and German airplanes bombing Spanish children. But suppose the Soviet Union had refused to sign the Non-intervention Pact? Then England would have pictured the war in Spain as a contest between Communism and Fascism.

The Soviet Union did not want to intervene in Spain, as Italy and Germany were doing, and could not have, even if it had wanted to, for simple reasons of geography. The Russian foreign policy was only to prevent aggression and thus general war in Europe. The Soviet Union had had to agree to the Non-intervention Pact, with the idea of trying to make the British Foreign Office really enforce it. The Russians could not sell us arms—they were energetically trying to make England stop the German and Italian invasion of Spain.

And so we welcomed the *Neva* which bore the terribly needed food but no arms. And in London, that same week, the silk-hatted diplomats of the Non-Intervention Committee met and refused to consider the Soviet charges that the Pact was being violated by Germany and Italy. The merest child knew that Hitler was bombing Spaniards even the Italian newspapers boasted of Italian aviators and troops in Spain. And yet in London, the British Foreign Office ignored these obvious facts. And in Paris, men who called themselves Socialists abandoned Spain to its fate. And in Washington, D. C., Congressmen who made speeches about how they loved democracy refused to lift the embargo on arms to democratic Spain.

The townspeople of Alicante knew nothing of the Soviet Union until the *Neva* steamed into the harbor. No "agents of Stalin" roamed the streets. And yet the people wept with joy in the harbor and we all cheered until we were hoarse, crying *"Viva la U.R.S.S."*

One people in all the world had not deserted us.

I think we needed not only the food the *Neva* brought us, but the hope and strength. For now the situation in Madrid had grown critical. Concha Prieto and President Azaña's pretty young wife and I began to discuss it in grave tones. They each had charge of a children's house, and presently Blanca Prieto, Concha's sister, joined us.

I had little news from Ignacio and Concha was too busy to hear very often from her father, the Minister of Air and Marine, but gradually we began to live with the tense military moment. In Madrid, General Franco's troops moved implacably forward.

Bombardment followed bombardment. And all over Spain bombs dropped on Spanish women and children.

And then, in the middle of October, I had a great shock. Concha got a peremptory note from her father. The military situation was tense. He could not work in peace with his daughters in Spain—in danger. They must leave. I could hardly believe my ears. The women of Madrid were fighting beside their men, building barricades, cooking food while the guns roared. We were comparatively safe, doing work, however unromantic, that was absolutely necessary. Why should the Minister of Air and Marine consider his daughters above the women of Madrid? I glanced at Concha as she told me the news.

We had all been disappointed and hurt when my friend Zenobia and her poet husband, who at first had helped us run homes for children in Madrid, had suddenly packed their trunks and left Spain. We considered it something of a desertion. Spain needed her poets. Zenobia might have been useful. She was needed. And yet Zenobia and her husband, like many Spanish intellectuals who thought themselves too delicate and too sensitive to stand the horrors of war, had gone abroad.

What about Concha?

"I'll never go," she said, her eyes flaming. "I don't know what father is thinking of."

And for day afterwards, she would tell me of new notes from her father and of her replies. I was amazed at Prieto's insistence when his daughter wanted, nay, demanded, to stay in her country and help in the fight. Finally the subject died down and I thought the incident was closed.

But the night watchman came to the villa where I lived very early one morning the next week.

"The cook at Concha Prieto's house says to come right away. Hurry!"

I was shocked out of my sleep. Frightened, I jumped into my clothes. Was Concha ill? What was the matter?

I heard the twenty-two children in Concha's house crying before I climbed the stairs. Inside, I found the youngsters in complete hysteria. The cook was huddled in a corner, also in tears.

Finally I got the story out of the cook, between sobs. "A car came last night," the poor woman began, "with one of Señor Prieto's secretaries. He said he had come to take Concha away. But Señorita Concha cried. She said she would not go. She said it was shameful for her to leave and she was not afraid and she wanted to stay."

"So?" I said impatiently, while the twenty-two children lifted their voices and wept afresh.

"Well, the Señor's secretary went away and presently he came back with the Civil Governor. And the Governor told Concha that her father had a very important job and he must not be worried and besides he had orders to send Concha with the secretary. So Concha wept again, and she told the Governor that her father should not be worried about her, did not all the men of Spain have to worry about their daughters?"

The cook quite dissolved again at these words, and the children wept hysterically, with the older ones crying, "We will all be dead, we will all be dead."

"Nobody is going to be dead," I shouted above the uproar, *"be calm, keep still."*

The cook finally stopped sobbing and went on with her story. "Well, they said Señora Azaña, the President's wife, and Blanca Prieto were leaving too, and Concha kept saying, 'No, no,' and I fell asleep, it was so late, and when I woke up they had taken her away anyway."

And from the three women leaving Alicante in the morning plane, the cook and the children and the townsfolk had drawn one conclusion: if the Minister of Marine and Air called the Civil Governor to force his daughter to leave Alicante, it must be that we were all in terrible danger. Not only Concha's twenty-two children were in panic that morning. The men started building barricades around the sea wall and the city. The women spent hours trying to think where they could hide their children from the bombs sure to fall.

I tried to quiet the children and the town. I did not like to tell the truth about Prieto, and I tried to explain that he was just a very doting father. But while I tried to go about calmly, inside I was filled with rage. That a responsible Government officer could behave in such a way, striking panic into the hearts of Spaniards, forcing his daughter to do such a remarkable thing—desert her country when she was needed! I have never believed that because a man has power in the Government he should not share the suffering of his country. Women and men of Madrid wept over their children, dead from the fascist bombs, but Prieto could not leave his daughters in Alicante!

By noon, some of the panic had died down and Alicante was just beginning to pick up its spirit when we all had another terrible blow, a real one this time. The first of the refugees from Cartagena straggled into Alicante. They stood about the quiet town streets and repeated, in dazed voices, the terrible story of Cartagena. The fascists bombed the town—and the bombs did not fall on the harbor, a naval base, but with awful accuracy ruthlessly bombarded the peaceful streets of the city. Nobody knew how many died in that bombardment, how many children and women.

When I heard the news my heart nearly stopped beating. Ignacio, I knew, had planned to visit the airfield of Los Alcázares only two days before. He usually stopped at an old hotel in Cartagena on these trips, for the barracks at the air field was crowded. And now Cartagena had been bombed!

I ran down the street wildly. At home I picked up the telephone, but my hands trembled so I could hardly hold the receiver. At last the operator answered me and began to ring Los Alcázares. The busy signal came again and again—ten minutes, fifteen minutes, twenty. I felt the fear growing in my heart.

"Get Madrid," I finally said, "the War Ministry."

Again I waited and tried to fight the panic. The morning newspapers lay before me. "The enemy is at our gates," the headlines said; "the workers' militia can force our foe to retreat!"

"Madrid. Hello, this is Madrid," I heard finally. The War Ministry answered at last. "The Chief of the Air Force," I said as calmly as I could.

A strange voice answered. Not Ignacio. "Who is this?" I asked. He replied, giving his name.

The name meant nothing to me—for a moment. And then I felt a wave of sheer, desperate fear. The man I was talking to I knew very well. He was a fascist pilot—a man who had written to Ignacio while we were in Rome, boasting of the good job the Air Force had done bombing the workers of Oviedo in 1934.

"The fascist 'Fifth Column' must be trying to seize Madrid," I thought, in a flash.

"Where is Hidalgo de Cisneros?" I shouted into the phone, above the noise of the bad connection. "Where is Ignacio?"

"I don't know," the aviator who liked to bomb workers replied.

"Give me Prieto!" I cried.

But my answer was a click. The man had rung off.

I got up from the phone, ran to the garage, begged Paco to drive me to the Governor. I did not want to spread more alarm, but I had to find Ignacio, and I had to discover if Madrid was falling. The capital could not, would not, fall into fascist hands. And yet—why did I get that fascist aviator when I asked for the Chief of the Air Force?

The Governor was busy when I arrived. But when I told my story to his secretary, all doors opened before me. The Governor had heard no rumors of a "Fifth Column" uprising in Madrid, but, he said, his voice trembling, "Call the Ministry of War in Madrid from my telephone!"

I walked from his desk to the telephone booth at the end of the office. He rose with me. On his table was a gun which he was not accustomed to using. Suddenly, in the excitement, the gun went off, luckily hitting no one. The people waiting in the ante-room jumped and some woman screamed. The panic spread outside.

But the sudden shot sobered me down. For some reason, I felt the fear melting away from my heart. I felt ashamed of my panic and I knew it was our duty to keep cool.

I got Prieto on the phone very promptly. Ignacio, he told me, was safe. The capital was in danger but it had not fallen and would not fall.

I tried to ask Prieto about the fascist officer I had spoken to, but he would not answer over the telephone. It appeared that he was an officer in good standing of the Republican Army—a piece of leniency that we were all to regret bitterly later.

I went home that night exhausted by the hard day of alarms. I was depressed, too, by the terrible news from Madrid.

I turned on the radio for the Government news reports.

And then I first heard the voice of Dolores Ibarruri, "La Pasionaria." This woman of the people, this living symbol of Spanish courage, spoke to the people of Spain at the grave moment when Madrid faced the enemy at its very gates.

The children at my home gathered around the radio. The cook came in from the kitchen. Paco came from the garage. We clustered around the little wireless set.

"They shall not pass! No pasarán!" Her beautiful voice, vibrant, strong, filled the room. We straightened up. After the long day of panic and fear, after the weeks of tense waiting which had weighed on even the children, this stirring voice called us all back to our faith in Spain, to our faith in ourselves.

"The fascists will not pass! They will not pass because we are not alone!"

I glanced at our cook. She had clasped her hands together in that beautiful, unconscious gesture which is native to all women of Spain. She was leaning toward the radio, her lips moving a little, repeating without sound, the words of "La Pasionaria."

"We must not conceal the fact that Madrid is in danger! The removal of this danger depends on the people of Madrid, and on them alone. . . . All the people of Madrid, men and women, must learn the use of arms."

Paco was nearly in tears. His hand covered his mouth. I saw him gulping hard.

The strong voice, powerful and sure, went on, growing more vibrant, more electric. *"The lives and future of our children are at stake! This is not the time for hesitation; this is not the time for timidity. We women must demand that our men be courageous. We must inspire them with the thought that a man*

*must know how to die worthily. Preferimos ser viudas de héroes
antes que esposas de cobardes!"*

"We prefer to be the widows of heroes rather than wives of
cowards!"

November 5, 1936.
In Alicante we did not know that this day Madrid fought
for its life. I had the use of a car and a holiday at long last. I
had not seen Ignacio for almost two months. He was stationed at
Albacete, the new air base the Government had built slightly
away from Madrid. I started early in the afternoon, before the
radio began to broadcast the news of the attack on Madrid.
The drive took four hours and when we reached Albacete, the
parched ugly little town was almost dark. Ignacio was not in
when I went to the Central Hotel but the porter led me to his
room. I was just inspecting the dreary, dusty metal furniture,
the taps marked hot and cold from which only cold water and
very little of that ever came, when the door opened and Ignacio
came in.

I turned to face him with a lump in my throat. Two months.
We had never even been separated for two weeks until the war
came.

His hair had turned from premature gray to white. That was
the first thing I noticed. His face had grown thinner. His eyes
mirrored a heavy worry.

For a moment, while he stood still, I was afraid he was ill.
Then when he spoke, his voice was full of energy. He had
just been promoted from major to lieutenant-colonel, but he
still wore his old overalls with a sweater sticking out under his
collar and his old major's insignias.

I think we were so happy to see each other that for a minute
or so, we actually forgot the war.

At last, Ignacio said, "I must work tonight, but now we can
have dinner, alone, and we will talk."

We had our coffee in the lobby. The place had the air of a
family encampment. The wives of the Air Force officers sat in
rocking chairs, knitting. The children played on the floor. Foreign correspondents sat at little tables, drinking and talking.

French, German, Italian, English rose from corner tables all around the room—conversation of the international volunteers, exiles from fascist countries, young doctors, lawyers, workers, from the democratic countries, men who had come hundreds and thousands of miles to fight for democracy in Spain.

Next day, Ignacio, who could spare no time from his work, sent me to visit the hospitals newly moved to Albacete. I found conditions very bad. The town had a very poor water supply and almost no plumbing. The doctors and nurses were struggling with inadequate buildings and supplies. Ignacio had asked me to visit the wounded of the Air Force, and that night I said thoughtfully to him, "We need some sort of a convalescent home for the pilots. Some place where they could grow strong after the first weeks at a regular hospital."

Ignacio grinned. "I wouldn't want to ask you, darling. . . ." I had the plans made in my mind for a convalescent home that first day in Albacete.

And then, for forty-eight hours, everyone in Albacete forgot everything else but Madrid.

Madrid!

The Moors and the "blond Moors," as Franco called his German troops, and the Italians were at the very gates of the city. Fascists fought at the barricades the people of Madrid had built. The whole city rose. Every man, every woman, leaped to the defense of their native Madrid.

And then, in this critical hour, on November 6, 1936, as the fascist planes rose over the city, defenseless from the air, a miracle (or so it seemed to all of Spain) happened.

For flying with impossible speed, swift, deadly, fierce, came a squadron of new planes, planes of the Spanish Government. While all Madrid looked on choking with excitement, the Government planes fought off the fascists.

Ignacio told me about it first. His face shone like a child's. "Connie! One country at least understands our fight. They sold us planes!"

I could hardly believe his story. The planes Spain had bought from Russia arrived at Cartagena on November 2—in parts of course. The mechanics, working almost without stop for four solid days, had assembled a whole squadron of pursuit planes, enough to save the capital from the merciless bombing Franco planned to synchronize with his attack on the gates of the city.

"The people call them *Chatos,* the pug noses," Ignacio said, grinning.

And that night, November 7, I had dinner with the young Russian pilots who had just arrived. The Spanish aviators were almost delirious with joy. Planes! At last! Ignacio had been trying to build an Air Force out of thin air, trying to train men with no planes to fly with. Now there were planes to save Madrid from bombing, pilots to teach ours how to operate the new planes, mechanics to school our mechanics and help us in our factories.

The dinner started off with a joke. One of the Spanish aviators turned to me with great pride and said, "I have already learned a Russian word. Listen!" Then, carefully setting his lips, he said, "Pro-peller!"

He was most crestfallen when I explained that the word was English. Probably some early American engineer had taught it to the Russians.

But although we laughed, our dinner was not hilarious but very solemn. Ignacio made a little speech, only saying that the people of Madrid were dying tonight, dying with the words, *"No pasarán"* on their lips. He did not need, he said, to ask his men to make the same great sacrifice. He knew that they were always willing to give their lives for freedom. But now, more than ever, the Republic faced danger. The Russian pilots who had come as volunteers to help the people of Madrid were an heroic example.

"Viva la República!" Ignacio said quietly. *"No pasarán."*

"No pasarán," the men at the table answered solemnly.

Then everyone went back to the air field.

Next day, little Albacete was filled with the sound of marching men and hurrying crowds. The international volunteers were being assembled in Albacete and rushed to Madrid. They needed translators and I stood for hours, handing out trousers, a short jacket, a sweater, stockings. The young men who stood briefly before me getting their supplies touched my heart. They had come so far to help us. No government ordered them to fight—on the contrary, most of them had had to use subterfuge to get to Spain. They were not mercenaries—the pay was nothing, and besides they had jobs and wives and homes in their native lands.

But these men had come to help Spain fight for freedom. And the only thing they wanted in return was a beret! Even the most unromantic looking of the volunteers turned down the caps the Spanish soldiers wore for the berets they felt were Spanish!

On the next day the International Brigade, marching smartly through the capital, went to fill some of the gaps in the defense lines where the men of Madrid had fallen!

The people all over the world who loved democracy had helped Spain to save Madrid!

When my week came to an end, I felt I could not leave Ignacio. The week had been a tense and difficult one. Madrid had been nearly lost and then saved again. I had spent hours talking to some of the foreign journalists I knew; I felt I was in the very heart of the struggle to save Spain. And yet I knew I could not spend my time knitting in the hotel lobby. I had to work to help save Spain.

"Couldn't the convalescent home be here in Albacete?" I asked Ignacio.

But of course I knew it couldn't. And then we both had to face a question we had kept away from all week. What about Luli? I couldn't run a convalescent hospital and take care of my daughter too. I couldn't very well leave her in one of the children's colonies—not when every place was needed to evacuate the children of Madrid. If I left Alicante—and after all, my job there was temporary—I couldn't take her with me.

We faced the terrible question that people all over Spain faced—what about our children? The fascists leave parents no time to bring up their daughters.

"I suppose," I said slowly to Ignacio, "that she would have good food and a good school in Russia." For the Russian Government had offered to take any Spanish children whose parents wished to send them, to safety and good care near Moscow.

"Yes, you are right," he replied, but my heart ached to think of the miles of sea and land between Spain and the Soviet Union.

Back in Alicante, I almost forgot our decision to send Luli to Russia—I was so busy preparing for my first Air Force convalescents. I had to arrange for doctors and nurses and cooks, get metal beds made, coax the one remaining plumber in Alicante to defer leaving for the front until he put an extra bathroom into the house I had chosen. And then, just after I had welcomed our first patients, the word came to send Luli immediately to the harbor—a food ship was sailing to Odessa and Luli and Charito, another little girl, the daughter of an Air Force pilot who had died in the early days, were to sail at once.

It was December in Alicante, but the weather was still quite warm. Luli had no woolen clothes and indeed I did not know where I could buy any for her. Our soldiers had the warm cloth in Spain. Besides, to tell the truth, Ignacio and I had no money to buy anything with. Since July we had not thought of money. I was paid no salary, but I needed none—I had my food and housing, and nobody thought of fine clothes or luxuries in Spain of those days.

So Luli had no trunks to take with her for the long journey. Ignacio flew into Alicante in his little two seater, alone, to bid his beloved foster-daughter farewell. He could only stay an hour and was off again. I went with Luli to the ship. The stewardess showed us the cabin the crew had prepared for the two little Spanish girls. It was gaily decorated and the sailors had made some little toys. On the desk were two pictures of smiling Russian youngsters, about eight and nine, little girls. The pictures were decorated with flowers.

"They are my children," the stewardess said, "and I put their pictures in the cabin, so that Luli and Charito will not be lonely for their playmates."

I kept saying to myself that I must not cry. No tears. Luli must not feel the separation is hard or the journey a tragic one. She must think it is a gay adventure, a wonderful trip to a faraway land.

I walked to the gangplank, Luli trotting along beside me. Charito's mother was speaking with careful casualness to her small daughter.

"Good-by," I managed to say to Luli, and kissed her on her forehead.

"*Salud!*" Luli replied.

There were no tears.

Her first letter, mailed from Odessa, was a diary of her trip on the Soviet ship. There were "three couples of eggs" every morning for breakfast, and the sailors played the gramophone and told Luli and Charito stories, and everybody on the ship loved Spain, and especially Spanish children.

The letter made Christmas easier. We had a party for our convalescents and our children, with a real Christmas tree and roast lamb that our Paco had somehow—we didn't like to ask how—wangled.

Christmas marked an ending and a beginning for me. The convalescent home was running smoothly. The children's colonies operated in careful routine. I was beginning to feel restless when one day I happened to be at the Alicante airport as a group of British Members of Parliament were embarking for Toulouse and Paris. They were having all sorts of trouble with their luggage and I helped out with a little routine translation. The plane was delayed and we fell into a long conversation.

These British gentlemen were obviously feeling very heroic. They had been through several bombardments in Madrid, and one of them said, not without modest hesitation, "Imagine, when we saw the *Chatos* we almost applauded. Indeed, I may say—between us only, you understand—we *did* applaud. Imagine!"

"Why not?" I said blankly.

"Well, of course they were sold to you by the Russians!"

I looked at him with amazement. "And why not?" I said again, "We are a legal Government putting down a rebellion—a fascist rebellion."

The gentleman spluttered. "Ah, yes, well—even so, if it were known in London we applauded the *Chatos!*"

"You think the English people would not applaud saving the lives of women and children of Madrid?"

The M.P. was disgusted with me. "Of course they would. But they were *Russian* planes."

"Then why doesn't your country sell us planes?" I asked.

That ended my conversation with M.P. number one. Now I was interested however, and I tackled some others. I discovered that these distinguished gentlemen had come all the way to Madrid—Madrid, the city of embattled democracy, Madrid, fighting off international fascism—to see if the fascist prisoners were mistreated!

It appeared that they had been more or less satisfied. The prisoners were treated well enough, although the food was very poor. Almost as poor, I discovered in asking them about it, as the food our own people ate.

"Of course we do realize the difficulties," one broadminded M.P. told me, "and the feeling of the people for those who sided with the Nationalists—naturally they feel the prisoners ought not to get better food than they do. Nevertheless, we were given guarantees that the food for the Nationalist prisoners would be improved."

I was never so astonished in my life. Why should we guarantee better food for the fascists than for our own? And what was all this about the "Nationalists"?

"Where did the word come from?" I asked. They said it was generally used in the British press—I suppose some bright young man in the British Foreign Office thought it up. "Nationalists" indeed! A fine name for a handful of generals who gave a Spanish front to an Italian and German invasion of Spain.

I found the British M.P.'s thoroughly infuriating. But I tried to be polite and explain, and before they left a Liberal M.P. Mr. Wilfred Roberts gave me his card and said, "I am sorry we did not meet you until now. Your English is so helpful and your explanations are most interesting."

I turned this over in my mind. My old friend, Jay Allen, had told me something of the same kind. "Connie, you should be in the Press Office," he said once, during a hasty luncheon in Alicante. "You speak too many languages to take care of children during a war."

Now, at Christmas time, I felt my job with the children and the convalescents was nearly finished. The Albertis, Rafael and Maria Teresa, came to drive me to see Ignacio for New Year's, and they too thought I should be using the only special knowledge I really had—languages and foreign countries. We talked about it all the way to the Army encampment where the Albertis were to speak that night.

I forgot the idea of my new job in the enthusiasm I felt for our host for the evening, Commander Juan Modesto. I had heard from Ignacio the whole story of the need to form a real People's Army, disciplined and trained. Now Modesto, one of the leaders of the famous "Fifth Regiment," was forming and training a new brigade. He was the first military leader I had met who belonged to the people—a man developed in the war against fascism. Unlike the Army officers I had known all my life, he was quiet, modest, jolly, and absolutely adored by his troops.

Modesto's brigade filled the Albertis and me with hope and excitement that night. For he had managed to combine the spirit of the first July days with the discipline of a trained Army. The men knew for what they were fighting and how to go about it. The officers, dressed like the men except for their insignia, were regarded as the technicians of the Army, not superior socially, not singled out for better food or special privileges, but only given the responsibility of leadership.

A few days after I returned from Albacete. Anna Louise Strong, an American writer who had lived for many years in the Soviet Union, called me on the telephone from Valencia. "I'm just back from Moscow," she said; "come down and let me tell you about Luli."

I couldn't resist hearing news from Luli and besides, the hospital and the children's colonies were running smoothly. Valencia had become the seat of the Government since early in November when the enemy approached the gates of Madrid— for it would have been useless to attempt carrying on the administration of the country under shell fire. I met Anna in Valencia and I am afraid that the first thing I asked her was: "Does Luli have warm clothes?" I had been haunted, in the midst of all the tragedies and tenseness of the war, by the picture of my daughter walking about the snow-covered streets of Russia in her light Summer clothes!

Anna laughed. "You should see her. She is wearing a gray squirrel coat down to her ankles and a fur hat and fur gloves besides. She looks like a miniature North Pole explorer."

I breathed a sigh of relief and settled down to listen. Luli and Charito were staying with Russian people, learning Russian and waiting for the rest of the Spanish children to come to Moscow. Plans were being made for an all-Spanish school. The youngsters would have Spanish teachers and Spanish lessons, exactly as they would have in their own country. In the meantime, Luli and Charito were the pets of every Russian who met them.

"She's having a marvelous time," Anna assured me, "she's healthy and happy and looked after by people who love her because she is Spanish and because she is Luli."

I felt my heart grow light for a moment.

While I was in Valencia I discovered we already had a Foreign Press Bureau, part of the Ministry of Foreign Affairs. Alvarez del Vayo, the Foreign Minister, and his wife, I already knew.

"You can really be of use in the Foreign Press Bureau, Connie," Señora del Vayo told me.

Next morning I started off to call on Rubio Hidalgo, Chief Censor and head of the Foreign Press Bureau. I found the address with some difficulty. The Foreign Press Bureau occupied a very old and dilapidated mansion. The offices themselves were up three flights of old wooden stairs, a suite of barn-like rooms with floors littered with papers, walls grim with peeling paint, old tables and chairs covered with torn posters, carbon paper, copies of Polish, Swiss, German, British, and French newspapers.

Half a dozen clerks scurried around in the mailing room, aimlessly picking at first a sheet of mimeographing paper, then a file-index. The foreign correspondents sat, when expecting their telephone calls from abroad, in an adjoining waiting room on an ancient high-backed sofa. Typewriters occupied the other overstuffed armchairs and tables and piles of discarded copy paper indicated that somebody used these typewriters frequently.

I began to feel timid and self-conscious as I settled down to wait for my interview. A beautiful young lady whom the reporters standing around the room addressed as "Gladys" made me feel very conscious of my clothes. For months I had lived in an old skiing jacket, a tweed skirt, some walking shoes, and a cotton blouse. Somehow I had stopped thinking about clothes the day the rebellion broke out. Now, as I sized up "Gladys," I felt a wave of admiration for her simple, very fashionable clothes—and a wave of apology for my own. The journalists, too, frightened me a little. Of course I had known many foreign correspondents in Madrid and Rome, but never professionally—always as friends.

Now I listened to the chatter of these reporters and felt baffled at the strange phrases.

"It's censored and they're asking for my call," one man sang out as he dashed through a door into the waiting room.

"My first take has gone through, but they're holding up my lead-all bulletin," somebody else told Gladys.

I felt much upset. I thought I knew English practically as well as my native tongue—but I had hardly heard a familiar word in fifteen minutes as I sat in that anteroom. These reporters apparently spoke a special jargon. It was all very baffling.

Then I was ushered in to meet Rubio Hidalgo, and I promptly felt much worse.

Señor Rubio—Don Luis as some of his faithful employees called him—lived like a mole in the middle of the Foreign Press Bureau. His office was practically pitch-dark. All the shades were drawn. The only daylight leaked in from cracks in the door. A shaded dim desk light made an eerie pool of green in the gloom.

In the midst of this darkness sat Señor Rubio, partly bald,

with a tiny mustache, pasty-colored face, and dark glasses. Dark glasses in the midst of the gloom!

"Do you know anything about journalism?" Señor Rubio began suddenly.

I felt myself growing hot with anger in the middle of the darkness. I gathered that Señor Rubio thought I was only trying to get a soft wartime job. He believed, I think, that I was only attempting to escape from the hospital and children's work in Alicante. At least he made it quite clear that a knowledge of languages was comparatively nothing in the foreign press work.

Finally, I noted what I took to be an expression of extreme disgust behind the dark glasses. "You can read these articles," he said glumly, handing me some manuscript, "at your house and bring them tomorrow ready to send off."

I had no idea of what he meant by "reading" the typed stories he gave me, but I was determined not to ask. I spent all of the rest of the day, until long after midnight, re-writing and polishing and improving the articles he had given me—both interviews with the only woman member of the cabinet, the Minister of Health.

Next morning, back in Señor Rubio's dim office, I was surprised to find he had just been "testing" me. I wasn't supposed to re-write the articles; just censor them for any military information, and so on. But before my anger could flare up, I was assigned to a desk in the outer office—a desk that had to be specially fitted for my long legs.

And then I settled down to be a "censor." I was supposed to sit in the office six hours a day, waiting for newspapermen to bring in their copy. My job was to look it over, and if it was approved, to let them send it either by cable—we had a crew of messenger boys waiting to rush copy to the cable office —or by telephone. The newspapermen telephoned their London and Paris offices all day long, and could call any foreign country except Germany and Italy from our booths. At night the Tass News Agency men used to call Moscow.

But for the first few days, unfortunately, I was ignored by everybody and had nothing at all to do—which made me terribly unhappy. There were three other censors, all men, two foreigners and one Spaniard. Then my Spanish colleague came over one day and offered to help me.

"It's very easy," he explained kindly. "The newspapermen can say anything they want to as long as it is true and as long as that truth is not giving information to the enemy."

I thought his words over carefully and began to feel more confident.

"We must naturally be careful about military information," he went on. "Things which the correspondents will consider trivial and of no military importance if allowed to pass can sometimes become precious information when read by the fascist. If they complain about this, remind them of the censorship during the World War."

I nodded. "As a matter of fact," he went on, "I personally think we are much too lenient with letting military details go by in their dispatches."

"But what about things not of a military nature?" I asked.

My teacher laughed. "You use your own judgment. But don't be frightened. It's pretty easy, really. The newspaperman brings you his copy. The first thing you must do is to make sure that what you are reading is perfectly clear, that it makes sense, that you know all the words. In other words, make sure the man is not writing code. After that, if it deals with ordinary news of a political nature, make sure it is true, not a wild rumor—a rumor allowed to go through a Government censorship is accepted as fact. This is very important and you will have to explain it over and over again to the reporters who will try over and over again to send through what they call 'dope' stories, articles based on their own feverish imagination or the wildest kind of café rumor."

"I see," I said slowly.

"One more thing. Some news of political nature is really of military importance. Anything that would strengthen the enemy's military position—a political dispute, for instance, as to whether we should press forward on this or that front—is out."

I gulped. This was a large order. I began to worry about the terrible moment when I would be actually faced with my first newspaper dispatch.

Fortunately I drew Burnett Bollotten, the United Press correspondent, for my first client. He was a hard-working, very keen, honest reporter, head and shoulders above the men who afterwards replaced him in the same bureau when he was transferred. But Bollotten was most absent-minded, for which I could only thank my stars. For I picked up his copy with fear, and lest he observe my embarrassment, I retreated to my desk in the inner room where I read and re-read it ten times, to make sure it was really only a very matter-of-fact piece of reporting.

When I finally returned, he was buried in a newspaper. He apparently hadn't noticed anything strange in the behavior of the new censor, the only Spanish woman with such a job. I put through his call to Paris with trembling hand. The operator answered quickly. I called him to the little booth newspapermen used for their telephone work, while I listened in from the desk. There was nothing secret about this, no eavesdropping. The newspapermen knew their conversations were being checked by the censor, to make sure they did not deviate from the copy already approved. We had a little key to pull down if we heard words which did not appear on the duplicate copy of the article we kept before us. With many of the correspondents we did not need to listen in on our phone—their howls could be heard practically all the way to London or Paris. The monotone of others was nearly as painful. The hours I have spent listening to some reporter chant: "Teruel. T for Tom. E for Ernest. R for Robert. . . ." And so on, for one thousand words of an article.

But on that first telephone call, I was hardly capable of listening and checking the copy at the same time, I was so frightened. When at last Bollotten hung up, I rushed out to the booth and found myself thanking him with a trembling voice. He looked slightly amazed and started to thank me, and finally we forgot the whole thing in a long conversation about Spain.

I found, as I settled down to my work and became more familiar with it, certain patterns emerging. Our office was overrun with well-meaning foreigners of distinguished reputation who had come to help us counteract the campaign of lies and slander the British Foreign Office and the Nazis were spreading about the Spanish Government. Actually, we needed no outside advice. We had decided, and properly so, that the only weapon we had against the lies told abroad about our Government was the truth. And the best way of getting the truth known was to give foreign correspondents every opportunity we could to see the truth, and then every facility possible for writing it and getting it sent abroad. Then we could hope the foreign newspapers would print what their reporters sent.

This sounds like a simple process but when I got my job, the Foreign Press Bureau was only just beginning to go about it correctly. For in the first days of the rebellion, some reporters, just because they were foreigners, were allowed to go about anywhere with the greatest of freedom. Spanish hospitality cost the Republic dearly. Mr. William Carney, the correspondent for the *New York Times* in Madrid, was allowed to travel about freely, for instance, although he was known to have fascist sympathies and fascist friends. Mr. Carney's curiosity took him to strange places and when he left Madrid for Paris, he wrote a series of articles giving the exact details of gun emplacements around Madrid, and so on. I myself have seen a pamphlet reprinting these damaging articles. How many hundreds of Spaniards fell by reason of his "uncensored" articles we can never know. Mr. Carney received later a fine fascist uniform.

This matter of Carney's articles was the subject of lively conversation among the foreign military attachés in Valencia; they severely questioned the wisdom of the Government's having given Carney such freedom of action. Mr. Carney's "impartiality" was further revealed long afterwards, when he signed a letter to the Primate of Spain congratulating the fascists on "their glorious victory."

The Carney episode brought its inevitable reaction. The Press Bureau placed foolish restrictions on honest reporters for a time, and when I arrived, the Government was just beginning to strike a sensible balance in its treatment of the foreign press. I realized at once that there was no need for reporters to know any more about gun emplacements, projected offensives, or the like than the rest of the population. On the other hand, we ought to make it as easy as we possibly could, in the midst of our own difficulties, for the correspondents to work.

Rubio was certainly, I gathered very quickly, not the ideal contact man for the foreign journalists. In the first place, perhaps because he had been a newspaperman himself for years, he hated all reporters, French, American, British, Swedish, or Russian. Next, although he read English perfectly—and rapidly—he really did not understand one word the American correspondents, with their Kansas rather than Oxford accents, and their journalese slang, said.

So he decided to keep all the correspondents at arm's length. His gloomy office, his strange forbidding manner, was all part of a scheme to discourage questions and requests for interviews with Government officials and demands for passes to Madrid or Barcelona or to the various fronts. The censors' relations with the press were rather formal—all they thought they could do was to pass on the requests the newspapermen made for information or help to Rubio. And Rubio usually promptly forgot the whole thing. As a result, newspapermen would wait for two days to get a permit they could easily have been given in two hours. Reporters idled for days on end in the waiting room, while Rubio kept on his desk their request for a car in which to travel to the front.

I felt this situation would not keep up. The irritated newspapermen began to write about "Spanish inefficiency" in their dispatches. Rubio's rudeness was reflected most inaccurately in the tone of the articles I had to censor.

Cautiously I approached Valentin, Rubio's assistant. I suggested that maybe—perhaps—it would be possible to help the newspapermen a little more. Why not? They could help us win the war by telling the truth, but we had to make it possible for them to learn the truth before they could write it. Wasn't it so?

So gradually we began to be more polite to the newspaper-men. Rubio was delighted to be spared the necessity of seeing the foreign journalists. We began to find rooms for the correspondents in over-crowded Valencia, ring up and arrange interviews with busy Government officials. We arranged more space in our office for the regular newspapermen to work.

As time went on, I came to know most of the regular correspondents in Spain exceedingly well. I knew their habits, their tempers, their styles, and their abilities.

I think I should say at the very outset of this that none of the good correspondents suffered from Richard Harding Davis overtones. Now and then some new agency man—sent, as is the wont of news agencies, direct from the police beat in Hoboken, fancied himself a Knight of the Typewriter. But most of the regular correspondents, particularly the staff men of the greater newspapers, were able, hard-working men who spent days chasing down facts on their own, complained about the food (as we all did), and sat in their hotels in Madrid, Valencia and Barcelona talking about the things that newspapermen talk about everywhere—gossip and politics.

I knew, as all of us did—that the cause of the Republic depended on the world knowing the facts. Consider how we were maligned at the outset of the war and how later on, as the tragic months wore by, understanding began to dawn even among the most unlikely people. We wanted the facts to be printed—all of them—not only those disagreeable to us. It is not easy to get the simple facts into print as newspaper readers must realize now that Hitler and Mussolini have admitted their participation in the Spanish war—participation the news of which responsible newspaper editors for months scorned to print on the grounds that it was "loyalist propaganda."

At first, I was not a little puzzled at the way correspondents shied at simple facts that were presented to them to make their work easier. I soon came to take into account this healthy, though sometimes paralyzing, fear of "propaganda" that is a part of every good reporter's nature. And so I accented my work towards helping them to find out facts for themselves by giving them whatever facilities we could scrape together for their work. Passes to the front, of course. Cars whenever we could get them. Gasoline for those who had cars.

Herbert Matthews, the correspondent of the *New York Times,* was one of the most familiar figures in our office. Tall, lean, and lanky, Matthews was one of the shyest, most diffident men in Spain. He used to come in every evening, always dressed in his gray flannels, after arduous and dangerous trips to the front, to telephone his story to Paris, whence it was cabled to New York. Like his colleague of the *New York Times,* Lawrence Fernsworth, who had lived in Barcelona for a decade and knew Catalonia as few foreigners alive, Matthews was at first exceedingly suspicious of me and of the Foreign Press Bureau. For months he would not come near us except to telephone his stories—for fear, I suppose, that we might influence him somehow. He was so careful; he used to spend days tracking down some simple fact—how many churches in such and such a small town; what the Government's agricultural program was achieving in this or that region. Finally, when he discovered that we never tried to volunteer any information, even to the point of not offering him the latest press release unless he specifically requested it, he relaxed a little.

Matthews had his own car and he used to drive to the front more often than almost any other reporter. We had to sell him the gasoline from our own restricted stores, and he was always running out of his monthly quota. Then he used to come to my desk, very shy, to beg for more. And we always tried to find it for him: both because we liked and respected him and because we did not want the *New York Times* correspondent to lack gasoline to check the truth of our latest news bulletin.

I came to admire terribly this passion for fact. I was irritated at first, I suppose, not to find myself believed. But I came to see that this, after all, was the way to get the facts into print, to have the men who sent them convinced of their accuracy because they themselves had got them. I have to smile when I hear stories of how we "influenced" the foreign correspondents! And now, of course, as one looks back over their coverage, one sees that if they erred it was on the side of understatement. Just as our Republican "propaganda" was pitched far too low, as we now see since the dictators have seen fit to reveal how they tricked the democracies.

A great favorite in the Foreign Press Bureau was Ernest Hemingway. He knew Spain very well, knew it and felt it perhaps more than any other correspondent.

Sometimes I used to think that he loved it for the wrong reasons, or at least for reasons which seemed very strange to me, but at any rate he loved it and understood it when the war came.

He too had his own car, and I think he got gasoline more quickly than any other correspondent, for all the girl secretaries in my office adored him and as soon as he walked up the stairs and opened the door, they would scurry around to find him permits and gasoline slips.

Of course, as Hemingway became a friend of ours, we used to have great arguments—especially about bull-fighting. I, like many Spaniards, have always loathed bull-fights. The people of Spain were brought up, in a world dominated by the landlords and feudal aristocrats, to find release from their hard and tragic lives in the drama of death and futility set forth so clearly in the bull-ring.

With the beginning of the war, bull-fights vanished by common consent in Government Spain. True, we needed the animals we had for food and the bull-fighters all went to war—there was a battalion of them at the outset. But it was more than that. The Spanish people now faced the future with hope. They were in love with life, not death. The bull-fight went out of the pattern of our existence. We no longer needed to forget our hopeless existence watching the matador—for we believed in the future.

We all liked Hemingway enormously—and everyone in the Foreign Press Bureau disliked and distrusted Sefton Delmer, whose car Hemingway sometimes used, when he left his own in Paris. Delmer was the correspondent for the London *Daily Express*. During part of his stay in Spain he pretended to be sympathetic to the Government, a piece of fiction he dropped when he went home to London. He would always appear in my office in ancient ragged clothes, dirty shirts, mud-caked shoes, trousers stiff with grease. We considered his strange clothing an insult for we knew that in London he was something of a dandy. Madrid, Valencia, and Barcelona were perfectly civilized cities —even if they were Spanish. Delmer always talked and behaved as though the Spanish people were some strange, benighted tribe of savages engaged in a rather silly, primitive type of bow-and-arrow contest. He was one of those Englishmen who consider any other race inferior and he had not even the grace to blush for what his Government was doing to Spain.

There were a few hard-working correspondents who never got much attention, which sometimes happens when men are so competent. There was Henry Buckley of the London *Daily Telegraph* and the *Chicago Tribune*. The others called him Enrique. He was a little sandy-haired man, with a shy face and a little tic at the corner of the mouth which gave his dry humor a sardonic twist. He knew Spain inside out from years of work and study there. He once told me that he had come to Spain as a salesman for some commercial firm and later on, in the early thirties, had gone to work for Jay Allen and the *Chicago Tribune*. He had lived the war from the very outset, Madrid, Valencia, Barcelona. His dispatches appeared under a Valencia dateline—his stories always carefully described the Spanish Government as mildly liberal. But the editorials in the same edition of the paper called the Spanish Government "communist" and the fascists "religious crusaders." It was a case of the left hand knowing not what the right hand doeth. I shall never forget how amused we were to hear that when he went out on his first vacation—to Lausanne, I think it was—he woke up the first morning in that smug Swiss picture-postcard setting to the sound of gunfire. His hotel, it seems, was next to the rifle range.

I never get over how little such men made. Buckley worked on some minuscular arrangement for the "World's Greatest Newspaper," as I believe the *Chicago Tribune* is called. With the *New York Times,* Lawrence Fernsworth had some strange contract by which they paid him on space. He began work at dawn, often driving hours to the front and back, then walking through dark streets to our Bureau to telephone his stories and so home again late at night. In one month of such work I am told that he made $90! This was apparently because the *New York Times* was inhibited about giving him free rein. His stories were under fire. The reason is obvious; Fernsworth, a devout Catholic, had been correspondent of the Jesuit weekly *America,* and his former employers never quite forgave him for insisting on covering the simple facts of the war instead of adopting their "line."

Few reporters stayed in Spain throughout the entire war, and many of the best newspapermen returned to their native countries to work brilliantly and passionately for the Spanish cause.

In Valencia, for instance, we all felt a great debt to Jay Allen, the American correspondent. He knew Spain as few Americans ever did. He was in Spain when the war broke out, and he was the first correspondent to interview General Franco when that worthy was an unknown, internationally at least. Jay Allen took real risks—few correspondents are actually in danger of their lives, but he most certainly was—to report in detail the horrible slaughter at Badajoz. After that he could not return to Franco Spain. His background knowledge of Spain helped him to aid our cause in New York, and he was always welcomed in Valencia and Barcelona on the short trips he made during the war.

Leland Stowe of the *New York Herald Tribune* came to Spain on his vacations. He too had an intimate knowledge of Spain and we could never understand why his paper would not send him to cover the war. His information on Spanish history alone would have made him invaluable to his paper.

Albert Rhys Williams, a delightful person and a good friend, was in Barcelona during the terrible March bombings. I watched him asking everyone and anyone he met those days, "What do you feel during the bombings?" "What are your emotions?" I decided finally that he must be preparing an article on the subject—"What Men Think of During a Bombardment," or something of that kind. Finally I asked him when the story would be finished, as I was curious to see it.

"Oh, I was just asking to see if they were as scared as I was," he replied.

Williams, perhaps more than any other person, helped to organize protests against the bombardments.

William Forrest of the London *News Chronicle* was, I always thought, one of the best all-around correspondents covering the war. He had a fine Scotch sense of humor, which turned up at the most difficult moments. I never saw him flustered or worried. I never heard him complain. Bombardments never gave him the jitters, defeats never shook his faith in the Spanish people. He knew Spain intimately and used his knowledge to give his dispatches an informative and understanding tone few reporters achieved. He moved slowly and silently around Valencia and Barcelona, apparently never in a hurry, never worried. Yet his dispatches were always on time and they always covered more facts than many reporters who stirred up lots of dust and trouble and got nothing for their pains.

During the early months in Valencia the *New York Herald Tribune* was represented by one of the best reporters covering the war, Don Minifie. For although George Seldes came about that time and did a splendid series of articles explaining the real causes of the war for the *New York Post,* he stayed only a short time, and Minifie's regular dispatches were among the few others which were really illuminating. But Minifie was a Canadian and the British Foreign Office put pressure on his paper to withdraw him. Minifie's dispatches were too clear to suit the gentlemen in London.

Perhaps the greatest competitor Herbert Matthews had in the number of his visits to the fronts was Joe North, the American *Daily Worker* correspondent. His paper could not afford a car as the *New York Times* and most of the other big newspapers did, but North always contrived to get lifts to the front, for he was extremely popular among all the other correspondents.

Vincent Sheean came to Spain for the first time during the war in 1938. The *New York Herald Tribune* sent him after they had been without a regular correspondent for quite a long time. He also became a familiar and greatly admired figure very soon. He returned to Spain a second time with his wife, Diana Forbes Robertson, an Englishwoman by birth. She was one of the most charming people who came to Spain during the entire war; we became very close friends. Mrs. Sheean was not afraid to accompany her husband to Spain every time she could; moreover, when she returned to England and later in the United States, she gave most of her time to work on behalf of the Spanish children.

Two other journalists with whom I grew to be warm friends during the war were Claud Cockburn and his wife, Jean Ross, who went with Richard Mowrer and me on our trip to Andújar. Claud was one of the many first-rate men and writers of all nationalities who came to Spain to report the war and after a very short time took part in our struggle, since they could not see the injustice done by their own governments towards the Spanish people and remain unmoved.

At about this same time, I began to see many of the visitors who came to Spain for reasons other than that of news gathering. I decided it cost me nothing to be amiable and helpful— and it might do Spain a great deal of good. Of course, I learned to take great precautions. Credentials had to be checked carefully. Sometimes I discovered a person of great importance— then we put cars at his disposal and outdid ourselves to be kind. More often I discovered our visitors were simply "war tourists." For, as time went on, we began to suffer more and more from this curse of sensation seekers, I had to put a careful check on my feelings. For I felt it simply monstrous that some people could come to Spain only to watch us die.

The stream of visitors kept increasing. We had politicians who wanted to curry favor with voters at home, and politicians who came to gawk at a suffering people and went home to fight our battles. We had writers and poets who came for inspiration and to find the truth; and writers and poets who came because at one time it was distinctly unfashionable in literary circles not to have visited Spain. I do not mean to say that most of the people who came to Spain did not come because they wanted to help us. Most of the stream of people who went through my office were honest men and women who worked hard and bravely for us in their own countries after they went home. Spain owes its foreign friends a debt it can never repay.

There was, for example, Dorothy Parker, dark-haired, small, and charming, who came to Spain with her husband, Alan Campbell. They, like nearly all my visitors that Fall, brought a lift to our hearts. They realized the difficult situation in Spain, wanted few favors, asked intelligent questions and behaved exceedingly well under trying circumstances. And they understood. Perhaps it takes first-rate people to understand simple values and obvious facts. David Lasser, the head of the Workers' Alliance in the United States, Sherwood Eddy, Herman Reissig, Lillian Hellman, and Leo Gallagher, the great American lawyer, all came about the same time.

We arranged a trip for our visitors from Valencia to the Madrid front. John Stuart and Bruce Minton, in Spain to collect material for a book and do special correspondence, went with Dorothy Parker and Alan Campbell to Madrid, and others followed shortly afterwards. Nearly all our visitors in the Fall of 1937 were impressed by the schools the Minister of Education had started in the trenches. I think Americans are especially touched and interested by education—they seemed to universally feel that a nation which has cut its illiteracy rate in wartime is a nation that has proved itself worthy to endure.

I had known Elliott Paul in 1932 when he lived at Ibiza. He was collecting material for a book on the life of a Spanish town; he did not then know that death would visit that same town four years later. I had met him at Jay Allen's home in the capital. When he came to Valencia in the Spring of 1937, he stopped in to see me immediately, his eyes twinkling, his short little beard jutting out. I sent my dear Coco to Madrid with him. I should explain that although Coco was only sixteen years old and thus under fighting age (although he often lied about his age and tried, in vain, to volunteer), he was one of the best guides I had on my staff. He spoke English fluently, for he had lived in America many years, and besides he was one of the most intelligent, able, and sweet-tempered boys I have ever known. We were all very fond of our Coco and it was a very special favor that Elliott Paul had him for his guide.

When Elliott returned from Madrid, he stopped in to tell me a strange story. He too had grown to like Coco immensely. He didn't know the boy's last name, but they became great friends and used to sit up late nights discussing the war and politics and literature and life in general. One night Paul began to talk about a writer he knew—John Dos Passos. Dos Passos had visited Spain a few days before Elliott Paul came to my office. His time in Spain was very brief and he left suddenly. I felt that he had hardly stayed long enough to understand the war, but we could not do more than we did for him.

"I don't know what has come over Dos Passos," Elliott Paul said to Coco one night. "I saw him in Paris and he won't even take an interest in Spain any more—says he doesn't care. He is full of some story about a friend of his being shot as a spy, some college professor from Johns Hopkins."

Coco regarded Elliott Paul gravely, his great black eyes unwavering. "I hope that will not make Mr. Dos Passos lose his interest in the fight against fascism in Spain. The man he spoke of was my father."

Elliott Paul asked me, "Is Coco the exception in his family? I never saw such sadness—and such firmness."

I told him no. Coco's sister worked without stop in the youth movement and during the last days in Barcelona when everyone had gone to the front, Coco's mother came to the office and with her knowledge of English was very useful. What John Dos Passos could not forgive the Spanish people, the man's wife and two children understood.

Congressmen Jerry O'Connell and John T. Bernard came to Valencia in 1937, too, with the charming and beautiful Mrs. O'Connell. They visited the fronts and the American volunteers at Albacete, and the soldiers were deeply pleased to see that such a lovely young woman was interested in the struggle for democracy. Martha Gellhorn, the American correspondent and reporter, always had the same effect on her frequent trips to the front. The soldiers loved to see her coming, her slacks setting off her slim figure, her fair hair, so unusual in Spain, blowing in the wind. She was one of those women, rare in any country, who managed to do a man's job well and at the same time look as lovely as a debutante. I never failed to marvel at Martha's clothes, always simple, to be sure, but always fresh and immaculate and charming—in the middle of a war.

The Congressmen and Mrs. O'Connell wanted to meet Pasionaria and I went with them all to visit a children's home. I think the American Congressmen were deeply moved to see our great political leader welcomed so passionately by the children and to observe her tender love for the young orphans of the war.

Josephine Herbst came when we were still in Valencia. She was specially interested in the people. I remember taking her to a big mass meeting on a Sunday morning. Pasionaria was one of the speakers and Jo Herbst seemed very impressed by the great love that Dolores Ibarruri inspired in her audience.

The Foreign Press Bureau liked the Americans who visited during those months. They came without fanfare; they stayed long enough to see what the war was about. They were modest and easy to get along with. They tried to bring their own food so that they would not consume our dwindling supplies. They did not linger to take up our time after they had learned what they wanted to know. And when they left, they usually told the truth of what they saw.

Naturally, there were a few visitors of another kind, notably those who came to Spain for personal publicity. I never failed to be amazed—and filled with deep anger—to find people who tried to utilize the terrible agony of the Spanish people for some cheap publicity trick.

I shall never forget, for instance, a tall handsome Hollywood movie star, Mr. Errol Flynn. He came into the Press Office at a moment when we were harrowingly busy, demanded a motor car, permits, passes, guides, and the like, to go to Madrid. We were very short of gasoline, every drop counted. The regular correspondents were trying to defer their business trips until we got a new supply of petrol. But Mr. Errol Flynn could not wait; his time was too valuable.

So he departed for Madrid with our precious gasoline in his

tanks. Two days later the Paris papers reported that he had been wounded at the Madrid front. We wired frantically—and innocently—to Madrid, wanting to know what hospital he had been taken to, how seriously he was injured. In Madrid our Foreign Office people combed the whole town looking for the dying Mr. Flynn. We spent hours furiously informing our guides in Madrid that the next time our orders were disobeyed and a visitor allowed within shooting distance of the front, we would fire them all. They roared back denials. They never saw this Mr. Errol Flynn, the movie star. And then just as we had decided that our Hollywood visitor must be lying in some morgue, one of the big news agency men drifted into the office.

"What's all the excitement?" he said casually to the wild-eyed censors who had been working long past hours trying to get to the bottom of the Errol Flynn business. "Your Hollywood friend isn't really hurt. Just a scratch with a penknife on his arm, or something like that. Just to fix it so that we could plant a story in Paris about it."

Fortunately for Mr. Errol Flynn, he did not visit the censors' office on his way back through Valencia. We would have really liked to have told him our opinion of his conduct, conduct peculiar under any circumstances, but most remarkable, if that is the word, at a time when men were dying for liberty all around him.

Of course, it is hardly fair to mention Errol Flynn without adding that other Hollywood stars worked earnestly and bravely for Spanish democracy. Many a Spaniard lives today because an ambulance, supplied by funds from Hollywood actors and actresses, was there to carry him from the front to the dressing station or the hospital operating room.

I had managed to move into a large double room with a bath at the Ripalda Hotel and when my working hours increased from six to sixteen I had my meals brought to the office. We still had rice at the hotel in those days—rice and horse or mule meat, a great luxury later on. I used to walk back to the hotel late at night, after a long day at the office, marveling that no policemen walked the darkened streets of Valencia. Even after the bombardments began in the harbor and the night and day were made hideous by the constant sound of bombs and sirens, I used to pick my way in perfect safety back to the hotel those pitch black nights.

I had been in Valencia a week or so when my phone rang one day. It was Ignacio! He was transferring his staff to Valencia and would I immediately have lunch with Prieto and him and a few other people?

I was so terribly pleased to be reunited with my husband I hardly noticed the first part of the lunch. I gradually woke up to my surroundings as I heard Ignacio speak heatedly to Prieto. Prieto had moved into a hideous Valencia house—the horrid gaudiness of the Victorian furnishings found in Valencia's houses of the rich is unequaled anywhere in the world, I think.

But the conversation over the luncheon table began to fascinate me more than the strange surroundings. Prieto had a certain weakness for false grandeur—and similarly, he was dazzled by the officers of the old Spanish Army, with their aristocratic traditions and high-sounding names. Unfortunately for Spain, many officers with very little faith in the Republic had been trapped, during the July days, by the collapse of the Rebel surprise attack. Rather than reveal their true sympathies, and so be shot by their men, they pretended to want to serve the Republic. Prieto believed the protestations of loyalty from these *señoritos*. And Ignacio did not.

Even, my husband argued, if these officers were really efficient—which most of them were not, for the Spanish Army had never been famous for its skilled officers—their doubtful loyalty made them poor officers for the People's Army. But Prieto could not be convinced. The luncheon ended with Ignacio temporarily defeated. Prieto meant to keep the old military caste Army officers. The decision was to cost us many lives and much suffering.

Ignacio and I settled down in the Ripalda Hotel. We both worked all day long and at night, too, but we tried to meet as often as we could for our late dinner. Afterwards, we both went back for a few hours' more work before bed. With my husband the Chief of the Air Force, and in Valencia with me,

I began to understand the military situation with great clarity and attention to detail.

Spain had morale, men, territory, and even money. But we lacked food. And we lacked guns, ammunition, gasoline, and airplanes—most especially airplanes. The *Chatos* and bombing planes we bought from Russia had to run the gauntlet of the Italian submarine blockade. After nearly nine months of the war, we were more poorly armed in comparison with the Italian and German invaders than we had been in September. For while we struggled to buy airplanes and supplies from the one country in the world that would sell them to the legal democratic Government—a country thousands of miles away, over hostile borders and enemy waters—General Franco had hundreds, not dozens, of brand-new fighting planes flown in daily from Italy and Germany. While we struggled to manufacture guns in our factories, so poorly equipped for the making of armaments, Franco had all the German and Italian cannons and guns he could possibly use.

"We are being blown out of our country by fascist guns," Ignacio would say gloomily over dinner.

The fall of Málaga, that dreadful tragedy, brought the foreign intervention home to every Spaniard. "We have written a glorious page at Málaga," General Mancini, Commander of the 15,000 Italian Army troops at Málaga wrote. The "glorious page" consisted of blowing hundreds and thousands of Spanish women and children to death, but, then, fascists have peculiar standards of "glory."

Málaga brought with it the slogan, "Out with the foreign invaders!" From this moment forward, every Spaniard understood the question was no longer one of a civil war, but rather the fight for independence.

And more. Spaniards woke up with a start to realize that the inefficient, badly officered Army of the first days was no longer enough. The fall of Málaga caused sharp criticism of the Republican generals who were supposed to defend it. An enormous public demonstration in Valencia the Sunday after the fall of Málaga brought huge crowds to the city, bearing the slogan: "A unified military command for the Army!" The brigades formed by trade unions and political parties were not enough. Spain needed an Army if it was to defend itself against the German and Italian invaders.

But Largo Caballero, Prime Minister and Minister of War, could not understand. The merest soldier, the most obscure peasant, realized that Spain must have—*must have*—an Army, a real Army. But Caballero looked out at the enormous Valencia demonstration, read of the similar demonstrations that Sunday in Madrid and other cities of the Republic—and decided that the people meant that *he* should be supreme head of the Army and single commander. It was like talking to a deaf man, signaling to a blind man.

For the Prime Minister whom we had welcomed with such hope in September, 1936, had proved himself a hopelessly ineffective leader by February 9, 1937, the day of the fall of Málaga. Surrounded by the slippery generals of the old military caste who dazzled him with their superficial knowledge of maxim-book military rules, advised by a corps of treacherous, boot-licking journalists, old Caballero had by this time succumbed entirely to his childish vanity. His narcissism had grown out of all reasonable proportions. He fancied himself a sort of modern Napoleon, Wellington, and George Washington all combined. He insisted on keeping in the Army the old regular officers who, he declared, knew more about military affairs than men trained in the ranks.

But now his generals had lost every battle. They had badly advised the Government, prevented the militia commanders from getting promotions.

The people clamored for a change that day in Valencia. "Out with the inefficient officers left over from the days of the Monarchy!" the people shouted. "Let only those officers who by their courage and loyalty have proved their desire to win the war remain!"

"One military command to plan and co-ordinate all military actions!"

"No more individual military actions!"

"Unified command in the Army!"

For six hours, half a million people marched carrying these

slogans written with huge letters on banners. Singing, chanting, cheering, they filled the streets of Valencia, streamed past the office of the Prime Minister. The demonstration was specific. The people knew exactly what they wanted.

And after it was all over, Caballero persuaded himself the whole gigantic parade was in his honor!

"He is really doddering—mad—insane," Ignacio groaned to me the next day.

And no measures were taken by the War Ministry for a generalized plan of action. The defense of Spain against a well-trained, heavily armed pair of foreign invaders had to be carried on, as always, by "individual initiative." The anarchists played cards in the trenches in Catalonia while the Madrid troops fought for their lives. The fascists could use all their airplanes in one sector to attack because there was no unified military command to order a military operation in the south while the troops were attacked in the north.

But the demand by the people for general mobilization was spontaneous and universal. Shopkeepers drilled after work and peasants practiced rifle shooting. The nation sprang to arms, in spite of Caballero. The Prime Minister was forced to recognize the wishes of the people, at least in some small respect. General José Miaja, Chief of the Madrid Defense Junta, was appointed Commander of the whole Central Zone, with Colonel Vincente Rojo as Chief of Staff. This was the first Army zone in Spain to have a unified Army command. No longer could brigades of one political party work at cross purposes to the brigades of another. No longer could supplies ear-marked for one battalion be deflected on the way by the commissary department of another sector of troops.

So far, so good. But Caballero, bowing to the demands of the people for a unified military command, left the Catalan, Northern Basque, and Southern Fronts untouched. Only the Central Zone was affected by the orders of February 28. And furthermore, Miaja and Rojo were both old-line officers, men who had grown up in the service of King Alfonso and Gil Robles. The people wanted the unified commands to go to the new military leaders who learned military tactics, not in a Monarchist school for aristocrats, but in actual combat in a people's war. Technical ability, the people said, was good, yes—but a general must be trusted. Had not this whole rebellion been started by generals?

But Caballero had yielded at least a little. And the first results of the new unified command were brilliant. The Jarama battle, where the American volunteers fought so bravely and effectively side by side with our newly trained Spanish troops, was a military success.

And then on March 8, the fascists began their greatest offensive of the war up to that time. The plan was easily understood. General Franco could not take Madrid. Very well. So he and his Moors and his Germans and Italians would try to cut communications between Madrid and Valencia by coming down the Saragossa road to Guadalajara.

When the battle began I was busy at the Press Bureau as usual. Ignacio was near the front, directing the operations of the Air Force. The newspapermen were full of what they called "feature" stories about the American volunteers at Jarama. They were somewhat inclined to overlook the fact that the Americans had numerically been very few compared to the Spanish troops at Jarama. In some of the dispatches it almost appeared as though the Americans had single-handed held back the enemy at Jarama. But I was inclined to be easy on my reporters—we were all so proud of the Americans who had come so far and fought so well for democracy. A little exaggeration was surely pardonable.

March 9 passed quietly.

March 10, I began to be worried. I knew the offensive was a big one. All our supplies and resources were concentrated on the winning of it.

March 11, I could not sleep. How could a battle last so long. Was it a defeat? No, no, it couldn't be. We *had* to have a victory.

On March 12, I went to the office, my eyes red from lack of sleep, my hands trembling with nervousness. No word from Guadalajara. The newspapermen were mostly at their hotels.

A few idled in the office, typing out articles on this or that political question.

The censor on duty called to me: "A long-distance telephone call for you. From the Chief of the Air Force."

I rushed into the telephone both, my knees nearly buckling under me. It must be very important for Ignacio to call me in the midst of a battle.

I heard his voice, hoarse from lack of sleep, loud over the noisy connection: "We have just had the first real victory of the war over the Italians!"

I felt like bursting into tears.

"We have defeated the Italian brigades completely. You can tell the newspapermen and they can send it. It is perfectly authentic. Today's victory is our victory over the Italians."

He rang off.

I dashed out of the booth to tell Rubio. A few seconds later the newspapermen hanging about the office were in a mad race to get their London and Paris offices. We had only two telephone wires abroad, and our correspondents had to line up to use them. I got on the wire to call the newspapermen at their hotels, as we always did in the case of a real news "break."

We were the first to have the news. Details came in rapidly. Our correspondents were filing their running stories of the battle even as Mussolini in Libya got the reports and started back posthaste for the Italian peninsula.

A great new wave of patriotism and hope swept the country. Our ill-trained, badly armed militiamen, fighting for the first time under a unified military command, had won the first victory of the war over the foreign invaders! Our patched-up Air Force, with its comparatively few airplanes, its remodeled transports, its newly trained pilots, had routed the finest brigades of the Italian Army. Spain would never bow to foreign invaders!

A few days after the victory, a great sackful of captured Italian army documents—orders of the day, letters, communications from the Italian Chief of Staff, etc.—was brought to our office. Our translators went to work to prepare the White Book the Spanish Government would present to the League of Nations

as absolute proof of the already completely public Italian intervention in Spain. The newspapermen were allowed to examine
the documents and given translations of them. Indeed, some of
the reporters took samples of the material, of which there was
an enormous amount, for souvenirs. All of the correspondents
filed complete stories describing these Italian documents.

And yet, even after all this, the offices in Paris or London of
the news agencies and newspaper bureaus continued to cable
their Madrid and Valencia correspondents: "Please prove
Italian troops are in Spain before mentioning them again in
dispatches. Do not be misled by Government propaganda."

The only "proof" we had were more than two hundred prisoners of war who spoke nothing but Italian, and thousands of
documents, written in Italian, seized at enemy headquarters.

Nevertheless, the international effect of Guadalajara was
enormous. Ignacio was in seventh heaven. "I told you the Italians are all bluff," he exulted to me when I finally saw him
again. "I always said so. With nothing at all in our hands, we
have made them run like hares."

He grinned. "Of course the rainstorm on the 11th made it
bad for their planes. Their air fields were flooded. We seized
the opportunity and brought out every plane we had in the
world, rainstorm or no rainstorm. I'll bet every military attaché
in Europe thinks we are getting new airplanes, lots of them—
and wondering why their spies haven't reported them. Well,
you know, we are still using those two old Potez that Malraux
brought over."

I blinked. "I wonder they held together at all," I said.

Ignacio chuckled. "And not only that. We used the old
Fokkers and Breguets that we had before the war. Yes, sir, we
used everything in Spain that had wings at Guadalajara and I
think some of the dead Italians died from shock instead of
bullets when they saw our bombers coming over. They were so
sure we only had ten airplanes which would still fly!"

Our correspondents had all left for the Guadalajara front in
automobiles, and the excitement at the Press Bureau over our
victory had hardly died down, when we got news from the

south of the Rebel offensive on the Pozoblanco sector. The Italians were moving on our coal, iron, lead, and mercury mines, hoping to recoup their loss of prestige at Guadalajara.

"General Government victory all along the line," the message to the Press Bureau read.

Richard Mowrer, correspondent from the *Chicago Daily News*, was sitting in the office, disconsolate at having arrived in Spain too late to accompany the other reporters on a tour of the Guadalajara front, when this bulletin came in.

"Cheer up, Mowrer," I said, showing him the message. "How would you like to go to Pozoblanco? It will be what you call a 'scoop.' Practically everybody else has gone north."

Mowrer was delighted. I offered a car to a few other reporters left in Valencia, too, but their offices in London and Paris would not let them go—either because they refused to pay the expensive premiums on insurance for reporters who went near the front, or because they momentarily, and in spite of everything the reporters cabled from Valencia, expected the "riots" and "street fighting" the Franco side was continually reporting in Government Spain.

How many times have I not read the incoming cable: "Burgos reports trouble Valencia. Please file." The reporter inevitably replied: "No disturbances here." To which the London office usually answered: "Please file 500 words discontent Spanish masses against Red Government." Sometimes the duel would go on, the reporter cabling furiously: "No discontent here except against Italian invasion of Spain," and the London office replying stubbornly: "Repeat. Please wire 500 words discontent Spanish masses against Red Government. New York requests."

So the handful of reporters left in Valencia had to stay on to cover the uprising against the Government their London and New York offices hopefully expected every day, and Mowrer and I and Jean Ross, a clever and charming Englishwoman working at that time for the Government news agency in Paris and London, started off in an automobile for the southern front.

Our first stop was at Alicante, where we spent the night at the convalescent home. My old friends gave us a great welcome, and next day I took Mowrer and Jean Ross around to the children's colonies. But we were anxious to push on to the front and the next day we arrived at Jaen, to find the little town crowded to the limits with the tragic refugees from Málaga. A month and more had passed since Málaga had fallen, and still the pathetic army of old grandfathers, women carrying babies, children—orphaned, weeping, lonely, forsaken—wound its sad way into Jaen. I translated for Mowrer and Jean Ross while they talked to some of the refugees. I found difficulty, sometimes, putting into English the passionate Spanish I heard.

"They killed my husband and my father and my three brothers," a woman would say, "and then I ran away somehow and then the bombs fell and my baby was killed. I had just put him down to rest my arms and then he was dead. It was on the road. Now I have nobody in the world."

I would repeat it, word for word, until the last terrible phrase, which I could hardly say aloud. "Now I have nobody in the world."

Jaen itself had been bombed a week before our arrival. The torn and wrecked buildings, the windows empty of glass, the heaps of bricks now piled up neatly in the gutters, were mute evidence of the fascist attack. A squadron of Junkers 52 had done the job. The city was entirely defenseless. It was not in any sense at all a military objective. No troops were stationed there. No supplies were being shipped from there to the Army. No ammunition was hidden there. Jaen was just a Spanish town of no importance, a little city where women and children lived—and where, just now, the refugees from Málaga had fled to hide themselves from the Italian and German terror.

Many people told us of the bombing, but we decided to call on an Englishman who lived in Jaen and have him repeat his version of the incident for Jean Ross. We spent nearly an hour in the driving rain trying to find our way to the house where he was staying in the country. He met us gladly, and identified himself as an English business man who had stayed on in Spain to attend to his red oxide concern.

"I saw the bombs destroy the house next to mine," he said. "Six people were in the house when the bomb exploded. I think they all were killed instantly except one—perhaps the father or the oldest son of twelve. I heard hoarse screams for some time, but we could not get to the buried voice. It stopped finally."

Jean Ross, who was doing the interviewing, swallowed. "Did you see the women and children killed?"

The Englishman nodded. "I went down in the city streets shortly afterwards. They were taking the children away to a special morgue where their mothers could come to look for them. But most of them could never be identified, even by their mothers—they were torn to bits."

We gulped. The Englishman went on: "I can swear to you that Jaen was not being used for military purposes in any way. This bombing was the most outrageous attack on defenseless women and children I have ever heard about, let alone seen."

Jean nodded and went on. "Has the Government confiscated your business?"

The Englishman laughed. "Certainly not. In fact, they sent workmen, free of charge, to repair the damage the bombs made. They have been most kind all through the war. I have to smile, reading my British newspapers, with all this talk of "Reds" in power in Madrid and Valencia."

I made notes on a piece of copy paper. Jean Ross said: "Do you have a London address that I might use in my story?"

The Englishman suddenly drew himself up. "You mean you want to use my name? Impossible! I will sue you for libel. I will deny everything I said!"

And then he gave a careful explanation of how a business man had to be "neutral" and how he could not offend "certain people" in London by making any statements to newspaper reporters. I went away amazed at a man who could see women and children die and then be so cowardly as to refuse the use of his name—his name, mind you—against these murderers.

We left Jaen sickened by the destruction—but encouraged by the quiet, matter-of-fact bravery of its Spanish population. Our car bumped along the Andalusian roads. The Spring was already passing into Summer in this southern region, and the fields were yellow and sunburnt. We went miles after mile without seeing anyone. Far away, peasants bent over the soil. Now and then, we passed a wrinkle-faced old woman trudging slowly along the dusty road. A war, a fierce, cruel, modern, efficient war, lay just to the south of these beautiful fields and quiet roads of Spain. But nothing disturbed the ancient peace of this countryside.

All the way from Jaen to Andujar we saw the olive groves, rising rich-green, symmetrical, sensuous, from the hot, yellowed plains. Even from the roadside, the olive groves had the look of concentrated, patient, and loving care. The meticulous spacing of the trees, the satisfying and exciting pattern of the groves, brought exclamations of surprise from my American and English companions.

But the olive groves gave me a sudden vision of another life, another woman with my name who had once lived in fine houses and called the rich and powerful by their first names. For I had come to this region in 1931 to stay at the elaborate hunting lodge of the Marquis of Cayo del Rey. It had been my last farewell to my old life, that hunting party. Two weeks later I was in Madrid with Luli, and the Cayo del Rey family no longer spoke to me because I was rumored to have Republican opinions.

I remembered the olive groves, the beautiful, dark trees on moonlight nights. I had a sudden sharp picture of the hunting lodge called Lugar Nuevo, with its forty-some rooms. I remember hearing Mass in its chapel with the *Marcha Real* (the Monarchist hymn) played during the Elevation of the Sacred Host to emphasize the loyalty of the Marquis. I remembered, too, the long walks, the canters on horseback our party had taken over the countryside. Once, I recalled, we had all driven up to the fortress of La Virgen de la Cabeza, a monastery built on a huge rock, overlooking the whole countryside.

As we came near Andújar, I began to feel very curious. The hunting lodge of Lugar Nuevo must have been in the heart of the recent fighting. I wondered what had happened to its stately walls, its beautiful grounds.

But I forgot my memories, once we had driven into Andújar. The three hotels, all equally dirty and primitive, were crowded to the limit. Our first meal in one of the hotel dining rooms was served in a buzz of loud talk from the tables crowded with men in uniform. We ate a three-course meal—two kinds of meat and one vegetable. The waiters replied to our amazed questions: "We have meat when nobody else does because our *guerrilleros* go into the Extremadura and bring back cattle!"

We soon got our bearings on the military situation. Colonel José Morales, an officer of the old military caste, was in command of all the southern armies. But his next in command were two young Republican officers. True, they too had been in the old Army, but now they identified themselves with the people's cause. Lieutenant-Colonel Antonio Cordón was in charge at Andújar, and Lieutenant-Colonel Perez Salas at Pozoblanco.

We met Cordón immediately after that first dinner of ours, and while we three bent over his maps with fascination, he explained the military situation in the southern fronts and added that Lugar Nuevo was at that very moment the last Rebel stronghold in the neighborhood. The Civil Guards, fascists here, had retreated to the stately old hunting lodge where I had stayed what seemed like so long ago, and to the sanctuary fortress above taking with them their wives and children. It was a trick they had learned from the "heroes" of the Alcázar. Cordón, like the Republicans of Toledo, had hesitated to blow up the beautiful manor house or the monastery while children and their mothers were imprisoned there.

"But I want you to go up and see my 'propaganda' assault," he said. "We'll have Lugar Nuevo by tomorrow."

We had just walked out to the car when Cordón came running after us.

"We have it already," he said, grinning. "The Rebels escaped during the night and took a back mountain road to the monastery. Now we'll get them out of there and the whole neighborhood will be cleaned up."

So Jean Ross, Mowrer, and I drove up the familiar mountain roads—until today under machine gun fire—to see the old house the Rebels had abandoned under cover of the night, only eight hours or so before. The automobile kept passing landmarks. Here was one of the old hunting posts where I had remained one whole day; here I had often walked, talking to the Marquis' daughter.

My heart skipped a beat when we rounded a corner and I saw the great square stone palace, for now windows were caved in, doors battered, the whole mansion bore the marks of machine gun fire and bullets. But the battered walls were only a foretaste. The Rebels had left the beautiful, luxurious palace in the most complete devastation. Filth littered the spacious drawing room. In the bedroom I had once occupied, soldiers had lit a fire on the inlaid hardwood floor and cooked a meal of lentils and beans. Rotted food lay in corners. Every picture in the house had been destroyed. Rags littered the floor—and among them I recognized the beautiful table linen of which my one-time hostess had been so proud. Most of the luxurious furniture, imported directly from London, had been burnt up and the large library existed no more for the Rebels had used the leaves of the books to light fires.

The house was a sickening sight. The Republican Army was under strict orders to preserve everything they found, and I could not help smiling wryly at the irony. For the fascists who fought to preserve the ancient privileges this hunting lodge represented were the very ones who had wrecked it. Those whom the Marquis would have called the "Reds" would have respected his library, protected his pictures. All through the war the Government spent time and money preserving Spanish culture, and at Lugar Nuevo I had an opportunity to see what Franco's followers did, even without the help of German or Italian bombers.

But then, I was not sure the Marquis would not have approved the wreckage, could he have seen it. For he was one of the many Spanish noblemen who, like Bolin's aunt and her baby carriage long ago, would have preferred the complete destruction of his library, his paintings, and his palace rather than have them afterwards used for a museum or rest-house for the people.

The only bright cloud in the whole palace was the joy of the *milicianos* who had found the entire collection of the Marquis's shooting arms carefully hidden in several oil tanks in the cellar. The Rebels had plenty of guns and had not bothered to search for these hunting pieces. The *milicianos,* many still unarmed, were delighted to find the old pieces, many of which still worked splendidly. We came upon them, mostly young boys, sitting in the cellar, cleaning the fine shooting rifles and shot-guns, patting the barrels affectionately as they worked. The Marquis had fled abroad to help finance the fascist revolution, but his guns were to fight for the people!

It was almost sunset when we left Lugar Nuevo and reached the troops besieging the monastery. Cordón had arrived and the sound truck had been moved into position.

"I think we'll get them to surrender with the truck," he said, "instead of with bombs or shells. Every evening about this time we come up here and read the Government's decree of amnesty. We guarantee their lives and promise freedom for the women and children."

Mowrer watched the truck warming up its loud speakers. "Why has it taken so long?" he asked.

Cordón looked grim. "The man in command up there is a fanatical Civil Guard. Cut off from the Rebel Army, he communicates with them every day by means of a heliograph. He still breeds hope by lying to his men—he tries to make them believe they will be rescued as the men at the Alcázar were. We tell them every day their position is hopeless."

The driver of the sound truck gave a signal. The speakers jumped inside the truck. Every evening at sunset, these men risked their lives to get close to the monastery. The speeches began. A priest started the program by reading the amnesty, assuring them he was under no duress and begging them to surrender. A second speaker gave a true account of the military situation, describing the recent battle and the Government victory.

We all stood about listening to the speeches. There was no reply from the monastery except an occasional shot. Now and then a bullet whistled over our heads, too close for my comfort, but nobody moved.

Darkness closed in. The night on the mountain was full with the enlarged, monstrous voice of the speaker. The words rolled over the whole countryside: *"We beg you, as Spaniards, surrender before we have to attack you with bombs. Save the lives of your wives and children. Do not let the deaths of the innocent ones rest forever upon your souls. . . ."*

"Aviation coming!"

The word crackled through the night. The great voice was cut off, like a sudden snap of a light switch. Somebody seized me by the hand. In the dusk, I saw Mowrer and Jean Ross running down the road. I began to run. The sound of the planes, the low roar of the motors, filled my ears and head and heart and throat. I ran faster and faster. I felt that I was running through eternity, on a treadmill in hell, that I ran but I did not move. My hand was held firmly by some stranger. I heard his feet running above the roar of the motor, but he must be caught on the treadmill too. My lungs hurt with the effort of drawing breath.

The hand in the night pulled me down, my feet stopped in the dust. I reached out and clutched for support. My hands touched somebody's legs, I tasted dirt in my mouth and spat it out.

"It is safe here," a man's voice said. The voice must belong to the legs. I sat up for a moment and looked at his face. He was a young soldier. It must have been his hand in the night, drawing me to this place, a gutter in the road.

"Down!" the young soldier said.

I threw my body in the gutter, and felt the soft dirt all around me. The sound of the motors was very close.

Suddenly the whole mountain exploded with a noise so hideous, so vast, that the ear was not shaped to comprehend it. The ground where I lay trembled, I felt it move against my body. The sound began to diminish. I even heard a stone rattling down some incline nearby.

Then the mountain was torn apart again with the explosion. I put my hands against my ears so hard that my head ached with the sharp pressure. But the third and the fourth explosions echoed in my brain, no less powerful than the first.

There was an interval. I lay motionless in the gutter, pressing my body into the still trembling dirt. The soldier said in the half-quiet, "Are you all right?"

"Yes." I could not believe the sound of my voice. All sounds had changed since the great noise.

Then the fifth bomb exploded, and the sixth and the seventh. After the last bomb there was a long interval. The sound of the motors grew small and faded away altogether. The earth grew solid under me. The noises of the night, the small, ordinary noises, came back. Voices, human voices, echoed on the road. The young soldier sat up.

"It was not so bad."

I did not answer. I did not like to say that although I had often been bombed in a city, this bombing in the open country had frightened me until I thought my heart would burst with fear.

I stood up in the gutter slowly, almost experimentally. I began to talk to the soldier and my voice did not tremble. I listened to my voice and it seemed ordinary, a commonplace sound. Jean Ross and Mowrer came down the road. We made jokes. Some new soldiers came to relieve the men on duty and took Jean Ross and me for women escaped from the monastery —we looked so frightful. This made us laugh. Soon after that we were on the way back to the town, and when I went to bed that night I fell asleep instantly and only awoke later, much later, to taste again the sound of that first bomb, making the mountain explode.

We three from Valencia grew accustomed to bombs that week at the southern front. The Rebels were angry because Cordón used propaganda to attack the monastery. General Queipo de Llano announced over the wireless that he "took great pleasure" in making the town of Andújar pay for Cordón's "tricks" with the sound trucks.

Nine times the German Junkers bombed Andújar in the few days we were there. Nine times the big bombers flew over the perfectly defenseless city—nine times General Queipo gloated on the radio over the dead of Andújar.

There was no possible shelter against these air raids. When the church bells pealed, announcing the coming of the planes, the best thing was to stay where you were. All the Government Air Force was busy over the Madrid front at the time, and Andújar never boasted as much as a single anti-aircraft gun, so the only thing was to sit and wait until it was over. If we happened to be in bed, we hid our heads under the pillow and hoped for the best. If we were in the dining room, we used to run for the kitchen—somebody had a theory it was safer, I don't know why.

The old cook and her more ancient husband, peasants who had escaped from a town taken by the Rebels, used to run into a tiny closet under the stairs. If a bomb had hit the hotel the closet would have been a perfect tomb for the old couple. But then, if the hotel were hit, it would have made no difference at all where you were. So Mowrer, Jean Ross, and I tried to resign ourselves to our fate and look as natural as possible when the bombs started to fall.

We left Andújar to visit various sectors at the Cordova and the Extremadura fronts. Pozoblanco, delivered by our troops after the Rebels had reached its outskirts, was a pitiful sight. Not one single building was standing. Electric wires littered the streets. The townspeople had fled from their homes. The houses were wrecked shells—one had been neatly clipped in half, and on a sagging wall, naked now to the street, hung a picture of the Sacred Heart of Jesus, with an iron bar piercing the Heart.

Of course, I think I should say here that "visiting" a front is not what journalists are apt to make their readers think it is. Actually there is little to be seen at a modern battleground. From the safe distance at which all visitors are kept, you can see the front trenches—scars on yellow fields. Trees are withered and torn. The scene is very lonely. Puffs of smoke dot the landscape—shots far away, now and then near. The air trembles with the sound of field artillery. The commandant of the sector has you to lunch in his headquarters, usually improvised from a peasant's farmhouse. You begin to ask him questions—but he breaks in: "How is the war going on other fronts? Aren't the English and the French going to help us? Is the United States going to lift the arms embargo?" Every soldier you meet is hungry for information.

Still, we saw the Spanish Government troops holding the southern front and Mowrer could verify with his own eyes the extent of the victory. Almadén and its mercury mines had been effectively saved and we were putting pressure on the Franco troops holding the coal and lead mines nearby.

But back in Valencia we had grave news. The Germans, more interested in the industrial north than in the southern regions, insisted on having their own way for a while. The offensive against the north started at the beginning of April with the announcement of the blockade of the harbor of Bilbao—the blockade the English Government was so eager to take for granted. Britannia decided not to rule the waves, at least not until the Nazis could seize the north of Spain.

I met Ignacio in Valencia. He was preparing to go to Bilbao to study the needs of the Air Force. The Basque country was cut off from the rest of Republican Spain; the geographical division made the transport of troops impossible. Until the fall of Irun we had communicated with Bilbao through France. Now we could only reach the Basque provinces by sea—but the Germans had blockaded the port with their superior Navy—or by plane.

The use of airplanes in Bilbao was almost humanly impossible. The country was mountainous; there was no place to build airports except a few spots very well known to the Nazi bombers. The most modern pursuit plane, light and fast, used to attack the slower and heavier bombers, has a small cruising radius. If Ignacio sent pursuit planes from airports outside of Madrid they would have great difficulty crossing the mountains shrouded in continuous fog and would have to refuel in Basque airports before they could be used against the Nazi bombers. But the few airports near Bilbao were as well known to the Germans as to us; it was unlikely they would allow a pursuit plane, down for refueling, to rise again.

The Basque officials made things no easier for Ignacio. For months they had disdained Government aid, lost in the absurd dream that England would sell arms to the Basque Government. The British had enormous investments in the north and the Basque officials believed that London would never let the Nazis seize her property. The Basques discovered they were wrong—too late. They called for help from the Spanish Government, but the hour was critical.

I waited for Ignacio's return with anxiety. It came sooner than I had expected. He had transferred a few of his precious planes to the north and left an officer in charge. He had returned because trouble was brewing in Catalonia.

I had heard Ignacio say often enough, "I am always telling Prieto that we should go to Barcelona and incorporate the Air Forces of Barcelona entirely into the Government Air Force. And if that goes for the Air Force, I would apply it to everything else dealing with the war. Until we have *one* Army, *one* command, we cannot expect to do anything serious. But Prieto seems to be afraid to undertake it because he knows Caballero would fight it. And we are letting things slip and so we are going to be faced with something very unpleasant."

I knew little about Catalonia in those days, but when Ignacio returned to Valencia from Bilbao I was to learn a great deal. Barcelona had been almost entirely untouched by the war since the first days of July when the people defeated the attempted fascist coup. Because Catalonia was not faced with the immediate problems of life and death which the rest of Spain had continuously wrestled with since July, Barcelona was a veritable breeding ground for "rear-guard" squabbles.

More important, Franco's "Fifth Column" operated more powerfully in Catalonia than anywhere else in Spain. Disguised as ultra-revolutionaries, these fascist spies flocked into Barcelona, mouthing left phrases, talking of overthrowing capitalism, all the while they sapped the strength of the Republican rear-guard. The fight against fascism in Spain required three things from Catalonia: food, grown by the peasants; armaments, manufactured by the workers; and disciplined volunteers for the Army. But the Trotskyites who acted as Franco agents, working through a political party called the POUM, wormed their way into high places.

The food situation had grown grave because these "leftists," who maintained an actual as well as theoretical connection with Franco, tried to force the peasants into badly managed "collectives." The only result was diminished crops, when we needed more food than ever before.

In the factories the POUM agents or anarchist workers whom they had misled talked of "seizure" and "confiscation." At a moment when Spain's very life depended on how fast we could manufacture guns, bullets, and airplanes, these "revolutionaries" were calling strikes. The productivity of Barcelona workmen fell to incredible levels at the precise historical moment when Spain needed its skilled industrial workers as never before.

The question of the Army in Catalonia was perhaps the gravest problem Spain had to face. Misled by these "Fifth Column" agents, the Catalonian officials tried to keep their Army separate from the Republican Government's. Under the Republican Constitution, Catalonia had about the same rights as a state in the United States—it could have its own language, its own local laws, and so forth. But the Army and foreign affairs were to be managed by the Central Government. Caballero had a perfect legal right—nay, duty—to enforce this article of the Constitution. The Army in Spain should be under one unified command. The Catalonian front had been absolutely inactive for months, while the Government troops in the north, south, and central zones had battled for their lives. Had the Catalonian front been efficient and organized, the Government could have executed movements to flank the enemy and divert forces from Madrid and the south. But Caballero was timid. His advisers were in touch with those in Catalonia influenced by the arguments of the Franco agents. Caballero believed that an attempt to unify the Army would cost him his popularity with the extreme "leftists"—something for which he was willing to sacrifice Spain's safety. His advisers were wrong, as it turned out. The majority of the people of Catalonia wanted the unified command of the Army and welcomed it with cheers when it finally was realized.

But in the meantime Caballero's weakness was to cost much in lives and blood.

Ignacio's return from Bilbao and the growing tension in Catalonia finally convinced Prieto that he must take steps in Barcelona no matter what the childish old Prime Minister said. Ignacio was to accompany Prieto on the trip.

On May 2, Prieto put in a long-distance call to Barcelona. He asked to speak to the head of the Catalan Government. The telephone operator, who was a member of the group of conspirators calling themselves "Friends of Durruti," replied that there was no longer a Catalonian Government—only a "Defense Committee." This Committee was most ironically named. It was headed by paid agents of Franco.

Now the Government could hesitate no longer. Caballero *must* act. But still the vain old man hesitated while his advisers buzzed about him. On the Aragon front, groups of POUM militiamen, the Trotskyite heroes who had played football with the fascists in the opposite trenches, started for Barcelona, this time in dead earnest about the fighting. They intended to slaughter the people of Barcelona on the streets—as they had never slaughtered the fascists.

The POUM soldiers returning from the front revealed the whole dirty game to the people of Barcelona. Franco could not win so easily. Some workers, misled by the "leftist" phrases, came out on the streets. They were armed by the Trotskyites with guns hidden all over the city—hidden guns, when brave men went into the attacks against the fascists using their fists because the Republican Government had no rifles!

Ignacio flew to one of the smaller Catalonian provinces, taking sixty men with him. These men, together with the people of the little town who came out on the streets as a body, prevented the fascist "Fifth Column" from doing any damage. He too saw the Trotskyites armed to the teeth with guns and even armored cars which the Republic needed so badly in its fight against fascism.

On May 7, Caballero finally yielded to the pressure put on

him by the rest of the members of his Cabinet and the people. He sent shock police forces to Barcelona. The abortive coup against the Republic was easily defeated by the people, who saw through Franco's tricks. But five hundred died in those May days and fifteen hundred were wounded, many badly.

This was the price Spain had to pay for Caballero's weakness. And Spain responded in kind. Caballero's days as a tenpenny dictator were finished. The Army must be unified and the rearguard strengthened. Caballero had failed as a leader of the Spanish people. And yet until the last, Caballero had not the slightest idea of the political situation. His reply to his critics was a proposal to give him more power!

All over Spain, in every village and in every great city, the cry was universal, "Caballero must go!"

And so the Cabinet was re-formed. Dr. Juan Negrin was made Prime Minister of a Government which included three Socialists, two Communists, two Republicans, one Catalan, and one Basque representative. The previous Government had the same grouping of political parties, except that the anarchists now withdrew to indicate their support for Caballero. Some months later they realized their error and took the two seats left open for them. The theory of this Popular Front Cabinet, with all the political parties represented roughly according to their strength in the country, was a simple one. Fascism can be fought only with democracy. The Government must truly represent the opinions and political beliefs of the people.

The new Premier believed in democracy—democracy in theory and democracy in methods of government. He came to power without the great popularity Caballero had enjoyed in his first weeks as Prime Minister. But Dr. Negrin had to wait only a few months before he became one of the best-loved men of Spain.

The new Prime Minister was a distinguished scientist. Before the war he had been the main support of University City in Madrid. His studies in physiology had interested him more than politics. A man of profound culture, he was widely traveled and had friends all over the world.

With the beginning of the war, he had left his laboratory to take the ungrateful job of Minister of Finance. Many were doubtful when they heard of this appointment. What did a physiologist know about finance and politics? Prieto and others with a long career in politics behind them were inclined to be condescending to Dr. Negrin from University City.

But Juan Negrin was a man of unusual talents. Modest, a little shy, he was never inclined to boast of his abilities. But gradually the other Cabinet Ministers awoke to the fact that Dr. Negrin was doing a brilliant job in the Ministry of Finance. As the war developed from a civil war to an invasion, Dr. Negrin became doubly valuable in Cabinet meetings. His wide knowledge of foreign countries made his advice enormously useful. More important, he was one of the few men in high office in Spain who never for a moment doubted our victory, who trusted the people, who was ready to rely on their heroism —and who was always firm as a rock, calm in the face of disaster. He believed in Spain, we knew—for his two eldest sons were in the People's Army, one a pilot in the Air Force. There were other Cabinet officials whose sons were conveniently far from the lines. Dr. Negrin, Prime Minister of Spain, asked no more for his sons than that they should have a chance to fight the invaders.

With Prieto now Minister of Defense, supervising the operations of the Army, Navy, and Air Force, Ignacio moved his headquarters definitely to Valencia. I began to look around for new living quarters, for the Hotel Ripalda had become more and more crowded. Ignacio couldn't eat a meal in peace— people lined up at our dinner table to ask questions, bring petitions, or talk business. We couldn't sleep, for Valencia was bombed nearly every night, and although we never bothered to go to the *refugio,* the hotel manager made all his guests get up and assemble in the hall. Sleepily, dressed in all sorts of robes or queer costumes, we stood about waiting for the nervous hotel manager to decide the raid was over. That often happened three or four times a night. Ignacio began to lose weight from lack of sleep.

So I went house-hunting in wartime. But I discovered that thousands of people before me had shared my opinion of living in a crowded hotel in Valencia. There wasn't a house to be had within forty miles of the city. The normal peacetime population had been nearly tripled. Valencia was crowded to the bursting point with all the civil servants, Government officials, the military staffs, the foreign journalists, the various attachés, and of course thousands of refugees.

On my third trip, I finally found a little house outside a village nearly twenty miles from the city. It had no electric lights or running water but beautiful mountains rose just behind it. The road ran near the house. I decided we would be able at least to sleep in this miniature house. Within a week, we had light and water and enough furniture to move in. The house had a dining room and kitchen on the first floor, four rooms above, and a few yards away another little house sheltered the chauffeurs, their wives, and the military guard to whom Ignacio, Chief of the Air Force, had finally resigned himself.

Living in the country saved Ignacio and me from the terrible nerve strain of Valencia. Seeing the green fields and trees in the early morning going into town somehow made the whole day easier. Eating out in our tiny garden those summer evenings was a real feast, although the food was always the same— lentils, rice, with sometimes tinned meat or fish, or on very rare occasions, real mutton brought from some distant part of the country.

The people in our village were mostly small farmers, each with his tiny orchard owned by the same family for generations. The orange and lemon growers of the Valencia valley were very different from most Spanish peasants, who had to till arid land usually belonging to a great landlord. Here the fertile soil could easily support whole families on very small acreage, and here the land was held by small farmers themselves.

We moved into the village just as the peasants were recovering from a bad attack of nerves. During the first months of the war, the anarchist trade unions, ill-advised and ill-prepared, had tried to force farmers into ineffective collectives. Naturally no one can argue with the fact that modern farming is more efficiently done in a collective—each farmer gains more from such an arrangement. But establishing farming collectives is a long job, requiring years of education and preparation. A collective without modern farm machinery, for instance, is quite foolish—and Spain was producing guns, not tractors, for the war. More important, the extremists finding support in Caballero had attempted to force farmers into collectives without any real educational preparation. The result was that the farmers were resentful and sullen wherever the Caballero Government had approached them.

Now, with Dr. Negrin as Prime Minister, farmers were promised freedom to till the land as they chose. Collectives were encouraged, especially in those places where the peasants were given huge tracts owned by the fascist landlords and where the peasants themselves wished to cultivate their lands collectively. But in the Valencia valley there was no reason to collectivize the land owned by the farmers and these were only asked by the new Government to produce food to the full extent of their abilities. Hoarding and price speculation were forbidden.

Vicente Uribe, Minister of Agriculture, tackled the problem of the rich *Huerta* in Valencia. He made the peasants understand their critical role in the war—save Spain from fascism by producing more food. Uribe solved the land question in different ways in different parts of Spain, suiting the policy to the circumstances. In some places he settled peasants on the old landlord's land, and in spite of the war, managed to find them credits, farm machinery, engineers to help them dam the rivers and irrigate their lands. Farm productivity rose sharply all over Government Spain—and this in wartime.

The success of Uribe's policies had their best proof in the great number of young men volunteers for the Army from the villages of Spain. Peasants do not go out to fight for a Government which has not successfully settled the land question. Indeed, only in Catalonia were the peasants restive and complaining. The Catalonian law decreed that agriculture must be directed by the regional Government. Uribe could not set up policies for the Catalonian agricultural regions and the local Government wavered between forcing collectives on farmers not prepared for such a policy, and, on the opposite side, allowing speculation and hoarding of food stuffs. Farm productivity fell greatly in Catalonia during a period when we needed food most.

The morning of May 31, Ignacio and I drove in from the green orchards to the hot, feverish city of Valencia. We went directly to our offices and I think we both had the news of Almeria about the same time. I could hardly believe it. The words on the piece of paper seemed to make no sense. The legal Government of Spain had bombed ships—ships, mind you, not people—in the Rebel port of Ibiza. Could anyone in the world argue that we had no right to bomb the ships bringing oil and arms to fascist conspirators trying to overthrow the legal Government of Spain? And in the course of this action, if we happened to hit a German pocket battleship, should not the question be asked, "What was the German ship doing in a Rebel harbor? Could it have been that the battleship was violating the Non-intervention Treaty?"

And so the German Government sent its battleships to Almeria, a peaceful little town on the Spanish coast, a city which nobody could possibly call a military objective—just a place where people lived, where children went to school and women hung up the washing and old men sat in the sun.

And the Nazis announced that they were going to take "reprisals" for the incident at Ibiza.

When the German ships steamed into the little port, the townspeople, menaced by the shining guns, fled to the hills and hid in the caves. A German officer barked a command, German sailors signaled the attack. A sheet of high explosives fell on the peaceful Spanish town.

In the hot, quiet morning the people huddled in the caves heard the guns roar, and roar again and again. And when the noise and the explosions stopped and the smoke lifted, the people looked down and saw their city all but destroyed. Ten minutes before this had been a quiet little street; houses stood here, houses filled with dishes and beds and pictures and chests full of clothes saved for weddings and fiestas. Now smoke curled lazily in and out of crumbling piles of chipped stones. The street no longer had houses; it was no longer a street. Almeria was a city of desolation.

I could hardly give this news to the correspondents. I felt sick as I read the dispatches from the Government that trickled in all day and the next day.

"Now the whole world will rise up and stop the invasion of Spain," I said to the correspondents. "Surely no one in the world can sit peacefully in his home and do nothing for Spain after this. Now the conscience of the world must speak!"

But although I waited breathlessly for nearly a week hoping that the Nazi bombardment of Almeria would not go unpunished, even in a world where the British Foreign Office lied regularly twice a day about the Spanish war—nothing happened. The Nazis could boast with safety about their "glorious triumph" over the peaceful Spanish town.

Almeria was of course only a beginning. German airplanes bombed the little Basque towns out of existence. Guernica, Durango, a dozen smaller villages, were blown into hell by the "brave" German aviators. We knew they were German because we had photographs; besides, every Rebel plane that crashed in the North was manned by pilots who spoke only German. In those days it was important for us to continue collecting the evidence of the invasion. Now, of course, we have better proof. We know it was the Nazis who blew the Basque country to death because Hitler now boasts of it.

I shall never forget the torture Ignacio went through those last weeks of the fight in the Basque country. It was almost impossible for him to send any planes at all to Bilbao and Santander. Our supply of airplanes was fantastically small. We simply had no airplanes while the Rebels had hundreds and hundreds. Perfect weather was required for the flight to Bilbao. Our planes, with their small cruising radius, had to start from an airdrome near the front lines in Madrid. The Rebels, who obviously knew our situation, bombed this airfield almost continuously. If the squadrons did take off, they had to fight fog over the mountains. If they were able to land safely in a northern air field, the Germans bombed them while they tried to refuel. Few people, even in Spain, knew how many planes we lost trying to save Bilbao. Every airplane we had, whether an antiquated model remodeled from a transport, an old Fokker, or what not, was very nearly worth its weight in gold to the Government of Spain. While the Italians and Germans sent new shipments of airplanes daily to the Rebels, we had had no new planes since November.

And yet, precious as our planes were, we had to make the attempt to save Bilbao, we simply had to. The loss was terrific.

But the fight was hopeless. We could not defend the Basque country against the invading forces of two dictators. The northern provinces were cut off from the Madrid front by implacable geography. Bilbao was lost—in the words of one correspondent, "admired but abandoned by the whole world."

With the conquest of the North by the rebels—or rather by their German allies—their internal troubles came to light. The different factions fighting under Franco could hardly be expected to agree on the spoils of any battle. How could the Falangists—the Spanish fascist party—have anything in common with the Monarchists, or either of them with the old Carlist branch, the Requetés—who fought the "constitutional Monarchy" of Spain finding it "too liberal" for their tastes?

After the victory in the North, the "left wing" of the Falange wanted their twenty-six-point fascist program put into practice, but the Requetés from Navarre, considering themselves the Lords of the northern provinces, resented the foreign "help." Navarre was the most backward of the northern provinces; the tradition of the two Carlist wars of the nineteenth century had not disappeared in that region isolated by mountain chains from the other three industrial Basque provinces. Now Navarre expected to gain predominance over its sister Basque provinces, like the stupid brother who gains control of the family fortune and tries to dictate to the enlightened members of the clan.

But General Franco had German and Italian masters from which he thought he could learn solutions for all his problems. He named himself the leader of the "unified" Falange and

Traditionalist Parties, the Requetés, combining the two most bitter enemy parties among his supporters and simply eliminating all the others by decree. But unity cannot be made by a stroke of a pen, even if Italian and German guns protect the penman. The empty title General Franco gave to his new fascist party, the "Falange Española Tradicionalista de las Jons," meant exactly nothing. The fundamental difference between the Navarre fanatics and the Spanish imitators of Italian and German fascism continued to exist after Franco decreed it did not.

And while on the Rebel side unity was decreed and dissension grew wider every day, the Spanish people were achieving real unity in the Popular Front Government of Dr. Negrin. For the tragic events in Barcelona in the early days of May had taught us all lessons of enormous value. We knew each other now. The traitors could be eliminated. The Negrin Popular Front Government, a more democratic and responsible and representative Government than Spain had ever known in its whole long history, raised the slogan: "All efforts to win the war!"

Spain had been tested in the fire of war; the Summer of 1937 found us a disciplined nation, fighting for our lives against the foreign invaders. And with the increasing intervention of Germany and Italy, Dr. Negrin formulated an important new policy; if there were any Spaniards living in fascist territory—and we knew there were many—who resented the invasion of their country by foreigners we must bind them to us. The fascist rear-guard was as much a battlefield as the front line trenches.

The long Summer of 1937 was climaxed by two great victories. The reorganized Army battled the Rebels at Brunete, west of Madrid. "If we only had twenty Modestos, instead of one," Ignacio used to say over the dinner table, as we talked excitedly of Brunete.

Brunete brought its inevitable losses, among them Gerda Taro, the little Hungarian photographer, the wife of Robert Capa, whose work has appeared in *Life*. She had been to see me in the office at Valencia just before the offensive. I was very busy with all the correspondents who wanted cars to go to Madrid and I couldn't give her the attention I wanted to. She wrote me a sweet little note and put it on my table with a bunch of flowers. "I'm so sorry to worry you when you're so flustered and busy and tired," she wrote, "but I must get to Madrid before the offensive is over."

She was a great photographer and she believed greatly in democracy. She felt she must show the world what was happening in Spain, show them with her camera. She was never afraid of danger; she only wanted to get pictures that would make the world know about Spain.

Gerda left that night for Madrid. When I saw her again, her body lay in state in a large room at the Intellectuals' Association in Valencia, waiting to be taken to France. I put some flowers in her hands.

In these days of the war, we had trained ourselves not to mourn for our dead. So many people we loved fell every day on Spain's battlefields. So many men we met grew into our hearts and then one day were reported dead. I remember so many who came—and went, never to come back. Ben Leider, a young American pilot whom Ignacio admired for his ability and heroism—I met him once with Ignacio. We talked, we would have been friends. And then he was killed. And others. So many others. I lived with the nightmare of Ignacio falling—his life had been nearly blotted out so many times. And we all made ourselves survive the agony of death. Work had to be done; there was no time to mourn.

And yet I could not forget Gerda Taro, so young and charming, with her sweet smile and her almost childish figure and face. I looked at the flowers I had put in her hands for a long time and then I went away and for a while that day I could not work but only sit silently at my desk, fingering the little note she had left me.

At the end of August, with the invasion of Spain now more than a year old, many of the Republican troops that had won the offensive at Brunete near Madrid were transferred to a very different front: Belchite in the Aragon sector. Here anarchist militia, undisciplined and uncontrolled, had been in full command for more than a year. The military situation on the Aragon front was shocking—the troops had been in complete idleness almost since the beginning of the war. Morale was low; results were what could be expected.

Now the disciplined brigades of the People's Army marched into the Aragon sector and the victory they won was not only of enormous military importance, but of equally great political importance. For the value of the People's Army was effectively proved. The best units of the old anarchist militia were pleased to serve under the command of experienced military leaders. The villagers received the Army enthusiastically. It was a timely revelation to the peasants to discover the People's Army had nothing in common with some of the groups of the so-called militia which had come to the villages in the early days of the war and lived on the fat of the land.

Ignacio rushed from Madrid to the Aragon sector with one night at Valencia. He was exhausted, but happy. The Air Force had behaved "gloriously" at Brunete, and already the Army and the people in Madrid were calling it "La Gloriosa." He had been promoted to colonel, but I had to laugh at his annoyance at his new rank. What did he care about promotions? He had only put on the insignia of his last promotion a few weeks before and if he waited as long to wear the colonel's insignia as he had the lieutenant-colonel's, the war would long since be over. He left the next morning for Aragon.

A week passed. We were very busy in the Press Bureau. My work kept me there day and night. I had large maps pinned on all the walls, mainly to help the correspondents in their work, but also to make their dreary room look a little more pleasant. Some of the less capable personnel, including the two foreign censors, had left the office. My work increased as a result, but my peace of mind easily compensated for the longer hours. The newspapermen themselves applauded the change. The Foreign Press Bureau began to take on the aspect of an efficiently managed office. Correspondents could get quick service.

Of course, I usually had what the reporters called "hot news" from Ignacio and with his permission I gave the reporters many "scoops" straight from the Army. The red tape of the roundabout Government news sources could be often eliminated. As time went on, the foreign journalists and I developed a working agreement, and during the first week of the Belchite offensive, for instance, the arrangement worked smoothly. Then late one night when the battle was seven days old and we were all standing around the maps, trying to understand the latest Government news report, Rubio called me into his office.

"You can invite the correspondents to have dinner tomorrow in Belchite," Rubio said, blinking at me behind his dark glasses.

"Belchite!" I said breathlessly. "We've taken it!"

Rubio allowed himself a faint, distant smile. "The War Ministry has just telephoned. All the foreign correspondents are invited to dine with the Minister tomorrow at Belchite!"

I dashed out of his office to spread the great news. If I had had time to think—or the energy, for I was very tired from the week of work and suspense—I might have realized that an invitation to dine in a city captured the day before is a most remarkable business.

But I was overjoyed at the news—and more, Rubio suggested that I accompany the correspondents to the front. That meant I could see Ignacio!

Prieto sent the cars for the correspondents over to the Foreign Press Bureau almost immediately, and with a lot of wild excitement—several foreign correspondents had to be rounded up from their hotel beds—our caravan left Valencia towards dawn. Around midday, sleepy and disheveled, our motor caravan stopped at Lérida. From there we took the road to Saragossa —still in Rebel hands—which would lead us to Belchite. Or so we thought.

For our guide, an obnoxious fat Spanish journalist, promptly lost us and we had to make for the village of Candasnos where I knew Ignacio was staying.

Candasnos was a small Aragonese village, typical of the dozens of little towns in the countryside, on the main road between Lérida and Saragossa. It was easy for us to find—and easy for the fascist planes. I still cannot understand why it was not blown to pieces during the Belchite offensive, for the Air Force had established its staff headquarters there. Perhaps the fascist espionage was not as effective as it was said to be.

Our caravan stopped in front of the Air Force headquarters in the old inn with its graceful courtyard and sagging white-washed walls. I found one of Ignacio's aides working in a room full of maps and papers. "The colonel is at the observation post near the front. He will return soon."

I turned to leave him to his work. But he stopped me.

"What," he inquired pleasantly enough, "on earth are *you* doing here?"

I pointed out the window to the caravan of cars standing in the hot sun, filled with bedraggled, perspiring, weary reporters.

"Newspapermen," I said.

The young man who had flown our old "crates" at the risk of his neck and had come through hundreds of bombardments, turned quite pale.

"*What?*" he shouted.

"Prieto has asked them to dinner today at Belchite."

Ignacio's aide sat down heavily in the nearest chair. "Oh," he said flatly.

I began to understand.

"There is still—ah—fighting in Belchite?"

He nodded.

"Whew!" I said, softly too, and also sitting down. For I realized with a sudden shock the perfect madness of that invitation to dinner. Dinner, in a town where our troops were still fighting the rear-guard action with the Rebels; dinner when the Army's commissary was working day and night to get emergency rations—and even water—to the Government vanguard.

It turned out long afterwards that Prieto had never asked our journalists to dinner or to any other meal at Belchite. He was still in Valencia, as a matter of fact, watching the offensive but also attending to other business. He had agreed to give the correspondents cars and permission to visit part of the Aragon front—not because he liked journalists especially but because someone had convinced him of the importance of impressing the world with our victory at Belchite. The invitation to dinner had been the imaginative work of some assistant, passing on the word about the automobiles and the permits.

I stayed at Candasnos, excusing myself on the grounds that I wanted to wait for Ignacio. I intended to duck the fury of the correspondents when they heard Belchite, which they had announced as a Government victory, was still being fought for.

But when I joined the journalists that evening to hear about their plans for the next day I found them all strangely subdued. They were so tired and hungry they welcomed a chance to eat and rest long before they reached Belchite. We broke the news about the rear-guard action in Belchite very tenderly and suggested that the next day, perhaps, they could see the city. Not a single journalist objected, or even asked questions. We found them beds and they were grateful.

Next morning, after spending the night with Ignacio near Lérida, I reported at the hotel at 6 A.M. to take my correspondents to the front. My fat Spanish journalist had conveniently disappeared and relinquished his authority. The night watchman thought me mad to arrive for an appointment at 6 A.M.—and, sure enough, my exhausted charges did not turn up for breakfast until 10 A.M., except for the three women, who were on time. Women are a very tough section of the human race.

Back on the Saragossa road, past Candasnos, we reached a rough barricade of trees. Beyond the barricade, two miles away, were the fascists. The Ebro river divides the road, however, and the bridge was blown up. Our troops had crossed the river at Pina, on the left-hand side of the bridge and road, and we motored over a bumpy sandy path which the soldiers were building as they advanced. A week before, all the land we were crossing had been in fascist hands.

We stopped to talk to the soldiers resting under the shade of the few scattered trees. They showed us the trenches the enemy had occupied last week. The men were filled with touching pride. They were eating as we talked to them—a plate of meat with potatoes and a big loaf of bread. They had newspapers propped up before them—the same newspapers we might have brought them from Valencia.

"How many of you learned to read in the Army?" one reporter asked. We had all heard of the cultural activities of the Army and this journalist decided to check up on the reports of the Minister of Education.

The soldier looked up from his newspaper. "Almost all the men in this battalion learned to read since the war," he said casually; "some could read a little, their names and a few words in big type, most could not read at all. I, for instance, could not read even my name, for I did not know how it looked in writing. Now you see."

He gestured towards his newspaper. With a little encouragement he took a notebook out of his back pocket. "I practice writing when things are quiet," he said, and his voice was soft with pride. "You see."

We all looked. His notebook was neat, filled with little essays on the war and his native village.

"This, of course," he said with an attempt to be casual, "is my third notebook. The commissar says I have learned very quickly. My first notebook was naturally not so good."

He took the notebook back from our hands and began to look at it again himself.

"When I go back to my village," he said, in a matter-of-fact tone, "I shall teach everyone to read. There is nobody now who can read, unless they have learned since I left. But I will teach them all very quickly because they all want to learn to read very much. I always wanted to learn, but there was never the opportunity, you understand."

I understood and I think the foreign journalists did too.

"Just at first," he said, and we could see that he had given this much thought, much careful planning, "the people in my village will not be able to read the newspapers. So I will read them aloud every day, so that they will know about Chamberlain and other such matters. Perhaps I will read the newspaper every day at a certain square, you understand. Everyone will come to hear, because the people in my village are very intelligent and like to discuss matters of importance."

We all nodded. The people of his village began to take shape in our minds—proud men, who "liked to discuss matters of importance," who would "learn to read very quickly because they have always wanted to know how to read but had never—you understand—had the opportunity."

"I have discussed this matter with our political commissar," the soldier went on, "and he has advised me on certain questions. The women, for instance, he says should be taught as well as the men, for women should know about such matters, too."

The three women journalists nodded.

"Just as soon as the war is over and we have defeated the fascists," the soldier said with quiet dignity, "I will hasten back to my village and begin. I have already told a boy who was wounded and was returning, to give the news to the village and to prepare for the study. He had not been in the Army so long as I so he could not write so well, but perhaps he will make a beginning until I return home."

We went away from the soldier under the tree, and I think we all wished most fervently that he would come safely through the war so that he might hasten back to his village and begin to teach people how to read and write.

It was very difficult to reach Belchite. The main roads were cut off; even those beyond the range of enemy guns were not possible to travel, for the fascists had blown up everything, every square inch of road, in their retreat. But as we haltingly felt our way along the countryside, we had the feel of being in fascist territory. For we were traveling through utter desolation. Our peasants farmed their lands right up to the front line trenches, almost. But the fascists had miles of unplowed land, vines left to die, uncultivated fields. They could not force the peasants, even at the point of a gun, to till their fields.

Our caravan disbanded as we plodded through the dusty paths and sandy ditches, cut through desert fields and rough dry land. We had to close all the windows of our car and even so our mouths were full of dust and our eyes burned with the sand. We were driving through the plain towards what we thought was Belchite when a caravan of trucks passed us. We all stopped.

The open trucks carried a load of women and children and four old men. The old men were silent. Their several days' growth of beard hid their impassive faces, masked the emotion, if the old men felt any. For the Aragonese peasant—like the Castilian peasant whom I knew much better—gets to a point in his austere life of hardship and tragedy when his body turns to lined parchment, his eyes burn hard and cold. It seems then as though he no longer cares about anything in this world, as though nothing he sees or endures could be worse than what he has seen or endured before.

Many peoples in the world reach this point of human suffering, but the Spaniard bears his sorrow with one great difference. The Spanish peasant is a man of such dignity that to the superficial observer he even seems to be proud of his suffering. But to the superficial observer only. For this austerity, this implacable dignity under hardship, is the fruit of the old Spain. Taught for generations that one could expect nothing better than sorrow from this life, the peasant withdrew into a shell of proud, unspeakable resignation.

The calamities of war, added to the fascist oppression in Franco territory, had killed the last rays of hope instilled by the young Republic in these old, old men. For the young, the war was a lesson learned in their hearts. But for these old men in the trucks, immobile, like statues, their eyes full of what they had just seen at Belchite, the lesson came too late.

The women in the trucks were different. They were of all ages, some young, some very ancient, all dressed in black. They had been told by the fascists and by some priests in Belchite that the "Red" armies advancing on the town would rape and kill all the young women, torture all the old ones to death.

Now they were being taken to safety in trucks by these same "Reds" who, to their enormous surprise, turned out to be Spaniards. For they had been told that the army taking Belchite would be composed exclusively of Russians!

"Why," an old woman said, plucking up her courage, "we all thought the world had gone mad. Russians were coming to kill us, and in the village the men were all bewitched, speaking some strange language of the devil."

"Don't be silly," one young matron said sharply, "those men were Italians, I told you so all the time, and those others were from Africa and the Captain, he was German. I told you so, but you *would* believe that story they told you about all those men being Spaniards from different provinces! Ha! I knew better all the time!"

The trucks passed on, leaving me very sad. For I suddenly realized what it must mean to these peasants to be involved in a war about which they know nothing. These women had been lied to from the beginning of the July days—told that all their sufferings were the result of "Red Russian" terror!

We passed one of the mixed brigades resting near Belchite and stopped to ask for news. But as usual we knew more than the soldiers did. Men at the front know only what their particular brigade has been doing—they must wait for the newspapers to find out what is happening.

At last we sighted Belchite. Obviously the town was still under fire. We stopped on the road about half a mile from the city and listened to the noise. The church was the target of one of our cannons, for the last Rebel forces were barricaded in the stone building. While we watched, the Rebel planes twice circled the town and then tried to bomb our troops stationed just outside the little city. But bombs dropped harmlessly into open fields.

We were alone in our car. The other cars had taken another little road toward Belchite, but they were also stalled outside, waiting for the fire to die down. It did not look as though we would sleep in Belchite that night.

We stood on the road, ducking down now and then behind mounds of sand and low bushes when the bullets came too close. A company of soldiers passed us.

"It's almost all over," they said. "They only have two machine guns inside the church tower."

Another soldier looked at us quizzically. "The town smells something awful," he said. "Those sons of b—— in the church tower have mowed down everything trying to cross the square, so it is full of human bodies and dead mules. We haven't been able to bury them yet and with the heat and everything . . ."

I rounded up the other cars. All the reporters had the same story. Should we wait another day for the entrance into Belchite? I decided to return to Valencia. I was needed in the office. Besides, I felt in my bones that I could not bear to see Belchite. It would serve no purpose for me to walk on those stones of the square. I would return.

I was right. The other reporters stayed over and returned a day later, shaken and sick with horror. Many could not eat or sleep for days—for modern warfare is not a pretty sight and Belchite, with the unburied corpses lying in the hot August sun, shook the nerves of even the most "hardboiled" newspaperman.

The Summer went by. The People's Army had won two great victories. The people were beginning to realize their own strength. If only the German and Italian invasion could be stopped in its tracks by the Non-Intervention Committee, we would have a quick victory.

But in Geneva the League of Nations met. The Non-Intervention Committee received reports. The opposition asked questions of the Foreign Office in the British House of Commons. In the United States, people cried, "Lift the embargo on democratic Spain." In France, the French people cried to the Blum Government, *"Cannons et avions pour l'Espagne."* Meantime, the Italians could read, in their Government press, Mussolini's words of greeting to General Franco on the occasion of the fall of Santander in the North.

"I am particularly proud," Mussolini wired Franco with brotherly affection, "that the Italian legionaries have, during ten days of hard fighting, contributed mightily to the splendid victory of Santander. Their contribution receives coveted recognition in your telegram. This brotherhood of arms, already close, guarantees the final victory which will liberate Spain and the Mediterranean from any menace to our common civilization."

The Italian press stressed that Santander was an Italian victory. Yet when the British Government, which ran the Non-Intervention Committee, made "inquiries" on this matter,

Mussolini flatly denied any "intervention." The British Foreign Office was then unable to proceed on the complaints of the Spanish to the Non-Intervention Committee, for, it said, it lacked information. We began to feel very sorry for England— a nation without a single man in its Foreign Office who could read and translate the Italian press!

Germany, too, was very backward about admitting its invasion of Spain. Once the Fuehrer made a little slip in a speech, mentioning how useful the iron ore of Bilbao would be to Germany. This slight admission was removed from the official copies of the speech handed to foreign journalists in Berlin, and, of course, the British Foreign Office was at a loss again, with no one to read German and report on Herr Hitler's remarks!

And all the while, Italian and German troops, Italian and German planes, Italian and German pilots, tanks, cannons, machine guns, rifles, ammunition, gasoline, kept pouring into Spain, "unobserved" by the Naval Control Commission and certainly viewed with satisfaction by those gentlemen in England and other countries who longed for a quick fascist victory in Spain—hoping against hope that after the defeat of democracy they would be able to come in and share the spoils with the victors.

Ignacio and I, sitting at home nights in our little house outside of Valencia, were worried. We knew that the comparative calm after Brunete and Belchite boded no good for Republican Spain. The fascists had been badly beaten. They realized they were no longer fighting raw militia, but a trained, disciplined, first-class fighting force. Accordingly the word had gone out to Mussolini and Hitler: more men, more materials are needed. This period of calm was really a period of reorganization of the fascist armies. Did the Republicans have a good army now? Very well—the fascists would put a larger army, with more guns, more tanks, more airplanes, more of everything into the field.

"We *must* get supplies for the next battles," Ignacio would say anxiously over dinner. "We used up almost everything we had at Brunete and Belchite. Barcelona must work faster. We must have materials!"

That Autumn the Government moved to Barcelona to be closer to our only factories supplying us with war materials. But this was not the only reason. A greater co-operation between all political forces was needed to make Barcelona, the largest city in Spain, into a second Madrid or Valencia. The whole population must be welded together into one unified group whose entire efforts should be organized under the slogan, "Everything to win the war."

Then, too, Barcelona was near the French border, the only means of getting material from abroad. Little enough came, but the Government with its unified Army command must be the first to get access to the meager amounts of war material crossing the border.

Valencia, the same city which had rather resented the arrival of the *Madrileños* in November, 1936, mourned our departure a year later. An understanding, lacking through centuries of Spanish history, between the regions and the capital had been achieved during one year of struggle together for a common end.

Rubio was worried about our transfer to Barcelona. Catalonia had a Censorship Office of its own, and one of the most important devices we had to use in Barcelona was tact. We must be careful not to encroach upon any of the privileges granted to the Catalans by the Cortes. But I knew that the scope of our office had greatly outgrown the mere censoring of dispatches. It was up to us to go on explaining the war, and helping foreign journalists and visitors to find out the truth about our country. These people would continue to come to our office for the help and information they required.

I was more worried about finding offices in Barcelona than finding our duties limited for us by the Catalans. For one of the main questions in the move to Barcelona was that of space. All the large important buildings were already occupied either by the Catalan Government, or by industrial committees who used them only to hold meetings—a survival of the board meetings, dear to the hearts of the anarchists, before most of the war industries were taken under the Government control.

We simply couldn't find separate headquarters in the over-crowded city of Catalonia for the Foreign Press Bureau, and we finally moved in with the Propaganda Department of the Ministry of Foreign Affairs. Rubio was most annoyed. Not only had the censorship duties been taken away from him—but more—our Bureau was to exist side by side with the Ministry of Foreign Affairs. We had been more independent, and, Rubio felt, more important, in Valencia. Overnight, Rubio decided to go to Paris to head the official Spanish News Agency. His post was vacant. Before I had time to even think of who was to fill Rubio's place, the Minister of Foreign Affairs had named me to succeed Rubio. I was the Chief of the Foreign Press Bureau!

The sudden promotion did not give me much joy, I am afraid. I was tired, physically tired, and, worse, on the verge of a nervous breakdown. Sometimes, in those last days in Valencia before our move to Barcelona, I could hardly bear to talk to some of my foreign visitors. The very sound of their rasping voices and their often foolish or heartless questions made me want to scream. I had to keep a close rein on myself. I found myself wishing I could be alone, alone for just a few minutes of the day, with no questions to answer, no foreign language to hear, no delicate matters of personalities to solve.

And on top of all this worry in the office, I had my whole household to move to Barcelona. I sometimes laughed a little at myself—in the middle of a bombardment, during a bitter battle between two foreign journalists which I had to patch up, I found myself worrying over whether to take the refrigerator to Barcelona or leave it in Valencia! Men do have one advantage over women in the business or government world—they never have to think of whether the bed sheets will last another six months, or whether the new cook was just self-conscious last night or simply no good.

Ignacio did go house-hunting for me on one of his trips to Barcelona and although he had to leave Valencia a week or so before I could close the Foreign Press Bureau, he arranged to leave me an old car for the moving. On November 17, I had everything in the office, all the files and clippings and type-writers packed; and everything at home. The old car was loaded down with the electric kitchen stove which I had rescued from Madrid, and the refrigerator, the radio, and our good mattress; two rabbits which we had bought to provide us with many generations of rabbit stew, only to discover later that they were both females; a few packages of dried and tinned food; my few clothes; an old chair Ignacio really loved.

The two girls who worked in our household had helped load the car. Now, on the morning of November 17, we all walked out of the little house and took a last look around us. The morning was bright with a kind of diffused yellow sunlight falling softly over the green orchards. The red mountains rising in back caught the sunlight and sparkled in the morning. I hated to look at the little house. We had spent nearly a year there, Ignacio and I, a hard year, of war and danger and terrible anxiety. Yet the small house had seemed a comforting haven and the mountains had often calmed my tired spirit and refreshed my taut nerves. Now we were leaving. When would I see this house again? How long before Spain would be free and I might return to see our beloved mountains again? In the vast misery of the war, it may seem a little thing to leave a house you have loved well; and yet my eyes were filled with tears as I left that November morning. How long must we Spaniards be driven from pillar to post, from house to house, from province to province? When could we rest again in peace and security, when could we settle down to live for years in the same well-loved valley, in the same little house?

The rain began pouring down in a thick blinding sheet as we drove wearily into Barcelona. A sentry at the Air Force headquarters, his nose dripping rain, directed us to the address Ignacio had given me before I left Valencia. We went slowly through the downpour to the suburbs of the city, past the medieval monastery of Pedralbes, to a large mansion looming great in the rain.

This was our new home. The house had belonged to a fascist eye-specialist, who, before he fled abroad and his sympathies became well known, tried to curry favor with the Government by turning his house over for the use of the Air Force officers. So we had legal possession of a completely furnished mansion.

And from that day when I stepped in out of the rain, I began to lead a collective life, which at first I found difficult and later on grew to like. The house was occupied by about thirty people —Ignacio's Air Force staff officers, their wives, odd Government workers and the like. The house had eight bedrooms besides the servants' quarters which had three more bedrooms. There was a large hall and dining room, pantries, a huge kitchen.

Ignacio and I, over our protests, were assigned the "master" bedroom—one of the most hideously furnished chambers I have ever seen. A life-sized copy of Botticelli's "Spring" hid the trunk closet, an over-generous use of gilt, mirrors, draperies, and figured carpets made us speculate endlessly on the character of the eye-specialist who had apparently liked living in this room—which looked—as a friend of ours remarked, "like the nuptial chamber of a Wagner Opera with a Catalan *mise-en-scène.*"

But our bedroom had its compensations. The windows opened out over the whole city of Barcelona which lay calm and lovely beneath us. In the background, the blue sea outlined the fort of Monjuich. And besides the fine scenery, we had a modern bathroom with an electric heater for the bath water. No one who suffers with rheumatism and has not lived through a year of ice-water baths can know what a hotwater heater really means!

The other bedrooms were all filled—not an inch of space was left in the house. At first, the communal life was something of a strain, but gradually the couples who were not congenial got other quarters. The few wives who only wanted to go to the cinema, complained of the food, and found political and military conversation boring, rented apartments in the city, and others took their places. Gradually the house began to fill with people whose friendship was cemented with common work and common hopes. The women all had jobs as well as the men. After hard hours of work in the city we all met for dinner late in the evening, and gradually we began to look forward to those dinners and the easy conversation. Of course, many of the men were away for long months—Ignacio often for two months at a time, and we women found a certain comfort in each other's friendship. As the war grew more difficult during the hideous bombardments of Barcelona, it was good to spend a few hours every day with real friends.

Ignacio had been smoking a great deal in the last few weeks. When I arrived in Barcelona I found him all on edge. He was a man of calm disposition and iron nerves, cheerful, witty, hopeful in the most difficult situations. I had watched him during fifteen months of this heartbreaking war; first flying airplanes no one expected would hold together, then directing the work of brave men faced with impossible difficulties. I had been with him during the tragic fall of Bilbao. I had seen him just after and during the big offensives, when he was straining every nerve to achieve victory.

And yet never until now had I seen his face so white and drawn, never had I observed his hand tremble as he lit one cigarette after another.

"Are you worrying about an enemy attack?" I would ask him.

"Yes, of course, we expect a big fascist offensive, after all this time they have had to prepare—but it isn't only that."

"What then?" I would say.

But Ignacio would never answer. One night he came into our bedroom—and slammed the door, a gesture so unlike Ignacio I looked up in distress. "We have traitors in the Army!" he burst out. "Traitors!"

And that night he told me what preyed on his mind. The high commands of the Army and Air Force were still filled with old-line military officers. Ignacio was convinced that many of them were not only unsympathetic with the Republic, but active agents of Franco.

"Only last week one of them crossed over to the enemy lines carrying plans for the whole surprise attack the General Staff had arranged for yesterday—an attack we had prepared carefully and thus had to abandon."

"What upsets you tonight particularly?" I asked.

Ignacio bit his lips. "I had a long talk with Prieto tonight and begged him to let me remove the officers from the Air Force whom I am unsure of. But he says he cannot allow me to do so until I provide absolute proof which would hold in a court of law! And of course I'll only get that proof when they betray us!"

My husband paced the room, his hands twisting behind his back. "Can't a democracy defend itself? Do civil liberties include leniency for our enemies?"

"Whom are you thinking of?"

The two men Ignacio hoped to remove particularly drove him wild with worry. One was the gentleman who had given me such a fright the day I called Madrid from Alicante—the man who had written Ignacio of his joy in bombing Asturian miners in 1934. The other was an Air Force officer whose wife was the daughter of a well-known Italian newspaperman, and an intimate friend of one of Franco's most important supporters.

I began to worry with Ignacio after that night—and then a few days later he came home all smiles. He had gone again to Prieto and this time convinced the Minister of Defense. The men were already under arrest and the police were even now carefully examining their papers.

But Ignacio's reassurance was short-lived. The following night he was called from dinner to the telephone to be told that Prieto had released his prisoners—why, we never knew. I never saw Ignacio look the way he did that night. His face was dead-white, his eyes burning with fever, his lips trembling. He lay in bed beside me and never slept at all. I woke up during the night, feeling his tense body on the bed.

"Sleep," I would say, but he did not answer.

In fact, I did not hear him speak at all after he got that terrible news.

Next morning he got up early and left, wordlessly, for his office. When I came home for lunch, Maruja, my old friend, who lived with us now too, met me at the door.

"Don't get excited and make a fool of yourself," she began sternly. "Don't make any noise or cry or sob. Ignacio has just been carried in from his office. He is ill."

I pushed her aside and ran up the stairs, my heart beating terribly. Ignacio lay in bed, motionless, his eyes staring. He had been looking at a map, talking of a new plan to some officers, when suddenly he had fallen. He had a stroke. His face was gray, really gray-color. I sat all day and night beside him. I did not talk, for I knew it would tire him. Sometimes I touched his hand. Watching him, I knew how much of himself he had given to our country, how sternly he had driven himself, the nights he had not slept, the days of worry and anxiety.

At last he slept. Doctors from Barcelona and a great heart specialist who flew from Madrid came in and out of the room. After the first days of fear, when we momentarily expected another attack of angina pectoris, an attack which would have been fatal—I began to breathe more easily. Even the heart specialist agreed that all Ignacio needed to make a complete recovery was absolute rest.

"Do not let him even *hear* of the Air Force or the military situation," the heart specialist said. "Keep him in bed, even after he feels very well. Let him have good food, music perhaps, books that will not remind him of his work, a change of climate and scenery as soon as possible—and mostly just sleep, sleep and rest."

But Ignacio scoffed. He got up one morning, announced himself cured, and went back to work. I watched him those days with awful anxiety. One day I returned home for dinner—and found that he was in bed again, with a second stroke, ill, very, very ill.

The doctor from Madrid flew again to Ignacio's bedside. This time he told Ignacio plainly: "I will not be responsible for your life—your life, sir—if you do not rest."

We pulled him through that stroke, but now I was thoroughly frightened. And the doctor convinced Ignacio that he was doing his country a disservice if he did not attend to his health—and life. So we decided to go to the Soviet Union.

No other country in Europe could cure Ignacio, I knew. For if we went to a good sanatorium in France or England, we would be surrounded by the rich sympathizers of Franco and

I knew Ignacio would worry himself into another stroke. Besides, I longed to see my Luli.

As soon as Ignacio was able to move after his second stroke, we took the plane to Toulouse. The first thing we saw in Toulouse was three fine, brand-new American fighting planes, belonging to the Spanish Government, paid for by our money, which the French Government would not allow to be flown across the border.

With this feeling of helpless injustice in our hearts, we went to the restaurant. We saw baskets of good white bread, whole baskets, placed on every table. Ignacio and I looked at each other—thinking of the lentils we had eaten every day for so long, thinking of what this good white bread would mean to our people in Barcelona. And we couldn't eat it. We tried, but it choked us.

Paris struck us a crazy city. We felt like men and women from Mars. What are these people doing, going about the streets, dressed so well, looking so well fed and happy? Do they not know their enemies are fighting at their border? Why aren't these people helping Spain? Are they mad? They will be next!

We tried to enjoy the good meals our friends bought for us—after the second day we began to eat the food, although its richness often made us ill. But we were glad to leave Paris, that beautiful city of the French—because it made us hot with anger to watch the people so indifferent to the fate engulfing them in a region so close. We only felt happy among the people of the crowded back streets who held meetings and cried, *"Cannons et avions pour l'Espagne!"*

We took the train to Antwerp to board the Soviet cargo ship. We couldn't fly to Moscow because the transports crossed Germany and should they be forced down we would be sent to Franco Spain. The little boat was not at all luxurious, but everyone tried to make us comfortable. We ate the same simple but bountiful and good food the crew ate. We spent most of our time resting and reading in the cabin. At meals, one of the officers who spoke a very little English—we spoke no Russian—

used to smile at us and ask us questions: "Like sea? Sleep good? Eat more?"

The young stewardess spoke nothing but Russian, but she used to beam at us with the most expressive smiles.

One evening as the crew was reading the wireless sheet radioed from Moscow every night for Soviet ships' crews all over the world, the sailors suddenly jumped up, turned to us, and began to wave the typed sheet.

"Republicans, Teruel," they said over and over.

We could not believe our ears. While Ignacio had lain sick in bed the Army had started the offensive so long delayed by the treachery of the spy in the officers' group. But Teruel! It was wonderful!

The English-speaking officer dashed up to confirm the news. He gave a sort of pidgin-English review of the battle, although we mostly got reports of the engagement in hasty drawings and gestures.

Ignacio and I were wild with joy—and then Ignacio's face fell. Ah, if he had only been in Spain! This victory would have cured him better than any rest. I tried to change the subject, thinking of the doctor's orders. And Ignacio, with his mind relatively at ease after the victory, did begin to think of other things beside the Spanish war.

We both talked a good deal about the country we were going to visit. We felt able to enjoy something in life for the first time in many months.

We reached Leningrad on the eleventh day of our voyage, well rested, happy to touch ground again, and grateful to everyone on board. I had never seen such kindness for strangers before.

We peeped through the porthole of our cabin as we dressed that morning and in the gray early light we suddenly spotted a Russian such as we thought lived only in story books. He was a harbor watchman. He wore a long gray overcoat, nearly touching the ground, and lined with fur which showed beneath the hem. His chin was snuggled into a huge fur collar, his hands buried in gray fur gloves and his head was more than covered with an enormously tall gray fur hat. We discovered afterwards he was something of an exotic. Most Russian men wore ordinary American caps in bright colors.

The great thing about Russia is that you can learn so much with your eyes. We drove to the Hotel Astoria—a large, conventional European hotel. We saw walking in the hotel lobbies peasants dressed in old sheepskins, chatting in the marble magnificence with sophisticated town people in clothes of yesterday's European fashion; smart Red Army officers better groomed and dressed than the officers of the old Spanish Army; marines in sober blue from merchant vessels and Navy ships. This, we understood with our eyes, as we watched the people talk and walk arm in arm with each other, was a "classless" society.

We only stopped for two days in Leningrad. I was anxious to get Ignacio installed in his sanatorium, and now that we were so near, I could hardly bear to wait any longer to see my Luli.

Our express train pulled smartly into the Moscow station. I looked out the window and saw on the platform a lanky young girl with fair hair and dark eyes lighted just now with impatience—a girl who reminded me so much of myself in those days when I went to the convent that I nearly wept.

When I held Luli in my arms, I saw how much she had changed. She was a head taller. The hollows of her face had filled in. Her arms were no longer match-sticks. The fleeting expression of anxiety I had watched crossing her eyes those last days of Spain was gone. She even seemed, in a way, a little younger, a little more carefree, as though she had regained her childhood completely in a country whose warm hospitality had sheltered her from bombs and food rations, death and privation.

I was astonished when I saw Luli's school. The Spanish children lived in beautiful, comfortable surroundings. A really lovely Armenian rug covered the floor of their large playroom. Children's drawings and newspapers hung on the walls. The Christmas tree was still up when I arrived—a beautiful tree covered with gilt-dust and chains of colored glass. A fine grand piano stood in the corner—a collective gift from the trade unions and the Soviet Government who together provided food, shelter, clothing, teachers for the two thousand Spanish children in Russia. The classrooms were light and well ventilated, filled with cheerful modern furniture, movable desks, window boxes of flowers, reproductions of famous paintings. The dormitories were small—only a few children to each room—immaculately clean, with cupboards and wardrobes for each child.

"But," I said haltingly to the headmaster, "it is so pleasant, even so luxurious. Not everything in Russia is so fine—our hotel is not so modern, the furniture is not so new and cheerful."

He looked quite genuinely astonished. "But you know, here the children get everything first. The furniture in the hotel will come last. Everything we have, we give to our children. It is an absolute rule—from the first days when there wasn't enough food for all, the children got what there was. Now, when there is plenty of food for everyone, the children are the first to get modern furniture, modern bathrooms, good pictures. Why not? They are the people of tomorrow."

Our Spanish children had grown quite fat and happy in these wonderful surroundings. I had always managed to send Luli to good schools in Madrid, but even she was deeply impressed by her Russian school. The other Spanish children, sons and daughters of Asturian miners, Castilian peasants, Madrid workers, orphans of the *milicianos*—they found themselves in a paradise of which they had never dreamed. They chattered furiously to us when we arrived, showing us their notebooks, telling us how they progressed in their Spanish lessons. For this was a Spanish school, conducted in Spanish, by Spanish teachers. The children were being brought up as Spaniards. They were told that some day they would return to their own country. They studied Russian as a foreign language, as other youngsters in other countries study French or German as the case may be.

I stayed a few days in the school and watched my Luli. I couldn't help laughing over her. At the age of ten she was quite a linguist. She spoke Russian fluently from having stayed five months with a Russian family before the school opened and still remembered her German and Italian. She headed her class in history and literature, too—but alas, she had terrible trouble learning how to ski while others of her schoolmates had developed into real masters of the art. She was no better at dancing. Charito, her bosom friend, was a beautiful and graceful ballet dancer, but not my Luli. I had to make up my mind that my small daughter was not going to grow up into an actress or dancer or an athlete or even a singer. For in spite of the good teachers and the modern methods, Luli eschewed artistic and athletic endeavors. She was, I could see, slated to be a scholar.

The headmaster at Luli's school and the Soviet medical authorities did a gracious thing for our small family. Knowing how limited our time was, they permitted Luli to stay with Ignacio and me at his sanatorium—a thing which caused major excitement at the rest-home, for children had never been admitted at this particular convalescent home before.

"But you are Spanish, and we are glad to do this little thing," the Soviet doctor said, while Luli, with shining eyes, interpreted.

I had gone with my parents to the best sanatoriums in Europe, in Germany and France. But I had never seen such a beautiful convalescent home before until we drove to the one assigned to us, about twenty-five miles outside of Moscow. It was a simple modern building, white and graceful, in the midst of a thick pine forest covered with snow. It looked like a comfortable modern hotel inside. The furnishings were simple, in beautiful taste; the furniture similar to what Americans call "Swedish modern."

We had a fine suite of three rooms in the sanatorium. The time passed very quickly. We skated and skiied, played volley ball, chess, and went to the movies three times a week. The sanatorium belonged to a trade union of Government workers, and we talked, through Luli, to porters and secretaries, Government officials and mechanics, all taking rests or recovering from illness at the sanatorium. Naturally none of these people had to pay at the sanatorium—but we were surprised to find that the sanatorium staff included specialists in almost every department of medicine. We all had our teeth looked after while we were there, Luli had her tonsils out, I was examined from head to foot.

Ignacio was allowed little exercise. He rested for two hours daily, lying on a couch on the snow-covered terrace outside our room, wrapped in furs. He used to sit in the fine library some days, too. Gradually he began to grow stronger, his face lost the strained expression to which I had grown accustomed.

And then the news from Spain grew worse, and Ignacio began to get nervous again. The enemy had concentrated an enormous supply of material near Teruel. It did not look as though the exhausted Republican Army, its supplies depleted, could hold the little town. Even worse, the officer Ignacio had left in charge of the Air Force was proving ineffective. The men Ignacio suspected as traitors, whom he had carefully isolated and put into positions of no strategical importance, were being promoted into positions of trust by Prieto, who seemed never to be able to learn a lesson.

"We must go back at once," Ignacio said one day after reading the mail from Spain.

The doctors tried to argue with him. He should stay at least another fortnight. But Ignacio would not listen and I did not try to make him. I knew he was needed in Spain and besides he would worry himself ill again so far away from the battlefront.

The farewell to Luli was very hard. I tried not to let the tears into my eyes. I tried to remind myself that no child in the world, in any country, could have happier surroundings, better teachers, better food, more love and kindness. And yet the parting was so hard. Moscow seemed so remote, such a long journey, and when would I see my little daughter again? I knew that I was fortunate; I did not need to imagine my child torn to pieces by bombs. The bombing of Barcelona would not mean Luli's agonized death. And yet—when the train pulled out of the station, and I waved my last good-by, as gaily as I could—I leaned back on the train cushions and wept very bitterly.

We returned to Barcelona in early February and were welcomed very gaily. We had saved our money and brought bags full of food back as gifts, and we sat down with all our friends that night for a gay reunion.

But Ignacio could hardly sit through the festivities. He

wanted to be back at work. The next day he flew to the front.

Before he left he stopped in to see me. "The enemy has hundreds of new planes, new fast pursuit planes and bombers. Our troops are taking impossible punishment. The situation is very grave."

Next day Maruja and I, almost alone in the big house with all the men gone and many of their wives gone back to different towns, settled down with all of Barcelona to fight the battle of Teruel by remote control. For Barcelona had changed. No longer the indifferent metropolis, the whole city lived through those days of Teruel with terrible anxiety.

The news came slowly. And always it was bad. The fascists bombed our troops at Teruel out of the very ground. Wave after wave of enemy planes flew over the trenches. Teruel became a terrible no-man's land. Once we got a note from Maruja's husband saying that the punishment our troops were taking was terrific and Teruel was no longer tenable.

Then one day a band of soldiers, shaken, without guns, wandered into Barcelona.

And we understood with a sense of awful shock that our Army was not defeated—but routed. For the open breach at Teruel was impossible to cover with troops that lacked arms, artillery, and airplanes. Our men were being blasted out of the earth itself.

The defeat we could understand. But the rout?

All Spain found the same answer we did. Prieto, the politician, had revamped the Army in the past months. The system of people's commissars had been torn out by its roots. The old-line officers whom Ignacio distrusted so, and who surrounded Prieto in his Barcelona offices, had pooh-poohed the military usefulness of what amounted to traveling teachers of the troops. "This is an army," Prieto would bluster, "not a picnic. Let the men obey orders. Soldiers don't need explanations—they need only obedience. The best soldier is the soldier who thinks the least."

Ignacio and the new military leaders trained in the war had fought this idea bitterly. "The best soldier is the soldier who knows for what he fights," Ignacio used to reply to Prieto. "The political commissars are the life-line of our Armies. They explain the *why* of things—they give examples of courage and discipline. Our people are fighting for liberty—they are not ordinary soldiers. We need a disciplined Army, yes. And we have one. But get rid of the commissars and you get rid of our one strength, our one superiority over the fascists. They have machine guns and airplanes but we have understanding."

The rout of Teruel was evidence, if evidence was needed, that *our* armies, at least, fought on understanding and understanding only.

The tragedy at Teruel brought two different kinds of response. The population took up the cry, "Political commissars for the Army!"

And Prieto and his group, who had never really believed in a people's victory against the fascist invaders, began to toy with the idea of capitulation.

The rumors of this attempt to surrender spread in Barcelona late one afternoon. That night Barcelona's greatest demonstration in history took place—almost by spontaneous combustion. Fifty thousand people, Catalans mostly, with a sprinkling of those from other parts of the country now living in Barcelona, marched on the Government building where the Cabinet was in session.

I had heard of the demonstration at the last moment. I was one of the enormous crowd that marched, singing and cheering, to the Government building. When we arrived, a loud speaker announced that a delegation of people from the various political parties would call on the Cabinet. Pasionaria's name was announced as delegate and I think the greatest tribute Dolores Ibarruri ever received was the heartfelt and wildly enthusiastic greeting she was given that night by fifty thousand Catalans.

The delegation came out of the building. "Premier Negrin," the leader announced, "has pledged his life that Spain will never surrender."

Our great demonstration turned about face, sober and orderly. We were marching down the streets towards the center when we learned, if we had not known before, what it meant to demand "no surrender." For suddenly the fascist planes droned overhead. The Germans and Italians had bombed Barcelona when we had taken Teruel. Forty-three school children had paid with their lives for the Republican victory. Now, on March 15, the Germans had no defeat to avenge. But the Nazis could never be convinced that bombardments could not demoralize the Spanish people. So several people peacefully eating their beans and lentils died in agony that night while the bombs fell and the night was hideous with explosions.

We did not know, when the explosions finally stopped, that the fascist General Staff had planned a three-day bombing of Barcelona to break the morale of Spain's civilian population.

But from the evening of March 15 until the evening of March 18, squadrons of fascist planes arrived promptly, like clock work, every three hours. Day and night. *Day and night.*

Ignacio had stopped overnight that first evening of the demonstration and flown back to the front the next day. I was glad he was not in Barcelona. I think he could not have lived in the city and kept his sanity; for the thought of a perfectly defenseless city, with not a *single* airplane to fight off the fascists, and only a few 'ineffective anti-aircraft guns, would have driven him mad. Our few airplanes—we had almost none, after Teruel—were at the front, so badly needed for military operations to defend our retreating troops that we could not spare even one squadron to defend Barcelona. I think Ignacio could not have lived through days and nights of agony and terror in Barcelona and kept his self-control, for he was the commander of the Air Force that could not save the lives of the children, that could not prevent the terror of the mothers, that could not ease the awful nervous strain.

I remember those three days with perfect clarity. I could wish I did not. Barcelona was a city of almost two million inhabitants. Most of the population lived crowded together in apartments, tenements, and built-up residential districts. Every three hours the planes flew over the city. Every three hours the sirens screamed, the fire engines tore out of their stations. And every three hours the helpless people stiffened, straightened up, and looked at each other.

Where should we go? What can we do? Will the bomb fall on us now?

On the second day we had counted over one thousand dead. On the third day nearly two thousand.

Two thousand dead. Thousands more in hospitals screaming with agony. Legs—just a leg, blown off some child's torso—lying on the bloody sidewalk. No shelter. No possible place to hide. No *refugio* that would not be a tomb.

The days were bad.

The nights were hell on earth.

At dusk, the people of Barcelona walked slowly to the foothills around the city, carrying their mattresses and blankets. For the work of the city had to go on and a man must get some sleep.

But there was no sleep. By the third day, we were crazy for sleep, shaken with fatigue, half-mad with wanting to sleep, only to sleep. But the city could not sleep. You went to bed. You lay there tense, tears of fatigue in your eyes. You fell into uneasy sleep. Suddenly you awoke. It is quiet. What time is it? You look at your watch. You have slept twenty minutes. There is still time to sleep before the next bombing. You lie still, perfectly still. You cannot sleep. Finally, after an hour of agony, you lose consciousness. You are awakened ten minutes later by the dreadful, ear-splitting, inhuman sound of a bomb exploding two blocks away. And then another, and another, and another, until you get up and dress and wander into the street, dull-eyed, shaking, trembling with the noise.

This was the bombing of Barcelona.

And yet military men have written in dry reports: "The Spanish war proved that civilian populations cannot be demoralized by bombing. The three-day bombing of Barcelona was a failure. The population responded with increased determination to fight the war."

It is true. Barcelona suffered during those three days as no other city in the history of the world has suffered. And yet the fascists could not break our spirit.

After the first day, we stopped speaking of the bombings. It was a serious breach of good manners to refer to the fascist planes at all. Nobody suggested this; no Government official asked the population to keep silent. By common consent, the population of Barcelona ignored the fascist bombs. We turned away from those who sometimes broke out into hysteria. We went about our work. The factories and offices of Barcelona operated almost at full capacity those three days. We ate our lentils and beans. We even went to the movies—why not? One may as well die in the movie as in one's bed.

You only saw the bombings in people's eyes and the stiff look around their mouths.

Even my newspapermen responded as well as they could to the situation. Their embassies offered them protection in a city thirty miles away—the diplomats had retreated to safety with the first bomb, and some even before. But the reporters had to stay. This was no ordinary bombing, worth a paragraph in the back page. This was front-page news. Two thousand dead, thousands wounded. This was a story. They had to stay.

The Hotel Majestic, where the newspapermen lived, could hardly be considered safe. The Ritz had been hit the first day and this time the fascists were dropping bombs in the smart districts as well as the poorer sections near the harbor. The newspapermen were mostly quite courageous. A few quieted their nerves with overgenerous amounts of brandy. But most of them watched the people of Barcelona and then went quietly about their business.

Day after day I had to sit behind my desk, looking calm and cheerful for my visitors. I could not be less heroic than the Spanish people. It would have been a pleasure to scream. Instead I had to sit, my face frozen into a smile, while foreign journalists sat across from me, chatting of this or that. I never saw so many people as during those seventy-two hours. Correspondents drifted into my office, wanting news from the front, or just nothing in particular. As we started to talk, the sirens would scream. We would move to the sofa. I had two large glass doors in my office and a large window. I was more afraid of flying glass than a bomb. The glass would blind you; after the bomb, there would be nothing at all to worry about.

I went to sleep that third night so exhausted I did not think of the next scheduled bombing. I dreamt of bombardments, of course. I think no one in Barcelona could dream of anything else. But this dream was strange. The bombing seemed to be under my window, and the city, seen from my room, was in flames.

It was not a dream. I woke fully. Two gasoline tanks in the harbor had been hit and were burning. All Barcelona was illuminated, bright and clear, in the high-leaping flames. I pulled down the blinds. I put my head under the pillow. But I stifled. I put the rug over me, to blot out the noise. I slept.

I awoke again, two hours later, with a terrible crash echoing and re-echoing in my ear drums. I held my breath. Another crash shook all the windows and the wooden frame of the house. I did not move. I tried to stop my breathing—as though any little noise would betray me to this hideous, merciless enemy outside my doors. A third crash. Broken glass smashed to the floor. Furniture fell. I sat up, stupidly, blinking, silent.

"Are you all right?" Maruja cried from the door.

"Oh, yes," I said politely. "Oh, yes. And you?"

"Yes," Maruja said.

Our voices were unnaturally quiet. The bombs had fallen in the yard, just missing the house. We got little sleep that night.

We all thought—hoped rather—that the bombings had ended with the night. In the morning the fascists let four, almost five hours pass. At my office I avoided seeing visitors. I just sat at my desk, staring into space. The office staff sat quietly, too, not working much, just sitting.

About midday every door and window in our office flung open violently. Bombs fell, heavy bombs, and very near. We all stood up. The newspapermen in the office rose. Nobody said anything. We just looked at each other. Each bomb seemed nearer. Once a correspondent said, "They are using bigger bombs than yesterday." I nodded. The girl stenographers did not scream or get hysterics. They just stood perfectly still, their hands white where they clenched the edge of their desks, looking into each other's eyes.

I think I learned what it meant to be a Spaniard that fifteen minutes on the eighteenth of March, 1938. We have been trained in my country to austerity. There was no place to run during that bombardment, and no reason to run if there had been a place. There was no hope of escaping the bombs. For three days and three nights we had gone without sleep, living with fear. Now let the bombs fall. We stood still, staring at each other with soundless intensity, waiting for death.

Then the noise stopped. The tinkling sound of glass—I will never hear it as long as I live without thinking of the bombardments—lasted for a few moments more. And then silence.

We were not, then, to die just now.

We sat down. One girl began to cry into her handkerchief and we all looked reproachfully at her. "It's nothing," she said. "I was only thinking of my brother who was killed."

We all nodded, grateful for her excuse.

At midday I went to a restaurant with my secretary and her husband. The restaurant was very crowded, every table was taken. We sat down at a table with a stranger. We ate. The food was worse than usual—water soup, a tiny piece of meat, lettuce and three nuts. The planes flew over again as we ate our meat. We could see them right over us through the little window by the side of our table.

For the first time in the three days I felt my nerves giving way. I began to fear surviving the bombs. We sat in a one-story building, with no floors above us to protect us even a little. The restaurant was so crowded. If the bomb fell, and I survived it, I would be alive in the midst of death. I saw the crowded restaurant after the bomb had struck. I began to clench my hands. Only to die when the bomb hit. Only to die at once, and not suffer, and not see the dead and maimed, and not hear their shrieks. Only not to hear them dying and see them. The thing began to make a pattern in my mind. Only to die. Only to die at once. Just that I might not hear it and see it. Only not to hear the shrieks.

A hush fell over the restaurant. Every person put down his spoons and forks and knives. The waiters stood motionless, their trays held on their arms. The heavy drone of the planes passed directly above us.

They faded, and the explosions sounded distant. They were bombing the residential suburbs.

People began to talk again. But I felt no words in my mind, only immense relief.

"Your hands," my secretary said.

I pulled my hands away from the side of the table. I had clenched the table until my palms ached with the effort. I rose.

"I will go back to the office," I said stiffly. "Thank you for dinner."

I walked back alone. The streets were torn and maimed. Great apartment houses were smashed into piles of mortar. Buildings still burned.

I went to my desk. I sat still. The telephone rang. I did not answer it. I was alone. The silence beat on my nerves. "Come again," I said to myself, "come again now. I am alone now, it doesn't matter. Come again, I can stand it for myself, it's only when I will die with all those others that I can't stand it."

I shook myself. I must get hold of my nerves.

I went home that night and fell asleep. I awoke in the morning. There had been no bombings in the night.

Next day Barcelona was "normal." We only mourned our dead.

One morning Barcelona awoke to find that all trains and trams had stopped. "Air raid?" people asked each other as they stood on the street corners. The city scanned the sky anxiously for the inevitable planes. But when hours passed without the familiar and dreadful drone of motors overhead, the news began to circulate: the fascists had captured Tremp, Catalonia's largest electric power station.

The people of Barcelona took the news with simple courage. For weeks they walked back and forth to their factories, and ate their meals at night in darkness. For there wasn't a candle or a lamp to be had in Barcelona. In our house we used a strange device nights—an eau de Cologne bottle filled with gasoline, giving a flame through the small hole in the stopper. The stench and the smoke were terrible, but it was better than eating in complete darkness. When Ignacio returned from the front a month later, he installed a small electric generator in our house. After a few months the Government imported coal, at enormous expense, to generate power for the Catalan industries and the Barcelona housewives had electricity again for a few hours a day.

The military situation grew more difficult in the early Spring of 1938 after Teruel. The fascists were advancing on three fronts. In the far north, they attempted to isolate Catalonia from France—this was why Barcelona went dark when Franco and his Italians took Tremp, the great power station. On another northern front, the fascists were advancing to Lérida on the main road from Saragossa, hoping to close in on Barcelona from this position as well. And finally the fascist troops, heavily armed, backed by light and heavy artillery and an enormous concentration of planes, were advancing in the south of Catalonia to the Mediterranean. They expected to cut off Catalonia from the rest of Spain by this implacable march to the sea.

The whole world held its breath during those dark weeks. But Prieto, the Minister of Defense, sat for days on end in his office, like a man paralyzed. He expected complete defeat momentarily. He had no faith in the people. He waited for his own pessimistic predictions to come true. The officers at the front, infuriated to see the Minister of Defense sinking into apathy at the very moment when he was needed most, begged Dr. Negrin to act. And finally after a few terrible days, when the commanders of the troops at the front could not even get answers to their frantic telegrams and calls to the office of the Minister of Defense, Dr. Negrin, who had been a personal friend of Prieto for years, now reluctantly had to take the reins of the Defense Ministry into his own hands. Prieto, sulking and petty, retreated to his own house.

Dr. Negrin's problem was far from easy. In a great speech, made just before he took his new office, he called on all the Spanish people to resist the fascists with their very lives. In his clear, unornamented prose he explained that victory was truly possible, if only we could stop the enemy *now*. Our war factories in Catalonia were beginning to turn out guns and airplanes. In a short time we ourselves would be able to begin an offensive—if only the soldiers and the rear guard understood that "resistance now was the first step to final victory."

These calm and hopeful words of Dr. Negrin rallied the people of Spain at home and at the front. But they were only the beginning. Prieto had left the Ministry of Defense in inconceivable confusion. Dr. Negrin had to reorganize the Army.

In the meantime the fascists with their enormous superiority of guns and bullets pushed through to the Mediterranean. They took Vinaroz on April 15, 1938—by a bitter coincidence, the day before the signature of the Anglo-Italian Pact on the status-quo of the Mediterranean.

Our revived Army, still badly equipped but now filled with determination, began to dispute the fascist plans to overwhelm democratic Spain. General Franco had planned to make a fan-like offensive from Vinaroz north to Barcelona and south to Valencia. But in the north our troops were able to hold the Italian invaders at the mouth of the Ebro. The front was established at the beginning of May at Tortosa, a little seacoast town.

In the south, the people of Valencia, inspired by Dr. Negrin's great call for resistance, helped the Army build fortifications to hold back the fascist invaders. Sagunto, Spain's last city of blast-furnaces after the loss of Bilbao, became the rallying point for our soldiers. From April until July, the furious battle raged almost without cessation. The fury of the fascist advance was expended on the brave defenders of Sagunto. And the battle of Levante which began as a fascist triumph ended as a democratic victory.

Spain's armies could never have made the enormous sacrifice necessary to defeat the fascist offensive without what we called in Spain "the Thirteen Points." Dr. Negrin, on May 1, announced these thirteen principles, the full, complete, and truthful program of the Spanish Republic. He explained that these declarations, drawn up by a Government of National Union, were designed not only to show the outside world but every Spaniard, both in our territory and in the fascist-held zone, what the Spanish people stood for. Here was our answer to the liars in London who called us "Communists," here was our appeal to misled Spaniards inside Franco territory who, we felt sure, abhorred the invasion of their country.

I put down the "Thirteen Points" in their entirety for this was the only formal, legal, and complete program ever put forward by our Government. This is for what we fought and for what we still fight:

1. The absolute independence and integrity of Spain.
2. The liberation of Spanish territory from foreign occupation and foreign influence.
3. A people's republic.
4. A plebescite on the form of government when the war ended.
5. Respect of regional liberties, compatible with Spanish unity.
6. Full social and civic rights for every Spaniard, including liberty of religious worship and conscience.
7. Protection of private property and the elements of production, but also prevention of such accumulations of wealth as might result in the exploitation of the citizens.
8. Complete agrarian reform.
9. Social legislation guaranteeing rights of workers.
10. The cultural, physical, and moral improvement of the nation.
11. A non-political Army as an instrument for the defense of the people.
12. Renunciation of war as an instrument of national policy and fidelity to the League of Nations.
13. Amnesty for all Spaniards who proved they desired to co-operate in the work of reconstruction—the amnesty to include common soldiers in the Rebel Army.

This program united Spain during the hard days after our territory was cut in two. For a food shortage in Barcelona followed immediately on the defeat. With the rich Valencia valley out of reach of supply trucks, with the advance of enemy troops into Catalonia and the capture of Aragon, Barcelona had to import all its food from France. The city grew more and more crowded with refugees, and the increased population faced worsening food conditions.

Communications with the southern zone were difficult, and it took us some time to begin radio talks, never very satisfactory for they became quite public. The coast was severely bombarded and ships going to and from Valencia and Barcelona were bombed and sunk by German and Italian submarines and pocket battleships. The airlines remained the only sure way of reaching the central and southern zones, but service had to be severely limited.

Every other morning at dawn a Douglas plane, one of the four owned by the Government—only one of which we had been able to buy after the war, and that second-hand—would leave Barcelona for Valencia or Albacete, returning the next day. How often Ignacio flew on that plane and how often I was left alone, thinking of an attack on the helpless transport by enemy pursuit planes! But the Rebels never brought down our Douglas transport, in all those months of flying over miles of Rebel territory!

Once, the Douglas in which Ignacio was flying back from Valencia was about to land at the Barcelona airport when suddenly the air raid sirens began their familiar wail. The city's scattered anti-aircraft guns started shooting at the Italian bombers flying overhead, when suddenly the big Douglas appeared in the sky. For a moment the enemy bombers and our Douglas seemed to merge in the air while the bewildered anti-aircraft gunners watched in horror. Then the pilot in the Douglas beat a hasty retreat and managed to land at an airport some miles from Barcelona.

In the midst of these difficulties, I got a new assignment. The Foreign Minister, Alvarez del Vayo, called me in one day to say that he was taking me with him to Geneva to handle the press when Spain made its appeal to the League of Nations. Not that we expected anything from an organization dominated by the British Foreign Office; Del Vayo was first and last a realist.

But at a time when every embassy in Europe felt that Spain was dying, we intended to show the whole world that Spain still lived. For after the fascist victory in mid-April, the knowing gentlemen in European diplomatic posts gave us three weeks to live. Now a month had already passed, and Del Vayo intended to demonstrate our vitality by making an important declaration before the League Assembly.

I went to Geneva on May 10 curious about the operations of the august body called the League of Nations. But I could not wait to return to Spain, I was so sickened by the shocking behavior of the English and French Governments. I think cynicism, and treachery reached their highest points at Geneva that early Summer of 1938.

We arrived to find the city filled with diplomats, their secretaries, reporters, Franco agents and their fascist Latin American friends, bystanders of every nation and kind. The correspondents, barred from the private meetings, crowded together for hours in the famous long marble corridor outside the Assembly Hall. Rumors and whispers passed rapidly up and down the corridor—talk of the Italian-British accord recently signed, pessimistic rumors about the coming fate of Czechoslovakia.

In the midst of all this intrigue, Del Vayo made his historic stand. He called on the League of Nations to end the outrageous "Non-Intervention" Committee which only served as a convenient mask for the invasion of Spain by Italy and Germany. Lord Halifax engineered Del Vayo's defeat. Cool, contemptuous, superior, Lord Halifax tried to steam-roller the Spanish question.

We saw him one night in our hotel dining room during the League sessions.

His Lordship had ordered fruit to end his dinner, as we had. The waiter brought us a basket of choice fruit and put it on the table before us. But Lord Halifax was not made of our common clay. A waiter brought him an enormous basket of lush and precious fruit. Lord Halifax waved his finger to indicate his choice.

Thereupon a uniformed page boy presented the head waiter with a box from which that dignitary drew a pair of spotless white gloves. Slowly, he drew the gloves over his freshly scrubbed hands, deliberately he took the piece of fruit Lord Halifax had selected from the basket and put it on his Lordship's plate. The whole staff then stood, their faces one great question mark, while Lord Halifax cut a piece of the fruit. Then they all relaxed—his Lordship had nodded, and everything appeared to be satisfactory.

This was the great English gentleman who sat with a supercilious smile on his face while Del Vayo begged the League to restore Spain's rights in international law. Somehow it would have been easier for us Spaniards if we had found a single human being in Geneva who thought us liars, or who disputed our facts, or who really believed us wrong. But nobody did—least of all Lord Halifax and his supporters. Every articulate person in Geneva knew that we had justice, international law, democracy, liberty—everything on our side. And everyone raised their eyebrows and said delicately—so delicately—"What of it?" Lord Halifax, for instance, did not bother to answer Del Vayo's charges that while the Italian-English accord was being drafted, Mussolini sent a whole new detachment of troops to Spain and the Italian press boasted again that Italian troops in Spain had been the first to reach the Mediterranean at Vinaroz. Bonnet did not even speak of the Spanish question. Why should these fine gentlemen waste their breath denying what everyone knew was true? Of course Spain was being invaded by Germany and Italy. Of course. And what rude, uncouth fellows we were to even bring the unfortunate matter up.

And the Halifax steam-roller worked. The vote on the resolution was four to two; England, France, Poland, and Roumania voted "no;" Spain and the Soviet Union voted "yes." Nine members of the Council abstained.

Immediately afterwards the American Government, following the wake of England, refused to lift the embargo on arms to Spain.

We returned to Spain abandoned by nearly the whole world to find that our Armies, in spite of treachery from abroad, were holding the fascist offensive.

In the midst of these trying days, Herbert Matthews came in the office with Jo Davidson, the American sculptor. Davidson had a brilliant—and generous—idea. He wanted to do a series of heads of Spanish leaders and afterwards present them in an exhibition in New York to tell Americans what sort of people were engaged in the fight against fascism in Spain. The idea I approved heartily. But my heart fell as I thought of how difficult it would be to execute. Naturally Davidson wanted to do the leading personalities of Spain—Del Vayo, Negrin, Pasionaria, and so on. How on earth could I get men and women struggling with life-and-death problems of defense to stop long enough to pose for their busts?

"And," Davidson said, "I want to do you."

I said "no" promptly.

"Well, if you think you're not important enough personally, then as a Spanish type. I want to do several heads of the people —just ordinary Spaniards."

I began to demur again until I had a sudden idea. I would pose immediately and in the meantime I would try to scare up a few more subjects for Davidson, who was in a great hurry.

I was tired, nearly ill from exhaustion in those days, and as there were no tram cars running I had to walk a mile from our office to the Ritz Hotel every noon during luncheon hour to pose for Davidson and then a mile back. So I must have looked very tired to Davidson, whose beautifully modeled head of me makes me seem an ascetic! But then, none of us laughed very much in Barcelona during the Spring of 1938.

But at that, posing was easier than getting others to pose. I had to beg, plead, threaten, and argue to get our leaders to take time off from saving Spain to pose for an artist, even as great an artist as Davidson. But finally he succeeded in getting nearly all the names on his list to pose for him. He took his plaster right up to the front lines to get some of his subjects. Only Dr. Negrin would not pose. But then, he never would. He hated personal publicity and assiduously dodged all camera men, sketchers, and the like.

One day about the middle of July, most of Barcelona was puzzled to observe hundreds of small fishermen's boats being carried through the streets on trucks.

"What on earth is the meaning of that?" I asked Ignacio that evening. Ignacio smiled. "This is a secret—we are going to start an offensive."

"When?"

"Tomorrow night."

I was puzzled. An Army that had been cut to pieces three months before, an Army without guns or airplanes! How could we start an offensive?

But Ignacio explained that our own factories in Barcelona were at last turning out the famous *Chatos*. And even better, the Russians had sold us more airplanes, the first since those November days so long ago. For after our first shipment of planes, France had refused to let war materials cross her borders. Now at last we had found a way to get some Russian planes to our borders, and Ignacio was in seventh heaven. An Air Force again! Or anyway, part of one! Of course, the fascists had five times as many planes, nay, probably eight or nine times as many—but what of that? We could beat them every time if we just had a *few* planes, a few guns, instead of none at all.

The crossing of the Ebro was the greatest news story of the Spanish war, and one of the greatest military feats of history.

Colonel Modesto, who planned it, and lieutenant-colonel Lister, who executed it, relied on surprise, quick timing, and the courage and discipline of their troops.

They used the fishing boats to sweep across the river, landing their troops long before the Italians knew they had a battle to fight. Indeed, our first two captured villages were kept a complete secret. The peasants, Republicans to the last man, helped us to keep up the Italian communications with false messages, and long after our troops had marched off, double time, to new villages, the peasants were cheerfully informing the Italian general staff on the telegraph key: "All quiet here. All quiet here." We even captured a German officer in bed.

When the enemy finally woke up to the fact that Lister was advancing deep into their territory they began to bomb the bridges our soldiers were setting up. But Modesto and Lister, men of the people, had lots of common sense ideas which often occur to ordinary men and seldom to generals. They stretched canvas across the river—and from the air the Italian pilots thought they were bombing bridges as they wasted explosives on our old canvas. The real bridges, covered with mud and dirt and branches, were hard to identify from the air.

Thus the four-month battle of the Ebro began with a great victory.

Our small Air Force responded to the situation with great bravery and skill. Our soldiers had a special admiration for our planes and their pilots. And with the first days of the offensive, Ignacio was made a general. He scorned the promotion personally and told his men it was really a recognition of their services.

The correspondents filled my office. The Foreign Ministry had resumed its censorship duties. I had simply asked the Catalan Minister of Interior to let our office handle the foreign press, including the censorship, and to my surprise, he had agreed. A very able Spanish professor and very intelligent linguist handled the Censorship Department, however, for my hands were very full meeting reporters and giving out news. My staff grew to include fifty-two people, mostly women, for the majority of the men had joined the Army. Most of the women had never worked before in their lives but their zeal and intelligence made our office efficient. We had none of the bureaucratic or formal methods of the ordinary Government office. Because we had started from nothing we did not have to break down old habits. Everyone in the office worked with one thing in mind—to win the war. Anyone who did not share the common goal soon left, or was asked to leave. As the months passed, my office staff grew into a solid group of women who were friends and Spaniards, united through air raids and death and personal loss—and common love of our country.

And we needed this feeling of solidarity to sustain ourselves, for the battle of the Ebro which began so brilliantly gradually turned into a heartbreaking tragedy. Our People's Army advanced two hundred square miles after crossing the Ebro. The whole world gaped—amazed that a people which had suffered such privation and terror, such defeat and difficulty, had the strength for this great offensive.

But the advance was halted—halted literally by a solid wall

of steel. The Italians and Germans, shocked and horrified by their defeat, threw every inch of cannon, every machine gun and plane they could hastily ship to Spain, into the conflict. Colonel Modesto said in August, "This is the most formidable front I have ever seen. The fascists used ninety-five tanks on a four mile section of the front and more planes than I have ever seen in the air at one time."

The world took our advance across the Ebro for granted and few realized that we had thrown all our strength and resources into this desperate effort to stop the fascist pressure on Valencia. Our few planes and guns and tanks and machine guns went into the splendid advance—all the supplies we had accumulated. When the fascists brought us to a halt and started pushing us back, inch by inch, we gave everything we had in courage and heart, every final resource our poverty-stricken nation could muster, to defend the Ebro.

Month after month we held the fascists. Think of what it means—almost without guns and planes at all toward the end, we stood our ground, day after day, under a blasting sheet of shells and bombs. The fascists lost 70,000 men in that battle. But we lost the picked troops of our Army. The fascists got new shipments of Italian cannon fodder from Mussolini, docile, bewildered Italians. But Spain could never replace the men of Modesto's and Lister's brigades, the soldiers who began the war as the famous "Fifth Regiment," who fought their way through battle after battle, and who finally died, having sworn to defend the Ebro with their lives, in the long, tragic battle.

When the General Staff finally, on November 16, 1938, ordered the troops back across the Ebro, the retreating soldiers left their bravest officers, their most heroic comrades in shallow graves on the enemy side of the river. Ignacio could never replace the pilots who performed such feats of bravery at the Ebro—nor the planes that carried them first to victory and then to death.

Europe had said Spain would die in May, 1938. But until November 16, 1938, we held the fascists on the other side of the Ebro. The world never knew what the battle of the Ebro cost us in courage, men, and supplies. We fought the last part

of that battle with our fists and the fascists fought it with heavy
artillery.

And still we did not despair. I heard the news of the retreat
across the Ebro before it broke in the world headlines—but I
heard it without flinching. For the offensive against the Ebro
had startled all Rebel Spain. We knew that the people of
Spain, whether in territory captured by Franco or not, were
never fascist. We knew they hated the foreign invaders. But our
offensive against the Ebro brought them all new hope. Riots
broke out in Rebel Spain. The Carlists fought with the Falangists. Franco faced unrest in his rear guard.

Meantime Dr. Negrin, at an hour when we needed our picked
troops, had the courage to announce the withdrawal of our
foreign volunteers. They were six thousand of these men, anti-
fascists from all over the world, who fought side by side with
our Spanish troops, bravely and with discipline.

The Chamberlain Government was trying to fool the world
again with another bogus plan for withdrawing the foreign
troops from "both sides" and Dr. Negrin forestalled that piece
of chicanery by withdrawing our six thousand volunteers from
abroad. No longer could Lord Halifax deliver mealy-mouthed
speeches about foreign troops on "both sides," while hundreds
of thousands of Italians battled our six thousand friends. We
hated to say good-by to the foreign volunteers. They had
fought with unexampled courage and discipline. We no longer
needed to learn from them, for our Armies had mastered self-
discipline. But our hearts were filled with gratitude as we
planned to bid good-by to these men from far-away countries
who had come to Spain to fight for democracy, leaving behind
so many comrades buried in the Spanish earth.

But before we could complete our plans to bid the Internationals farewell, Spain suddenly forgot its own agony in the
Czechoslovakian crisis. I can never forget those dreadful days
of suspense. We knew intimately the treachery of the British
and French Foreign Offices. And yet we could not believe they
would abandon the Czechs as they had abandoned us. And if
only the Czech frontier held, our own cause was reborn.

Day after day the radio held us fascinated. We felt our fate being settled far away. We felt with the Czech people hour after hour. And then Chamberlain played the drama of the great betrayal.

Long after the rest of the world had given up Czechoslovakia, we Spaniards sat beside our radios, sick with suspense. For we thought that the Czechoslovak people would fight, despite their political leaders, despite their betrayal. Only think of the guns and airplanes and forts they had! Surely they would turn those guns on the Germans! Surely it is better to die fighting than live on your knees.

Even after the first German troops had crossed the frontier, we Spaniards still thought the Czechs would fight. The Army, in those splendid forts, manned with those fine guns, would defend the country. But the same discipline that saved Spain betrayed the Czechs. The Army fell back without fighting. We could only thank heaven that the Spanish Army had revolted against its officers in our own July, 1936. Discipline is all very well at the right time. We believed that a little less discipline in the Czech Army would have saved the country.

And so Chamberlain betrayed another democracy to the fascists, and another people were made homeless by the scratch of his pen.

And the Spanish people, alone in Europe, were left to carry on the fight against fascism. We resolved, after Munich, to carry on our struggle, not only for our own freedom, but for the liberty of people everywhere.

And we thought we would win—unless all the cards were stacked against us. They were.

It took us a few days to recover from Munich. And then we began to make plans for bidding a fine farewell to the International Brigades. Ignacio dreaded the parade. He was afraid that the fascists would get wind of the demonstration and slaughter the cheering population. For that reason, the hour and even the date of the parade were not scheduled. People watched the decorations on the Avenue of April 14th carefully for signs of the intended ceremony. Every florist in Barcelona had orders from workers, trade unions, girl secretaries, for the great day.

Finally on the afternoon of October 17, Ignacio came home to lunch to say the parade would be held that afternoon. And as I went back to work the streets were filling with people, everyone carrying flowers. There were no Moors to keep them from the curbs, no secret police to line the avenues and prevent the people from even seeing the parade. Franco has never held a "victory" parade without calling out half his Army to keep the "celebrators" at a safe distance.

But all of Barcelona turned out that day to bid a fond farewell to our Internationals—and not a policeman in sight. Our political leaders. Pasionaria among them, walked right through the crowds to the platform, while the people pressed close to see and cheer them. Dr. Negrin's car drove right along the curb and the young girls impulsively began to pelt him with bouquets. Nobody searched the bouquets for bombs. The Spanish people were united with one common aim and one common hope— liberty for all.

The parade began with a detachment of picked soldiers and sailors from the People's Army. I could not keep the tears from my eyes. Our Army looked so strong, so well trained, so healthy. Our soldiers marched smartly, with their heads up, often singing as they passed. The people knew we were still holding at the Ebro, and they cheered these troops madly. But alas, I knew our position was already untenable—most of the guns these paraders carried were for looks only. Every gun that could still fire was at the Ebro and they were not enough.

And after the Spanish soldiers came the Internationals. They were greeted with touching and profound enthusiasm. From the start of the march girls piled flowers in their arms. They carried no guns, but roses and great sweet-smelling blooms covered their hats and battered old uniforms. Many of them had little Spanish boys perched on their shoulder—so that when the boys grew up their mothers could say: "When you were four years old, one of the heroes of the International Brigades carried you down the Avenue in the parade!"

I think I have never seen such enthusiasm. The Spanish people said good-by to their friends from abroad with a mighty display of gratitude. And when, at the speakers' platform, they blew taps for the Internationals who would never return home but always stay with us in Spain, all Barcelona bared its head and wept.

Governments betrayed and abandoned us but men from all over the world came to die in our country—that democracy might live. The Spanish people were given new hope and strength and pride because Englishmen and Americans and Poles and Germans and Italians and Frenchmen came to our country and laid down their lives so that Spain might be free.

History has no greater story to tell than the record of the International Brigades.

The bombardments of the coastal towns became continuous. Barcelona suffered almost daily air raids. Dozens of small Spanish harbors were very nearly bombed off the face of the earth. Food ship after food ship was sunk by Italian and German planes.

The Spanish Government at last announced to the world that we could no longer suffer these terrible raids in silence. We could not retaliate by bombing towns in Franco territory—for Spaniards were not to blame for the children we counted dead, the mothers dying of starvation.

No, we would retaliate by bombing those who murdered our school children and starved our people. The industrial triangle of Turin, Milan, Genoa was only 480 miles distant from our airdrome at Gerona.

With our announcement, the British Government took a sudden interest in the bombing of civilian populations for the first time in the whole war. A commission was formed and sent to Toulouse to investigate complaints of bombing of civilians "from both sides." Naturally the Rebels had nothing to bring to the commission, but the English gentlemen were kept busy acting on the Spanish Government's complaints. No sooner had they started investigating the slaughter of non-combatants, than news would come of another. The commission was always a dozen bombings behind schedule. And of course, having investigated the bombings, nothing was ever done about them—Mussolini's wrist wasn't even slapped. The commission was only a fake to prevent the Spanish Government from bombing Italian industrial regions.

Along with this bombing commission, the British Government decided to "humanize" the Spanish war. The Spanish people, cold, starving, watching the British ships bringing them food sink in their harbors, mourning their children destroyed by fascist bombs, regarded the attempts of the British to "humanize" the war with some irritation.

Still, one English commission after another arrived in Barcelona. Although we knew these commissions hunted opportunities to "mediate" a peace at the expense of the Spanish people, we had to welcome them all, as best we could. One, I remember, was headed by Field Marshal Sir Philip Chetwood; its task was the exchange of war prisoners. Sir Philip, his lady, his secretaries, and the rest of his retinue arrived in Barcelona as the English always arrive when visiting their huge empire, carrying immense mounds of baggage containing everything not to be found in semi-civilized countries.

Dr. Negrin assigned three Spanish officers to meet Sir Philip; immaculate in their dress uniforms, speaking exceedingly correct English, they met the English delegation and drove them to a small palace next to the Premier's home. Later the officers reported to their Spanish friends with considerable hilarity that our English guests had apparently expected to be lodged in a tent and were much surprised by the elegance of their living quarters!

Next morning I took Lady Chetwood for a drive through Barcelona. Our whole household had contributed items to my wearing apparel and I turned up at the palace sporting gloves (for the first time in the war), the last pair of silk stockings any woman in our house owned, and a fashionable tailored suit. And more. Not for nothing had I grown up in one of Spain's haughtiest families. It had been years since I had left calling cards on silver trays and looked down my nose.

But now I trotted out all my old-régime manners and Lady Chetwood, who began our conversation in a somewhat casual manner, was soon toeing the mark I set.

"Shall I give you a few figures on the war?" I enquired icily.

"Pray do," Lady Chetwood replied somberly, obviously much astonished.

"Over four thousand men, women, and children—mostly children—have been killed by fascist air raids in Catalonia alone," I began while Lady Chetwood winced, "and in Barcelona, 5,963 buildings have been completely destroyed."

Later I shifted to Gothic architecture and took Lady Chetwood on a tour of historical buildings until I think even her English feet were tired. And in the course of the morning I gathered that Lady Chetwood was surprised that (a) our ruffians had not stripped the palace where she was staying of all its valuables, (b) that the Spanish officers had good manners and did not wear overalls, and (c) that her husband had not been met by Dr. Negrin himself.

"Well," I said very politely, to this last, "of course Dr. Negrin is so very busy with the war—otherwise he would have seen Sir Philip last night, I am sure."

"Ah," Lady Chetwood said thoughtfully.

When I took her back to her palace, a formal invitation to dinner awaited Lady Chetwood and her husband. "Black tie requested," the invitation said in the best English manner.

But it developed that these gentlemen had omitted from their enormous baggage the one item required by Englishmen who expect to have any dealings with their equals. For that night Dr. Negrin presided over a formal dinner at which the Englishmen present were the only ones not wearing dinner jackets! And it was not the Spaniards who mentally squirmed. We all felt that Lord Chetwood would take his dinner jacket to Spain the next time he came.

The visiting Englishmen were a sort of ironic relief in the face of the increasing tragedy of the war. For as our troops retreated across the Ebro, the fascists prepared for a great offensive on the Catalonian front. They realized, as we did, the immense importance of holding the French border.

On Christmas night, four Italian divisions started the drive in the north of Catalonia between Lérida and Balaguer. Three days later Ignacio remarked, over our usual dinner of lentils and beans, "They have massed six hundred planes on the Segre front alone."

We all put down our forks and stared at him.

"How many do we have?" I said finally.

"About ninety, including the 'Krone circus.' "

The "Krone circus," named for a famous European traveling menagerie which used to visit Madrid, was a wonderful collection of ancient and peculiar airplanes, remodeled transports, slow old boats that often just fell apart from age, in the air, and so on.

"But never mind," Ignacio said, eating lentils again, "we can still give the fascists plenty of trouble."

We all dutifully tried to smile and turned back to the lentils.

The fascists began their advance from Tortosa up the coast towards Barcelona early in January, 1939.

Our troops, most of them raw recruits and poorly armed, fell back. Colonel Modesto rushed the remnants of his famous Army Corps, decimated at the Ebro, into the breach. Rifles were our worst need. Machine guns, of course, were an unheard-of luxury. All—and this is no exaggeration—all our heavy and most of our light field artillery had been used up in our attempt to hold the Ebro.

The fascists were attacking us on three fronts of Catalonia, on the north, on the west, and on the south. Never before in the war had our enemies been so well armed. Our intelligence service reported that they were using completely new stores of war materials for the offensive. On all three fronts our troops were being blasted with heavy shells, light artillery, machine guns, tanks, and of course the airplanes—six hundred alone on one front, nearly as many on the others.

And against this onslaught of steel and high explosives, we could only offer our bodies for defense. Our best troops had fallen at the Ebro. New recruits with little training, men of over thirty-five and boys under twenty, had to stand this withering fire of shells and bombs. One out of three men had a rifle—

the other two stood beside him, waiting for him to fall before
they could fire a shot at the advancing enemy.

Our people abroad had tried since the beginning of the war
to buy arms and get them delivered. Now we made final desperate efforts, in a kind of agony, as a smothering man gasps
for air. We were the legal government of Spain. Our country
was being invaded by Germany and Italy. Our fight was the
fight of the world—democracy threatened by fascism. Would no
one help us? Surely the United States would lift the arms embargo? Surely the people of England would force the British
Foreign Office to end the treachery? Surely the men of France
would not see us strangled?

The Soviet Union, alone in the world, would sell us arms—
but how could we get them delivered?

New Year's Day, 1939.

We awoke in the morning and ate the inevitable lentils and
chewed on the bad bread. We went to our work and came home
again at night and tried to sleep. And always we had the feeling of being choked, almost a physical feeling of an enemy's
hands at our throats. Day and night, all Barcelona could think
of nothing but the front. All Spain lived in helpless agony
through the first days of the new year.

That first week Ignacio flew to the various fronts every day
and seldom slept at home. Then the fronts changed so rapidly
he stayed in Barcelona at the Air Ministry offices. But he hardly
slept at night at all, and he seldom spoke at meals.

At my office the newspapermen came in and sat down at my
desk, mentioned the weather, mentioned some piece of gossip,
and then sat, in heavy silence. Sometimes they would say, "What
do you think, Constancia?"

And I would reply, "Their offensive cannot last forever. Even
they cannot use guns and shells and bombs at this rate forever."

Usually the newspapermen would nod and go away. Sometimes they went on, speaking heavily, looking away from me to
the floor, or the ceiling, examining their fingernails. "But if
the fascists continue to supply the offensive at the present
rate . . ."

And then I could only answer, no longer glib, no longer in military terms, but only from my heart: "Spain will be free. Spain will never be fascist."

I have never changed my mind.

A little after the New Year I sent away the child-refugees we had taken into the house. The bombardments never stopped now. Day and night the sirens screamed, day and night the skies were lit with fires. Ambulances clanged through the streets at all hours; hearses collected the mangled bodies of the latest casualties. Hour after hour and day after day the fascists bombed Barcelona, destroying the children, maiming the women, shattering the nerves.

The news from the front grew more grave. The year before the news from the front had been even worse, for the Army had been routed. Our troops were not running now. Our Army was not demoralized. It was only that our men had no arms, not even any rifles. An unarmed man is killed, and then the fascists step on his body to advance. That was the advance on Barcelona. The crack Italian divisions, well trained, magnificently armed, smartly uniformed, advanced under cover of heavy artillery and airplane bombs. They waited until they had killed all the men in one trench; then they walked over the bodies to the next trench.

Many of our troops in the Barcelona defense had been called to the colors only a week or two before. They had no time to receive military training. We had to send them to the front without uniforms or guns—a human wall between us and the fascists, nothing more. Our best officers had been killed at the Ebro. Even the crack regiments were far under-officered. The new troops hardly had leaders at all. More, these men drafted at the last minute were those who obviously had not understood the struggle very well or they would have volunteered before. Yet we had to draft them. Our cause was a common one. We would either be all slaves or all free.

Early in the evening of January 23, I attended a women's conference. Our men were at the front. The women of Barcelona organized to fortify the city.

The fascists had passed the last ring of fortifications protecting Barcelona. Now we planned to tear up the city pavement and build barricades within the city limits. Women were to be supplied with oil—to be lighted and poured on the heads of the fascist invaders. We would sell our lives dearly.

But the conference was heavy-spirited and the plans for the fortification of the city limits seemed fanciful even to those of us who made them. Nine times during the evening we had to suspend our meeting during a fresh bombardment and nine times we stood alone while the bombs crashed, each of us reflecting on what none of us would say aloud.

For Barcelona, in all truth, was untenable, and we knew it, but we could not say it—the words stuck in our throats.

The city lies in a beautiful natural hollow, surrounded by hills, and easily accessible from the south where the river Llobregat flows. The enemy was advancing and once they held the heights, Barcelona would be completely cut off from the rest of the world. The fascists could make short work of it by sea, air, and land.

The whole Army, of course, might be brought into Barcelona to defend it, but already we were starving in the city and with the population nearly doubled and all escape cut off— what then? And if we brought the Army to Barcelona, the rest of Catalonia, up to the French frontier, would be in fascist hands.

The choice was a terrible one. In the end it came down to a simple question: Shall we all die in Barcelona, or shall we try to fight to the last in northern Catalonia on the French frontier?

I have heard people say: But they held Madrid, why not Barcelona? The war was young when Madrid was defended. The best and strongest men and women leaped to fight the fascists at their gates. In Barcelona almost two million people had lived for a year and more with only lentils and little else to give them life. In Barcelona almost two million people had lived for a year and more with the whine of the air raid siren and the crash of the falling bomb never for one moment out of their minds and dreams.

The women's conference asked the people of Barcelona, the people still left in the city, the very old men, the very young boys, and the women: Will you die fighting or will you just die? And these people answered: We will just die. Human beings reach a point of suffering when death is better than any effort against it. The best and the strongest men of Barcelona had gone to the front months and years ago—or had been killed in the incessant air raids.

We could not defend Barcelona any longer. All the strength and will to live of the Spanish people were concentrated in the Army—and the Army could not save the beautiful city of Catalonia.

The end was very near. I went home from the women's conference and lay sleepless in bed, too sick at heart to even shed tears. The bombardments went on all night, but I hardly heard them, thinking only of Spain, my country, dearer than life itself, stretched now on the rack of fascism.

Next morning, January 23, I went to work as usual. The newspapermen came and sat in my office. We had little to say to each other. The girl secretaries sat quietly. Now and then the air raid sirens screamed, but we hardly noticed.

At eleven o'clock the Under-Secretary of our Department called me into his office. The Minister of Foreign Affairs, Alvarez del Vayo, had left for Geneva nine days before to make another appeal to the League.

"You will immediately begin packing the papers and other valuables in your office," the Under-Secretary said.

His voice was heavy and he could not look at me. He rubbed his hand nervously over his cheek. I rose from my chair and walked slowly back to my office.

As I entered my private office I stopped at the desks of my most responsible assistants. "Come with me."

When they were all assembled, I rose, and steadying myself with the palms of my hands pressed hard on my desk, I said very quietly, "We must now pack all the really important papers. Those which we can leave must be burned. We must make absolutely sure that we leave nothing behind which can help the enemy or hurt our friends."

The girls—the men had long ago left for the front—looked at me in silence. And suddenly I realized that what I had known now for days, they had never guessed. Somehow, they did not think Barcelona would fall—somehow, someway . . .

And now they knew.

"The newspaper files should be burned?"

I was grateful for that steady voice. I looked at the girl—she was young. Her brother and father had been killed at the front. But her eyes did not flicker as they met mine.

"Yes, we cannot take the newspaper file with us—obviously, it would occupy too much space, and space is very precious."

There was silence after her question. Many thousands, perhaps more than a million Spaniards, had been driven from their homes by the fascist advances in the last two and a half years. Yet these girls and women had never quite thought before of what it meant to leave everything you own, everything dear and familiar, and set out for a strange and perhaps hostile place.

But there was no hysteria in my office that morning. After the first silence the girls rose and walked, their carriage more dignified, their tread more steady than I had seen it before, to start the work of packing. Half an hour later I walked out into the offices and found my assistants clearing up their files and desks, working rapidly—and in silence.

"We have a lot of territory left after Barcelona," Ignacio told me. "This by no means is the end of the war."

I repeated this to my staff and they all brightened as they considered it. For the first time after my announcement I heard them talking in their normal voices.

But after they had packed, the more restless ones began to ask questions:

"When are we leaving?"

"Can we take our furniture or clothes with us?"

"Are we going alone or can we take our families?"

"Do we have to take food with us?"

And I could not answer them—I did not know myself. These

humble questions, asked without cease from morning to night, tortured me—and tortured the Under-Secretary.

That afternoon I went to his office and suggested that he should inquire from the Government when we were leaving. My staff was growing more restless by the hour.

But the Under-Secretary, a brilliant architect and a charming man, simply could not cope with the terrible problem of evacuating three hundred civil servants and all the documents and papers in the office not only of the Foreign Press Bureau, but of the entire Department—documents which simply had to be preserved.

He accepted my offer to go to the colonel in charge of military transportation—a man whom I knew quite well. I told the colonel that we had three dilapidated cars, which we really needed to take the foreign journalists out; but perhaps they would ride with those newspapermen who had cars. And that was all.

"For three hundred people?" the colonel said.

"And the documents."

The colonel turned red in the face. "Documents! I can let you have one truck today, perhaps two tomorrow—no more. Why don't you charter a special train as the other Government departments did?"

The Under-Secretary started to work on getting a train for us. We found that, with the families of our staffs, we had seven hundred people to evacuate. Some went with friends, but most of them had no means of transportation. They had to leave— any of the seven hundred would be liable for Franco's reprisals.

Ignacio kept calling up all afternoon. "When are you leaving?" he kept saying. "Try to get home early."

But I couldn't leave. I kept telling people the train was arranged for the next day, but we still had no word, in truth. I couldn't go home while the question of the train was not settled. I felt responsible for my staff.

At ten that night I still sat in my office, tearing down from the wall next to my desk a set of pictures of Luli, tacked up there so that I could see them as I worked—Luli reading; Luli playing; Luli listening to the radio.

As I worked a messenger boy came into the office. I tore open the envelope. The message was brief. No trains and no trucks would be available at all, tomorrow, or any other day. And if there were trucks or trains they would be used for the Army which faced terrible problems of transportation.

I rushed across the street to find the fat old professor who was taking Del Vayo's place while the Minister was in Geneva. "You *must* let my people on the train you have for the Foreign Office people."

The professor was more than calm—he was exasperating. "Why not?" he said, shrugging. "There won't be room for nearly all who want to go, but we will find more trains later on —don't worry."

I felt like slapping him. "Don't worry!" When the colonel in charge of transportation said quite flatly there would be no trucks and no trains available at all—and if any should by any remote chance turn up, the Army needed them!

But at least I had his permission to get some of my people aboard his train. Next I tried to get the Under-Secretary to sign the traveling permits for my staff members. He was at a meeting, a very important one.

And then I thought of another staggering difficulty. The train left at eight and my people came to the office at nine. How to let them know? We had already destroyed our files and with them the telephone numbers of the staff. I sat at the telephone, desperately trying to remember phone numbers. We grabbed a messenger boy passing, told him our story and he started out, with his bicycle, to inform the few whose addresses we could remember.

It was midnight. Two soldiers appeared in the door, as I worked with three staff members who had stayed on with me.

The sergeant said: "The general's car is outside. We have orders to take you home at once."

I could no longer argue. I had done everything I possibly could for my staff, and I could only hope against hope that they would all make the train the next morning. I could not help matters by staying and I dared not take Ignacio's time by keeping him waiting. He was badly needed at the fronts; his wife could not hold up his work. I bid farewell to the girls still working.

I hardly recognized the house when I arrived. Everything was turned upside down. My poor maid was in tears trying to carry out Ignacio's orders: "Pack the most necessary things in two suitcases; we have room for no more."

The cook and the laundry-woman were sobbing. They were staying behind; their husbands and old fathers were in Barcelona; they could not leave.

"Never tell anyone you worked for us," I warned them. "No one at all. Otherwise you will be shot."

They nodded and hung on my neck, sobbing.

The house was filled with people, who were going to make the trip with us, including a stupid old lady, the mother of the Under-Secretary of the Army. She kept muttering about her son who had ordered her to pack all her belongings in one suitcase. My heart sank when I heard her silly quaverings. I had promised her son to look after her in the exodus, and I could see she was going to be a problem.

I kept saying, as we sat down to a hasty midnight supper, the first food I had eaten all day, that I could not leave until I saw my staff people on tomorrow morning's train. Nobody paid any attention to me; the trip had already been arranged and I had nothing to say about it.

A few minutes later the Under-Secretary of my Department came and told us Dr. Negrin had advised the Cabinet to start for Figueras and in any case not to spend the night in Barcelona.

We planned to spend the night, therefore, with the Under-Secretary of the Army at his country house about thirty miles outside of Barcelona. We had often gone there before for a good night's rest during the bombardments. We tried to pretend now that we were only going, as we so often had, to spend the night with our friend. Perhaps, Dr. Negrin had suggested as an afterthought, we could all return to Barcelona in the morning to help supervise the evacuation.

But we knew better, really.

It was after three when we got into the cars with our luggage. Ignacio left to spend the night with the General Staff. Nobody knew where the enemy was, exactly, how near or how far from Barcelona. Our drivers were not certain of which roads were open and which closed by fascists.

Our three cars started out in the dark night. There were no moon and no stars, no street lights. The whole city lay black and silent around us. We hardly talked in the cars. Some of us shed a few tears, but most of us sat stiffly upright, our faces drawn with fatigue.

Approaching a crossroads near the big hospital of Valcarca on the outskirts of Barcelona, the sound of voices just ahead of us made our drivers stop. We all got out of the cars and found Dr. Negrin, whose car had halted just in front of ours.

Dr. Negrin was speaking loudly in the darkness when we came up to him. He was addressing several hundred soldiers whom he had found wandering on the dark road. They were elderly men, of the last draft. They had been waiting in the barracks outside of Barcelona for a few guns and orders to go to the front. The guns never came; the men were completely defenseless. Late in the evening their officers had deserted them. Panic-stricken, they had run from the barracks out into the night toward Figueras, not knowing what to do, where to go.

"Men! Soldiers of Spain!" Dr. Negrin said, in the darkness, to the men who milled before him filled with fear. "Because your officers have deserted you, you must not be cowards. Do not be afraid. There is nothing to fear."

They quieted as he spoke. The Under-Secretary of the Army rushed up. "Send an officer to the barracks of these men," Dr. Negrin told him, as the soldiers listened. "See that he is there by ten in the morning."

"Yes, sir," the Under-Secretary said.

The men began to talk among themselves. "The officer will be there at ten in the morning. He will lead us to fight. At ten in the morning."

The old lady who sat beside me was hard to keep quiet. At every sound on the road she would scream in my ear, "It's the

Moors! The Moors are coming! Don't you hear them?" She kept this up while Dr. Negrin spoke to the soldiers.

But it was easy for me to keep my self-control. I felt as though I were moving in a dream, and the shadowy soldiers, with their blankets folded over their heads, surrounding the Premier, seemed dream-like too.

The noise of the voices died away. The Premier got back in his car, still surrounded by the soldiers, who watched him silently and respectfully. The Under-Secretary of the Army drove back to Barcelona to find the officer for the soldiers, and we drove on.

"Where are we going? What do you think we will do tomorrow? Where is my son going to live now?" The old lady kept up her steady drone all night long. The driver and I lapsed into silence and she asked her questions of the wind.

For I had grown to love Barcelona in the past year, grown to love the spirit and the beautiful buildings of the Catalonian city. But that didn't matter now. Through the whole long drive I kept thinking of the million people in Barcelona who had no way to escape, no car to drive them from the fascist fury, no train, no truck—nothing. They would be caught, for they had not the strength to walk. The year of starvation had taken its toll. They could not walk and so they were trapped.

We reached the country house at dawn. Every room in the old mansion was crowded. Strangers slept on the floors. I wandered in the main part of the house and somebody led me to a bed in a room with another woman—the wife of a political commissar. She was nervous and began to chatter as I undressed, and I fell asleep as she talked.

When I woke up and went to the kitchen for hot water I found Ignacio snoring in an armchair in the hall. His chauffeur told me they had just driven in after a sleepless night and he was resting a few minutes before he went on to join the General Staff at Vich.

Half an hour later the big old house emptied. I stayed on, waiting for somebody to take me to Figueras. There was no question of returning to Barcelona. The roads were jammed with traffic—all leading from the city. It was humanly impossible to return to the city. I must get to Figueras at once and set up press headquarters.

But I waited all day long in growing impatience for the car to take me to Figueras. The country house was about two miles from the crossroads at Granollers where all the traffic from Barcelona had to pass. All day long the house shook as the fascists bombed the fleeing people. The bombs fell on the crossroads, halting traffic, setting fire to gasoline stations. Huge clouds of smoke hid the countryside again and again as the bombs fell.

At six o'clock Ignacio sent a car for me. I joined him where his staff was installed in a country house flying a Swedish flag. Every other house in the whole countryside was occupied; we could not be careful of international law in this emergency. But we swept the house carefully and took care to even make the beds. The caretaker who had protested our entry turned out to be an able housekeeper and ended up helping us.

January 26. At four in the afternoon, nine Italian light tanks bumped down the empty, silent streets of Barcelona, greeted by a hurricane of old paper, blown up in the wind.

Shots rang out. The tank crews dismounted and tried in vain to find the snipers.

I stayed three days at the Air Force villa. Maruja was with me again. We cooked a little food for the men. We had no news, for the radio could not work without electricity. Ignacio told us of the occupation of Barcelona. We received the news silently.

January 29. I started for Figueras with a Catalan Air Force officer. Ignacio had to be with the General Staff, but he had finally found a car for me.

When we left the country roads and turned onto the main highway to the frontier we found the people of Barcelona, hungry, wretched, cold, desperate, fleeing from General Franco.

The road was absolutely jammed with people in cars, in trucks, on donkeys, on foot. Peasant women holding a child or a goat or a chicken to their breasts; young women trailing their children behind them. We stopped to talk to some of them—a young woman with four children. Her husband was at the front; she had left Tarragona with all her household goods and now she walked with nothing but the shawl over her head.

We had a small car, but we filled it with people. The families would not separate—who knows what might happen to them, and we carried only the strays or the lonely ones.

The people cursed the fascists who drove them from their homes. But they were not broken people, or demoralized. "We shall come back," the women said and the children echoed them, "We shall come back, and then let them tremble!"

As we neared Gerona the traffic jam became worse. Truckloads of children from the children's colonies were stalled on the road with no gasoline. The gas stations were empty.

My driver knew the back streets of Gerona; we threaded our way in and out of the town, avoiding the traffic jam. I kept looking at the sky. Suppose they bombed Gerona now? The children would be slaughtered.

We drove on to Figueras. Just as we came to the outskirts of the town we saw the fascist planes bombing the defenseless city. We backed up. No use to drive into Figueras during an air raid.

We drove around and around the outskirts of Figueras, looking for a house where I could stay until Ignacio joined me. The villages were poor and miserable. There were no houses. We came dangerously near the French border, went back on our tracks.

Finally my Air Force officer grew angry. "Pick a house you want and I'll move you into it."

I protested; we could not move people out of their own houses.

"I haven't much time," the officer said. I pointed to a house. The officer told the captain of *Carabineros,* in command of the village, that I was a government official. Shortly afterwards the peasants who lived in the little whitewashed house moved out quite cheerfully when I explained why I needed their house.

The Air Force officer left to tell Ignacio where I had found quarters. I stayed alone with Ignacio's soldier guard. It was almost night. I turned the electric light switch and saw a square

room with a red-tiled floor, covered with half an inch of dirt.
A square dining-room table stood in the center covered with
dirty oilcloth. The walls were covered with calendars, all out-
dated and fly-specked. There were two bedrooms and four
beds. Ignacio, I, Maruja, her husband, one of Ignacio's aides,
two chauffeurs and three soldiers were going to stay in that
house. I took time to wonder where we would all sleep.

We dined on tepid cocoa and a few sardines that night. An
electric light burned dully, giving almost no illumination in
the dirty, shadowed room. I stumbled into bed exhausted and
fell almost immediately asleep. I awoke several times during
the night. Once I heard loud voices under my window, arguing.
"The road is cut. We must leave," one man shouted. "No, no,
it is a lie, you're just afraid," another would answer.

But I fell into a deep, dream-troubled sleep before I heard
the angry reply.

The Winter sun streamed yellow into my room next morning. I struggled out of nightmares to hear banging at my door
and the soldier of Ignacio's guard calling, "The Air Force officer requests urgently to see you."

"Tell him to wait while I dress."

There was a pause. I lay back on my bed, my forehead wet
with perspiration, feeling no sense of refreshment after the
night of troubled sleep.

The soldier banged again. "The officer says he cannot wait
for you to dress. It is a matter of life and death."

I jumped out of bed and threw on a few clothes, a skirt and
blouse, a pair of dusty shoes.

"Yes?" I called from the dark, rickety stairs.

Ignacio's officer shouted, his voice trembling with hysteria:
"Come at once! We are leaving! The road has been cut below
Figueras. We are trapped! Hurry!"

"What?" My voice was still sleepy. I still could not move
rapidly. I came carefully down the stairs, squinting to see the
officer in the dark peasant house.

"My wife and child are outside in the car. I have come back
for you, but for their sake, I cannot wait. Come at once!"

Now I began to fumble to understanding. San Clemente, the

little suburb of Figueras where I had spent the night, where I had intended to set up living quarters for Ignacio and his staff officers, was very close to the French border. When I went to bed the night before, the Government had held a narrow wedge of Catalonia, bordered by France and the sea. Figueras, ten miles from the coast, was about the center of this district. Our troops were fighting to the west and south of Figueras. Now, if the main road had been cut by the Rebels between Figueras and Gerona, our front, we were trapped indeed.

"But how could the road be cut?" I said stupidly. "We traveled over it only last night. The fascists were nowhere near."

The officer trembled with rage. "The captain of the *Carabineros* says the road from Gerona has been cut. Do you not take his word for it? The whole village is fleeing—we are nearly the last people left. Hurry!"

I went out into the open. The village streets were indeed nearly empty. A few last stragglers were running towards the country road. I climbed into the officer's car, already jammed with somebody's old mother, the wife and child, an old mattress, children's toys, strewn clothes.

Our car started out with a jerk. We left a cloud of dust in the village street. We turned into a back country road, headed north, for the Pyrenees and the border.

"The main road from Figueras to the border is too crowded to travel." The officer's voice was still breathless.

"Who said it was?"

"The captain of the *Carabineros* says so. He knows."

I began to turn this over in my mind. I was slowly waking up, collecting my wits.

We bumped along a country lane, passing farmers riding on donkeys, peasant women lugging their children.

"The captain of the *Carabineros*," I said slowly, "is probably a traitor—you know that. How do we know that he is telling the truth? Surely you aren't depending on this captain's word?"

The Air Force officer shouted at me. "Don't start arguing. The road has been cut. The *Carabineros* came to the village and said the General Staff had left Figueras. The people were left to their own devices."

Now I began to really think. "That's nonsense. The General Staff would not just abandon the people here. They would first evacuate those who had to leave."

"Well, they didn't."

I began to feel anger choking my throat. Ignacio had no confidence in this officer—otherwise he would have been at the front instead of driving women and soldiers around to look for quarters. And besides, I myself had heard Ignacio order this officer to return to staff headquarters the moment he had found us a place to stay.

"I don't believe the road is cut!"

I said it loudly. The old grandma in the back seat began to cry. The child wept. The officer drove faster. We were going uphill now, the car groaned in second, then in first, gear.

"I think that *Carabineros* officer was a traitor and deliberately started a panic to crack our rear guard—and I believe that you were a coward to believe him!"

The officer didn't answer.

"Stop the car and let me out."

The officer threw on the brakes and the car jolted to a halt. I climbed out.

I was alone in a great crowd. The road was jammed with people, all trudging to the frontier. I began to ask questions. Nobody would stop to answer me. Could I have been wrong? Perhaps the road was really cut? How far had we gone? Could I walk all the way back to Figueras? I tried to retrace our footsteps, but the panic-stricken crowd forced me slowly ahead. Finally I gave up trying to buck the flood. Slowly I was forced up a little hill—and then suddenly I was face to face once again with the officer. His car was stopped. The road had ended. The mountain path lay steep ahead, up and up, then down—into France.

"What are you going to do?" I asked the officer. "It is all right if you show your wife and child the way to France. But you—you are an officer in the Army. You are deserting!"

My voice was loud. The crowd began to slowly gather around us.

"Where is your husband?" somebody called out.

I bit my lip. "Where any man who is not a coward should be," I answered, and then, to my own surprise, burst into tears.

At that moment fascist planes circled overhead—looking, no doubt, for the fleeing villagers the *Carabineros* had touched with panic. The crowd scattered, running for ditches and trees. I stood still, wiping my eyes. No bombs fell.

"Constancia!" I turned. Maria, a young girl stenographer who had worked in the Air Force headquarters, was running towards me.

"Oh, heavens, I am glad to see you," she began breathlessly.

I looked at the three-year-old child, a curly-haired little girl, she held in her arms.

"The baby belonged to a railroad worker who lived in my house in Barcelona. The mother had six other children. I carried the baby for her when we left—and now—we were separated. The last thing she said to me was, 'Take care of her for me.' And I have, and I am always going to."

I smiled. I felt an enormous love for Maria and her newly adopted little daughter. I touched Maria's hand, smoothed the baby's curls. Suddenly it spoke: "Good day, madame." Maria and I had to laugh.

Ignacio's faithful soldier, his personal guard, had turned up out of nowhere. He had orders to insure my personal safety and apparently nothing, either panic or flight or confusion, could stop him.

"I will take you to the French border and then inform the general where you are."

I began to argue. But the soldier was firm. "You cannot return to Figueras safely now. I have a rifle. I can return. But not you."

There was no answer to this. Maria and I and the baby, followed by the little soldier, began to climb. The mountains were not very high just here. But the stones were very sharp, the mud thick. We shifted the baby back and forth. The little girl never cried even once; she kept her black eyes focused on the trees, and sometimes she cried out, "Ah, only see! A bird!"

We seemed to be alone, although now and then voices floated

to us on the wind. We climbed one mountain, came down in a little valley where we rested, went up another mountain. Here the soldier bid us farewell.

"France is just ahead. I will tell the general you are safe. *Salud.*"

"*Salud,*" we echoed—and I tasted tears. Where was I going? What madness had brought me here to this mountain valley? I half started after him. I must return to Spain and Ignacio.

"Later," Maria said.

We walked down the mountain path, quite alone. We made a little hammock of our hands for the baby to sit on, for our backs and arms ached cruelly, and our feet were bruised with the stones.

The path suddenly became a narrow country road. At the very end of the road we saw an old red car, filled with wood. Beside the driver's seat was a dark-eyed young woman, holding a beautiful baby. We watched a man, apparently her husband, climb behind the wheel. Then they saw us.

"They look like Spaniards," I heard the man say in French to the girl.

The girl glanced at us. Then she called, in Catalan, "Madame, madame, would you like us to take your little girl into the town? It is six miles, and you look very tired."

Maria and I could only nod. I felt the terrible fatigue creeping up my back and legs and arms and neck.

"We will leave her with the Mayor. The town is called Port Vendres."

We passed our little girl to the dark-eyed woman. She smiled at us and the red car vanished in a cloud of sudden dust.

We walked a little faster. Only six more miles. It was nearly dusk. I had eaten nothing since the sardines and cocoa the night before, and I found a bar of chocolate in my pocket. Maria and I munched it as we walked.

Suddenly we faced our first French Guarde Mobile.

"Are you armed?" he called out.

Maria gave him a toy revolver she carried in her purse. I had no gun.

"Now go on without stepping from the road," he ordered, "until you overtake the others."

His harsh voice and his peremptory commands troubled me. We walked on, weary and desperately tired, and at a bend of the road we found the villagers whom we had passed in the morning. They had taken a shorter path across the frontier, and now they waited, patient, tired, for the hospitality of the French.

The Guarde reappeared. Night was falling. No more refugees would cross until morning. He was brisk.

"Very well. Now women and children over here. Hurry!"

The Spanish peasants stared. I translated. Still they did not move. The Guarde Mobile shouted, but the Spanish families would not separate. I began to understand—with fear. I had a diplomatic passport, with a visa good for France, but I did not intend using it unless I got in trouble. What was this Guarde Mobile planning to do, taking wives from husbands and children from their fathers?

At this moment, while the crowd milled about, the old red car reappeared, emptied of its wood. The driver argued with the Guarde. "Let me take a few into town. I will deliver them to the Mayor. Only they are so tired, and these ladies"—he pointed at Maria and me—"have a child who weeps for them. They must go to her."

We clambered gratefully into the car. Six others held on somehow, including a young boy in shabby corduroy trousers who had lost his family in the flight from Barcelona and was alone.

"The blacksmith will want him for a son," our host said. "He has been wanting a Spanish refugee for so long. He will be so happy."

The boy smiled, when I translated.

The rattling car swerved into a narrow street, and we looked at Port Vendres, a typical fishing village. The car stopped under a street light. The smell of the salt air astonished me. We were on the sea coast.

"Go to the Mayor—down that road—and good luck!"

Our fellow passengers started off.

"Please come into the house," the Frenchman said to Maria and me, "and please hurry; do not let anyone see you."

We ran into the house. We climbed steep steps in silence, the Frenchman cautioning us not to speak. Then he flung open a door on the landing and we were inside his home, neat, bright, and shining. His pretty wife turned from the stove and said softly, "This is your home. Be at ease. Do not worry. Your child is at my mother's. I will bring her after supper. Now sit down and rest—and be at home, please be at home."

Maria and I looked at each other. I felt the tears in my eyes.

The husband said, "We will not give you up to the authorities, do not worry. We are proud to have you in our home."

I gulped and said timidly, "Well, I have a diplomatic passport and a French visa, and Maria is a government official."

The Frenchman shook his head. "It will make no difference. There have been others before you. Those who walk over the mountains are treated the same." And he swore—a black oath against the French Government which welcomed the Spanish refugees with terror instead of kindness.

"Now do not worry," the wife said softly, still in Catalan. "Now you must eat." We sat at a clean scrubbed wooden table and ate fresh white bread and butter and drank coffee. I think I never tasted food so good.

After supper the grandmother brought the two babies, the French child, only a little over one year old, and our Catalan adopted daughter. Our infant was already happy, playing with the toys she had seized from the younger child. And every time the little Marie tried to reclaim her property from our Isabel, the whole family, father, mother, and grandmother, would shout in French: "Give it to the little Spaniard! Can you not see she is a little Spaniard? Give it to her!"

And the small French child, considerably abashed, would hand the toy to our crowing Isabel, only to attempt to reclaim it a moment later.

The Frenchman's brother came in as we were watching the children. Our host was a gardener; his brother worked in the dynamite industries nearby. He had brought a wonderful mattress and the wife made us a great double-mattressed bed in the next room. I shall remember that sleep always—the feel of the fresh, spotlessly clean heavy linen sheets, the soft mattress, the smell of clean linen on the pillow. . . .

Next morning our host rushed out and got a paper while we drank coffee from great steaming bowls. The paper confirmed my doubts of the day before. Our troops were still holding at Gerona. The road was not cut! Ignacio must be at Figueras! And I must go to him!

Maria and I decided at once. The war was not over, not even in Catalonia. We could hold south of Figueras. Our place was in Spain. We must find a home for the baby and return at once.

Our host had stayed home from work—and what it meant to lose a day of work I could see from the spotlessly clean, bare, frugal little household—to attend to us. Now I had to gently put aside his advice. "Do not go out," he repeated, but I sought out the Mayor, whom he described as a Socialist and fairly decent.

The square in front of the town hall was filled with exhausted refugees, including hundreds of men.

"These people have been betrayed and deceived," I told the Mayor, "the *Carabineros* officer, who was a traitor, lied and spread panic. The men must be told they should return to Spain to fight for their country."

The Mayor shrugged his shoulders. "Tell them yourself if you like."

Maria and I began to circulate among the men, showing them the newspaper. The men were excited. Yes, they agreed, they should return. Yes, yes.

As we went through the crowd, cheers and the buzz of excited conversation followed us. The Guarde Mobile rushed up.

"One more word from you and I will throw you both in jail."

I showed my papers. "I am not a refugee. I have a legal right to be here."

I went to the commanding officer of the Guarde Mobile and told my story. "The men want to return to Spain to fight. They were deceived. They want to return. You have no right to keep them."

"Madam," said the commandant of the Guarde Mobile, "if I hear one word more on this subject from you—either said to me, or said to the men—you will go to jail. And I don't care that"—he snapped his fingers—"for your diplomatic passport. It is probably no good. I shall be forced to take it from you to examine it and sometimes documents of that kind get lost."

"But the men themselves wish to return. It is not I who is asking them. I only explained their mistake."

The Guarde Mobile beckoned to a sergeant. I bit my lip and turned away. Maria and I wandered to a café on the square. There a Franco agent, unmolested by the Guarde Mobile, was offering the men one hundred francs and a free meal to sign on for fighting in the Franco armies. The men listened to the recruiting agent's spiel and turned away. I heard one say, "If only, somehow, we could get back to Spain—our Spain."

But we did not entirely give up. I found the Air Force officer who had driven me away from the suburb of Figueras the day before. He was heartily ashamed of himself indeed, and he fell in with our plan easily. He and a group of other soldiers and officers, misled like the others, would stand up in the village square and announce they were returning to Spain to fight. In the meantime Maria and I would drive to the next town where the Mayor was a loyal friend of Spain and get him to call off the Guarde Mobile, to give orders to let our men back over the frontier.

We had some difficulty finding the Mayor of Cerbère, one Monsieur Cruzel. He was frantically busy, passing out food and clothing to the women and children who had arrived the day before. While we searched for him, I ran into another of Ignacio's officers, driving a car. He had come across the frontier on orders and was returning shortly. And he promised to drive me back to Figueras next day.

With my heart much lightened after this—I would see Ignacio and be back in Spain tomorrow—I approached the Mayor with confidence. And he was another stroke of good luck.

"Of course the men must return to fight!"

But when I asked him to call off the Guarde Mobile, his face darkened. "One can try," he said, but his voice was savage. And he nodded. The Guarde Mobile were pushing Spaniards around like cattle while we watched.

The Mayor led me into his office, and from his window I glimpsed several Spanish ambulances, painted the typical green. I cried out in astonishment, "What are they doing here? We need every one at the front for our wounded and to evacuate the sick. Ah, if only we had had a few more in Barcelona!"

The Mayor raised his eyebrows. "You think so?"

"They must be driven back at once!"

The Mayor examined his hands. "I think not. They were driven here on January 27, some days ago, you see, before the Army had retreated to anywhere near its present position. And they arrived, filled not with sick or injured, not with the children from your colonies, not with disabled soldiers or the aged, but filled with the files and household goods of certain of your politicians."

My face turned red. I could feel it burning.

"No! It cannot be so. Not at this time."

The Mayor nodded. "Oh, yes, it is so. You can examine the ambulances yourself if you like. You will see certain files, fine lamps and rugs, and other such things. We have not disturbed them. Luis Araquistain, his wife, and Largo Caballero came themselves in a large limousine and their drivers brought the ambulances behind them. It was quite a procession."

I could find nothing to say. I felt sick with shame. Caballero and the Araquistains had blackened the name of the Spanish people. Ambulances filled with lamps and rugs when our wounded lay dying on battlefields for want of transportation! Ambulances for linen and silver when a wounded soldier in Franco's hands faced the firing squad as soon as he could walk.

"Do not be ashamed," the Mayor said softly. "We know, here in France, what the Spanish people are. You are not to blame for people like the Araquistains and a senile, foolish old man who once had power."

It was night when we returned to Port Vendres to complete our plans to lead the Spanish men refugees back to fight. The

Guarde Mobile hung on our footsteps but finally we threw them off the track and went back to our French friend's house. All night long, Spaniards came and went, unshaven, tired, dirty— and ashamed.

"We are deserters. We should be shot when we cross back into Spain," one officer kept saying.

Next morning our plan began to work according to schedule. A group of three hundred men were ready to march down the road and across the frontier.

Suddenly a man in civilian clothes stood up in front of the crowd. I recognized him—he was the officer of the *Carabineros* who had started the whole panic-stricken flight in the first place, with his lying tale of the road being cut below Figueras.

"She is an *agent provocateur*," he yelled, pointing at me. "She wants to lead you back to your sure death. Figueras is in the hands of the fascists. You will all be killed."

The men hesitated. "He lies," I shouted.

Maria said hastily, "Let me start with the twenty I have in my group, we have no time to lose."

"Form in ranks of five," the Guarde Mobile began to shout above our voices.

"Do not believe her, she lies," the *Carabineros* officer yelled.

The men were bewildered. A few went with Maria—about thirty in all. They got away. The others formed in ranks of five, still talking and asking questions.

And then they were marched away under the guns of the Guarde Mobile—to what destination they did not know. At the same time trucks bearing their wives and children started in an opposite direction, and I heard the pitiful and tragic good-bys of families about to be separated, perhaps forever.

The Guarde Mobile and the fascist conspirators inside France had outwitted us. There was nothing more for me to do in France. I must return to Spain.

We found a French couple to adopt our little Isabel and about three in the afternoon I left for Spain in a car Ignacio had sent. Ignacio had also sent a letter by the driver, to say I was to stay in France, but I disregarded that.

I drove back into Spain feeling very optimistic. What I had read in the French papers did not make our cause seem hopeless, even in Catalonia. We could hold at Gerona. The General Staff could stay at Figueras. We still, of course, had the central zone. The civilians who had fled into France were fewer mouths to feed. We were strong; we could hold out in northern Catalonia, I knew we could.

It was dusk when we reached San Clemente, the little suburb of Figueras. I stepped down from the car and faced the little house I had fled from so unwittingly three days before. I felt a wave of shame. Well, I had been a victim of panic. Now I knew what it was like—and never again would I act on rumor and fall prey to foolish fear.

The soldiers on guard laughed and greeted me cheerfully. "Ho! The General will not be so glad to see you! You should see how relieved he was when he heard you were in France!"

I climbed the stairs and found Maruja, my old, dear friend, Maruja, sitting knitting in the one rocking chair by the light of the feeble electric bulb.

"Oh, Connie," she too began, "Ignacio will be furious."

"But," I stammered, "I have come back because I have work to do at the Press Bureau, and to take care of him, and . . ."

Maruja looked up at me and said softly, "Connie, our position here is hopeless. We have no guns, no supplies, no food, nothing. We are fighting a rear guard action to cover the evacuation of the population. That is all. It will be all over in a few days. Then we will all return to Madrid and fight from there." She paused. "Ignacio thinks we have a chance in Madrid and the central zone. We have a much shorter line to defend."

"Ah," I nodded. I had not realized that it was all over in Catalonia. I had not really thought of it at all, not really. A man who suffocates slowly hardly realizes when the last air is gone.

"We were all supposed to leave yesterday," Maruja said, "all the women, stenographers, wives, and all that."

"But who will cook for the men and attend to them?" I said. "They must eat."

Maruja was overjoyed. She too could not bring herself to leave.

We went into the kitchen to cook. The food had improved the last days. The peasants brought out their last chickens and their hoarded supplies of food and sold them—they were already leaving for France.

Ignacio found me at the stove, stirring a chicken in its broth. He pretended to be angry for a moment, and then he put his arms around me and said simply, "How good to see you."

At dinner we joked over my adventures. Maruja and I promised that we would leave when Ignacio and her husband said it was absolutely necessary. Until then we would stay.

"Our men are fighting as they have never fought before," Ignacio said. "Modesto and Lister's men are wonderful. They fall back in perfect discipline—because they have orders to. They would like to advance, I think, but they are making a rear guard action. Still, you would cry to see them. What men!"

The three days I spent at our little peasant house outside of Figueras were the three most tragic—and yet, almost happy —days I ever knew. I saw Ignacio hardly at all, only late at night, when he came home exhausted and sick with worry and sorrow. Yet I knew that those tragic three days were easier for him because I was beside him. We had shared all our life together for so long that now I wanted to remain beside him as long as I could.

In the daytime Maruja and I did housework. We cleaned the peasant house from top to bottom, not because we expected to stay but for want of something to do. We washed and ironed. We cooked—such meals as we cooked! But nobody could eat them.

Maruja and I went into Figueras the morning of February 3. With all my mishaps, I had not yet seen my Press Bureau staff, although I had sent letters by messenger to my immediate superior, the Under-Secretary, reporting on my whereabouts and adding that I couldn't get a car to transport me into the temporary headquarters.

Figueras was one of the most appalling sights I have ever

seen. The little town, which normally counted 15,000 inhabitants, now sheltered at least 100,000 persons—perhaps many thousands more, there was no exact way of telling.

The building where the Under-Secretary had his temporary office was typical of Figueras in those terrible days of the evacuation. Exhausted women and children slept sprawled on the steps in the lobby. Soldiers elbowed clerks for sleeping room on the sidewalks. Cars abandoned for lack of gasoline blocked the streets. Every nook and cranny of the old building I went into was packed—absolutely packed—with human beings; people eating, sleeping, singing, arguing; children whining, playing games, crying, "I'm hungry!"

The castle, half a mile out of Figueras, was the only refuge from the human ant-hill the village had become. A fortress built in the eighteenth century of solid stone, it had been used in past wars as a munition dump, and once Felipe V and his wife, Maria Luisa, the Italian princess, had lived within its thick walls. Now the castle housed the whole Spanish Government besides all the paintings, works of art, and jewels private citizens had deposited with the banks of Barcelona during the war.

I should explain, perhaps, about these jewels, for they were to bring tragedy within a few days. The Government, quite early in the war, had asked all private citizens to deposit all jewels and valuables in the bank for safekeeping. Wartime means insufficient police protection; the Government successfully forestalled robberies by getting citizens to deposit their valuables in banks. I had deposited the pearl necklace left over from the days of my wedding and debut, for instance, along with a ring and a few other pins and brooches. In return I got a receipt.

Now when the evacuation of Barcelona began, the Government sent trucks to take all this treasure from the banks to Figueras where it was stored in the castle vaults. The Government acted on perfectly ordinary sort of banking procedure. They had guaranteed to return my necklace on presentation of my receipt. But only citizens who sympathized with the Government had deposited jewelry and other possessions with the banks. Obviously Franco would not honor my Government receipt for my pearl necklace. The Government had to take this treasure out of Barcelona if it was ever to be returned to its proper owners. Moreover, why should we hand Franco a vast treasure to pay for the guns which would kill us?

The treasure filled many trucks, for each depositor had his own little sack, with his name attached to it. Naturally, inside each individual sack was much that was worthless, of only sentimental value, and only now and then a really valuable piece. If the Government could have sorted out the treasure and reticketed it, it might have been able to move the most valuable part of the jewelry in one or two trucks. But the evacuation of Barcelona was no time to sort out jewelry; with the enemy advancing to the gates, the best the Government could do was to dump all the small sacks into big sacks, and throw the whole load into trucks.

But the fate of the jewelry was not yet settled. When Figueras in turn was evacuated, there were not enough trucks to carry the load, and it was left to Lieutenant-Colonel Lister, whose troops were the extreme rear guard, to transport the jewels into France. He scoured the neighborhood for trucks; found a few, took what he could of the treasure, put soldiers to guard the trucks and had them driven into France. And at the border the soldiers who had been ordered to take this property of Spanish refugees to safety were arrested for thieves and sentenced to long prison terms—a detail which Franco agents arranged while seizing the jewels themselves!

I heard about the question of what to do with the jewels that morning at Figueras, but I confess I hardly listened to the story—Figueras frightened me. These thousands and thousands of people, jammed into every available building like olives into a can, were the perfect target for enemy bombers. If an air raid hit Figueras the slaughter would be so appaling I could not bear even to think of it. Figueras had exactly one anti-aircraft gun. We had thirty-four planes in Catalonia then and twenty in the central zone. Of our available thirty-four, Ignacio had all but six trying to fight off Rebel bombers harassing our retreating troops. The other six lay in an air field near Figueras.

Ignacio hoped he could fight off the inevitable bombers and prevent the desperate refugees in Figueras from being blown to pieces. He hoped—but little more.

I had a reunion with my office staff that morning in Figueras. They had left Barcelona on a fantastically crowded train very late on January 24. Twenty hours later they reached Figueras— a distance the train usually covers in a few hours.

I discovered that my mishaps had made little difference to the Press Bureau. Work was impossible in Figueras. There were no tables, no chairs, no typewriters, no wire-service, no cable-service, almost no telephone service—and no reporters anyway. The newspapermen had gone to the French border.

The Under-Secretary asked me to set up a skeleton office at Le Perthus, on the French border, where the newspapermen could file stories. In Perpignan, at our consulate, another man would set up an office and I would have a motorcycle courier from Figueras and a car to our consulate. We made careful plans as though Figueras were to be a permanent capital, our front at Gerona a permanent front. But that is the only way work can be done in wartime. You live in the present and make elaborate plans for a future that may never materialize.

Maruja and I left Figueras about noon. I had to return to our suburb of San Clemente to pack and say good-by to Ignacio. We had just driven out of the town when we heard the terrible, the familiar, the everlasting, sound of bombs. Our six planes took to the air immediately. They fought all afternoon, hope-lessly outnumbered, while Figueras was bombed, again and again, again and again. Nobody knows how many times Figueras was bombed that afternoon; people lost count. The Italian bombers came in wave after wave, the sky was black with them. Nobody knows how many hundreds died that afternoon in Figueras. The slaughter was so frightful men could not speak of it; they returned from Figueras white-faced and muttering, "They lie all over the streets; the buildings are filled with screaming children caught in mortar and brick. It is . . ." And then men stopped and could not continue.

The Government had to evacuate Figueras. That night four

thousand people slept inside the castle. Nobody could say how. Thousands of others walked a few miles out of the doomed city and slept in the fields, more cruelly hunted than any wild beast.

Next morning, although the enemy was still being held at Gerona, the Government began to send the people who had survived the bombing of Figueras to the French border. And all day long the fascists bombed the roads on which the women and children walked.

Maruja and I waited very late that night for our husbands to return. The food we cooked grew cold. We had no more wood to feed the stove. We sat waiting, to grow more nervous as the long hours passed.

When Ignacio finally came in the door, I knew the dreaded moment of leaving Spain had come. Maruja's husband went to her side. We both stood up, and I felt my knees tremble.

"Let's have dinner at once," Ignacio said, with an attempt at briskness. "The captain is outside with the car to drive you to the border. He cannot wait long."

I swallowed. "Why do we have to leave now?"

"Don't be silly," Ignacio said, sitting down at the table. "Don't make a drama of this. It is very simple. The Government is moving to La Agullana, and the General Staff with it."

He saw my question before I asked it. "No, you cannot come with me. There is no question about it."

Maruja and I said nothing. "Don't be sad, darling," Ignacio said after a pause. "This is not the end by any means."

Half an hour later, Maruja and I drove to the French border at Cerbère. As we reached the border, the road showed signs of the passage of thousands upon thousands of refugees. The night was dark and the roads now almost deserted; but the headlights of our car picked out a discarded suitcase, lying on the side of a road, or a pile of rags, a doll, a dead mule. Hundreds of old cars, carriages, and carts, each with a punctured tire, a broken wheel, or a smashed-in front.

These limp, discarded, broken souvenirs of men and women and children uprooted, homeless, fleeing, touched my heart and made my throat feel tight with tears. This is what the foreign invaders, what Hitler and Mussolini, had brought to the Spanish people—these poor carts, these mules dead of exhaustion and starvation, these dolls dropped by some child too ill and tired to carry them any further. These were the mute and humble souvenirs of a people hunted by fascism.

We reached the border at 3 A.M. After some difficulties, our car, with its French papers and passports in order, was allowed to pass.

I had four hundred francs—about $12.

No Spanish cars, even with their papers in order, were allowed to pass beyond Cerbère—and Cerbère looked like Figueras the night before. People slept on benches, in the streets, on the beach, in the railroad station—with one difference. This was France and they would not be awakened by bombs.

By giving the address of our French friend at Port Vendres, we got permission for our car to pass. At dawn we came into the little city and found a small hotel on the same street as my French worker. We did not wish to waken him.

Next day I awoke paralyzed with rheumatism. Our French friends came to see us, and were sad because we had not broken their sleep the night before. But next day they drove me to the station in the little red car, and with body aching and my head splitting, I took the train for Perpignan to try to set up the Press Bureau.

The train was crowded. We kept our little suitcases, all that we had salvaged out of our varied wanderings, in our seat, and sometimes we looked down at the slender cases and reflected that out of all our past lives, these few things, a skirt, a blouse, a package of letters, a box of powder, a thermometer, a little piece of lace, a few pictures—were all that we had to call our own. These—and about 350 francs.

Perpignan was a madhouse. Our consulate was crowded; not a very pleasant place. Those who left Spain first had pre-empted shelter there, and those who bravely stayed until the last got scant courtesy. Hotel rooms were very nearly impossible to find, but after a stroke of good luck in meeting a Dutchwoman I knew, I accepted her offer and moved into her room. A day later, the little room, number 16, had become official Spanish headquarters, practically speaking.

A dozen Spanish girls I knew quite well had crossed the border to wait for their husbands, and we pooled our hotel room and our money. I had had a great windfall; a friend who owed me two thousand francs sent me the money from Paris. With this comparative wealth, my countrywomen and I were able to feed a very large number—I lost track of how many—refugees.

The three days I spent in Perpignan waiting for Ignacio seemed like three years. We all knew that the Army officers would return to Madrid as soon as the rear guard in Catalonia had been completed. We faced the future with a kind of grim hope. The Government of Spain still held one-fourth of the country, including its capital and one of its largest ports. Eight million Spaniards still lived in democratic territory. We believed we could still hold out for months, and perhaps win in the end, if the collapse in Franco's rear guard which we expected developed rapidly enough.

But in Perpignan those three days we had to wait without news, our anxiety prey to any rumor. For the consulate had no news; besides, it was dangerous to approach it. The French Guarde Mobile raided the environs of the consulate regularly and dragged off to concentration camps any Spaniards they could find still waiting to get passports.

The word "concentration camp" began coming into our anxious conversation again and again. I had heard of concentration camps in Germany and Italy—I had heard of them in Franco Spain. We had no concentration camps in Government Spain; not even for our prisoners. For the captured soldiers volunteered to fight the fascists either at the front or behind the line. But now we were to hear indeed of concentration camps for Spaniards in France.

For our room was filled day and night with men who had managed to escape from French "hospitality," men who told of the horrors of the camps with shaking voices. The French concentration camps were the ultimate in brutality—men crowded together like animals along a beach where the wind blew the sand into their eyes and hair and skin ceaselessly; men fed on less than nothing; men surrounded by barbed wire and guns on one side, the sea on the other, and nothing in between except human beings packed together like animals.

We bought a little alcohol stove and started to do mass cooking in our room, number 16. Refugees, men who had escaped from the camps, friends, or just anyone who was Spanish arrived to eat scrambled eggs and bread and drink coffee. For our pooled funds were running low and we couldn't afford to feed our comrades in the restaurants. The hotel proprietor eyed me with anger and suspicion; I was running an amateur restaurant obviously in competition with his dreary little café downstairs!

With our pooled funds, we bought two quite smart hats. The hats were used by whomever had to go out on the street, for we found that the police seldom arrested women wearing hats and speaking French—the women of Perpignan look not unlike Catalonians and the Guarde Mobile didn't want to infuriate local citizenry. In the midst of all the tragedy we had many laughs about the famous two hats, for they were becoming to some of us, and quite appalling on others. One of the hats, a smart brimmed affair, was in great demand, while the other toque was shunned by everybody.

The foreign correspondents, Matthews, Buckley, and a few others were stationed at the Grand Hotel in Perpignan. They helped us rescue our friends and many a Government official from the concentration camps those first few days. Often they would drive down to the border and help us rescue people from groups being taken to one of the very worst camps.

The evening of February 8, I drove to the border with the foreign correspondents to watch our last troops march across the International Bridge into France.

I was safe with the reporters; otherwise I would have been snatched by the Guarde Mobile and sent to a concentration camp. My diplomatic passport was no safeguard, any Spaniard could be rushed off to die of pneumonia or starvation in the terrible ocean camps, as the spirit moved the Guarde Mobile.

We spent the night at Le Perthus. The frontier runs through

the little village. On one side of the line the Government and the General Staff occupied a row of peasant houses. I called out to a soldier: "Where is General Cisneros?"

Ignacio answered me. He came to a little balcony and waved. "I will be in Perpignan tomorrow."

We drove slowly along the frontier. Our Army seemed immense, stretched out in the darkness, their fires lighting the faces of a few groups here and there.

All night long, trucks and ambulances bearing our wounded crossed the frontier. All night long, our troops brought the few guns and the little ammunition we had to France to be safe, we had hoped, from Franco. We had expected to take it to Valencia.

At dawn I watched the troops march into France. They marched with their heads up, keeping perfect time as the regimental bands played. This was an orderly disciplined Army which had fought to the last against terrible odds. Column after column marched to the border, not a routed or panic-stricken Army, but an Army which had fought as only brave men defending their country can ever fight. A last column of Internationals, disarmed long before the battle and waiting for transportation when the evacuation of Barcelona began, crossed into France, singing.

At three o'clock on February 9, the rumor went through our hotel at Perpignan that the Monarchist flag had been hoisted at Le Perthus. I rushed into the street to confirm the news, and saw Ignacio passing slowly by in a staff car with three other officers!

I called out and Ignacio saw me.

Ignacio wanted a bath and sleep more than anything else in the world.

He and the other officers of the General Staff left Le Perthus half an hour before the Monarchist flag of the Rebels went up. They were the last to cross the frontier.

He had been so busy worrying about the rear guard action he had not stopped to think of how the Spanish refugees would be treated in France. At the border he was robbed not only of his side arms and his general's insignia, but also of his field glasses, which he loved better than any other possession he had in the world.

There was a brisk trade going on at the border in the articles the French border guards had robbed from the helpless Spanish refugees. Ignacio and I reflected bitterly that our little radio and his field glasses were a good haul for some guard.

But I suppose we should not have been very surprised. After all, the Government of Daladier and Bonnet was guilty of robbery on a considerably bigger scale than field glasses and radios —they had robbed the Spanish people of 41,850,000 francs in gold.

For the deposits of the Bank of Spain with the Bank of France had been withheld from the Spanish Government. When we decided to bring suit to recover this gold, we had a most interesting offer from persons in the French Government:

An oil monopoly suit in which the French Government was much interested had been dragging through the Spanish courts since the beginning of the Republic in 1931. The oil monopoly was trying to recover thirty-five million francs from the Spanish Government.

Now, if Dr. Negrin would settle this suit, not for thirty-five million francs but for two hundred and fifty million francs, the Spanish Government might be able to recover its gold, with or without a lawsuit!

I am afraid the French Government found our reply brusque —putting aside diplomatic language, we indicated that bribery was not a method of government we could condone.

And so we never got the gold which belonged to us.

Field glasses and radios are nothing compared to 41,850,000 gold francs.

Ignacio came out of Spain exhausted and tired. He slept like a man dead that night in the crowded little hotel room—and woke up next morning with one fixed idea: "We must return to the central zone—at once."

And so we went to Toulouse the next day to prepare for the Government's and General Staff's exodus to Madrid. I think the next ten days were the most anxious, confused, and agonized days I have ever spent in my life.

Spain's situation was grave indeed. Dr. Negrin was calm and determined in the face of this dreadful crisis, but none of us could overlook the facts staring our country in the face. The central zone, we knew, could be defended, and successfully, for months. But we desperately needed the few guns, the airplanes, the stores of ammunition our Army had taken out of Catalonia, with such difficulty. And Ignacio discovered, when he arrived in Toulouse, that the French Government had no intention of returning the property of the Spanish Government to us. Our few planes flown from Catalonia to the nearby French airports were confiscated. Our few rifles, guns, and ammunition stores were seized.

Even worse, our armies, the men of Modesto and Lister, our best-trained troops, pilots, technicians, were interned in the French concentration camps, and Daladier and Bonnet made very clear that our men could return to Spain only if they threw themselves on the mercy of Franco. Spaniards could leave the French concentration camps for fascist Spain—but most certainly they would not be allowed to board any ships we might be able to charter for democratic Spain.

Ignacio raged at this final treachery of the French Government. Betrayed on every side, treated like enemies, the Spanish Government on French soil tried desperately to rally its forces and prepare for its return to the central zone.

But now Dr. Negrin faced difficulties within the central zone itself. For days the armies of Madrid had been without news of the situation in Catalonia. Communications had been cut during the retreat. Bombs in Figueras had destroyed a hastily constructed radio station. We all knew that the military commanders in Madrid must be prey to every rumor and every anxiety.

"Now the foreign agents will get to work," Ignacio said anxiously. "And now is the perfect time for the traitors in our own ranks to come to the front. If only we can get the Government and the General Staff to Madrid in time!"

But this was no easy task. The French Government had allowed us to keep our four old Douglas transports—that was all. In these four antiquated planes we would have to transport all our Government officials across miles of Rebel-held territory, through districts filled with Rebel planes patroling the airways.

I sat beside Ignacio in Toulouse when he got the final word that out of the thirty-eight Spanish planes on French soil, we had the use of only the four transports. I saw his face tighten and his eyes go black with anger, and for a moment I only thought of what this meant to Spain. And then, because I am a woman and cannot help thinking of such things, even in a moment so grave, I realized that with only four Douglas transports I could never go back to Madrid with Ignacio. I kept thinking: "Ignacio will be in Madrid, and I will not be with him. Ignacio will be . . ."

For eight days I lived with this idea. I worked frantically all through those days, reaching newspapermen, telling them the new policy of the Government, helping Ignacio arrange a hasty trip to Paris—and yet in the back of my mind, through all the days, ran the steady chant, "Ignacio will be in Madrid, and I will not be . . ."

The foreign correspondents wanted to know the new Government policy. One afternoon I stood up before a group of them and acting as a sort of impromptu Government spokesman, outlined it as best I could.

"First of all," I said, "the war is not over; the fight goes on. The Government is returning to Madrid and we will defend the central zone. I have no less an authority than the German colonel Von Xylander for our opinion that the central zone can be defended."

The newspapermen made hasty notes. "The German colonel said in the newspapers, 'The Germans must not expect a hasty victory over the Republicans in central Spain. In the first place, the fascist internationals will have to reorganize their forces, and in the second place the territory held by the Republicans is vast and difficult.' "

The foreign correspondents grinned and somebody said something about the Devil's advocate. I laughed. "The colonel is only wrong in assuming there will be any kind of a victory."

Everybody sobered, and I wished in my heart that I believed as deeply in the brave words as my voice indicated. Still, we had a chance, and we would fight to the end for that chance.

"Has Dr. Negrin formulated any new peace terms?"

I knew the question was inspired by the rumors Franco and British agents had fed the press for days—that Republican Spain was ready to surrender.

"Yes, we have peace terms," I said. "Dr. Negrin has outlined them again—at the meeting of the Cortes held in Figueras. The meeting was held ten days ago on February 1 and the peace terms have not changed since then. They are: first, a guarantee of the independence and sovereignty of Spain; second, freedom from all foreign influence and the right of the people to chose their own Government by means of a plebescite; third, guarantees of no reprisals and no persecution of the civil population."

One of the reporters looked up from his notes, "May I ask a question?"

I nodded.

"There are rumors that France and England will recognize the Franco Government now."

I tried to keep my voice steady. "Only rumors?"

The reporter's voice was sympathetic. "Well, yes. But if such a thing should happen, would it be correct to say that the Spanish Government hopes this recognition will be on the basis of the three points of Dr. Negrin you have just outlined?"

I hesitated. "I cannot answer that question for the Government or any other way, since we cannot believe France and England will recognize the invasion of Spain by foreign powers. Still . . ."

And that was as far as I could go.

"I think that's all," I said hesitantly.

Another correspondent called out: "Who will return to Spain?"

I drew a deep breath. "We have only the four Douglas transports as you know. Of course Dr. Negrin and his whole Cabinet."

"What about the military commanders?"

I hesitated. I knew that some of our military leaders, lost in pessimism, had decided not to risk their lives by returning to Madrid. And the Government wanted no half-hearted generals in Madrid. Still, I hated to reveal to foreign correspondents that some of our generals were not ready to return to Madrid, perhaps to die for their country.

"Those who will return," I said slowly, "include Colonel Modesto, Lieutenant-Colonel Lister, Colonel Cordon, the Under-Secretary of the Army, General Cisneros"—I stopped on that name, for a moment—"and a number of others."

The correspondents seemed satisfied. I turned to go. I was to escape without being asked the question I could hardly answer.

From the back of the room somebody called out casually, "Of course, President Azaña returns with the Government?"

I turned back. "Well," I began slowly, feeling my face grow hot and red, "well, no, not immediately."

The correspondents straightened up. I could see them writing leads in their mind's eye to stories headlined, "Azaña Deserts Republican Cause." In my heart I felt such an anger I wanted to cry. President Azaña had been of no use to the Republican Government for the whole two and a half years of the war. Everybody knew he had predicted defeat for the people from the very beginning. Now he was in Paris, staying at the Spanish Embassy—when all that was expected or asked of him was that he should be brave in the eyes of the world, at least, and return to Madrid with Dr. Negrin and the Cabinet.

I drew a deep breath. "President Azaña is carrying on absolutely necessary talks with the French and British Governments," I said loudly. "It is essential to our cause that he remain in France at the present."

To my infinite relief, the reporters seemed satisfied. "What kind of talks?" somebody asked, but that question was easy to turn off.

The press conference had been a success.

I saw little of Ignacio those eight days, and when we met late at night, exhausted from work and anxiety, we could hardly talk to each other. I could not speak of the moment when we would be separated—and he never mentioned the day when he would have to leave.

One night I came in late and said: "Ignacio, only think, I am going to America!"

We both tried to smile. Since the Spring of 1938 I had been invited time and time again to come to America and plead the cause of Spain before the American people. I had always refused the invitations, work was too pressing in Spain. Now we needed foreign help as never before. The Government decided to make a last effort to convince America to send more food—and arms, arms!—to help the Spanish people. We had to tell our friends in America that the fight was not over, the central zone could be defended. Spain still lived. I was chosen to take this message and this appeal to the United States. I would leave shortly after Ignacio departed for Madrid.

"You will like America," Ignacio said that night. But I couldn't answer. I was afraid to speak, for fear I would be betrayed into tears.

February 20, 1939.

Ignacio's plane left for Madrid at ten o'clock in the evening. In the dark the Douglas transport could fly over Rebel territory in some safety.

For days we had been gulping hasty meals at cheap little bistros around the corner from our ancient and dirty hotel. Now, this evening, I took pains with my clothes, dressed in the best I could find in my meager wardrobe.

About seven we started out for dinner. Ignacio chose a new restaurant—a sixteen francs (fifty cents) restaurant. We were to dine in great style. We studied the menu with exaggerated care and Ignacio amazed the waiter by ordering the best bottle of wine (none too good) in the whole restaurant.

We talked of silly, matter-of-fact things. I asked him not to smoke too much. He smiled. "Not enough cigarettes in Madrid anyway." I suggested that he go around and look at our apartment, abandoned so long ago, with the furniture still piled in the corners so that the painters could do the floor. He said he certainly would.

Dinner seemed so short. We paid our check—what an extravagance. We went back to the hotel. I opened our suitcases and began to pack. We went about it silently.

When Ignacio closed the suitcases, the snap of the locks made a small noise in the room, a sort of final sound.

I was not to come to the airport. The French police was still busily picking off Spaniards from odd places and taking them to concentration camps. The airport was distinctly not safe for me.

We paid our hotel bill. I stood beside Ignacio and watched him with great care, trying to memorize every gesture.

He called a taxi. We stowed our suitcases beside the driver. We rode in silence for a time, and in the back of my mind, in the silence, I heard the words, "He will never come back. I will never see him again. Madrid will fall and I will never see him again."

Ignacio said in the silence, answering my unspoken words: "There is nothing else for me to do. I could not leave you, if I did not have to. You would have it no other way."

I nodded. It was so. I would not have Ignacio desert our country. If he had to die in Madrid, then I must resign myself. He had to go, there was nothing else for a decent man to do.

The taxi stopped. Ignacio leaned over to kiss me and felt my tears.

"Don't cry," he said softly. "Just think, in a few days you will be sending from America all the planes we need to win the war. And eating hot-dogs."

I tried to laugh. And then he was gone.

That night I left for Paris to take the boat-train for America.

V. EPILOGUE: VIVA LA REPÚBLICA!

I NEVER had a chance to ask the American people to send food and arms to help the people of the Republican central zone in Spain.

On March 5, as I sat in New York listening to the radio, I heard the first news of the coup that was to mark the betrayal of the rest of Republican Spain into the hands of the foreign invaders.

The only news allowed to trickle out from Spain was either censored in Madrid or distorted abroad. But I was able to grasp the meaning of the dispatches from the first. For I knew all the persons concerned and their conduct during the two and a half years of the war. I knew their suspect connections with those foreign Governments whose objective was to finish the Spanish war quickly: with a Franco victory.

The details of the plot I learned much later.

I knew, of course, that in the central Republican zone we still had powerful reserves. Sixty divisions, almost a million men under arms. Eight hundred cannon, tanks, besides munitions and some planes. A Navy superior in number and strength to that of the Rebels (not counting, of course, the ships supplied by their German and Italian allies), and a territory rich in mineral and agricultural products. But above everything else, the Spanish people had unity, unity achieved under the National Government of Dr. Negrin, a Government which included all political parties and organizations.

Dr. Negrin arrived in Madrid on February 12, and his first appeal to the entire population living in Republican Spain was: Maintain unity! Join in the effort of resistance! Force the Rebels to accept the conditions laid down at Figueras on February 1!

For general Franco had just issued his law of "political responsibilities" and the Spanish Government could agree to no peace terms as long as Franco insisted that every soldier who fought for democracy, every woman in the rear guard, every child over fourteen years of age, who had not been active on behalf of Franco during the years of war, was liable to reprisals. These were the Premier's own words: "We will continue to fight until we insure the independence of Spain. Only by fighting for Spanish independence can we prevent our country from being submerged in a sea of blood, hatred and persecution. Otherwise foreign domination, violence, and terror will be for generations the only means of keeping the country together."

Newspapers voicing the opinions of all political parties and organizations welcomed the Government. A wave of enthusiasm swept the Republican zone. Women volunteered in thousands to take the places still occupied by men. Women unloaded the ships at the four important harbors still held by the Government. Women worked in the fields together with the old men.

After a thorough visit to the Madrid fronts, Dr. Negrin left the capital for the Levante fronts. The traitors in the capital realized that they must act quickly for the Government's presence had strengthened the people's determination to resist.

Julian Besteiro, a pseudo-Socialist, had waited for that moment to come ever since his return from the coronation of George VI. His personal friend, President Azaña, had sent him to England to represent Spain at that ceremony. In London, Besteiro had started "talks" for surrender. Now he was pressed to put them into practice. For many years Besteiro had led an isolated existence even within the Socialist Party. He had no mass following; he lacked the confidence of the people; he could not hide his animosity and jealousy towards other Socialists who had attained a high degree of public approval. During the time that Dr. Negrin was Premier, Besteiro never gave up trying to overthrow the Cabinet. The Government had reliable information of his "appeasement" contacts in England and France. But Besteiro would have been powerless if he had not found an ally in colonel Segismundo Casado.

An officer of the old school, Casado was in command of the Central Army. On March 4, while Dr. Negrin was still inspecting the Levante fronts, a revolt started at Cartagena. This naval base held by the Government was coveted by the Rebels for their enforcement of the blockade. The Cartagena revolt was fascist. The usual "Fifth Columnists" started it and it would have been easily subdued had the garrison not received orders from colonel Casado to support the rioters. This provoked enormous confusion until the Government sent from Levante loyal troops who put down the fascist revolt. But Casado prevented Madrid stations from broadcasting the Government's account of what had actually taken place. Instead, he represented the Government troops' rescue of the Navy and civilians as a "communist" revolt. The Republican Navy had time to leave Cartagena before the Rebel ships arrived. When these came, the fascists within had been dominated and the Republican artillery was able to sink one Rebel submarine and another ship sent by Franco to help what he thought were the victorious Rebels at Cartagena.

These events brought terrible confusion among the people and provoked the disunity which was necessary for the plans of the capitulators. On the night of the fifth, Casado formed a "National Council of Defense" in Madrid. With Besteiro, Mera, and other members of the Council, Casado issued a demagogical manifesto attacking the Government.

At a meeting of Popular Front representatives held in Madrid a few days after the Government's return, the F.A.I. (anarchist) delegate present had proposed the formation of a similar "Council of Defense." This man's nationality and name were never disclosed and his plan was rejected by the rest of the delegates who were all Spanish. This failure, together with the rapidity with which the Cartagena rebellion had been dealt with by the Government forces, moved the traitors in Madrid to act promptly. The British and French agents present at the time in the capital, as well as Franco himself, were pressing for quick action.

But the events at Cartagena had shown plainly that there were traitors in our own ranks. The Government then decided to centralize the command of all the military forces in the person of Dr. Negrin as Minister of Defense. The executive power remained with the General Staff. Certain higher officers were shifted and replaced by other military chiefs who had proved their loyalty to the cause of the Republic. But it was too late. Lieutenant Colonel Cipriano Mera, an anarchist and military commander of the IV Army Corps, placed his men at the disposal of Colonel Casado to arrest the Government and all those opposing the plans of the capitulators.

When Dr. Negrin, at a small town near Alicante, heard of the coup carried out by Besteiro with the help of the military traitors, he sent a message to Colonel Casado. He offered even to get in touch with the newly formed "Council of Defense" in the hope of preserving the unity of the Army and the civilian population.

Then the Government tried to establish contact with Valencia and other cities in the central zone. But they discovered the plotters had been thorough. Casado's men occupied the strategic posts in the central zone.

Casado did not answer. Again, Dr. Negrin begged Casado: "Do not surrender our people into General Franco's hands. Get a promise of mercy, at least. Save the lives of our people."

There was no answer. Only silence.

Ignacio came into the Cabinet meeting that day. "Casado's troops are marching upon us," he reported briefly. "You must leave at once."

Dr. Negrin rose. "Never. I and my Government, the legal Government of Spain, will not leave our people to the mercy of Franco. There is still hope."

Ignacio shook his head. "Don't you realize that the terms Besteiro and Casado have arranged with Franco include their surrendering you and the entire Government?"

Dr. Negrin sat down heavily. "It is not possible."

Ignacio replied very grimly, "It is true. I talked to Casado half an hour ago. He still trusts me—you know I was a military officer of the Monarchy. He thinks I am betraying you, and he has indicated that he has to hand you and all the members of the Government over to Franco."

Dr. Negrin had no answer.

Del Vayo asked: "But suppose we surrendered to Franco ourselves. Could we not save the lives of our soldiers and people? Suppose we agreed to surrender on such terms?"

Ignacio shook his head again. "Besteiro and Casado and their fellow-traitors have been promised their lives if they turn over the members of the Cabinet and some others of us to

Franco. But Franco and his German and Italian allies will not even discuss any guarantees of safety for the Spanish people—not under any circumstances whatsoever."

Dr. Negrin began, "But surely Casado will . . ."

A messenger interrupted him. Dr. Negrin read the teletype message aloud to the members of his Cabinet and the General Staff. "Miaja has joined Casado."

There was a moment of silence and then Ignacio said, "Miaja is in Alicante. It is a matter of hours, perhaps minutes, before he will be in this room."

Dr. Negrin said slowly, "The world will not understand Miaja." And his voice was bitter. For the fumbling old general, who had been left by the fleeing Caballero to die in Madrid, had been made a hero—to his great surprise—when the people of the city rose up and defended their homes almost with their bare hands. After that, Miaja had been a newspaper headline, "hero" of every government victory, although the old man, never a good general and increasingly a feeble and useless one, had never actually participated in any military victory after the defense of Madrid in November, 1936.

Now Casado had made a dupe of the old man. Miaja was led to betray the Government and the people who had made him a hero by the promise of the exchange of his son, a fascist prisoner.

Dr. Negrin rose. "If there is no other way out," he said with dignity, "I feel that we should adjourn and meet again in a foreign country to carry on our fight, which we will never give up for a free and democratic Spain."

The Cabinet and the General Staff rose.

Ignacio led Dr. Negrin and the other officials to the airport. He had four Douglas planes and two bombers which he had hastily transformed to carry passengers.

It was three in the afternoon. It was dangerous to fly over fascist territory in the broad daylight—but even more danger-ous and useless to remain. Miaja was a half an hour away. Casado had ordered him to arrest the legal Government of Spain.

Dr. Negrin, Del Vayo, and others left in the first two Douglas planes bound for Toulouse. The bombers, with a smaller cruising range, could only make Oran on the French-African coast.

It was dawn next morning by the time Ignacio had completed the arrangements to evacuate the Spanish Government and other persons who had come to the central zone after the defeat in Catalonia. He left on the last plane, together with the Minister of Agriculture, Vicente Uribe, who had stayed with him to make sure all the others were flown to safety. Modesto and Lister were also passengers in that same last plane.

The story I put down here I learned weeks after the betrayal of Madrid. I spent days of anguish in New York, after March 5, trying to find out if Ignacio had been arrested and shot or whether he had escaped to safety.

The newspapers in New York told of fighting in the streets of Madrid. Afterwards I learned the truth about this fighting. As soon as the "Council of Defense" was formed, the IV Army Corps commanded by the anarchist Mera received orders to arrest all those military leaders who had recognized Casado's treason behind his demagogical promises. Over two thousand military leaders and political persons opposed to the betrayal were arrested during the first few hours. But before they were able to arrest them all, those military commanders, who were ready to resist the fascist invaders until the end, counterattacked against the new rebels.

Officers and troops betrayed by Casado with promises that he would resist Franco, turned against the traitors when they learned the truth. The "Council of Defense" was forced to hide in the old cellars of the Ministry of Finance, dreading the people's anger.

But the treason was well timed. Franco's forces at University City on the Madrid front initiated a powerful offensive. All military leaders fighting Casado gave orders to their troops to remain at the front and not open their ranks to the invaders. It was these loyal troops that stopped the enemy's advance and even captured some war material.

While they were carrying out this last fight face to face with the enemy, the traitors at their backs were preparing the last touches for the unconditional surrender. At the same time the Republic was being adroitly undermined and disarmed. Confusion, disorder, and panic spread like wildfire. When the people realized the betrayal it was too late. Unity, their best arm, had been taken away from their hands. And this rendered the Spanish people powerless.

Some officers and several civilians were shot. Over twenty thousand patriots were put in jail at Casado's orders.

A group of Spanish cowards and traitors delivered Madrid— and after Madrid the rest of Republican Spain—tied hand and feet, to Franco, Hitler, and Mussolini.

After the first shock of the betrayal and surrender of Madrid, I turned back to my work in America. I was distressed and bewildered to find that men such as Don Fernando de los Rios, our Ambassador in the U. S. A., had sent a telegram of allegiance to the rebel "Council of Defense." Here was another of those Spanish representatives who lived comfortably abroad on their generous salaries while understanding little of what was happening in their own country.

I did not allow that to make any difference in my work. Although I could no longer ask my American friends to send food to the defenders of Madrid, I was now trying to help the hundreds of thousands of Spanish refugees.

Some months have passed since General Franco and his Italians and Germans marched into Madrid. By now nobody in the world can doubt what we said over and over during the two and a half years of the war: the Spanish war was not a civil war, but the invasion of a peaceful democracy by Hitler and Mussolini. For both these dictators have boasted in public speeches of the triumph of fascism in Spain; they have outlined in great detail the role they played in the defeat of my country since the first days of July, 1936.

And now, more than ever, I know that Spanish democracy is not dead—but still lives—and will always live.

Franco had executed thousands. Even as I write these words, the firing squads are still shooting men and women who believe in democracy, at the rate of one every nine minutes, for twenty-four hours of the day.

Thousands more still live in French concentration camps, hungry, suffering in forced idleness and misery.

But twelve million Spaniards lived in democratic Spain for two and a half years while the foreign invaders bombed our children and slaughtered our people.

Franco cannot shoot the twelve million.

They will remember.

Even now, the little news that comes out of Spain is always of the fight that the Spaniards inside the fascist boundaries carry on day and night against the foreign oppressors.

"Spain for the Spaniards! Viva la República!" These are the slogans that my countrymen fight under inside Franco Spain. In a dozen little newspapers still published in secret places, in the prisons, on the streets, in the homes, men and women write and sing and whisper these slogans.

The fascists cannot make Spain fascist. We are a democratic people. We shall always be a democratic people.

I know that Spain will soon again be free. Nothing can prevent it—for the united people of Spain will make a democracy with their blood and their courage.

Viva la República!

INDEX

427

Uribe, Vicente, 323, 424
U.S.A., 158, 189, 228, 255, 292, 306, 316, 318, 337, 365 f., 377, 415 f., 419, 424 f.
U.S.S.R., 256, 265-67, 274-81, 300, 345-51, 367, 377; Red Army, 348

Valencia, 205, 219, 245, 280 f., 288, 291-93, 295, 298, 302 f., 306, 316 f., 321-24, 327 f., 329, 330-32, 337-41, 361-63, 409, 422
Vich, 386
Vigo, 205
Vinaroz, 361, 365
Volunteers, International, 274-76, 303, 370-73, 409

War, Spanish. *See* Airforce; Army; Invasion; Rebellion; Republicans; etc.; World, 15, 19 f., 22 f., 174; after World, 33, 36, 43
Wedding, 98 f., 177 f., 402
White Book, (Italian documents), 304 f.
Workers, 7, 22-4, 55, 58, 116, 154-56, 185, 187, 192 f., 202, 206 f., 217, 229 f., 232, 238, 242, 317-19, 349, 362, 372. *See also* Reforms; Strikes; Trade Unions; Wages; etc.

Yeste, 218

Zamora, Niceto Alcalá, 130, 144, 149, 186, 204, 214

CANTABRIAN

(COAL MINES)
ASTURIAS

SANTIAGO

GALICIA

VIGO

LEON

ATLANTIC OCEAN

SALAMANCA

SEGOVIA

LA GRANDA

AVILA

EL ESCORIAL

LA ALBERCA
LAS BATUECAS

BRUNETE

LAS HURDES

TALAVERA

PORTUGAL

TOLEDO

EXTREMADURA
(CATTLE BREEDING)

BADAJOZ

ALMADEN
(MERCURY MINES)

POZOBLANCO

SANCTUARY

PUERTOLLANO
(COAL AND LEAD
MINES)

RIO TINTO

ANDUJAR

(COPPER MINES)

SEVILLA

RONDA

MALAGA

CADIZ

TORREMOLINOS

GIBRALTAR

ALGECIRAS

TETUAN

ALHUCEMAS

SPANISH MORO

A000012417889

REINHARD